Politics and Welfare in Birmingham, 1900–1975

POLITICS AND WELFARE IN BIRMINGHAM, 1900–1975

Edward Shannon LaMonte

The University of Alabama Press

Tuscaloosa and London

Copyright © 1995
The University of Alabama Press
Tuscaloosa, Alabama 35487–0380

Manufactured in the United States of America

∞

The paper on which this book is printed meets the minimum requirements of American National Standard for Information Science-Permanence of Paper for Printed Library Materials, ANSI Z39.48–1984.

ISBN 0-8173-0754-0

Library of Congress Cataloging-in-Publication Data

LaMonte, Edward Shannon.
Politics and welfare in Birmingham, 1900–1975 / Edward Shannon LaMonte.
p.   cm.
Includes bibliographical references and index.
ISBN 0-8173-0754-0
1. Public welfare—Alabama—Birmingham—History.   2. Birmingham (Ala.)—Social conditions.   3. Birmingham (Ala.)—Race relations —History.   I. Title.
HV99.B53L35   1995
361'.9761781'0904—dc20   94-7186

British Library Cataloguing-in-Publication Data available

For Jennie, Brad, Rachel, Matt—and especially Ruth

Contents

Part Four: 1962–1975

Preface

THE CITIZENS OF Birmingham, especially its civic boosters, were understandably distressed when the August 1937 issue of *Harper's Magazine* appeared. They had, of course, known that their city would be featured in the magazine, as writer George R. Leighton had been in the area collecting information. But they scarcely expected and deeply resented the treatment Leighton gave their hometown.

Birminghamians had come to regard their city as "the Magic City," a unique American city poised on the edge of municipal greatness. Many were convinced that Birmingham would in the future outstrip rival Atlanta and become the preeminent city of the South. And all were impressed by Birmingham's history. They pointed to its post-Civil War origins as a purely industrial city, the only city in America to be built on the surface of all the raw materials essential to its economy. More often they marveled at census data: incorporated in December 1871 with an estimated population of 700 to 800, Birmingham registered 3,086 inhabitants in 1880. By 1890 the population had increased nearly 750 percent to 26,178. The turn-of-the-century count rose nearly 50 percent to 38,415; and then a major annexation sent the population skyrocketing to 132,685 in 1910. By the time Leighton visited, the city claimed over 259,000 residents.[1]

But to the chagrin of most local residents, Leighton did not write about "the Magic City"; rather, he titled his article "Birmingham, Alabama: The City of Perpetual Promise."[2] Instead of documenting the city's undeniably impressive physical development, he emphasized its equally undeniable shortcomings: the fact that Birmingham ranked ninety-fourth out of the ninety-four cities over 100,000 in population in per capita public expenditures; that it had more illiterates than any other city in the 200,000–300,000 class; and that its citizens had among the lowest spendable incomes in the nation.[3] He speculated on the causes of the unfulfillment of the perpetual promise.

Part of the unfulfillment during the 1930s was attributable to the Great Depression; the Roosevelt administration had found Birmingham to be "the worst hit town in the country."[4] But more fundamental to him was the history of the city and its raison d'être. "In a mountain wilderness, laid in a region devastated by war and inhabited by bankrupts, a group of speculators and industrialists in 1871 founded a city and peopled it with two races afraid of each other."[5] This city was to be "a place where speculators by ruthless exploitation might wring out a fortune."[6]

Leighton may have been harsh on his subject, but his analysis points to many of the same factors that loom large in the following study of politics and welfare in Birmingham throughout most of the twentieth century: the rapid growth of a young industrial city clearly dominated by a political culture favorable to further economic development; the paucity of both public funds and public services; the extreme vulnerability to external economic and political influences; and the presence of a large black population that was virtually excluded from political activity during most of the period under study and that received distinctly inferior public services. And because so little was provided publicly and so many were excluded, the role of private groups in the area of welfare emerges as an important topic for investigation.

This study, divided into four parts, explores the relationships between politics and welfare in Birmingham during four time periods in the twentieth century that illuminate the development of these relationships: 1900–1917, 1928–41, 1954, and 1962–75.

I selected the period 1900–1917 to examine the young Birmingham during a formative period of city building. During most of this period, welfare was regarded as an activity appropriate for the private sector. In 1915, however, local leaders recognized the failure of private agencies to meet local need and established instead a city department of relief and correction.

The 1928–41 period permits a review of the impact of the Depression on the caretaker-style local government and the city's limited welfare programs. Of particular interest are the massive federal intervention and the impact of New Deal programs on both social welfare services and the distribution of benefits to needy persons in the community.

I chose the year 1954 to determine the lasting impact of the New Deal reforms before turning to the dramatic 1962–75 period, which witnessed significant local government reform, the civil rights movement, and a new federal intervention in the form of the War on Poverty.

Welfare services are defined as those activities providing jobs, money, or services—such as education, recreation, counseling, child care, and health care—to low income residents. The distinguishing factor in this definition is that the service is designed specifically for low income residents, or at least that it includes a significant number of these residents in its clientele. The particular activities I examine during the four time periods are different, reflecting the abandonment of some efforts and the creation of new programs.

Focusing my study on welfare services, I examine the following five questions:

1. Who participated in the decision-making process concerning delivery of welfare services for each of these periods?
2. What was the pattern of services for each period? Specifically, what services were available and who received them?
3. What significant changes occurred in the way decisions were made in these different periods, and what caused those changes?
4. What effect did changes in the decision-making process have on the pattern of services?
5. How does Birmingham seem to compare with other major cities in the area of welfare services, and how can significant differences be explained?

Politics in this study includes a general description and analysis of local government during the four periods under review, with a focus on the following questions for each of the periods:

1. What was the form of government and who were the occupants of offices?
2. What characterizes the general performance of government as it functioned routinely? Specifically, what did government do and who benefited from government action?
3. What major governmental decisions were made, who were the key public and private participants (as nearly as can be determined), and who gained from these decisions?
4. What significant changes occurred in local government in the different periods, and what caused those changes?
5. What effect did changes in government have on the participants in and beneficiaries of government decisions?
6. And finally, how does Birmingham seem to compare with other major cities in the area of local government and politics?

My study reveals a fundamental congruence between local politics and welfare services, both public and private, during the four time periods. It was possible during the Depression to achieve a major change in welfare services by an external intervention that did not have a significant impact on local government. When the intervention largely ceased, welfare returned to basically the same pattern that had prevailed before the economic crisis. During the 1960s, however, external intervention and fundamental change in local government occurred simultaneously, each reinforcing the other. As a result a major reform occurred in both public and private welfare services—a reform that has persisted even in the face of sharply reduced external intervention.

Part One, 1900–1917: The Formative Period in the City's History

Birmingham is a young city, having been established in 1871. Between 1900 and 1917 local government was still concerned with the building of the city; much of the agenda of local government was devoted to issues dealing with the provision of basic services. There emerged a political style similar to what Sam Bass Warner, Jr., calls "privatism" in his study of Philadelphia: government should meet the demands of business and industry, attempt to provide services inexpensively to neighborhoods of the city, and recognize that "the business of the city was business."[7]

This was an era of predominantly private welfare; the city's early response to human need was confined to maintaining a referral service directing clients to private agencies. The county played a somewhat larger role, managing an almshouse for the indigent. But until 1915 the prevailing assumptions were that welfare was not a major responsibility of local government and that the private sector would render most services necessary to cope with the perceived needs of the poor. As this first period of study draws to a close, however, the provision of welfare services is recognized as a public responsibility in light of the manifest failure of private agencies to meet local needs.

Part Two, 1928–1941: Stable Polity, Unstable Economy

The Depression had a particularly devastating effect on the single-industry economy of Birmingham; and the political history of those years is the history of a local government swamped by national economic events and struggling to remain afloat, supported largely by national policies conceived and directed at national and state levels. The formative years had passed, and government prior to the Depression fit the caretaker role—still leaving the widest possible latitude to private activity. But local government and privatism were both inadequate during this crisis.

This part not only describes a caretaker-style local government and local welfare activities as they functioned immediately before the Depression; it also discusses the efforts of both to respond to the crisis during the Hoover years and the adequacy of these efforts. The main topic of this part, however, is the massive federal intervention in local affairs and the significant changes that this intervention caused in the distribution of welfare benefits. Most dramatically, Blacks now received benefits that reflected both their proportion in the population and their critical need. This dramatic redistribution of benefits in favor of Blacks reflected the bureaucratization and professionalization of social services in Birmingham as general, impersonal rules of eligibility were applied by social workers in a relatively nondiscretionary manner.[8]

Part Three, 1954: Stable Polity, Stable Economy

One year has been selected between the 1928–41 and 1962–75 periods in order to determine what lasting effect the New Deal welfare programs had on the services in Birmingham. This part discusses the continuation of caretaker government in the midst of a continuing political culture of privatism. It also discusses a private welfare sector that largely resumed its pre-New Deal ways of distributing benefits, thereby substantially excluding Blacks. Illustrative of this exclusion of Blacks by white social welfare policy makers are two brief case studies, one dealing with the unwillingness of white leaders to allow an Urban League affiliate in Birmingham, the other dealing with their unwillingness to tolerate a biracial discussion group sponsored by a Community Chest agency.

Part Four, 1962–1975: Political and Economic Maturation

The year 1962–63 was a revolutionary period in Birmingham's local politics. In late 1962, reform-minded white leaders began promoting a change in the form of government from a three-man commission to a mayor-council form with a nine-member council chosen in nonpartisan, at-large elections. Two motivations lay behind the reformers' program: (1) the desire to attract wealthy suburbs into the city by "modernizing" local government, and (2) the desire to replace the commission, dominated by Police Commissioner Eugene "Bull" Connor, with a regime more responsive to both the local black community and mandates from the federal government concerning desegregation. The new form of government was chosen, but the assumption of office by newly elected officials was delayed by a court challenge from the commissioners. During that awkward time when it was unclear legally who governed in Birmingham, Blacks demonstrated and conducted an effective boycott of downtown stores, making clear to all the severity of the crisis in race relations in the city and its impact on the well-being of white-owned businesses. The new officials were confirmed in office by the courts, and there followed an extended period of transition toward a more active city government, one that explicitly recognized the social and economic needs of Blacks and that responded cautiously to those needs. In an early, significant public policy decision, the mayor established a citizens' committee to seek funds under the Economic Opportunity Act of

1964. The remainder of this part analyzes the relationships between the antipoverty program and local government and the antipoverty program and private agencies.

This analysis develops the argument that Office of Economic Opportunity (OEO) programs reinforced the preexisting political reform effort in Birmingham aimed at extending new benefits and new opportunities to black citizens. Thus, the antipoverty program is seen as one aspect of local government's effort to make a clear and fundamental break with the past.

In addition to discussing the significant governmental reforms in the period 1962–75, Part Four also analyzes the local antipoverty program, examining those who initiated it; the nature of its board; its programs and their beneficiaries; its relation to public authorities, private agencies, and private powerholders; and its role as a source of black political leadership. This analysis documents changes in both the public and private sectors caused by, or at least consistent with, the OEO effort. Thus, Birmingham implemented an extensive citizen participation plan under the Housing and Community Development Act of 1974. The debate surrounding this plan reflected the impact of the antipoverty program and especially its insistence on maximum citizen participation; several of the debaters had served political apprenticeships in OEO programs. Private agencies also reflected the impact of OEO in changed board composition, substantially modified programs, and experimental efforts at shared decision making with clients.

In summary, local government in Birmingham had begun radical reform prior to the advent of OEO, largely in response to demands from and unmet needs in the black community and pressure from white business leaders to resolve the racial conflict and end its economic disruption. The antipoverty program reinforced this reform and carried its major themes into the private welfare agencies, which made major efforts to modify both decision-making processes and programs largely in favor of Blacks. Despite the weakened external intervention, these local reform efforts continued unabated.

Acknowledgments

I AM GREATLY INDEBTED to many people for the important contributions they have made, directly and indirectly, knowingly and unknowingly, to the writing of this book.

My parents provided much to me, but probably the greatest gifts were the emphasis they placed on good schooling for their three sons and the sacrifices they made to assure it. Rainey S. Taylor, a true master teacher, taught me and many others to appreciate the importance and joy of history as he stimulated and endured his young charges at the Columbus Academy from my eighth grade year through high school.

John U. Monro, my undergraduate dean and later beloved family friend, first introduced the idea of Birmingham to me when he encouraged a group from Phillips Brooks House Association at Harvard University to travel south during the summers of 1964 and 1965 to teach in a variety of programs sponsored by Miles College, located in Fairfield just west of the city. I strongly believe that no institution of higher education in the United States was more exciting or more important during that period than Miles; and I shall always be grateful to John Monro for getting me there and to the late president of the college, Lucius H. Pitts, for encouraging me to remain for longer than I had planned and learn so much about his college and his community while serving as his assistant.

My stay at Miles during the 1965–66 academic year was possible only because J. David Greenstone, my adviser at the University of Chicago, where I planned to enroll that same year, not only allowed but virtually required me to accept what he immediately recognized was an extraordinary job offered at an extraordinary moment in time. David Greenstone was my mentor during graduate school, chair of my dissertation committee, and source of intellectual renewal until his tragically premature death. My wife and I cherish our several visits with him during our infrequent trips to Chicago and often recall both his personal kindness and his stunning intellectual powers.

At Chicago my interests and activities were greatly shaped in urban history seminars with Richard C. Wade, who challenged us academically and also challenged his students and colleagues to play significant roles in public affairs. After John Monro introduced me to my future employers at the University of Alabama in Birmingham, David Greenstone and Richard Wade cooperated by

xv

helping me define and then later supervising a Birmingham-based dissertation that allowed me to join the University's Center for Urban Studies while completing my doctoral program. Both my employment and my academic research now directed me to an exploration of the history of Birmingham and its past and contemporary public policy choices.

Throughout my research the holdings and personnel of the Birmingham Public Library have been invaluable. I am especially indebted to the following persons for not only their professional assistance but also their personal interest and friendship: George R. Stewart, the recently retired director of the library, whose knowledge of the Southern Department saved me many hours of searching; Marvin Y. Whiting, archivist extraordinaire; Mary Bess Kirksey Paluzzi; Yvonne Crumpler; Anne Knight; and Don Veasey.

David Orrell, former executive director of the United Way of Central Alabama, permitted me complete access to the records of the Community Chest and Red Cross and also generously provided me with working space in the offices of the United Way. G. David Singleton, former executive director of the Jefferson County Committee for Economic Opportunity, allowed me to use his offices and all of the agency's documents.

The people whom I interviewed all gave freely of their time and information; I note them by name at the end of the bibliography. I wish to extend special thanks and pay tribute to Charles F. Zukoski, Jr. Readers of the following pages will note that at critical moments in Birmingham's history, Charles Zukoski offered remarkable leadership, ultimately at great personal sacrifice. His life would be my answer to the question of what it means to be a citizen of one's community, and indeed of the world community.

Neal R. Berte, president of Birmingham-Southern College, has appreciated the importance of this project to me and provided the flexible schedule and other support that made possible its completion. Gail Morris and Vonda Fulton typed the manuscript with great accuracy and good humor.

Richard Arrington, Jr.—academic dean at Miles College during the year I worked there, Birmingham city councillor from 1971 to 1979, mayor from 1979 to the present, and good friend throughout—invited me to work on his staff after he was elected mayor; I agreed to join him for one or two years and stayed for eight marvelously exciting and rewarding ones. That experience intensified my interest in understanding our city and gave me a unique vantage point from which to reconsider its history and be involved in its public policy making. I hope this book sheds some light on the daunting challenges confronting those who would lead Birmingham.

Malcolm MacDonald, director of The University of Alabama Press, has been persistently encouraging throughout a period of preparation that I suspect he thought might never end. His telephone calls and letters at key moments prodded me to refocus on the completion of the text. Suzette Griffith, project editor, guided me skillfully through the final stages of preparing the manuscript.

To our four wonderful children—Jennie, Brad, Rachel, and Matt—now adults, I am grateful for the required patience and periods of peace. To my wife Ruth I am indebted for that and very much more indeed.

PART ONE

1900–1917

1

Birmingham, Alabama

The Historical Background

BIRMINGHAM, ALABAMA, was incorporated 19 December 1871 with an estimated population of eight hundred.[1] The new city was located in the sparsely settled hill country of Jefferson County, an area avoided by enterprising farmers because the rocky, sterile soil was unsuited for the staple crops of corn and cotton. There had been a hint of the future in the crude industrial furnaces in the area that had been used during the Civil War to produce pig iron for the Confederate arsenal at Selma.[2] But the furnaces had fallen into disuse, and Jefferson County offered no attraction to newcomers until two railroads were projected through it shortly after the Civil War ended. Where the railroads crossed, Birmingham was laid out. Land speculation provided the impetus for its early development.[3] Reconstruction laws gave Birmingham an early boost by providing conditions favorable to a manipulated election that established the new city as the county seat, removing it from the neighboring village of Elyton. "Construction trains were brought into service on the morning of the election and hundreds of Negro laborers were hauled to town, as were large groups of white people."[4] Local historians support the story that Blacks were duped into voting for the change of location by Col. James R. Powell, one of the town's most avid promoters, president of the Elyton Land Company and later Birmingham's first elected mayor. Mounted on a splendid horse, this impressive figure is said to have ridden among the Blacks, identifying himself as General Grant and urging them to vote for Birmingham as a personal favor to him.[5]

But 1873 nearly brought ruin to the newly designated county seat. A cholera epidemic in the summer killed 128, and this disaster was immediately followed by the Panic of 1873. Driven by the fear of disease and economic stagnation, early settlers abandoned Birmingham; the population declined from an estimated 4,000 to about 1,200 in 1878.[6]

Birmingham's fortunes began to improve in 1876 with the demonstration that coke pig iron could be manufactured in the district, using coal rather than the usual charcoal. Two years later speculators opened the first coal mine in the district and began operation of the first blast furnace in 1880.[7] Northern money flowed into the district between 1880 and 1884 to establish additional furnaces, as word spread in financial circles that Birmingham was able to produce pig iron more cheaply than anywhere else in the country. By 1890 the population had increased to over 26,000 citizens, who had been attracted by a vibrant economy based upon mining, 25 blast furnaces, and 437 real estate offices.[8] The profits of the Elyton Land Company skyrocketed; in 1887 the company paid dividends representing a 2,305 percent return on original investment. One-hundred-dollar shares of stock that sold for $17 in 1875 were marketed for $6,400 twelve years later.[9]

In the midst of this boom the powerful Tennessee Coal, Iron and Railroad Company entered the district in 1886 through purchase of several existing operations; nine years later the company produced the first successful basic pig iron that could, in turn, be made into steel. Birmingham entered the modern era of steel production when two open-hearth steel furnaces were built in 1897.[10] At the turn of the century three northern-based companies dominated the Birmingham economy: the Tennessee Company, the Sloss-Sheffield Coal and Iron Company, and Republic Iron and Steel Company. The Tennessee Company absorbed Republic in 1906, shortly before the Panic of 1907. When the Tennessee Company itself nearly went bankrupt during the Depression, the local economy was rescued by a special exemption from antitrust laws granted by President Roosevelt to United States Steel so that it might purchase the huge Birmingham facility.[11] This $50 million acquisition was the single largest financial transaction in the history of Alabama, and the decision of United States Steel to enter the district was undoubtedly the most significant decision, public or private, affecting the city's early development.[12] As one historian notes, "Birmingham thus began its life as an adjunct of a land company owned by southern land speculators and ended its first forty years as an adjunct of an industrial corporation owned by outside capitalists."[13]

During the period 1900–1917, Birmingham stood as the preeminent example of industrialization in the New South; a very young city, it owed its strength and development to its position as one of the nation's leading steel-producing centers and as the center of the country's cast iron pipe industry.[14]

Birmingham did not escape economic distress during this period. Plunged into a serious depression during the Panic of 1907, the city experienced another serious downturn in 1914. It was estimated that 40 percent of the work force in heavy industry was unemployed in the fall and that 50 percent of black workers were idle. For the first time in its history, the city created work to aid the unemployed, paying men to cut wood.[15] Private charity also strained to meet the crisis; the Associated Charities handled 5,589 cases during December 1914 and the first quarter of 1915. The load for the corresponding time one year earlier was 1,180.[16] But conditions improved through 1915 and 1916, and at the close of the period Birmingham was once again a thriving industrial center, caught up in the heavy demands of a wartime economy.

While the successful operations of the huge steel mills employed many of Birmingham's residents, the strength of the private sector did little to bolster the public economy. City boundaries had been drawn with great care to exclude many of the largest plants, especially the U.S. Steel works, thus exempting them from municipal taxation.[17] From the beginning, the city operated under constitutionally imposed tax and debt limits that prevented it from meeting the demands imposed by rapid growth. The 1875 Alabama Constitution allowed a tax rate of $.50 per $100 of assessed value, forcing the city to issue bonds in order to finance necessary public projects.[18] The 1901 constitution doubled this rate, but Birmingham in 1914 still had the lowest tax rate of the thirty-eight American cities in the 100,000–300,000 population class.[19] Coupled with this low rate was an equally low assessment figure. Central-business-district property was assessed at 18.5 percent of market value, while residential property was calculated at 20–35 percent. When the county proposed a 60 percent assessment schedule consistent with the recommendations of the state tax committee, large real estate developers, as well as the Birmingham Real Estate Association, mounted a vociferous protest; the assessments remained unchanged.[20]

Citing the financial plight of the city in his 1907 annual message, Mayor George Ward lamented "the failure of the city government to carry on modern legitimate municipal functions." He particularly mentioned the need to increase charity appropriations: "The city of Birmingham probably donates less to work of this nature than any city of similar size in the United States. While we can continue to repudiate such obligations, the duty ever resting on the strong to take care of the helpless is upon us, notwithstanding."[21] To compensate for its limited revenues from real and property taxes, the city adopted a stiff license schedule for local businesses; it was the only city in the nation where license collections exceeded real and property taxes.[22] In Ward's opinion, the only satisfactory solution to the financial dilemma was a constitutional amendment increasing the maximum allowable tax rate, but this relief eluded Birmingham until 1920.[23]

The financial problems of the city prior to 1910 were sharply intensified after the 1910 consolidation of Birmingham with surrounding municipalities. Birmingham in 1900 covered 11.4 square miles and had a population of 38,415. As a result of the consolidation, the city in 1910 had an area of 48.3 square miles, a population of 132,685, a large and growing deficit, and service demands that far outstripped the government's capacity to provide services.[24] Each year the situation grew more serious.

In 1911 the newly formed city commission faced a deficit of over $560,000. It promptly reduced the city's payroll by $80,000 per year and turned over responsibility for operation of the municipal parks to the women's garden clubs, which were aided by an advisory committee from the Chamber of Commerce. The public schools were serving 2,500 additional students from the suburban neighborhoods in 1911, but the commission was compelled to reduce its appropriation to the board of education by $30,000.[25]

Continuing deficits forced the commission to drop twenty-six men from the police department in 1913; the 115-man force was one-half as large as it had been immediately after consolidation and before the economy measures.[26] Birmingham now ranked twenty-first out of the twenty-three cities above 100,000 in population in per capita expenditures for local government; still the city continued to fall behind at the rate of $1,000 per day. The deficit at year's end was nearly $2 million.[27]

The year 1914 saw the city reach the constitutional limit of its borrowing power, a figure fixed at $800,000.[28] Current operating expenses were reduced by another $100,000, lowering the annual deficit but taking a huge toll in the level and quality of services. The commission completely eliminated the city's recreation, welfare, and smoke control departments; halted all public improvement work; and reduced school appropriations $340,000 by cutting teacher salaries, discontinuing night and vacation schools, discontinuing free textbooks and supplies, and closing the kindergarten program. In order to keep the public schools open for the full term, the board of education charged monthly fees for all students in attendance. Commissioners drastically cut public library appropriations, reduced the police and fire departments by one-third and instituted twelve-hour shifts, and halted all street sprinkling. During this time of general economic depression, they also discontinued all aid to private charities.[29]

The *Birmingham News*, which prided itself on boosting the city, reviewed the commission's economy measures of the summer of 1915 and glumly wrote:

> So, in one week, the city of Birmingham will be changed almost visibly. Its Fire Department will be too small to handle large fires; its Police Department, already insufficient, will be cut further; its library, already admittedly beneath the dignity of Birmingham, will suffer materially; officially there will be no recreation, welfare, or humane department; one-third of the present lighted places at night will be dark; there will be no street sprinkling and no street repairs to speak of; the parks will be without care of keepers; there will be no charitable appropriations; and

the schools will be without free textbooks or supplies and facing the graver contingency of a term shortened under the standard.[30]

The city's auditing company, after comparing the finances of Birmingham with other cities, concluded that "the appropriations for practically all the main departments are clearly inadequate for truly efficient service, and that if such a condition is allowed to continue indefinitely serious injury will result."[31]

It would be tempting at this point to conclude that Birmingham was a potentially progressive city in the early 1900s, but that her development was thwarted by a rural-dominated legislature and statewide electorate that clamped restrictive limits on her tax and debt limits. And there is some measure of truth in this position.

Most notably, George Ward, mayor from 1905 to 1909, commission president from 1913 to 1917, and dominant public figure throughout the period, repeatedly advocated a constitutional amendment raising the tax limit as "fundamental and necessary to the success of any administration."[32] Supported consistently by the city's leading newspaper, he asserted that "progressive cities with high tax rates always outstrip the older centers with low tax rates."[33]

But the position of Ward and the local press was clearly not shared by either the business community or the voters of the city. Seeking solutions to the financial plight of the city, Commission President Ward in 1914 joined the president of the Chamber of Commerce in appointing a citizens' committee of one hundred to review municipal finances and recommend future actions; this committee included virtually the entire economic leadership group of the city.[34] The committee was divided into three subcommittees, one concerned with a plan of permanent relief for the city. This subcommittee recommended a legislative prohibition against the city's expenditures exceeding its revenues in any fiscal year and called for the equalization of assessments. Significantly, the business leaders recommended that the permanent tax rate remain fixed at 1 percent.[35]

This recommendation by the elite was endorsed by the voters at large in December 1915. The state legislature had authorized a statewide vote on a constitutional amendment to permit municipalities to raise their tax rates from 1 percent of assessed value to 1.5 percent; Commission President Ward himself led the local campaign in behalf of the amendment, supported by the Birmingham newspapers. Not surprisingly, the amendment lost by a majority of 8,480 across the state. But even the local vote was against the measure, which lost in Jefferson County 1,386–2,634.[36] One is forced to conclude that the city's business elite and voting citizenry consciously chose to maintain a level of public services that was uniformly recognized as being deficient, the commission president and media notwithstanding. In a postreferendum editorial, the *News* said:

"It will take some teamwork to awaken a city which apparently lost all of her old 'magic' yesterday but it must be done!"[37]

Birmingham residents throughout the 1900–1917 period received an inferior level of general municipal services, which declined in quality toward the end of the period as the financial condition of the city worsened.

Early in the century the police force was inadequate. Late in the nineteenth century seventy-two men had patrolled the city; in 1903, fifty officers covered the same geographic area and an increased population. Birmingham's force was one-half as large as those of other southern cities with comparable populations, and all but Birmingham had comprehensive telegraphic communication systems. A ratio of one officer per one thousand citizens was regarded within the profession as being minimally acceptable; typical ratios were 1:300 (Chicago) and 1:500 (New York City) in the North and no more than 1:1000 in the South. Birmingham's ratio was 1:2000.[38] Reductions in the force during the teens resulted in a force of 115 in 1914 as opposed to the 50 men of 1903.[39] However, in the interim, the geographic area to be protected had more than quadrupled and the population had increased almost as much.

Birmingham ranked last among southern cities in parks in 1907; six years later two park commissioners issued a statement of complaint: "Birmingham has probably a smaller developed park area on the whole than any other city of its size and population in the United States."[40]

Education was notoriously bad throughout the South in the early twentieth century, and Alabama ranked last among the states in per capita expenditures for public schools.[41] Although Birmingham ranked at or near the bottom of each year's list of major cities in this category of expenditures, local officials noted with pride the fact that expenditures per pupil were, in fact, declining. The 1883 per-pupil expenditure by the young school system had been $17.20; this figure had dropped to $13.29 in 1893 and further to $11.41 in 1903.[42] Lest this be interpreted as regression, the *News* assured its readers that because of better teaching methods and superior physical facilities, students received "vastly more" from their schooling than they had twenty years earlier.[43]

The 1916 school situation was reported to be more bleak. City Commissioner John R. Hornady pleaded for a bond issue for education, saying, "As matters stand now, many of our schools are mere shacks, unsafe, crowded and ill-adapted for school purposes."[44] Comparisons with other southern cities were discouraging. Richmond, Virginia, for example, spent $750,000 per year on thirty-five schools for 22,459 pupils. Birmingham spent only $450,000 on fifty-five schools for 25,248 students.[45] And the city's fiscal crisis had caused administrators to curtail basic services like kindergarten and free textbooks and supplies.

The provision of health care services by the city also lagged badly. Noting that the two private hospitals serving charity patients were unable to meet local needs, the *News* advocated a municipal charity hospital: "There are few cities in the country so large as Birmingham without a city hospital and a city ambulance corps." The city, it urged, should proceed toward establishing such "a useful public institution."[46] Data presented to the board of aldermen in 1906 emphasized the city's deficiency in this area. Birmingham in 1904 had allocated $3,557 to health care; within the state, Mobile spent $7,885 on the same category. Chattanooga owned its own charity hospital and was reported to spend $7,200 besides; Cincinnati, also maintaining a municipal hospital, spent $175,789 on health; the Memphis city hospital received $45,112 from local government; and Nashville spent $28,993 on health.[47]

The city did maintain charity beds in the local Catholic hospital and supported Hillman Hospital, a private charity institution; but the public response to the health needs of the community fell to others. The Jefferson County Board of Revenue assumed control of the seventy-eight-bed Hillman Hospital in 1907, along with its $9,000 debt and $17,000 per year operating expense.[48] And the University of Alabama School of Medicine opened a free dispensary for the walking sick that was financed by public subscription.[49] Even the federal government extended aid to the district in an early example of federal intervention in a local service area.

During a serious typhoid epidemic in 1916, the surgeon general of the United States was asked by U.S. senator Oscar Underwood to detail a staff member of the U.S. Public Health Service to Jefferson County; this request was supported by the Jefferson County Medical Society, a private organization that served as the county board of health. The federal health service also conducted a sanitary survey of the county, assisted the board of health in designing a unified city-county health department, and cooperated in funding the first county health officer, drawn from the staff of the service.[50] Though the city initially refused to merge its own health department into the newly designed agency, and though there was great opposition to the first health officer because he was Catholic, the Jefferson County Health Department was established and later achieved national recognition for the quality of its work.[51] But at the end of the 1900–1917 period health conditions in the city were still poor; of cities in the 100,000–300,000 class, only Memphis with 21.3 deaths per thousand population exceeded Birmingham with 20.3 per thousand.[52]

Statistical data about the entire population of Birmingham are somewhat misleading because they fail to recognize the vast differences between services and conditions in the black and white communities. The Birmingham death rate is a case in point. This single figure masks the fact that Whites in Birmingham, as in most other southern cities, consistently had a death rate that was about one-half the rate among Blacks.[53] The black death rate from tuberculosis of 349 deaths per 100,000 citizens was four times the white rate. In every area where information is available, it is clear that the level of services and quality of life for black Birminghamians were significantly below the admittedly low standards for the community as a whole. The black-white comparisons in public education are particularly telling.

The public school system in Birmingham was established for Whites. Early in 1873 the Elyton Land Company donated to the city land for its first public school. The deed specified how the school was to be utilized:

> To have and to hold to the Mayor and the Aldermen of Birmingham in trust as follows. For the use and purpose of erecting a schoolhouse and school buildings and improvements to be used under the management of the Mayor and Aldermen of Birmingham for the purpose of a free school for the white children now residing in, and who may reside hereafter in said city and for no other purpose and use whatever. The school is to be taught by white teachers.[54]

The city responded to a petition for support from the black community in 1877 by paying for a teacher for a school bought and supplied by civic-minded Blacks.[55] But by 1885 neither of the two black schools then existing offered more than six years of instruction, while white children could complete the eleventh grade.[56] In the 1880s and 1890s the building of schools for Blacks had roughly kept pace with the building of facilities for Whites, though the black plants were demonstrably inferior. But the expansion of schools in the first decade of the twentieth century brought virtually no benefits to the black community. According to one historian, "It was almost as if the Board [of Education] completely forgot about them."[57]

"As a matter of fact," Mayor George Ward observed in 1907, "the Negroes are not as well provided for now as they were ten years ago."[58] No new school had been built for Blacks between 1891 and 1907, while the Thomas School for Negroes in East Birmingham had burned in the mid-1890s, causing one thousand pupils to stop school.[59] The board of education had collected insurance for the school but had not replaced it. Instead, the board rented space in the basement of a neighborhood church, a location which frequently flooded, causing classes to be dismissed for days at a time. The *Birmingham News* commented that "the place is a menace to the public health, and if it were a private house would long since have been condemned as a nuisance."[60]

In 1905 Birmingham had eight elementary schools and one high school for white pupils; all were brick. The city had three elementary schools for black pupils in addition to the Thomas School; all were frame.[61] At least one of these frame schools was totally inadequate. Wrote the *News*: "The east end Negro school is in miserable quarters. It has about five hundred pupils who are packed in five rooms without light, without heating facilities, with a distressing ventilation, and without desks."[62] The *News* commented in the same editorial that no reasonable results could be expected from students working under these conditions, no matter how efficient the teachers and willing the students.

But inadequate physical facilities were not the only obstacle to comparable education for Blacks and Whites. The teacher-pupil ratio in white elementary schools was 40:1; in black schools it was 73.1.[63] The school attendance figures reflected the relative conditions of the schools. The 1906–07 school census showed that there were over 7,600 white children of school age living in the city, with 4,903 seats available in the schools; average daily attendance for Whites was 3,483. There were over 6,200 black children of school age, with 1,607 seats available in the schools. Average daily attendance for black pupils was 1,646, exceeding the seating capacity of the schools.[64] The school census figures showed an increase in black children of over 1,500 in fifteen years, but the number of these children attending school increased by only slightly more than 550.[65]

Black citizens had petitioned the board of education for improved facilities in 1905, expressing concern over racial prejudice in the allocation of school funds. The board, however, felt the petition to be "ill-advised" and "a practical insult."[66]

Mayor Ward joined the black community in pressing for improved school conditions. In his 1907 annual message he wrote: "It appears to me that we are not doing our duty to the Negro population in the matter of school facilities."[67] The final report of Ward included the recommendation that $100,000 of the $300,000 bond issue be appropriated for black schools. With considerable foresight he wrote:

> I wish to say here that in my opinion the city authorities are not doing their duty to the colored population nor pursuing a wise or just course in holding colored schools down practically to a worse condition than they were in fifteen years ago. . . . There will doubtless be discussions of this question for years to come but the sweep of the tide is toward elevation and better conditions through education and its force will ultimately prevail. The colored people are so intertwined in the life and traditions of the South that they must either be elevated by the whites or the whites will be affected injuriously by them through bad health and sanitary conditions.[68]

Blacks had cause for some hope in 1910. By that date a high-school department had been started in a rented building. The board of education had earmarked funds for improving black schools, recognizing the need for brick structures; and finally, in 1910 construction began on a new brick building for the Thomas School, the first brick building erected in Jefferson County for black students.[69]

But still black schools lagged, and official school reports indicated no sense of urgency to remedy the situation. Supporting a board of education request for a bond issue for new buildings in 1912, the superintendent summarized "the recommendations made in this and previous reports as to the most urgent and immediate needs of the white schools of the city."[70] His summary included no recommendations for improvements in black facilities. It was left to the newspaper to record that only one black school was in a modern, safe, and proper building; the remaining twenty-two were described as "shacks." "Common justice" required change, not only because of the economic debts owed the black community—"the foundation of much of this city's industrial structure"—but also because of the "superior race's moral duty."[71] Four years later twenty-five hundred Blacks held a mass meeting to protest conditions in Birmingham, particularly the conditions in the schools.[72]

Although data for other areas of life among Blacks are scant and often unreliable, all indicators point to the period 1900–1917 as one of either increasing exclusion from services or increasing segregation, by private action or with public sanction.

Parks, for example, had been used by Blacks and Whites alike when the city system was established in 1883.[73] In 1901 the park commissioners officially permitted Blacks to picnic in one of the parks, saying it was "a public place, dedicated to the people." However, citizens in the neighborhood formed a "walking delegation" and persuaded Blacks to cancel the event.[74] Two years later a black civic organization protested to the city council that the park superintendent himself had denied them access to a park.[75] After 1910 Blacks were not allowed in any of the parks except as servants unless specifically granted permission by the city commission.[76] Even when this was done, as in the case of a church group in 1914, hostile residents succeeded in discouraging the picnickers. The rejected congregation wrote to the commission expressing the hope that "this affair may lead to the provision of some suitable place where the Negro children may go in this sultry weather from the narrow and germ breathing alleys of our city."[77] The park commission did request $300 for two black playgrounds, but this compared poorly with the $15,375 sought for the seventeen existing and five proposed white areas.[78]

Until 1910, although neither local nor state law required segregation in public transportation, the streetcar company separated Blacks and Whites, often by partitions. But that year the council made official the customary practice by enacting a Jim Crow streetcar law.[79] The city fathers also explored officially for the first time laws to segregate the races in residential districts. One bill was presented to prohibit Whites and Blacks from living on the same block, but it was not passed pending court cases in other cities.[80] Brought up again in 1916, the housing segregation law finally was enacted in 1926.[81]

Wherever possible, the races were strictly separated toward the end of the period. The renovations in the Louisville and Nashville railroad station waiting room included one that was "somewhat of an innovation in this district, that of the absolute separation of the white and colored people and a private dining room for the colored people, as well as for the whites."[82] In 1912 Hillman Hospital services were rendered to Blacks and Whites on a segregated basis in the same building, but a new annex was projected that would allow a complete separation of the races in different buildings.[83] Similarly, the medical school established a new clinic in 1913 primarily because Whites, influenced by the crowds of Blacks in the single waiting room, were making less use of the existing facility. Fearing that the clinic might become "almost a strictly Negro service bureau," the school raised funds to "have everything in duplicate, one set for white people and one for Negroes."[84]

And at certain critical times, Blacks received no services at all. During the depression of the teens, the *News* commented that "not more than 10 percent of that [the black] population is assured of its daily bread without a hard struggle" but said "the whole matter has been shunted to disused tracks of the mind."[85] With unemployment among Blacks estimated at 50 percent, about 100 each day were leaving the city for the coal mines of West Virginia and Pennsylvania.[86] But when the city sponsored its only public works project designed specifically to aid the unemployed, a wood cutting program, no Blacks were included among the 115 beneficiaries.[87]

Throughout the period 1900–1917 there was an undercurrent of white concern that Blacks were being neglected in virtually every area of municipal life to the clear detriment of the race and the potential detriment of the entire community. Illustrative of this undercurrent and the mixture of condescension, religious concern, and self-interest that sustained it is the following editorial comment of the *News*:

> The white race has fallen away from its duty to colored people. The kindness and sympathy of the antebellum regime, with its paternal restraints, discipline and character training of the Negro, has to a large extent been supplanted by a feeling of indifference, cynicism, or downright antagonism on the part of the white people toward their unavoidable neighbor, their black burden of weak brothers. This situation is indeed out of keeping with the spirit of Christ. It is also a great blunder from a standpoint of enlightened selfishness.[88]

But white concern over the plight of Blacks in Birmingham never extended to one important arena, local politics. Blacks were virtually excluded from active participation in Alabama politics; and that was precisely what the white community, including its most liberal elements, wanted. Locally, Blacks had been barred from municipal politics in 1890 when the white Democratic primary had been instituted.[89] They continued to vote in state and national elections until the "disfranchising constitution" of 1901, which included "the most complicated and undemocratic suffrage article in the United States."[90] Local leaders claimed that the county board of registrars applied the property and education requirements fairly to both races and that well-educated Blacks were allowed to register. But the number of black registrants was inconsequential during this period. Of 5,240 voters registered by officials during the spring of 1902, 76 were black.[91] The following analysis of local politics and decision making in Birmingham is therefore an exploration of power and participation solely within the white male community.

2

Politics and Decision Making

A T THE VERY BEGINNING of Birmingham's history, political leadership was assumed by the same men who controlled the Elyton Land Company and thereby dominated the financial life of the community. The first elected mayor of Birmingham was James R. Powell, the election manipulator and president of Elyton Land Company; serving from 1872–74, he was succeeded by one of the principal stockholders of the company, W. H. Morris, who resigned near the end of his two-year term. The board of aldermen filled the vacancy by appointing the new president of the Elyton Land Company, Dr. H. M. Caldwell, who served until 1878. Powell was challenged in the next municipal election by Thomas Jeffers, a local businessman who won the election, served four years, and was then succeeded by A. O. Lane, a successful local attorney. Other mayors in the nineteenth century included B. Asbury Thompson, broker and former city treasurer; David J. Fox, retail grocer; James A. Van Hoose, wholesale grocer who was also president and general manager of a local steel railway; Frank V. Evans, newspaper founder, broker, and former city treasurer; and Walter M. Drennen, president of a dry goods and department store. Thus, after 1878 political leadership passed from associates of the Elyton Land Company, the dominant economic entity in the community, to men of means who were still of lesser economic rank.[1]

The separation between political leadership and economic power increased as major outside investors entered the district, starting with the Tennessee Company in 1886, and gradually changed the economy into an extension of primarily northern financial interests. The new economic elite consisted of absentee stockholders and the managers whom they dispatched to Birmingham to supervise their investments. Characteristically, this elite avoided participation in day-to-day local politics and surfaced as a political force only when its immediate interests were involved.

A major factor that differentiates the political history of Birmingham from that of many communities is the absence of a massive influx of immigrants. While the city did develop identifiable ethnic neighborhoods and had at least two foreign-language newspapers, the ethnic influence on local politics was negligible; the foreign born residents in the population never exceeded 4.3 percent.[2]

For local industry the functional equivalent of the immigrant as a source of labor was the Black. The proportion of Blacks in the Jefferson County population had risen from about 20 percent in 1870 to about 40 percent in 1890 as migrants from rural counties settled in the Birmingham district and worked in the mines and mills.[3] Throughout the twentieth century, Blacks accounted for between 30 and 40 percent of the population of the city itself. However, disfranchisement of this substantial proportion of the population prevented Blacks from playing a significant role in politics in the early twentieth century.

The following analysis of local politics includes an examination of the socioeconomic characteristics of local officeholders, a brief review of the routine decision-making process of city government, and a study of three "key issues" during the period 1900–1917.

Officeholders and Elections

In 1900 Birmingham had a mayor-council form of government with aldermen elected by districts. The mayor served a two-year term and aldermen served four-year terms. Each district elected two representatives who served staggered terms; one-half of the board of aldermen was elected every two years. From 1900 to 1 January 1910 the city was divided into nine wards. On that date surrounding municipalities were consolidated with the core city, and the number of wards increased to sixteen. This expanded aldermanic board served only fifteen months, at which time the mayor-council form of government was replaced by a three-man commission.

An analysis of the occupational backgrounds of the mayors and city commissioners indicates that throughout the period, executive leadership was provided by successful local business and professional men. Their occupations provided these men with economic security and in some cases with recognition as outstanding business leaders in the community. None of them, however, was associated with an institution that could be said to dominate the local economy; the most economically powerful mayor was probably Walter M. Drennen, president of one of Birmingham's three leading department stores, manager of a coal and coke company, and president of a cracker company. Prominent and respected as a business leader, he was not among the economic elite who could potentially have influenced politics by the threat of closing his operations and leaving the district. That kind of potential power rested only in the hands of the owners and managers of the major industries; these men were not represented among local officeholders.

Drennen, mayor from 1900 to 1905, was succeeded by George B. Ward, who had left his position as paying teller of the city's leading bank to open a successful stock and bond company. That company survives today as the influential security investment company of Sterne, Agee, and Leach; but then as now it was only one among several such firms in the community. During his public and later private life, Ward was regarded as a leading spokesman for the progressive element of the local business community; but he, too, could have closed his firm and left the community without posing a serious threat to the economic welfare of the total district. Frank P. O'Brien, one of the leading building contractors in the district, served as mayor from 1909 to 1910; upon his death he was succeeded in office by Harry Jones, head salesman for a local hardware company.

The commission form of government was established in 1911, and the occupants of these offices maintained the pattern of political leadership by men of local prominence but not of overwhelming economic power. The first commission, appointed by the governor, consisted of Culpepper Exum, president of a powder company and a fertilizer company; A. O. Lane, mayor from 1882 to 1888, lawyer, and circuit court judge; and James Weatherly, lawyer. George Ward returned to local office as first elected president of the commission in 1913. Others serving on the commission before 1917 include the proprietor of a drug and seed company, a civil engineer, a newspaper editor, and a physician.[4]

An analysis of the occupational backgrounds of aldermen serving from 1900 until the change in the form of government indicates a similar pattern of dominance by established local businessmen. However, also on the board were occasional representatives of the business—but not industrial—elite and of the skilled working class. The following listing of candidates during the 1903 Democratic primary (table 1) is representative of aldermanic races during the period.

The public officials in Birmingham between 1900 and 1917 were not a rising class of entrepreneurs displacing an established elite of old families from office, because there was no such elite in the young industrial city. Neither were they representative of the most powerful economic institutions in the community in general. Rather, most of the officials were either professionals or businessmen who had achieved modest wealth in a local economy that was dominated by nonlocal influences. These local officials experienced no real challenge from the working classes; neither were they leavened by representatives of the huge industrial complexes that dwarfed even the largest of the purely local enterprises.

Municipal elections present a welter of detail about personalities, charges

Table 1.   Candidates for Alderman, 1903.[5] (First candidate listed in each ward was winner.)

Ward 1—Skilled worker in rolling mill
            Saloon operator
Ward 2—Head of leading mercantile firm; past president of board of trade;
            past vice-president of commercial club
            Official of loan company
            Liquor merchant
Ward 3—President of plumbing company
            Attorney
Ward 4—President of coal and coke company; coal mine operator; un-
            opposed
Ward 5—President of furniture company
            President of savings bank
            Paying teller, bank
Ward 6—Lawyer
            Lawyer
Ward 7—President of coal and lumber company
            Commercial agent for railway
            Secretary, waterworks company
Ward 8—Head salesman, hardware company; unopposed
Ward 9—Bookkeeper for brick company
            General manager of iron company
            Insurance agent
            Physician
            Liquor merchant

of maladministration, and promises of more and better services. In general campaigns dealt with few broad issues; in at least three the *News* made comments similar to its observation during the 1908 primary that "perhaps never before in the history of the city has a city campaign been so devoid of interest."[6]

The majority of issues that did arise in the various campaigns saw candidates differ not on matters of principle but rather on matters of detail. Throughout the period candidates advocated municipal ownership of public utilities, especially the waterworks. They differed as to whether the city should try to purchase the company's existing plant or should construct a new one. They also differed as to whether or not the city should operate its own electrical light plant or continue to contract with a private utility; Clement R. Wood, an avowed Socialist running for mayor in 1913, urged extension of public owner- ship to street railways as well.[7] But in regard to the issue of public utilities, the candidates for mayor or commission between 1900 and 1917 fit the general pat- tern in municipal politics in the United States during the Progressive Era of favoring an expanded governmental responsibility for basic services; only one was formally a Socialist, but all were "sewer socialists."[8]

When the issue arose, the candidates for mayor also favored political re- form, even when it meant abolishing the office they sought. In 1910 when a popular movement was under way to adopt the then-fashionable commission form of government, all three mayoral aspirants endorsed the change.[9]

Candidates regularly charged that the opponents were part of a political "ring," and challengers claimed that municipal services were declining while deficits rose. The latter was usually a matter of fact, given the extended periods of municipal financial crises. Challengers variously promised cleaner streets, more street paving, better health services, lower streetcar fares, and better schools. But the fiscal restraints imposed upon the occupants of office made such campaign statements little more than a campaign litany. A less popular but repeated promise was one of fiscal restraint. Voters showed no consis- tent preference either for advocates of better services or for advocates of re- trenchment.

In only two campaigns during the period did issues of real consequence divide the candidates. The 1907 race for mayor between George Ward and Frank O'Brien produced two topics that occupied large amounts of newspaper space and appeared to generate considerable popular interest: police adminis- tration and the regulation of liquor.

The Birmingham police department was managed by a popularly elected commission that was responsible both for the selection of officers and for the day-to-day operation of the force. The chief was appointed by the mayor and board of aldermen, occasionally in accord with the preferences of voters as ex- pressed in the Democratic primary. Ward had consistently argued, in opposi- tion to the elected police commission, that the mayor and aldermen should set general policy for the department, since they were responsible for the good governance of the city and the police were an instrument necessary to its achievement. As mayor, Ward had preferred charges of corruption against the commission and had issued orders directly to the chief regarding enforcement of saloon and gambling regulations. Standing for reelection in 1907, he advo- cated abolition of the commission and assignment of full responsibility for the department to the mayor and board of aldermen. O'Brien countered with a proposal that the force be placed under civil service; he argued that Ward's plan would give the mayor undemocratic control over the police and would turn the department into a political machine.[10]

The second issue was closely intertwined with the first. Ward favored strict regulation of saloons, primarily by means of high licenses and their segregation in specific neighborhoods. He repeatedly charged that the police department colluded with saloon owners and permitted flagrant violations of municipal gambling laws. O'Brien was generally regarded as the candidate of local liquor interests.[11] Though he did not speak publicly in behalf of open and unregulated saloons, this issue was perceived by Ward forces and local newspapers as basic to the campaign. Ward won the 1907 election and then retired from office two years later. At that time O'Brien was elected in an issueless campaign in which he faced no serious opposition.[12]

The 1917 race for president of the city commission was a heated campaign between Ward and N. A. Barrett, a physician from one of the suburban neighborhoods that had joined the city in 1910. Several of the outlying areas had expressed hostility toward the city government, particularly citing inadequate public services as justification for their occasional threats to withdraw from Greater Birmingham. Barrett claimed that the great influence of the Birmingham Railway, Light and Power Company, the provider of criticized basic services, was the major campaign issue.[13]

But anti-Catholicism emerged as the most publicized issue of the vicious 1917 campaign, which included the theft and photographing of city hall documents and implications by Barrett that Ward was the tool of a Roman Catholic conspiracy to take over Birmingham's government. Barrett promised that if elected, he would exclude Catholics from appointive office and particularly from positions as schoolteachers.[14] The True Americans, a secret nativist organization, supported the suburban challenger, though Barrett's leading campaign aids denied any connection with the group. Ward delighted the two thousand supporters who filled a downtown theater to attend his final rally when he showed motion pictures taken from a parked automobile recording local leading citizens and Barrett supporters entering the headquarters of the True American Society.[15]

Barrett won the election by virtue of his overwhelming margin in the outlying neighborhoods; Ward easily carried the central city. The election was widely interpreted as a serious blow both to the efforts to unite the city and suburbs of Greater Birmingham and to religious tolerance. The cleavage between core and outlying area was noted by the *News*: "Ever since the formation of Greater Birmingham [in 1910] there has been a tendency for the component parts not to cohere; this election has emphasized that tendency."[16] That tendency had been muted when the mayor-council form of government was replaced by the commission shortly after the consolidation of 1910; had the board of aldermen been continued, fourteen members would have represented the suburbs as opposed to eighteen from the central city. But suburban protests prior to 1917 had been confined to complaints about inadequate services and occasional threats of withdrawal from the city, especially by Ensley, which had been included in Greater Birmingham by the governor in an executive amendment with no opportunity for local residents to express their preferences. It was not until the Barrett campaign with its clear appeal to the suburban vote that the sharp differences between core city and peripheral neighborhoods became real issues in local politics.

The campaign also introduced religion into local elections for the first time. Anti-Catholicism had already surfaced in the form of opposition to the Catholic health officer recommended for the newly created city-county health department by the federal health service; this opposition came from the county board of revenue, the medical society, and city hall. Barrett was obviously appealing to a strong anti-Catholic sentiment, and the True Americans received newspaper coverage for the first time during the campaign. Ominously, one of the first acts of the city commission was the demotion of the highly respected chief of police to the rank of patrolman; he was a Roman Catholic.[17]

The campaign of 1917 offered a forecast of the intense anti-Catholicism that would sweep the district in the 1920s, encouraged and sustained by a strong Ku Klux Klan, which became the dominant power in the county and city politics during that decade. So powerful was the Klan that no aspiring politician could hope to get elected unless he had been endorsed by it. Klan affiliation during the 1920s haunted the later lives of a number of prominent citizens, chief among them Hugo Black at the time of his nomination to the Supreme Court.[18]

Birmingham at the end of the period resembled older northern cities in respect to an identifiable division between center and periphery. Urban historians and political scientists have both noted that the periphery, largely inhabited by white Anglo-Saxon Protestants of middle or upper income, was the source of ethnic and religious hostility and reforms such as prohibition that were directed at lower income, working-class residents of the center.[19] The Birmingham data tend to support the local application of this generalization.

It is important to note topics that did not emerge in local election campaigns between 1900 and 1917. First, no questions related to race emerged. What discussion there was on racial issues was conducted during routine aldermanic or commission meetings and dealt with new legal measures to enforce customary segregation in housing and public transportation. Suggestions that Blacks were being slighted came primarily from outside government, especially from the newspapers. The only notable public figure to speak in behalf of the black community was George Ward, and his remarks generally came in the context of annual reports containing general observations and not specific proposals. The outstanding exception to this pattern was his detailed recommendations concerning the allocation of a $300,000 school bond issue in which he urged that one-third of the total be spent in upgrading black schools.[20] Electoral politics in Birmingham turned not at all on questions of race. And when they turned on questions of religion, as they did in 1917, the thrust was toward additional exclusions from politics.

Second, the welfare of Birmingham's poor did not emerge as a serious electoral issue. Clement R. Wood, Socialist candidate for the commission in 1913, did cite "miserly economy" in areas like health and housing and called for the establishing of a municipal employment bureau.[21] But his opponents did not respond to these ideas, and Wood was badly defeated in the election. In no other race did topics specifically relating to the poor emerge; in no campaign was the city welfare department or the level of support of private charities a matter of controversy. Again, public discussion of problems of the poor was stimulated by others, especially by those groups concerned with their condition and by reform-oriented newspapers like the *News*, which carried an extensive analysis of housing among the poor in 1913.[22]

Routine Operations of Government

The most extensive information about the operations of local government on a day-to-day basis is found in newspaper accounts of official meetings. There are additional fragments that give insight into routine governmental behavior, such as insurance company reports on major fires that point to inefficiency and lack of training among firefighters; complaints of misconduct against members of the police force; reports of directives to the force from the chief to arrest vagrants during times of economic depression; and reports on school curriculum.[23]

Every public meeting of the board of aldermen or city commission was reported in the newspaper, usually in great detail; and many meetings included disagreements that could be analyzed in an effort to understand local government. Detailed analyses of particular strictly local controversies do not significantly further an understanding of the most important characteristics of local politics. However, there did emerge over time a pattern of types of questions that appeared before city officials; general examination of these various types of decisions is a more productive approach for understanding the local scene.

The mayor and board of aldermen, and later the city commission, regularly confronted six types of decisions, which related to (1) the municipal budget; (2) the organizational structure of offices; (3) the occupants of offices; (4) whether or not to provide basic services; (5) the manner of providing these services; and (6) the regulation of behavior.

Establishing the city's revenue and expenditures for each fiscal year was a procedure that consumed considerable time and received extensive newspaper coverage; throughout each year, officials made incremental changes in the basic budget. The revenues from real and property taxes were fixed by the constitution and therefore were not subject to local decision once the maximum permissible rate was reached, as it was in Birmingham. Only property reassessment could increase the amount received at the prescribed rates, and this function was assigned to county government. The revenues from taxes were supplemented by revenues from licenses on businesses; and fixing the license schedule was an annual activity that consistently generated controversy, as business spokesmen urged reductions for their categories of enterprise. Executives of major utilities and traction companies, large retail operators, small retail operators, and saloon owners were familiar actors in this budgetary drama; major industries were not represented because of their location beyond the city limits. Eventually, the utilities and traction companies paid substantially higher licenses, reflecting growing public antagonism to their increasing profits and inefficient service. For example, between 1904 and 1907 the license fee of the huge Birmingham Railway, Light and Power Company increased from $9,000 to $35,000 per year; the waterworks fee increased from $1,000 to $15,000; and that of each street railway rose from $500 to $1,750.[24] In general, when the rates of retail operators were increased, delegations of notable businessmen succeeded in persuading officials to reduce them. This process occurred most frequently during periods of economic distress when the city needed additional revenues but when businessmen could legitimately claim that their own ability to pay was reduced because of declining sales. Liquor license rates fluctuated greatly, reflecting shifts in power between those favoring restriction/temperance/prohibition and those opposed to such policies.

Expenditures were limited by expected revenues on the one hand and by the constitutionally imposed debt ceiling on the other. Within these limits, city fathers made incremental adjustments in departmental budgets and acted upon the annual requests of the procession of private welfare organizations that were the recipients of public support. The departmental budgets, including the schools, fluctuated predictably with anticipated revenues; the appropriations to private organizations present a more complex process, which is examined below. A recurring matter of decision was the calling of elections authorizing the sale of bonds for capital improvements such as the construction of new schools, a sewerage system, and a new courthouse. Discussions on bond elections seldom involved disagreement over the question of need; the issue was rather a question of timing.

Reflecting the increasing need of the young and growing city for municipal regulation of various phases of life for public health and safety, local officials made several apparently uncontroversial changes in the administrative structure of government. At various times during the period new departments were created for building inspection, plumbing inspection, electrical inspection, parks and playgrounds, smoke regulation, and welfare. Financial crises saw periodic reductions in these new offices, and occasionally a department was at least temporarily abolished. But the long-term tendency was toward increasingly complex local government.

More controversial than the number of local offices was the question of who occupied these positions. The municipal record is pockmarked with disputes over who should be appointed to office or who should serve on boards, most notably the board of education. These controversies appear to have centered on personalities rather than principles; they reveal no enduring divisions within the city, but rather periodic charges of official incompetence that were rarely documented at the time and are virtually impossible to evaluate, given available information.

Because of the rapid development of the city and its persistent financial difficulties, a recurring theme in local politics was the provision of basic services to its citizens. Elected officials received a stream of requests for extension of gas, electricity, and transportation; more fire stations and hydrants; additional schools; road grading and street paving; viaducts over railroad tracks; and additional sewers. The decision of whether or not to meet a service need depended on the current financial condition of the city; the decision as to what area in particular would benefit seems to have been a function of economic class. It is clear that the black community did not receive an equitable share of public services. Instead, improvements were made chiefly in the newly developed neighborhoods that lacked services and in the downtown area. The new neighborhoods were the domain of the upper and middle classes who could provide their own transportation or utilize the street railways, while downtown was the location of commercial activity and therefore received special attention from a city government committed to encouraging conditions favorable to economic activity.[25]

Once the decision had been made to extend a service or upgrade it, controversy frequently surrounded the subsequent question of who would perform the work. The awarding of franchises and the terms of these contracts occupied a large portion of the officials' time and stimulated intense public interest; this is true particularly in the awarding of street railway franchises and in the terms of contracts for gas, electricity, water, and telephone service. Each specific decision involved a complex cast of actors and masses of detailed and often technical evidence. Rival companies would present claims prior to the awarding of contracts, while consumers and company executives would tangle over specific contract terms and revisions.

The final category of local government decision making involved the regulation of behavior. Two themes underlie this activity: the interest of religious groups in particular in temperance, moral behavior, and observance of the Sabbath; and a concern for racial segregation. Officials acted upon requests for segregation of saloons and houses of prostitution in designated districts, generally granting them.[26] They also enforced the ban against Sunday movies and sports in the face of opposition by theater owners and less traditional elements who felt that working men should not be denied entertainment on their only free day. And, as noted earlier, they passed ordinances enforcing racial segregation on public transportation and explored the possibilities of laws to segregate residential neighborhoods.

The kinds of decisions reviewed above were not related to the public issues that most stirred Birmingham residents between 1900 and 1917 or that most clearly illuminate the distribution of political influence in the city; in short, they are not the "important," "key," or "critical" decisions that were made during the period. Three "important" public issues did occur during this period that reveal a consistent pattern of decision-making activities, a similar set of actors, and an identifiable political culture that characterized the era. These issues were municipal ownership of the waterworks, the Greater Birmingham consolidation of 1910, and the change from mayor-council to commission form of government in 1911.

All three of these issues were important to contemporaries, judged by the amount of newspaper coverage given them, by the amount of time and money devoted to them, by the number of public and private figures involved in them, and by the common understanding that they affected the lives of many people and were significant to the future development of the Birmingham district. They are significant in historical perspective because they shed light on the nature of the decision-making process in nonroutine situations, on the political culture of the community, and on political conditions that are especially influential in the later history of Birmingham.

The reconstruction of decisions is a difficult and frustrating task in which the comments of President Kennedy become painfully meaningful: "The *essence of ultimate decision* remains impenetrable to the observer—often, indeed, to the

decider himself. . . . There will always be dark and tangled stretches in the decision-making process—mysterious even to those who may be most intimately
involved."[27]

The inevitable uncertainties involved in the analysis of any issue are increased greatly when research is conducted many years after the event and is
largely dependent on newspaper accounts. In the absence of the opportunity
to interview participants or observe parts of the decision-making process, one
must accept the possibility of journalistic bias or error as a given. Furthermore,
the available data do not allow the researcher to specify in detail the particular
roles of all the individuals and groups involved, much less make accurate judg-
ments about the relative influence of the various actors on the events studied.
The following case studies are therefore necessarily rather general.

There is, however, justification for believing that the newspaper accounts
are in the main accurate and that the conclusions drawn from the studies are
valid. First, the journalistic record can be checked against official documents
such as meeting minutes and court cases at several key points in the history
of each issue; the official record in all cases supports the newspaper accounts.
Second, the three case studies present results consistent with each other,
thereby increasing confidence in the general conclusions drawn from each
about the nature of local politics in important issues. Third, the work of other
researchers dealing with both Birmingham and other cities tends to support
these reconstructions of key decisions.[28] Finally, the results are consistent with
the subjective evaluations of local politics made by knowledgeable citizens
both at the time and in later years. Neither scholarly research nor im-
pressionistic data suggest that any unnamed actor may have played a
significant behind-the-scenes role, nor do they call into question the sequence
of events presented below.

Municipal Ownership of the Waterworks

An enduring issue throughout the 1900–1917 period was municipal ownership of the waterworks. Like many other American cities, Birmingham in its
early days relied heavily upon private enterprise to provide essential public
services. Garbage collection, gas, electricity, transportation, and water were all
privately provided in 1900, though the city did assume responsibility for garbage collection in 1901.[29] Large utility and traction companies continued to
supply the other services, even though public protests over rates and service
indicated a growing disenchantment with the corporations.

The focal point of the general controversy was the American Waterworks
and Guaranty Company of Pittsburgh, which in the first decade of the century

operated forty other municipal systems throughout the country.[30] Birmingham had entered into a thirty-year contract with the company in 1888, with an established rate to be paid by consumers. As years passed and the city grew rapidly, the waterworks company enjoyed increasing profits while consumers continued to pay the same high 1888 rates. As in many other American cities at this time, both public officials and private business and citizen groups began to press for municipal ownership of the waterworks.

Mayor Walter M. Drennen pointed to the city's water supply as a health menace as well in his 1900 message, citing a typhoid epidemic the preceding summer. To seek lower rates he announced that the mayor and council would initiate court action against the company. "Public interest is impatient of the contract system, and public interest demands public service. . . . This city is beset with the power and influence of private corporations."[31]

Drennen's call for municipal ownership was not supported by all major elements in the city. The *News* opposed the plan because of the great cost it believed would be involved, while the Commercial Club, representative of local industry and large merchants, also favored a contract with the company. The Board of Trade, a strictly mercantile organization, favored municipal ownership.[32] Joining forces with the board of aldermen, the Board of Trade collaborated with officials in 1903 on a survey of cities with populations of 100,000 or more to determine the extent of municipal ownership; results showed that twenty-nine of thirty-eight cities owned their systems. After receiving this report, the aldermen instructed the city attorney to draft an ordinance nullifying the water contract, but this bill apparently was never voted upon.[33]

The Commercial Club soon abandoned its previous opposition to the Board of Trade's position. The two organizations formed a joint committee to draft a bill establishing a water commission for all of Jefferson County, claiming that $6 million in funds for industrial development had been invested elsewhere because of an inadequate water supply. The *News* expressed satisfaction over the fact that the whole question of water for the district was now "in the hands of able and farsighted businessmen." And the county board of revenue both expressed its approval of the water commission plan and agreed to pay a portion of what it would cost the Commercial Club–Board of Trade Committee to have enabling legislation drafted. The Commercial Club also became a supporter of municipal ownership of the Birmingham system.[34]

Official activity on the question resumed in 1906 when a council committee reviewed prevailing rates and found them to be "exorbitant and unreasonable" in comparison with those of other cities. It called municipal ownership the only satisfactory solution to both the rate problem and the need for a larger supply of inexpensive water for industrial use; the *News* endorsed this position.[35] In

January 1907 the Birmingham Municipal Ownership League was established under the presidency of the city attorney and organized on a ward basis, with each district canvassed by a subcommittee of six of its residents. Additional leadership for the league was provided by a newspaper editor, a leading minister, and prominent lawyers and merchants; businessmen constituted a majority of the league's most active leaders.[36] The immediate objective of the league was the calling of a referendum on a $3 million bond issue for the purpose of building a new plant or buying the existing one; the citizens' group promised a one-third rate reduction under municipal ownership.[37] The board of aldermen acted favorably upon the league's petition, signed by 750, in a resolution both setting the referendum and endorsing municipal ownership. But then the board reversed itself without explanation; accounts give no hint as to why this about-face occurred or who might have sought it.[38]

Confronted by this setback, supporters of municipal ownership undertook a nine-month study of the question, conducted by a joint committee of members of the Board of Trade, the Commercial Club, and the board of aldermen.[39] The Board of Trade assumed the leadership role in 1910–11, canvassing candidates for the state legislature to determine their positions on the issue, establishing a committee of eight prominent merchants to work with Birmingham officials in behalf of municipal ownership, and drawing up a bill for submission to the state legislature that would empower the city to own and operate its own water and electric light plants.[40] The *News* assisted the movement by conducting a survey of southern cities that showed that Birmingham paid among the highest rates in the region. Editorially supporting municipal ownership, the paper concluded that the profit motive was incompatible with the public needs of the developing city for improvement of existing service and extension of lines into new areas. The *News* also sent reporters to visit southern cities that had taken over their water systems, emphasizing the savings to consumers and the superior services.[41] Organized labor, through the Birmingham Trades Council, began a petition campaign asking the city commission to authorize a bond issue; from this time forward the Trades Council played a secondary but supporting role in the effort.[42]

Beginning in 1912 the waterworks company and the city commission tangled in a series of highly complex battles that were conducted by means of local ordinances, private conferences, and court cases. After the company had refused to negotiate an agreement in secret session with the commission, the city initiated a suit against the company in state court. The legal action prompted the company to negotiate a new twenty-five-year contract with reduced rates, which the commission submitted to the voters in a referendum. An active campaign against the proposed contract was led by the Municipal Ownership League, and the measure was overwhelmingly voted down.

Assuming the revised contract was invalid, the commission passed a new ordinance, not subject to referendum, cutting rates 50 percent below the 1888 scale in a deliberate effort to test the city's power to regulate rates by ordinance. The company, in turn, sent out bills based on the terms of the defeated contract and filed suit against the city in federal court. The Municipal Ownership League, aided by the city attorney, organized a legal division to prepare a countersuit and urged customers to sue the company individually, with league support, when they received their bills. A newly formed Water Consumers Protective Association mailed postcards to all residents of the city, asking them to indicate the amounts of their water bills in an effort to strengthen the case against the company.

Between 1912 and 1915 the city and the company were engaged in multiple court cases. In general, the company argued that its actions were all consistent with the terms of the 1888 contract. The city argued that the contract had in fact been violated, that it had an inherent right to regulate public utilities, and that long-term contracts binding succeeding administrations were unconstitutional. Lower courts ruled against the city; appeals were pending when the issue was settled by mutual agreement. The company agreed to reduce rates and to give the city the right to purchase its plant at a figure to be set by a jointly appointed appraisal committee; the city in return agreed to drop all court cases. The end of the period saw disagreement over the assessed value of the plant and a decision pending over whether to buy it or issue $4.5 million authorized in a bond election to build a new plant.[43]

The Greater Birmingham Consolidation

Local agitation for consolidation of Birmingham with its suburbs began in 1900 with "quiet missionary work" by unnamed citizens for what came to be called Greater Birmingham. This activity received immediate support from the newspapers, which noted that the 1900 census would record a population of under 40,000 when in fact 100,000 lived in the district.[44] The Commercial Club also favored the consolidation and demonstrated its support by participating in a joint Commercial Club–Board of Aldermen Greater Birmingham committee established by Mayor Drennen. After two of the suburbs voted against merger, the mayor expanded this committee by appointing one representative of each outlying community to it.[45] The position of the large steel makers was also staked out early in the campaign by the executive of the Republic Steel Company facility: "If the vote is in favor of incorporation of Elyton and to include our rolling mills, I shall close down the mills and move them away."[46]

The *News* launched an intensive editorial campaign in behalf of Greater Birmingham in 1902, saying that "the injustice of the census figures of 1900 must be wiped out."[47] There followed a series of "Pull for Greater Birming-ham" editorials, each ending with the boast "Great Is Birmingham and the *News* Is Its Prophet." The Board of Trade now went on record as favoring the plan, also.[48] And the Commercial Club–Board of Aldermen committee, led by Mayor Drennen, met in Montgomery with county legislators and suburban officials to try to produce a consolidation bill that would be acceptable to the outlying areas. A Greater Birmingham bill, drafted by the city attorney, was passed by the house—providing for an election upon petition of 25 percent of the voters in the affected area and tax exemptions for the large corporations, which were included in the proposed new boundaries. However, the custom of senatorial courtesy in the Alabama legislature enabled the bill to be killed when a single Jefferson County senator, Hugh Morrow, opposed the measure, citing a constitutional technicality and—more significantly—the fear of ex-empted industries that they would be taxed soon.[49]

Leadership for Greater Birmingham was now provided by the Commercial Club, which convened supporters in the fall of 1905 to formulate a campaign for enabling legislation during a special session that was to be called by the governor; endorsements were received from city officials, the Board of Trade, the Jefferson County Board of Health, the Jefferson County Board of Revenue, the Birmingham Board of Education, and the Birmingham Trades Council. They reported that consolidation would offer protection against epidemics by extending over a greater area the police power of the city to require connection of property to the sanitary sewer system. Second, consolidation would lead to uniform police services over the entire metropolitan area. Third, suburbs would gain the benefits of Birmingham's school system. Fourth, industries could be more easily recruited to the larger city. And fifth, Greater Birmingham could borrow money at a lower interest rate. The *News* consistently maintained that the need to improve public health was the prime motive behind the in-tensified consolidation drive, but hurt pride at the city's population rank clearly played a large role in the movement. The Commercial Club report rec-ommended that the property of the major steel producers be designated non-taxing districts. A committee opposed to the club's report was immediately formed, headed by the local executives of the Sloss-Sheffield and Republic steel companies and the mayor of North Birmingham.[50]

Greater Birmingham legislation was next introduced in 1907 and was ac-companied by an intense lobbying campaign conducted by the Commercial Club and the Board of Trade, both of which sent several delegations of sup-porters to the capital during the course of the session. Their case was strength-ened by a typhoid epidemic during the summer of 1907 that motivated physi-cians to issue a statement calling passage of a bill "absolutely necessary for the public safety."[51] Bills embodying various plans for referenda, tax exemptions, and exclusion of industries were considered. The bill preferred by the Board of Trade and the Commercial Club finally passed, excluding the major steel plants from Greater Birmingham. Before deciding whether to sign the bill or not, Governor Braxton Bragg Comer met in Birmingham with one thousand supporters of the plan at a meeting sponsored by the Commercial Club in its headquarters; the owner of a large textile plant in the district and a personal opponent of consolidation, the governor agreed "to stretch his conscience as it had never been stretched before" to sign the bill. A key supporter, commenting on the special privileges granted industries, made the revealing statement: "It is not that we are subservient to the corporations but we cannot live without them."[52] Upon their return to the city the legislative floor leaders for the plan were greeted by a brass band and a cheering crowd estimated at one thousand in "one of the most remarkable demonstrations of public approval of the official act of public servants ever witnessed in Birmingham."[53]

Once the legislature had acted, a ninety-three-member Citizens Committee for Greater Birmingham promoted consolidation through public meetings and newspaper advertisements, pointing to the chance to "remain in the race for municipal supremacy." The Commercial Club and *The Labor Advocate*, newspaper of organized labor, endorsed the plan. The referendum produced a vote in favor of consolidation with majorities in both old Birmingham and the suburbs.[54] Ironically, however, the bill was declared unconstitutional by the Alabama Supreme Court because of a legislative clerk's technical error in reporting it in the senate journal. This unexpected setback caused another round of bill-drafting, debate, and lobbying in the 1909 special session before a new bill was properly passed and signed by the governor, establishing Greater Birmingham without referendum effective 1 January 1910.[55] Ten years earlier, Birmingham had covered 11.4 square miles and had had a population of 38,415; the consolidation resulted in an area of 48.3 square miles and a population of 132,685. Image-conscious boosters noted with pride that Birmingham had advanced from the fourteenth-ranking city in the South to the fourth, trailing only New Orleans, Louisville, and Atlanta.[56]

The Change in the Form of Government

Students of municipal reform in the early twentieth century have noted that adoption of the commission form of government was one of the most popular changes sought, particularly by the business community. Reformers were attracted to the plan because it replaced many unpaid aldermen representing districts with a few, usually five, paid officials elected at large who gave full time to city government. Because aldermen were unpaid, it was felt that they would attempt to gain personal profit by exploiting their official positions. Because they were only part-time public officials, it was felt that they could never truly master the intricacies of government in a large city. Because they represented districts, it was felt that they would serve narrow neighborhood interests at the expense of the more general interest of the city as a whole. It was apparent that reformers hoped to attract candidates with backgrounds in business into politics under the commission plan.

Support for a commission in Birmingham appeared at the same time that its popularity spread across the nation. The *News* gave editorial praise to the commission of Houston and observed, "Business methods are what are most desirable in municipal government."[57] Mayor George Ward, a product of the business community and frequent spokesman for its progressive members, also endorsed the commission form: "A strong centralized government will produce results the people want. Our present system has not done it yet and never will."[58]

Birmingham's board of aldermen in 1908 provided civic reformers with more than adequate cause for wanting radical change in city government. Three of its eighteen members were simultaneously under investigation for corrupt practices, two for profiting from city real estate transactions and the third for violating the municipal code's prohibition against working for a company holding a franchise from the city. A fourth alderman escaped indictment on charges of graft only because the indictment was technically deficient; the grand jury, which returned no bill, was chaired by a Birmingham alderman.[59]

When these abuses were publicized, the city experienced what seems to have been a grass-roots movement in behalf of a city commission. One hundred thirty-seven leading citizens issued a call for a mass meeting "for the purpose of considering municipal affairs, and what can be done to improve same."[60] Meeting in a packed auditorium, speakers attacked the inefficiency of the aldermanic system as well as the corruption of the aldermen, which were seen as the inevitable results of a system of government in which unpaid amateurs decided complex questions. Others praised the commission plan, reviewing successful experiences in neighboring cities like Memphis. After over two hours those in attendance went on record as wanting enabling legislation that would permit a referendum on the issue.[61] The *News* supported the movement by reviewing the history and operation of the commission in Galveston, the city of its founding, and by printing a series of articles on its use in other cities.[62]

Representative W. E. Urquhart, an attorney from Birmingham, announced that he would introduce a commission bill during the 1909 session including the initiative, referendum, and recall. To get help in drafting it, he called a meeting of the mayor and representatives of the Commercial Club, the Board of Trade, and the Business Men's League.

> Representative Urquhart had not Saturday decided upon the number of commissioners, the manner in which they shall be appointed or elected or the length of terms they shall serve. These questions, together with the division of the city government into departments and other matters will be settled at the conference [of the above-mentioned groups] to be held next week.[63]

Consultation in the capital with the Mobile and Montgomery delegations resulted in the introduction of a bill acceptable to the representatives of the state's large cities.

In the extensive maneuvering that followed, three leading businessmen from Birmingham spoke in opposition to the commission plan before a legislative committee, as did a delegation of six aldermen and the city's street commissioner. The interest of the public officials in preserving the existing government was apparent; the businessmen were later shown to have had significant business relationships with the incumbent administration. For example, the president of the bank in which the city deposited its revenues opposed the commission plan. Another committee of five journeyed to Montgomery to testify for the commission plan, speaking in behalf of a larger group of twenty-three supporters that included leading businessmen, lawyers, doctors, an alderman, and a former police chief.[64] The legislative committee, however, rejected the commission bill, killing it for that session.

The *News* resumed its prominent role in the campaign, stating, "There is very little political principle connected with city government. It is a business corporation."[65] Claiming that "nothing will contribute so much to Birmingham's prosperity and growth," the paper dispatched its associate editor on a tour of five cities that had adopted the commission form to do a profile of each.[66]

In Birmingham a municipal league was formed in 1910 by 150 citizens of the newly annexed suburbs, which were particularly critical of the provision of services by city government.[67] It quickly endorsed the commission plan and campaigned for it in an advisory referendum held prior to the 1911 legislative session, during which voters favored the change by a margin of nearly eight to one.[68] A majority of the Jefferson County delegation now endorsed the plan, and the Chamber of Commerce created a special committee to aid the lawmakers in the passage of the necessary enabling legislation.[69] The bill cleared both houses without any opposition, providing for gubernatorial appointment of the first three commissioners and generating new controversy over who would be chosen. Additional delegations, including one of one hundred businessmen, now visited with the governor in private sessions concerning implementation of the plan, and especially who his appointees would be.[70] Usually their names and viewpoints were reported, but historical analysis is frustrated when "the closest inquiry [by the *News*] . . . [fails] to reveal the names of the members of the Birmingham delegation, or what matters would be discussed [with the governor] at that time."[71]

The following general observations about decision making in Birmingham can be made based upon the above three case studies and information about additional decisions during the era for which detailed information has been gathered.[72] First, representatives of the dominant economic institutions in the district did not dominate the decision-making process in general. This is partly because city boundaries were drawn so that major steel plants lay outside the city and thereby escaped municipal taxation. But even the heads of major industries inside the city failed to participate in most decisions, routine or unusual. The exception to this generalization occurred when the immediate economic interests of the major industries were affected by public policy, as in the case of the 1910 consolidation. Then economic power was translated into political power with results favorable to the industries, and the process was anything but hidden. The heads of industry openly threatened to leave the community if their wishes were refused; no politician was willing to challenge the seriousness of the threat and risk the potential drastic consequences to the local economy.[73]

In the three decisions examined above, approximately sixty local private citizens played significant roles in the decision-making process, according to the newspaper accounts. Of this number fifty-three were active in only one of the three decisions; six were actively involved in two; and only one was involved in all three. Yet this individual, a lawyer, should be credited with unusual political activity rather than with extraordinary power, as he was on the losing side in the commission issue.

In addition to private citizens, various public officials were significant figures in the three case studies, including the mayor and board of aldermen, the city commission, the local legislative delegation, and the courts. But these public officials also were limited in their ranges of influence. Only the incumbent mayor was active in all three; four different men occupied the office of mayor during the time when the three issues were being considered. The city attorney was a key figure in two issues, participating in the negotiations among various parties concerned with consolidation, serving as a leader of the Municipal Ownership League, and drafting legislation in both cases.

The private citizens identified as playing significant roles in one or more of the three issues were overwhelmingly representative of the leadership of the local business community or of the legal profession; and with the exception of the few who opposed the commission plan, they were united in their public positions. The most notable exception to this occupational pattern was the aggressive leadership provided by a local minister to the Municipal Ownership League during the waterworks controversy.

The prominence of business leaders is also reflected in the participation of private membership organizations in the cases. Only two were involved in all three issues, the Commercial Club and the Board of Trade, which merged in 1912 to form the Chamber of Commerce. The *Birmingham News*, which viewed itself as a spokesman for progressive businessmen, also took strong positions on all three questions. The Birmingham Trades Council took public stands for consolidation and municipal ownership of the waterworks, but these came late in the decision-making process and were not accompanied by other types of reported overt political activity. Moreover, the mayors who as public officials played central roles were themselves products of the business community. In short, the numerous leaders identified in the three case studies reflect a relatively homogeneous socioeconomic background; they emerged from that segment of the population that produced leadership in the legal profession and in the local economy, which was in turn overshadowed by the absentee-owned major industries that had a national orientation.

But the influence of the business community was limited by the institutional arrangements of the political system by which the important decisions were processed.[74] All three issues were dependent at critical points upon enabling legislation at the state level. Here practices such as senatorial courtesy allowed a single local legislator to thwart legislation favored by business interests, as in the case of the early consolidation bill. The rural-dominated legislature could easily override the urban representatives, as in the long-established opposition to revisions in formulas for distributing state revenues that allocated funds equally to each county rather than on the basis of population.[75] In addition to the state legislature, the courts figured significantly in the waterworks issue; here legal constraints limited the power of all interested parties.

The power of the electoral majority during a referendum is theoretically an additional factor circumscribing the influence of the business community. However, in Birmingham this remained a theoretical rather than a real limit during 1900–1917. All three of the issues reviewed above were put to popular votes, and in all three referenda the electorate supported the position of the business community. Furthermore, there were no issues on which the business community took a position where the popular vote was in opposition; and the only controversial question that the Board of Trade and the Commercial Club avoided was prohibition. Here individual businessmen supported both sides of the controversy.

With their virtual monopoly of local officeholding and their great influence on important decisions, the business-professional leadership class appears to have established firm control over Birmingham's politics in both its routine and nonroutine functioning. In part this dominance can be explained by the resources of flexible work schedules, access to information, political sophistication, and money that they possessed. Men who owned stores with several employees or who engaged in law practice were freer to attend morning council and commission meetings than were laborers or proprietors of one-person shops; the former also were more likely to participate in the daytime meetings of civic organizations and to have the time and money to lobby in Montgomery.

But beyond the fact that it was more convenient for the business-professional group to participate in politics, their dominance was consistent with a political culture that saw businessmen as the natural leaders of the community and policies favorable to the business community as the appropriate outcomes of local governmental activity.

As political scientist James Q. Wilson points out, the term "political culture" is extremely difficult to define precisely, and any community's individual culture is difficult to measure. Yet he observes

> that however maddeningly vague it [the concept of political culture] may be, we seem increasingly unable to do without it. Very broadly, a political culture might be thought of as a widely shared, patterned view of the proper scope and behavior of public institutions and specifically of what ways of behaving on public matters (getting votes, casting votes, proposing programs, administering services, managing conflict) would be thought legitimate.[76]

One of the most provocative attempts to describe the political culture of one community is historian Sam Bass Warner's *The Private City: Philadelphia in Three Periods of Its Growth*. In this work, Warner develops the concept of "privatism," described as "the most important element of our culture for understanding the development of cities."[77] This tradition held that "the business of a city was business."[78] Suggestively, Warner describes it as follows:

> Its essence lay in the concentration upon the individual and the individual's search for wealth. Psychologically, privatism meant that the individual should seek happiness in personal independence and in the search for wealth; socially, privatism meant that the individual should see

his first loyalty as his immediate family, and that a community should be a union of such moneymaking, accumulating families; politically, privatism meant that the community should keep peace among individual money-makers, and, if possible, help to create an open and thriving setting where each citizen would have some substantial opportunity to prosper.[79]

In practice, according to his analysis of privatism at work in Philadelphia, it meant a lack of concern for raising the level of living among the poor, an interest in meeting the requests of business and industry, and a cheap uniform level of services to all neighborhoods of the city.[80] Employing this same concept in his study of Boston, Warner concludes: "Education, health, transportation and plentiful land were tools to encourage individuals to work effectively as private profit makers. The works of the individual private profit makers were to be the return for the public costs and effort."[81]

The entire history of Birmingham during the period 1900–1917 reflects a primary concern for the prosperity of the business and industrial communities. The configuration of the city boundary lines testifies to the fact that the desire of the steel mills to escape municipal taxation played a more important role in local politics than did the city's need for additional revenues. No public official during the period had a more clearly articulated philosophy of the role of local government than George Ward, who advocated a strong government playing a far greater role than the mere performance of housekeeping tasks in a businesslike manner:

Libraries, school parks and playgrounds, watchfulness for better health conditions, care for the welfare and well-being of its inhabitants, these are the things that make a city grow and hold its people. And these are the things for which this commission has stood as supplementary work to the usual municipal function.

For the things that truly make a city great, this commission has stood steadfastly. It has given of its inadequate resources when able, and has contributed liberally from its moral support and official sanction.[82]

But by Ward's standards Birmingham did not become a great city precisely because of inadequate resources. Yet even he vehemently opposed redrawing the city limits so that the huge U.S. Steel plant would be within the boundaries, arguing that the city should not "heckle" industry but rather should offer encouragement to plants desiring to come into the district and build up the community.[83] Clearly for George Ward and the other leaders of the era, the principal objective of local government was the creation of an environment favorable to private enterprise, and this meant that merchants and manufacturers had a right to expect "a municipal government that does not try to regulate every-thing from Panama to Maine."[84]

There was, in fact, great realism in the sensitivity of public officials to the industries; the city would have suffered intolerable economic loss had the major producers followed through on their threats to cease operation if brought into the city. But the business orientation went beyond the recognition of reality. Businessmen and the press regarded the business-professional class as the appropriate occupants of public office, and its representatives were looked to as governmental advisors whenever the city faced a serious problem or launched a municipal project. Joint committees representing city officials and representatives of the Board of Trade and the Commercial Club were regu-larly established to recommend municipal policy on important issues such as the waterworks. Businessmen were asked to spearhead campaigns in behalf of bond issues for the schools and a new municipal auditorium; public rallies were jointly sponsored by the city and the Chamber of Commerce.[85] Officials often turned to business leaders for advice on financial matters, taking the po-sition that policy recommendations and initiatives should emerge from the business community. For example, concerning legislative remedies for the fi-nancial crisis of 1914, Ward said, "The proper course, as I see it, is for the com-mercial bodies to appoint committees to work with the [Jefferson County] dele-gation. The Commission will render any assistance possible."[86] And when the committee of one hundred appointed by Ward and the head of the Chamber of Commerce to recommend local policy during that crisis issued its three re-ports, they became official city policy. Businessmen virtually made public policy even when not elected to office.[87]

Moreover, there appears to have been no sustained opposition within the community to either the values or roles of this business-professional leadership group. On two separate occasions the electorate ratified the expressed wishes of the business community, voting down locally the constitutional amendment permitting increased property taxation and endorsing the commission form of government by a margin of 4,962–693.[88] The first referendum perpetuated the city's uniformly low level of public services, while the second, neither opposed nor endorsed by organized labor, indicated massive support for a form of gov-ernment that virtually guaranteed that the diversity of representation found in the council would be eliminated.

These comments are not intended to indicate that Birmingham's social and political culture resembled in every detail that of Philadelphia as described by Warner or of any of several other cities that have been studied in detail by his-torians.[89] However, his notion of privatism is helpful in looking at the routine functions of local government, at its major policy objectives, at its officials and those upon whom they relied.[90] Another element of Warner's privatism was a general lack of concern by local government for raising the standard of living among the poor, evidenced in a low level of public services and in a heavy dependence on private organizations to meet the needs of the poor.[91] This study now turns to the subject of poverty and Birmingham's response to it.

3

Welfare Services

FROM THE TIME of Birmingham's founding until World War I, those concerned with relief of the poor in cities across the nation engaged in a controversy over the relative advantages of private and public means of aid. Though Birminghamians were confronting for the first time a question experienced for decades by older cities, their efforts mirror well the thinking and activities of the era. In the area of aid to the poor there was no lag between developments in the North and in Birmingham.

Surveys of relief in American cities during the depression of 1873 indicate that there was no consistent pattern in the provision of services.[1] Some cities relied exclusively on private agencies to meet the needs of the poor, often supplementing funds raised by private subscriptions with municipal appropriations. Other cities undertook public works programs as an emergency measure in addition to the ongoing, uncoordinated activities of the numerous private charities. Yet other communities attempted to rationalize the work of both public and private programs by establishing clearinghouses for the processing of cases and by joint planning of programs. From the varied approaches used during this depression, there emerged a consensus among welfare workers as to the superiority of private relief. Cities that relied heavily on publicly operated programs were accused of introducing political patronage into the provision of relief, giving aid on the basis of political loyalty rather than objectively established need. The private agencies, on the other hand, generally conducted investigations to save people from "the injurious effects of indiscriminate aid."[2] The more progressive, such as the New York Association for Improving the Condition of the Poor, increasingly employed paid staff members to supervise the field work of volunteer visitors. Private agency personnel were not alone in proclaiming their superiority; state public welfare officials repeatedly endorsed this position in annual meetings held between 1874 and 1891.[3]

Publicly provided outdoor relief was abolished in major cities between 1875 and 1900, reflecting the view that corruption in the public relief system fostered unnecessary dependency.[4] The almshouse became the public response to need; intentionally so miserable as to discourage applicants, these facilities cared only for those who were totally helpless because of age or infirmity. All relief outside the almshouses became the responsibility of the private agencies.[5]

The response of the private agencies to their postdepression responsibilities was the charity organization society movement. Begun in Buffalo in 1877, the movement spread quickly in both the United States and Canada, producing ninety-two societies by 1893. The institutional purpose of each society was to bring all outdoor relief under the control of a single reform-inspired agency; the ultimate goal was to end all such relief entirely. The movement was informed by the belief that need reflected personal deficiency; "friendly visitors" were used to verify real immediate need, but more importantly to help redeem the poor and lift them from their dependency. The societies often reduced the total amount of aid given, as visitors detected fraud and prevented duplication of services to an individual by collecting data for a centralized record bureau.[6] Charity organization society workers were not concerned with alleviating poverty, seen as a temporary misfortune that was natural, unavoidable, and a positive goad to human achievement and character development. Rather, they wanted to eliminate pauperism, a condition of wasteful permanent dependency encouraged by sentimental, indiscriminate aid to the poor. This moralistic emphasis on individualism coupled with the scientific accumulation of data led organized labor to oppose the movement and led one poet to lament

> That Organized Charity, scrimped and iced in the name of a cautious, statistical Christ.[7]

Private organizations remained virtually the sole providers of aid outside of almshouses until the second decade of the twentieth century, though they frequently received public funds to help with their work. Starting with the Kansas City Board of Public Welfare in 1910, cities began establishing municipal departments of social welfare, some under the direction of trained social workers.[8] During the depression of 1914–15 municipal governments increasingly assumed a role of leadership in providing special programs and in integrating the public and private responses to the crisis. This new public thrust apparently reflected both the obvious failure of the private agencies to aid the unemployed and that confidence in the capacity of government to meet local needs that typified the Progressive Era. With a large percentage of the labor force experiencing poverty, which was viewed by the movement as salutary, newspapers and reformers turned on the charity organization societies. They were labeled "minions of the rich who supposedly sought through charitable gifts to maintain the status quo in society," and it was charged that through "interlocking directorates" the agencies had become one great "charity trust."[9] But when the depression ended, public efforts sharply diminished; cities again displayed a marked preference for private charity.

The experience in the Birmingham district in responding to the needs of the poor broadly paralleled the national trends, reflecting the various stages of the debate as to the relative merits of public and private agencies. The basic poor law of the state, written in 1807 when Alabama was a territory, placed upon county governments the responsibility of caring for the poor.[10] The first record of this responsibility's being met in Jefferson County is found in 1883, when the court of county commissioners "let out" paupers for care "to the lowest and most responsible bidder."[11] The commissioners thus provided minimal protection to the totally helpless, while the bidder sought to profit from his contract. By 1884 the county had built an almshouse, a wooden structure with six wards: two for white men, two for white women, one for black men, and one for black women. In addition, there were eight rooms for tuberculosis patients and a separate building for the insane.[12] The practice of contracting with private bidders to care for indigents ended in 1897; all were now assigned to the almshouse except children, who were sent to the private Mercy Home. Between 1897 and 1932 the county provided virtually no outdoor relief directly; it did, however, subsidize several of the private agencies that were created starting in 1896. County support of all private agencies was terminated in 1917 when the county solicitor ruled that such payments were unconstitutional by virtue of an amendment enacted that year that prohibited allocating public funds to private organizations.[13]

The city had no legal obligation to aid the poor though it, too, allocated funds to private agencies throughout the period. In addition, prior to 1882 indigents from the city could apply directly to the mayor and board of aldermen for aid, especially in the form of charity transportation from Birmingham to their hometowns. The city continued to give public aid to those wishing to leave the area; but after the United Charities was established in 1882, it became the official investigating agency for the city.[14] From 1913 to 1917 the city played a larger role in the area of welfare, experimenting alternatively with regulation of subsidized private agencies and direct provision of public services. This four-year period saw city officials trying to cope with the local effects of a national depression after private agencies, by their own admission, proved unequal to the task of meeting dire need.

This study makes no effort to assess the public services rendered solely by public agencies prior to 1913. The county almshouse attempted to provide only a minimal level of subsistence to the totally helpless or incompetent. It made no effort to respond to need caused by economic conditions and was never seen as a rehabilitative facility. It was never an issue in local government and seems never to have been the object of concern of private citizens. Rather, the focus here is upon the various private agencies established in the Birmingham district specifically to meet needs that individuals could not meet themselves because of poverty or racial exclusion. The relationship between private agencies and public authority is also examined with special emphasis on the 1913–17 period, when the role of the city was greater than simply providing subsidies and charity transportation.

The following review of private agencies is based upon newspaper reports of agency activities during the period 1900–1917. Most records from this time have long since been lost or destroyed, and those that remain lack consistent statistical data. Thus, only the most general observations can be made about the recipients and adequacy of services locally. This same dearth of data exists in other cities, making detailed intercity comparison impossible.[15] As services were consistently judged inadequate even by those responsible for directing agencies, and as agencies were often in serious financial distress, it can be assumed that the private agencies in Birmingham failed to meet even the most obvious need as measured by the none-too-generous standards of the day.

The agencies are grouped into those providing services to Blacks only, to Whites only, and to both races. They are with one exception treated in the order of their founding to give a sense of the elaboration of private services as the city matured. The exception, discussed last, is the agency that most clearly illustrates the changes in private welfare administration during the period as well as the interplay between private welfare and public responsibility. Each description briefly reviews services offered, recipients of services, sources of support, and governance.

Omitted are all programs sponsored by individual churches, all private colleges, private schools for wealthy Whites, groups serving primarily the white middle class (YMCA, YWCA), and a group of private hospitals operated by physicians that generally had short existences.

Of the programs omitted, only those of individual churches may have had a significant concern with the needs of the poor. However, most churches—and especially small neighborhood ones—lack systematic church records; a review of church activities would be anecdotal at best. Moreover, church work among the poor would have been only part of the institutions' overall programs. This study focuses on agencies established specifically to meet the needs of the poor, including ones sponsored by religious groups.

Private Agencies Serving Blacks Only

St. Mark's School for Negro Children (established 1892)

This school was established by the Protestant Episcopal Diocese of Alabama to offer both elementary and secondary education to black children. It was the first school, public or private, to offer secondary education to Blacks in metropolitan Birmingham. Governed by the diocese, the school received substantial financial support from northern white women and from one prominent white Birmingham businessman, wholesale grocer and former mayor J. A. Van Hoose, who had been instrumental in its founding. Offering academic, industrial, and home economics programs in a three-story brick building, the school had a student body of between 165 and 200. St. Mark's closed in 1940 when the diocese noted "the advancement of public school education in the higher grades for Negroes in the city schools of Birmingham."[16]

Birmingham Colored Kindergarten Association (1900)

This association was organized by the principal of St. Mark's School and sponsored a program for forty-five children. It apparently dissolved shortly after the kindergarten was begun, and no successor organization appeared until the Negro Kindergarten and Day Nursery was established in 1911. The leadership for both programs was black, though the latter group was actively supported by a prominent white charity worker, Mrs. C. P. Orr, and by Dr. Henry M. Edmonds, the leading Presbyterian minister. Funds were privately raised for both from unnamed sources.[17]

Alabama Colored Orphans and Old Folks Home (1900)

This facility was founded amid high praise from the mayor and superintendent of schools and a financial crisis that plagued it throughout the period. A black board of directors comprised of businessmen, ministers, and physicians was headed by Dr. W. R. Pettiford, president of Birmingham's one black bank, The Alabama Penny Savings Bank; regular financial support came from black ministers and secret societies. Three special appeals for funds had to be conducted during the period to meet outstanding debts or mortgage notes, but creditors took control of the property in 1912 when the directors defaulted on mortgage payments. Black women organized a temporary civic league to redeem the property, seeking white support by means of a newly established advisory board composed of prominent white women, several of whom were active in other charity work. The permanent Federation of Colored Women's Clubs assumed responsibility for directing the facility, aided by a monthly subsidy of twenty-five dollars from the city.

In addition to providing shelter for the elderly and orphans, the home managed for varying periods of time a hospital unit served by black physicians and aiding up to one hundred patients a year, a nurses training school that had a maximum enrollment of forty-three, and a school for domestic workers. Admitting that the hospital was being run "at a very low rate," the board president unsuccessfully sought to have public authorities operate it as a charity hospital.

Built for a capacity of two hundred to three hundred in 1900, the home clung precariously to life in 1916, serving a resident population of only nineteen.[18]

Colored Women's Mission Congress Hospital Association (1901)

The association laid the cornerstone for a charity hospital for Blacks at a ceremony in 1901 highlighted by a speech of praise by Mayor Walter M. Drennen. A two-story frame building with four wards was planned to be built on two and one-half acres of land donated by a physician with funds from various black churches and clubs. The enterprise was directed by a board of black women. Five years after the cornerstone was laid the hospital still had not been built; the association is not mentioned in the newspaper after 1906.[19]

Colored Catholic Mission School (about 1906)

The Catholic Sisters of Mercy operated this school with funds provided by the order and supplemented by tuition payments of fifty cents to one dollar a month, depending on grade level. No information is given about the number of students or grades; the school probably offered work up to the high school level.[20]

Carrie Tuggle Institute (1908)

With the active help of two local judges and a leading white merchant, four black fraternal organizations established the institute as both an orphanage and a school. A white advisory board of prominent men and women continued to work with the institute, leading its most famous alumnus, Dr. A. G. Gaston, to recall with affection the "devoted and efficient inter-racial action of concerned adults."[21] With an enrollment of two hundred, it was the only institution in the state that educated black orphans. A mass meeting in 1915 was held to raise money to meet a seven-thousand-dollar debt; prominent black and white citizens addressed the audience, including a city commissioner. The institute closed in 1933 because of insurmountable financial difficulties; like St. Mark's, some of its functions had been made unnecessary with the rise of public secondary schools for Blacks.[22]

Private Agencies Serving Whites Only

Jewish Charities (1883)

The first recorded organized relief by a private charitable agency in Birmingham was offered by the Hebrew Ladies Benevolent Association to Jewish immigrants in 1883; in the 1890s the Birmingham Hebrew Relief Society was organized by leading Jewish men. These two groups merged in 1904 to form the United Hebrew Charities, which that year offered $675 in cash relief, extended credit to others, and found work for over one hundred needy Jews.

The Daughters of Israel and Hebrew Aid Society were both established in the 1890s; the former was particularly active in assisting Eastern European Jews, mainly those from Russia. During the depression of 1914 the Birmingham Hebrew Sheltering and Free Loan Association was incorporated for the purpose of giving interest-free loans as well as temporary shelter and meals to the needy.

The various Jewish charities established the Federation of Jewish Charities in 1915 to coordinate their fund-raising and relief-giving activities. The federation spent $3,594 in 1917 aiding the Jewish community of Birmingham, which numbered about 3,500 individuals—or 1.8 percent of the city's population.

Relative to its population size and to other charities, the Birmingham Jewish community sponsored a large number of agencies characterized by comprehensive services and progressive administration of programs; the Federation of Jewish Charities anticipated by nine years a similar rationalization of programs by the community's non-Jewish agencies.[23]

Mercy Home (1896)

The Mercy Home for Girls, established by the Women's Christian Temperance Union, was probably the best known and most generously supported agency in Birmingham during this period. Governed by a twenty-one-member board of prominent women and aided in fund-raising by an equally large advisory board of men, the home by 1900 owned a two-story brick building val-

The Mercy Home, established by the Women's Christian Temperance Union in 1896, acquired this two-story building to house its free maternity wards, home for delinquent girls, kindergarten, and accommodations for the chronically ill and elderly. (Mercy Home Papers, Birmingham Public Library)

ued at $15,000. Included in its services were free maternity wards, care of the chronically ill and the elderly, a home for "delinquent and defective girls," and a kindergarten. Serving 55 adults and 82 children in 1900, its average daily population was 49; the over two thousand dollars that it spent annually was provided by donations and subsidies from both the city and the county of fifty dollars and thirty dollars a month, respectively. In 1905 a successful fundraising drive raised the $1,250 needed to add a two-room hospital to the building. Three years later the board launched a $50,000 drive to build an industrial school for girls as a counterpart to the already existing facility for white boys who appeared in juvenile court; the county board of revenue donated five acres of land for the new facility. When the drive still lacked $8,000 in 1910, the female board of directors and the male advisory board supported the introduction of a bill in the state legislature to provide $4,000 for each of four years for operation of the industrial school, plus $20,000 for new buildings; they pointed out that the state already provided $20,000 yearly to the boys' industrial school. The state agreed to the $4,000 per year appropriation, and the school opened

for 25 girls between the ages of twelve and eighteen. The city stopped supporting the Mercy Home in 1915 as an economy measure, and the county board of
revenue ended its subsidies in 1917 after the grand jury recommended termination of aid to it and six other charities, which the jury said had not been
properly investigated to determine real need. The managers of the home,
therefore, sought additional private support to maintain services for the 90
children then in residence.[24]

Alabama Industrial School for Wayward Boys (1898)

The boys' industrial school was a state institution chartered by the legislature and supported by both public and private funds; it was regarded by contemporaries as one of the city's most worthy charities and is therefore included
in this discussion. Built on land purchased with funds raised by the Birmingham Commercial Club, it operated under stable leadership provided by a board
of directors of leading white women appointed by the governor. In 1900 the
school received $3,500 for the year from the state, $40 per month from the city,
and slightly over $4 each month from the county for each white boy from the
county between six and eighteen years of age who was in the school. In 1906
it received $8,000 from the state, supplemented by $4,000 from other sources,
to house 112 inmates. The school began a new building in 1907 for 250 boys
with a state appropriation of $50,000 and continuing support from both the city
and county. As with the Mercy Home, city support ended in the 1915 financial
crisis and county aid was stopped as a result of the grand jury recommendations in 1917.[25]

The public and private concern for delinquent white boys and girls was
not matched by an equal concern for black youngsters. There was no industrial
school for Blacks during this period. Wayward black youth were placed in a
special school class supported solely by funds collected by black ministers. The
black community also raised funds to support a youth officer for Blacks who
worked with the police department in disposing of juvenile cases.[26]

Birmingham Free Kindergarten Association (1899); later Birmingham Social Settlement Association (1912)

The association was formed by a group of prominent local white women
and was supported entirely by private donations. Though its funding was precarious, the association ran three centers for 113 children in 1901; three years
later nearly 400 attended at six locations. The work of the association reached
its peak in 1911 when fifteen centers were supported, offering both child care

and teacher training. The work of the association ended when the public schools assumed responsibility for the free kindergarten program in 1912.[27]

The women involved with the kindergarten association expanded their board in 1912 and formed the Birmingham Social Settlement Association. Their motivation to turn to this activity came from a talk delivered by Jane Addams before the National Child Labor Conference, which met in the city in 1911. After this speech interested women established a milk station and day nursery for the children of working women. These women soon merged with those of the kindergarten association to form the settlement association. Under the direction of the association, this project was expanded into a settlement house serving two hundred children; five additional settlements were begun by the association. The county board of revenue supported the organization from its founding in 1912 until the 1917 grand jury investigation.[28]

By 1917 there were seven settlement houses in the Birmingham district. One served Blacks; apparently directed by Blacks, it received support from interested Whites but not from the Social Settlement Association.[29] The remaining six received general support from the association. In addition, each was the special project of another organization. The City Board of Missions, organized by Methodist women in 1903, spent about five thousand dollars yearly on two settlement houses. The ten leading downtown churches supported one settlement house, which was managed by a board of one minister and women representing each of the congregations. Finally, the United States Steel Corporation contributed to three of the houses, which were located near company facilities.[30]

The settlement houses of the Birmingham district offered a comprehensive range of services including kindergartens, sewing and cooking classes, supervised playgrounds, Boy Scouts, Camp Fire Girls, Bible training, adult recreation, industrial training for girls, day care for working mothers, and night literacy school for working boys. They also distributed free milk to babies during at least one summer. By 1912 the settlement houses were staffed by fully trained social workers.[31]

Salvation Army (1902)

The Army began its Birmingham program with a small residence for men that could house fifteen at one time with provision for additional care for the sick; in its first four months of operation fourteen hundred men lodged there. Within the year a workingmen's hotel for seventy opened, followed by a rescue home for "unfortunate women" that opened in 1905 after a successful five-thousand-dollar drive. In 1907 the Army opened a free employment bureau for men and women that seems to have been maintained for only a few months. Both the city and the county supported the Army's work, but finances were inadequate for the local program. A special drive to wipe out indebtedness was held in 1912, and the situation worsened when county support was withdrawn in 1917 upon recommendation of the grand jury. The Salvation Army apparently had no formal lay leadership in Birmingham but rather was governed from southern district headquarters.[32]

Boys Club (1903)

The Boys Club was founded by an all-female board of managers who raised enough funds by selling tags on the downtown streets once each year to hire a male manager to supervise their program. The club was housed in a room in city hall, where both a school and recreation center were available to working boys, especially newsboys. Later the club operated at various times a dormitory, an employment bureau, a playground for working boys in the downtown district, a summer camp, and a "big brother" program for orphans. In cooperation with the police court, the club sought foster homes for "neglected and dependent white boys." The club also funded a black probation officer who worked with black youth appearing before local courts, but none of its other programs served both races. The women's board of managers received support from an advisory board of leading men, especially in preparing for the annual tag days. These two groups announced plans to open a Boys Club for Blacks in 1912, but by 1917 they had not done so.

When a separate juvenile court was established in Jefferson County in 1911, the leadership of the Boys Club played a central role in establishing a Children's Aid Society, which served as a clearinghouse for placing dependent and neglected children under the supervision of the court. Prominent men and women served together on the society's board, but their only function seems to have been to raise funds. Actual placements were made by field workers employed by the court. In 1913 the city employed two black probation officers, and hope was expressed that a Negro juvenile aid society could be established in the near future. However, none is mentioned in the press by the close of the period.[33]

Girls Home (1908)

The Girls Home was opened by Methodist churchwomen who responded to the plea of a local judge that such a facility be established as an alternative to prison. Five churchwomen constituted a board of trustees, while another nine served as the board of managers. As with several of the other agencies, prominent men belonged to an advisory board that aided the women in fund-raising. Supported initially by many small monthly donations, the home had a capacity of about thirty; an attorney and two physicians donated their services. Within two years the city and county subsidized the home, which received girls given short sentences by the court and also offered financial relief to the needy.

The legislature of Alabama chartered the Girls Home in 1911 as the state reformatory for white girls, operated by a board of managers of twelve women appointed by the governor; the initial board consisted of the same women who had directed the institution as a private agency. At the close of the period, the Chamber of Commerce was trying to raise fifteen thousand dollars to build new quarters for the home, a sum required by the governor before he would release twenty thousand dollars in state funds for construction. County aid terminated in 1917 after the grand jury report criticizing inadequate county investigation of subsidized private agencies.[34]

Holy Innocents Hospital (Children's Hospital) (1911)

The hospital was founded by the Episcopal Church with five leading men serving as trustees and prominent women serving as officers with responsibility for fund-raising. The women sought a large number of small monthly private subscriptions, which were supplemented by a subsidy from the county. With a capacity of twenty-five, the hospital provided free care to children under fourteen years of age referred by social agencies or approved by an admissions committee; Birmingham physicians volunteered medical services to the hospital.[35]

Octavia White Home for Aged and Infirm Old Ladies (1911)

The Daughters of the Confederacy opened and managed the home, which received support from local churches and the city and county. The home could accommodate only nine residents, and it was one of the institutions that the county stopped subsidizing in 1917.[36]

Pisgah Home (1911)

This home was established as a rescue agency for men by the Pisgah Evangelists, a sectarian organization that operated similar facilities elsewhere in the United States. Originally supported solely by voluntary contributions, the home offered food, clothing, and lodging to a maximum of twenty-five men and boys. Subsidies were soon received from both the city and county, enabling the home to open a center for women and girls. Criticizing the investigations conducted by other agencies, the home proudly claimed to offer "immediate relief without red tape or delay."[37]

The home was technically governed by a board of five men and two women that included the founder of the agency, but the charter specified that full control of the institution would rest in the hands of the founder during his lifetime. A ten-thousand-dollar fund-raising drive was announced in 1912 to purchase three new buildings for the home, and one was bought, to the dismay of neighbors, who protested that the moral lepers of the city would be concentrated there. Because of this protest, or for some other unidentified reason, the home was reorganized. In 1915 the Pisgah Home's new management announced, "The doors of the home are open to all white unfortunates in need of food, lodging, and clothing."[38] Finally, the city assumed full responsibility for the home in 1916 when it developed its municipal welfare program, discussed below.[39]

Private Agencies Serving Blacks and Whites

Hillman Hospital (1897)

Although Hillman Hospital was officially incorporated by its Board of Lady Managers in 1897, its origins dated back to 1888. At that time T. T. Hillman, prominent executive of the Tennessee Coal, Iron and Railroad Company, donated $20,000 worth of bonds for the purpose of establishing a charity hospital with the stipulation that the gift be equally divided between black and white patients. That original requirement governed Hillman's delivery of services thereafter. The income from these bonds, plus grants of $400 each per month from the city and the county, constituted the hospital's operating fund. When the city and the county were unable to maintain these payments in 1894, the hospital was forced to close for several weeks; it closed for two years after a fire destroyed the buildings at the end of that same year. After being briefly operated by two local physicians, the hospital was incorporated under its Board of Lady Managers, who succeeded in raising $40,000 for a new building that was opened in 1903 with facilities for one hundred patients, including private as well as charity cases. Separate wards were constructed for black and white patients. The Board of Managers requested monthly appropriations of $1,000 from the county and $500 from the city, arguing the reasonableness of these amounts for the new plant in light of the $400 per month subsidies a decade earlier. When each unit of government allocated only $100 per month, the women of the board announced that they would close the unit on 1 March 1904. Collections at a mass meeting in behalf of the hospital enabled it to operate beyond that date. At this meeting a committee of twenty-five business leaders agreed to argue before local public officials that Hillman should be a charitable hospital fully supported by the city and county with all expenditures supervised by an advisory board of five; the Board of Managers ratified this proposal. The county board of revenue initially rejected this plan, admitting its legality but claiming inadequate finances; the city, too, continued its same level of support. Finally, when it seemed that the board would, in fact, close Hillman, and after intense pressure from businessmen, the county accepted the facility as a gift and continued to operate it as a charity hospital serving equally both races with an annual budget of about $12,000.[40]

St. Vincent's Hospital (1900)

St. Vincent's was built at a cost of $250,000, most of which was provided by the Catholic order that managed it. One-third of its two hundred beds were reserved for free patients; the city maintained five at public expense. Each year until 1908 the hospital served about 1,250–1,400 patients. Between 550 and 700 each year were charity cases; about 350 Blacks annually were treated. The hospital also operated a free clinic that served an additional 650 each year. A $50,000 drive led by businessmen and physicians permitted an expansion of services in 1908, including food and clothing distributed as outdoor relief. The city now contracted with St. Vincent's to handle the overflow from Hillman. However, the two hospitals combined were unable to care for the black indigents of the district, many of whom were refused admission because of lack of room. St. Vincent's reserved twenty beds for Blacks, but demand forced the hospital to place carts in the wards to increase the capacity to thirty-five. This situation was aggravated by the closing of a private hospital operated by black physicians. Minimally adequate care for black indigents was recognized as a pressing unmet need by both the press and the medical profession at the end of the period.[41]

Sisters of Charity Home (1903)

A Catholic priest raised the $11,000 needed to purchase the building and nine acres for this home, which was managed by the Sisters of Charity and opened to children of all creeds and both races between three and fourteen years of age. The sisters established fund-raising committees of four from each ward and suburban community to raise nearly $3,000 each year, which was supplemented by the county and later by the city. By 1912 both Protestant and Catholic congregations aided the home, which consistently served more non-Catholic than Catholic children and was turning residents away because its limit of one hundred twenty was reached. The sisters also turned business and fund-raising responsibilities over to a lay board of managers and an orphans home association of over two hundred women.[42]

Anti-Tuberculosis Society (1910)

The twenty-four-member board of directors of the society included leading members of the business community who joined with ministers, physicians, and three women to combat this disease by establishing a mountaintop non-residential camp for its victims. From the beginning the incidence of TB among Blacks was a concern to the society, whose paid executive director expressed the hope that more would take advantage of the camp and the concern shown for their welfare by the society's other programs. In 1912 the society opened a fresh-air school for poor anemic black children as a preventive measure and also a sanatorium for Blacks as a supplement to the mountain camp; these additions reflected the board's awareness that of an estimated four thousand cases of TB in Birmingham, three-quarters of the victims were Blacks. Responding to the absence of treatment facilities for advanced cases, the society opened a residential hospital on land donated by the city, but this served only Whites. The race line ultimately was drawn even by this one organization that actively solicited black clients, although Blacks accounted for three-quarters of the deaths from TB each year. However, Blacks were served by the society's dispensary and often constituted a majority of its monthly caseload; visiting nurses called at the homes of about three times as many Blacks as Whites.[43] All together twelve hundred persons were reached by the society's various programs in 1916. The organization was commended at that time by the city health officer, who said that the society was responsible for a reduction in the tuberculosis death rate during the past five and one-half years of from 108 deaths per 100,000 citizens among Whites to 74/100,000 and from 519/100,000 among Blacks to 360/100,000.[44] Still Birmingham had the second highest death rate in the nation from the disease. And the society's program was clearly inadequate, despite support from private donations, the sale of Red Cross Seals, patient fees, and subsidies from the city and the county. It provided only thirty-three beds, while conservative estimates placed local need at about three hundred.[45]

Social Services of the Tennessee Coal, Iron and Railroad Company (1912)

Probably the most professional social welfare services in the district were provided by the area's major employer, the Tennessee Coal, Iron and Railroad

Company, which was owned by U.S. Steel. The motivation for this work was primarily the goal of increased profits rather than humanitarian concern. A company investigation in 1912 into the causes of the unacceptably high annual turnover rate of 400 percent among its over twenty thousand employees revealed two major factors: illness and dissatisfaction with life in the company's villages. Six thousand cases of malaria were reported that year among employees and their families, due mainly to the presence of stagnant pools of water in the communities. Understanding the economic impact of this turnover, the company established a health department of the same status as the firm's other operating departments. The department's sanitary division improved drainage and sewage conditions in the villages, virtually eliminating malaria and typhoid. The medical and dental divisions maintained clinics in each of the fifteen villages: forty-six physicians and fourteen dentists offered treatment and preventive care to employees and their families at minimal cost. The company built a 310-bed hospital that was maintained by the hospital division and its staff of twenty-five house physicians; services of equal quality were provided both races in separate sections of the hospital. The hospital also maintained training schools for both black and white student nurses. Managed by Dr. Lloyd Nolan, a gifted and dedicated physician who gained national recognition for his work, the company hospital was widely regarded as one of the most comprehensive and excellent health facilities in the South. Pointing to increased productivity, decreased labor turnover, and decreased labor-management hostility, the company president pronounced the health department a "very profitable investment."[46]

The company later established a social science department staffed by twenty workers who carried out various nonmedical programs such as the operation of ten kindergartens, four for Whites and six for Blacks, and libraries for Whites in all villages. The company also supported county-administered public education in the villages, providing and maintaining buildings for eight white and fourteen black schools and paying part of the teachers' salaries. It is interesting to note that several of the district's most prominent social workers who played important roles during the Depression began their professional careers in the social welfare programs of the company.[47]

United Charities (1886); Became Associated Charities (1909)

No private agency better reflects the changes within and ultimate failure of private social work during this period than the United Charities, established by leading white women and supported from its inception by city funds. The organization functioned virtually as an official department of the city in serving the poor within its boundaries. Thus, it became the agent of the city in determining who would receive charity transportation tickets because, in the words of the mayor, "The United Charities is better prepared than a district representative of the city to investigate the merits of each application for such relief."[48] The hallmark of the organization was personal investigation of each applicant to determine merit. The city was divided into nine districts, each supervised by a district chairman aided by a committee of visitors; meritorious poor were aided from funds raised from the membership dues of interested women, combined with the city's monthly appropriation. But funds were never adequate to meet verified need. Reporting that it had aided seven hundred clients in 1905–06, mainly the old and infirm, the United Charities noted that it "lacked sufficient funds to provide adequate relief in some cases where heads of families were stricken down."[49] The officers of the agency urged greater support from government and the community for purposes such as the opening of a work house for the willing poor, but they met with no favorable response. While men contributed to the work by giving commodities such as coal and clothing or professional services, their overall lack of concern for the administration of welfare services was openly criticized by the agency's president. She was supported by the head of the counterpart organization in Atlanta, who said that Birmingham was the "only large city in the South which has not organized its charity and placed their giving on a business basis."[50]

Finally, in early 1909, a conference was convened to review the inadequacies of the United Charities and to discuss reorganization into an agency staffed with a paid executive and agents to make investigations; various other private agency officers, as well as several businessmen, attended the session. This conference was followed by visits by a field representative of the Russell Sage Foundation, which had established a department to encourage the charity organization society movement in cities across the country. In April the Associated Charities of Birmingham was formally organized as the successor of the United Charities. Men now moved to the forefront of organized charity in Birmingham, as the vice president of the Tennessee Coal, Iron and Railroad Company, James Bowron, headed an eighteen-member board composed of leading business and professional men.[51] The first task of the new organization was to raise funds to employ a secretary and acquire office space by spring 1910. Reflecting upon these developments, Mrs. Wallace Ward, the president of the United Charities, talked about

> the indifferent support we received from our people. At last it came as an inspiration, that instead of asking the business men for a pittance occasionally, the manner of securing aid could be systematized, men could

be asked to serve upon the Board and with the aid of an experienced, paid investigator, problems could be solved, which had been enigmas to us and instead of unlimited and indiscriminate alms giving people could be taught to help themselves.[52]

At the time of the founding of the Associated Charities, sixteen agencies were accepted as members and granted representation on a central council of charities, along with representatives of the mayor's office and the county board of revenue.[53] The function of this council was to advise the board of directors, who were responsible for financing the work of the new organization. The stated purpose of the Associated Charities was to maintain a central registration bureau to which applicants for charity could be directed for investigation by skilled paid workers. Relief would be given only when the staff determined that it was necessary; the businessmen who directed it felt that well-intentioned volunteers were likely to engage in "mere dollar giving" that encouraged idleness.[54] Churchmen apparently agreed as the Associated Charities investigated all applicants for charity from churches as well.

Three major factors distinguished the Associated Charities from its predecessor, the United Charities. First, it was directed mainly by businessmen who assumed responsibility for fund-raising; as a physical statement of the changed character of its leadership, the agency established its headquarters in the Chamber of Commerce building. Second, it had a professional staff dedicated to dealing with the individual's personal problems that caused need; the executive director once stated that the agency would be a complete success if all its funds were spent on personal services and not relief.[55] And third, the scale of charitable activity increased significantly. The United Charities spent a maximum of $1,569 in 1909, serving 369 families and 880 persons; 212 of its families were white and 157 black.[56] In 1913 the Associated Charities spent its maximum of $11,635 on relief and $4,000 on administration, serving 3,228 cases and making 6,000 investigations.[57]

But success did not favor most of the fund-raising efforts of the Associated Charities, nor did universal acceptance greet its program. The first general appeal for private funds to supplement the $400-per-month subsidy of the city set a goal of $10,000. Personal letters sent by the businessmen of the board of directors to 6,300 selected citizens netted only $1,000. The board sought to raise $12,000 during November 1911 but collected only $5,000. One year later a $15,000 drive produced but $11,000 in the organization's most successful single effort. Repeated failures forced regular emergency appeals to both public and private sources as well as program reductions. Thus, during the depression of 1914–15 the Associated Charities was forced to close its woodyard where men could earn lodging and food; one hundred men were made homeless by this action.

The Associated Charities was criticized by other agency heads as having too high administrative costs; was refused by the city commission when it requested authority to investigate applicants for charity transportation as part of "scientific charity"; and was rebuffed when women established an emergency relief committee to provide aid directly during the 1914–15 depression—bypassing the agency. With a debt of $10,000 and mounting criticism, the board of directors investigated its own organization. Defending the 34 percent administrative cost and blaming the city government for inadequate funds for relief, the board denied charges that its charity work was "drifting and in serious shape."[58] Still, the businessmen requested that the city take over the organization and run it as a city department.

One year before this request by the Associated Charities, the subcommittee on city affairs of the committee of one hundred businessmen appointed by Commission President Ward to review Birmingham's financial crisis had issued a report critical of the city's method of dispensing charity "without any apparent rule for determining the needs of each one."[59] The subcommittee members urged greater municipal control; two groups representing the business community thus favored government replacing private agencies as the focal point of local efforts to aid the needy. In the summer of 1916 the city officially assumed responsibility for the activities of the Associated Charities through its recently established department of relief and correction, inaugurating a new era of public responsibility for a heretofore private activity.[60]

It would appear that the business leaders who willingly disbanded the Associated Charities chose this course of action because of the inconvenience caused them by fund-raising drives and because of their own lack of commitment to the work. The sums of money sought clearly did not exceed what the board alone could have provided, in light of the wealth of several of its members. And there could be no real hope that public management would increase benefits; the city was in the midst of its austerity program forced by the financial crisis that followed consolidation and was aggravated by the depression of 1914–15.

The brief agency descriptions provided above support the following generalizations about private welfare services in the Birmingham district during the period 1900–1917.

First, there were fewer agencies concerned solely with the needs of the black community than of the white, and these were supported either by black citizens, churches and civic organizations, or white northern churches, with the exception of the Colored Orphans and Old Folks Home—which briefly received a subsidy from the city. The emphasis of the black organizations was upon education; four of the six were concerned solely with this activity, and these were the most stable of the black agencies. The Orphans and Old Folks Home tried to provide both welfare and health services, but by the end of the period its financing was extremely precarious and its population only nine persons. The Colored Hospital Association was established to administer a hospital, but none was built by the end of the period. Thus no stable agency offered health and welfare services to Blacks only. The dearth of these services does not reflect an absence of need, since it was widely recognized that poverty and poor health were widespread in the black community. Rather, it reflected the lack of resources in the black community to fund such expensive services and the funneling of white church money into education. It also reflected the absence of local white support for black agencies; prominent Whites served on advisory boards to the agencies and attended ceremonial events but did not extend financial support.

Of the ten private agencies serving Whites only, nine were concerned principally with welfare services, although one—the Social Settlement Association—had organized as the Free Kindergarten Association. The Holy Innocents Hospital was the sole health organization. Whereas public subsidy had been extended to only one of six black organizations, eight of ten serving Whites received funds from either city, county, or state. The Jewish charities were totally dependent on private donations, as was the Boys Club. No clear criteria governed the selection of agencies to be supported or the amount of the subsidy. Thus the Boys Club served dozens each year in highly praised preventive work without public aid, while the Octavia White Home was supported by the city, though it housed fewer than a dozen elderly persons. The white agencies reflected the concern with personal transformation and improvement that characterized private charities generally during this era. Special interest was shown in redirecting the lives of juvenile offenders or "unfortunate women"; the Mercy Home for women and girls and the industrial schools for boys and girls received aid from all three levels of government: city, county, and state. The Boys Club phrased its public appeals in terms of the earnings of "redeemed" boys representing a favorable return on investment, and the religious thrust of the Salvation Army was always stressed.[61] Only the Jewish charities and later the Pisgah Home seem to have given outdoor relief freely without attempting to improve the character of the recipient.

The work of the white agencies reflected the civic activity of women; seven of the ten were managed and governed entirely by women. "Strange to say," noted the president of the Mercy Home, "the men of our city and state are indifferent to this question of the care of the dependent and defective; and most of them seem to consider all effort for this class a kind of woman's 'fad' instead of an important social obligation."[62] The exceptions to female governance were the Salvation Army, which seems to have had no local volunteer board; the Pisgah Home, which had five men on its board; and the Jewish charities supported by male congregation members.

Dozens of women made contributions to the charitable work of the district during this period. The clear pattern that emerges from reviewing board memberships is one of specialization; women adopted agencies as their special concern and tended to remain active in only one, often for extended terms. Thus, the four women who were incorporators of the Mercy Home in 1892 were all active board members for at least twenty years. The support given by men consisted of membership on advisory boards that usually were active only in promoting annual operating fund drives or special building-fund efforts.

The agencies serving both Blacks and Whites, all governed by Whites, were especially concerned with health care; and it was in these that men were most active prior to the establishing of the Associated Charities. Exceptions to this pattern were the United Charities (later Associated Charities), which served both races, and the Sisters of Charity Home, which was open to children of both races—though racial breakdowns were given in none of its reports. The fact that disease in any person threatened the entire community probably accounts for the roughly comparable health services extended to both races; and the impact of poor health on the community's reputation and economy may account for the unusual activity among males. The profit motive was clearly at work in the health and welfare activities of the Tennessee Coal, Iron and Railroad Company. When the Board of Lady Managers of Hillman Hospital faced serious financial difficulties, leading businessmen spent considerable time in meeting with them and later in the successful effort to have the hospital maintained as a public institution. The business community gave active support to the sisters of St. Vincent's Hospital when they launched a campaign for a substantial addition. And the board of the Anti-Tuberculosis Society was predominantly male. These health programs were also the recipients of the largest public subsidies given by the city and county.

The brief leadership provided by men to the Associated Charities is the most interesting factor that emerges from the review of this period; it is not entirely clear why they made their initial commitment to this relief work or why they abandoned their efforts so quickly in favor of municipal control. However, the nature of the changed leadership is dramatic. Of the fifty-eight different individuals who served on the board of the United Charities between 1900 and 1909, forty-three were women and fifteen men. The sixty-two directors of the Associated Charities who served between its founding in 1909 and the 1916 municipal takeover were all men, including the leaders of both industry and commerce. The president and vice-president of the Tennessee Company played active roles in the organization, as did the president of the powerful Birmingham Realty Company and the heads of several locally owned mercantile houses. The economic power structure of the community was well represented on the organization, as were ministers, educators, physicians, and lawyers. There was also an overlapping of those who played major roles in the important political decisions analyzed earlier and those who played a major role in establishing the Associated Charities. Eight of the sixteen original board members who incorporated the agency had been active in one of the three political decisions. In short, the leadership of the Associated Charities included prominent members of Birmingham's industrial, commercial, professional, and political elite.

Looking at the private agencies as a group, it is apparent that they partially filled a void in the life of the community by providing a range of necessary services that government either could not or would not provide. But two other additional facts are apparent: they did not provide services adequate to meet recognized need, and they did not wish to confine welfare activities to the private sector.

The annual reports of virtually all of the agencies refer to eligible applicants who were turned away because of overcrowded facilities and/or inadequate finances throughout the period. But the inadequacy became most noticeable during periods of economic recession, and particularly during the depression of 1914–15. Then the relief-giving agencies offered new emergency services and conducted more ambitious drives. But private donations did not sustain the special activities; the Associated Charities' woodyard, established in December 1914 to permit the able-bodied unemployed to earn food and lodging, closed three months later because of lack of funds, putting one hundred men on the street.

The most ambitious private fund-raising effort was a joint campaign for $24,500 conducted during the spring of 1914 by the Associated Charities, the Anti-Tuberculosis Society, and the Children's Aid Society. The *News* noted, "each one of them is now behind in its obligations and is inadequate to its responsibilities."[63] One hundred and fifty men volunteered to canvass the city, which was divided into fifteen districts. Luncheons were held on each day of the drive to maintain volunteer enthusiasm and focus publicity on the effort. Only $10,000 was raised during the drive, less than the amount raised by the Associated Charities alone in 1912.[64] Although this and other failures do not statistically measure the inadequacy of the relief and welfare services, they do give a significant indication of the extent to which private sources failed to measure up to their self-established goals in a community largely dependent on them for aid to the needy. When public officials refused to help the over-burdened Associated Charities, it resorted to bank loans and soon made its appeal that the city assume its responsibilities.

This appeal for public responsibility was not the first to be heard from leaders of private agencies, though its origins in the male leadership made it particularly striking. When the Birmingham Free Kindergarten Association was established, its president stated that it would function only "until the state has learned its duty, and taken the development of the child from the age of four to six into its keeping."[65]

The president of the Mercy Home called for a state board of charities and for greater city involvement in the screening and supporting of charities. The responsibility of providing institutional care and relief fell upon private agencies by default, only because "the city still ignores its responsibility to these things."[66] And George Ward noted, "Voluntary contributions cause worry, dangerous delays and uncertainty"; he argued that specific state taxes for charity, particularly in health areas, represented the only solution to the community's needs.[67]

The city government that agreed to take responsibility for the work of the Associated Charities had but limited experience in the area of welfare services. The predominant mode of public involvement from the beginning of the period had been subsidies to the array of private agencies in the district. Each year from 1901 through 1910 the city had appropriated between $4,700 and $7,000 to charities in monthly allocations ranging from $25 per month to the Colored Orphans and Old Folks Home and $50 per month for the white nonhealth agencies to a maximum of $200 per month to combat tuberculosis. The total appropriation for charity ranged from .8 percent to slightly more than 1 percent of the municipal budget; this category included all the health, education, and welfare agencies supported by the city. Birmingham's per capita expenditure for "hospitals, charity and prison" was $.27 per year in 1911; this compared poorly with other southern cities such as Louisville ($1.05), Atlanta ($.90), Memphis ($.41), Nashville ($.42), and Richmond ($.60).[68] The *Age-Herald* observed in 1907: "It will thus be seen that with all its greatness, Birmingham is doing little toward helping the sick and poor in her midst. Many other cities, smaller by far, own and support hospitals, homes, and all sorts of institutions."[69]

After the consolidation of 1910 with its resulting population increase, the city increased its support of charities, reaching an annual maximum of nearly $20,000 in 1913, which represented about 1 percent of the municipal budget.

But in the severe depression year of 1914, charity subsidies declined to just over $18,000 or .71 percent of the budget. In 1915 the city spent $15,102 on private agencies during the first six months of the year but then terminated all such aid in July as an economic measure to reduce the annual deficit; this action was taken despite continuing need and serious financial difficulties among the private organizations. The city supplied no further aid in 1915 and a total of just over $2,000 in 1916.[70] Clearly the men of the Associated Charities turned to the city for relief that year for reasons other than the superior financial capability of local government.

Prior to its experience as administrator of welfare services, the city had also had brief experiences as a source of referral and regulation and even as a direct provider of services. The services took two forms. First, the city throughout the period provided charity transportation to indigents wishing to leave Birmingham; investigations were made first by the United Charities and later by the city itself. Second, during December 1914, the city employed over one hundred white men for chopping wood and cleaning parks during the depths of the depression. This work project terminated within one month; the city offered no additional direct services to needy residents during that crisis.

The city's referral activities were provided by its welfare department, established in November 1912 and said to be the first such office in a southern city. The department referred clients to existing private agencies; its principal concern was with aiding single women and children. In 1915 the department was reorganized as the city department of relief and correction; directed by a minister with a staff of four, the department received contributions from private citizens, which it then distributed as relief to the needy.[71]

The inconsistent and inadequate performances of private agencies and city government had troubled both the professional social workers and the city commission. The commission in 1913 briefly discussed the possibility of taking over charitable work or at least stimulating the development of a central organization, citing "wars and rumors of wars among charity organizations of the city" and agencies "scrapping among themselves."[72] Wishing not to discourage private acts of charity, the commission decided only to pass an ordinance requiring all publicly supported charities to file monthly financial reports and maintain open books and accounts.[73] This measure proved ineffective and was supplemented by the informal creation by the city commission of a five-member advisory board of public welfare with one member each appointed by the city, the county, the Chamber of Commerce, the Interchurch Association, and the Medical Association. This board examined the books and reports of twenty-six agencies aided by city and county; discovering loss of efficiency due to duplication of efforts, it recommended the consolidation of similar agencies and their individual fund drives.[74] These criticisms were also made by the business-men investigating the city's financial operations; they urged that all public distributions to private charities should be made through the board of public welfare.[75] When both the city and the charities ignored its recommendations, however, the board resigned, urging the city to create by ordinance a board with the authority to compel consolidation of charities and to supervise these reorganized agencies. They recommended a five-member city-county board and an executive secretary with responsibility for all agencies receiving public funds or conducting drives.[76] But further discussion of this proposal was made unnecessary by Birmingham's termination of public subsidies in mid-1915.

The city reentered the welfare arena one year later when it appropriated $3,750 to purchase the nearly defunct Pisgah Home, that sum matched by contributions from local women; there is no information presented in the newspapers as to why the city took this step. When it had acquired the facility, the city announced that it would be the nucleus of a new department of relief and correction staffed with competent persons who would administer outdoor relief to the proven needy. The costs of the staff and the relief extended were to be met largely through private contributions to the city comptroller; the city had in fact assumed total administrative but only partial financial responsibility.[77] It was to the new department that the functions of the Associated Charities were assigned, once the commission finally agreed to accept them.

At the end of the period the city had what appeared to be a comprehensive department of relief and correction whose stated purpose was to provide immediate relief to the needy through a public institution, thus eliminating the delay and inefficiency of the previous system of private charity. Those who had supported the Pisgah Home or the Associated Charities now either gave to the city or were directed by it to families in need. The work of the department was carried out through five divisions:

1. Welfare—responsible for aid to adult females and children who had appeared in juvenile court by means of referral to public and private agencies and to physicians; 457 were aided during the department's first six months of operation.
2. Pisgah Welfare Home—a residential facility that housed 225 individuals in the first six months and served over 11,500 meals.
3. City relief—outdoor relief that provided $2,482 to 1,610 clients in six months. Additional aid was given in the form of coal, clothing, groceries, and medicines that had been donated to the department, which said that no legitimately needy applicant had been turned away.
4. Employment—aided 152 in locating jobs during the six months.

5. Industrial—furnished work to indigents who were paid to remove the stigma of charity. Apparently none were served during the first year.[78]

After twelve months of operation, the department claimed that it had served 5,941 persons and conducted 2,957 investigative visits while spending about $8,400—of which $2,500 was for salaries.[79] The available data indicate that only Whites benefited from its programs.

By the end of 1917 it appeared that the debate over private or public responsibility for aid to the poor was being settled in favor of an enlarged governmental role. But the events of that year were only one phase of a continuing debate that resumed almost immediately thereafter. The data of the department itself indicate that its services were none too munificent; it spent about $8,000 in one year, whereas the Associated Charities alone spent more than this amount during each year of its existence. Within eight years the Pisgah Home had been closed as a health hazard, the business leaders had reasserted themselves in the welfare area by creating a Community Chest, and the department of relief and correction had been abolished—its work turned back entirely to private agencies.[80] The major issue of public or private responsibility for welfare thus continued to emerge with particular vividness during the second period of this study, 1928–41.

PART TWO

1928–1941

4

Politics and Government in Birmingham

THE ROOSEVELT ADMINISTRATION regarded Birmingham as "the worst hit city in the nation," and the history of the city between 1929 and 1941 is largely the record of a community overwhelmed by an economic catastrophe totally beyond its control and aided by a federal response to that disaster.[1] The actions of local public officials and the controversies of local politics during much of the period had less impact on the day-to-day life of the citizenry than the actions of federal relief administrators, whose directives determined what programs would be carried out, how much external aid would flow into the community, and how many people would receive desperately needed help. In a fundamental way the city was nationalized during the Depression; the most significant policies locally reflected mandates from the nation's capital. This nationalization of policy-making had a significant impact on local behavior in the area of services to the needy, changing the institutional structure that provided relief and the characteristics both of those offering and of those receiving it. It had little impact on other aspects of local politics and government, which continued during this period the same traits and tendencies that had characterized them during 1900–1917.

Throughout the 1920s Birmingham had maintained a political culture similar to that described earlier. Blaine Brownell, in a study of local ideas and attitudes based upon analyses of local newspapers during the 1920s, details a "complete acceptance of business middle-class priorities and business middle-class leadership."[2]

This general viewpoint was spread throughout the community by the newspapers and "found wide acceptance among their readers."[3] Blacks and Whites shared the same urban ethos, whose principal values were cooperation, unity, stability, and physical and economic growth; this ethos supported the ideal of a "corporate-expansive" city.[4] Like progressives elsewhere, local leaders often compared their city to a business corporation and concluded that the task of local government was little more than the application of management skills to the problems of the city; leadership was expected to originate in most cases in commercial and civic organizations rather than in government. Like the political culture of privatism that Warner found in Philadelphia, Birmingham's was "a brand of progressivism that looked to economic growth as the primary means of solving social ills, and hardly touched the deeper problems of race relations, the economic plight of the disadvantaged, and other social problems that would become increasingly severe in subsequent years."[5]

Along with other businessmen across the nation, Birmingham's civic leaders were ideologically unprepared for the Depression; from their positions of prominence they merely joined in the plea for more federal aid to prevent total chaos locally and looked forward to the quick passing of the storm. But as analysis of later periods will indicate, Birmingham's political culture was suspended but not replaced, not even seriously challenged; it reemerged vigorously in the post-Depression era and characterized the city in the 1960s and 1970s. The preoccupation with poverty in the 1930s was due to its magnitude and not to any new sensitivity on the part of local civic or political leaders; it did not reemerge as a significant topic of concern until the era of the anti-poverty program when the city was again inescapably affected by national programs.

Both before and during the Depression the city maintained its pattern of low taxes, low expenditures, and low-level public services; and the distribution of funds among services reflected the relative lack of concern for social welfare activities. Between 1921 and 1928 the per capita expenditures for general government operations doubled in the city, while the per capita outlay for "hospitals, charities, and corrections" actually declined from twenty-five cents per person (about 1.9 percent of the budget) to twenty cents (or less than 1 percent of the budget). Birmingham was unique among major cities in the South in experiencing a decline in this category.[6]

Although its per capita expenditures had doubled in the previous seven years, Birmingham in 1928 still had the lowest per capita tax rate of the ninety-three cities in the 100,000–300,000 population class.[7] This ranking was partially due to the city's relatively meager revenues from property taxes, since the rate during the period continued to be the lowest, or among the lowest, of all cities above 100,000. The problem of a low rate was aggravated by low assessments; property could legally have been assessed at 60 percent of market value but was actually assessed at only 42 percent.[8] While major cities averaged about 65 percent of their revenues from property taxes, Birmingham typically received about 41 percent; taxing property at the maximum allowable assessment would have doubled the city's income from this source. But the county persisted in its earlier unwillingness to reassess property, compelling the city to maintain one of the highest license schedules in the nation. Nearly 20 percent of the city's revenues were derived from license sales at the end of the period, compared with an average of 2 percent for the nation's major urban areas.[9]

Birmingham's limited revenues dictated corresponding limitations in the city's expenditures for services. In 1934 Birmingham ranked ninety-first among the ninety-three cities above 100,000 in population in per capita operating costs for general departments; the average was $30.86, while Birmingham spent only $15.29—well below the average even for southern cities.[10] Other cities were averaging 9.2 municipal employees per one thousand citizens, while Birmingham employed 4.6 per thousand. Elsewhere the average salary for each worker was $1,709 per year, compared with $1,100 in Birmingham.[11] Birmingham ranked ninety-first in number of policemen in proportion to population with .9 per one thousand citizens, compared with the average of 1.61. The city's fifty square miles were patrolled by 239 officers, compared with 407 men for Atlanta's twenty-five square miles.[12]

Birmingham in 1934 spent only $.17 per capita on public health, while the national average was $.70; it had one-fifth the number of public health nurses recommended by the public health service and allocated only one-half as much as other major southern cities to public health activities.[13] The county bore a major share of the responsibility for providing health care services through Hillman Hospital, and the area compared poorly with other cities in this category as well. After the new wing was opened in 1928, Hillman had a bed capacity of 382 for a population of 300,000; with roughly the same population Atlanta had 500 charity beds.[14]

The city continued to have one of the highest death rates from tuberculosis in the nation, ranking behind only Denver. In 1940 the national death rate from the disease was 45.9 per one hundred thousand citizens, while in Birmingham the corresponding figure for the population as a whole was 77. This overall number masked the extreme severity of tuberculosis among Blacks, who fell victim to it at a rate of 149.9 per one hundred thousand compared with an incidence among local Whites of 30.6.[15]

When the United States Bureau of Education conducted a survey of thirty-five major cities during the 1927–28 school year, it found that Birmingham ranked at the bottom in per pupil expenditures with a figure of $59.02 per year compared with the average of $113.69; twenty-nine of the cities spent at least 50 percent more per pupil than Birmingham. In 1936 the city ranked ninetieth of the cities above 100,000 and twelfth of fifteen southern cities in that class, even though it devoted over 40 percent of its budget to public education, against about 29 percent for the national average.[16] When George Strayer from Columbia University visited the local school system, he praised both the efficiency and quality of the administration, noting that the great deficiency in the schools was a shortage of money.[17]

In short, Birmingham during the period 1928–41 continued the pattern of paying little per capita for public services and receiving little in comparison with other major American cities. Except for dissatisfaction with health care, neither public officials nor private sources prior to the Depression objected to the fact that Birmingham ranked at or near the bottom of every comparative listing of per capita expenditures for any purpose. And the financial limitations imposed by the Depression throughout the period precluded improvement in any service. Between 1930 and 1933 the city reduced its general operating expenditures by 37 percent, and the municipal budget at the end of the period had not yet reached the 1928–29 level.[18]

The relative status of the black community as the recipient of public services also followed the pattern described for the 1900–1917 period. Though the health department described services for Blacks in the city as "meager," Blacks fared reasonably well in this area, again reflecting recognition of the fact that disease was no respecter of racial barriers. "Birmingham's Health," the monthly publication of the Jefferson County Board of Health, noted that of the cities above 100,000 in population, Birmingham had the largest percentage black, 38.2 percent in 1930. Referring particularly to the large number of black women working as domestics in white homes, the bulletin argued, "Even regardless of any humanitarian considerations, all citizens of Birmingham must for their own self-interest and self-protection be interested in the problems of Negro health—in mere selfish self-defense we must do something."[19] The majority of Hillman Hospital patients each year were black, and the antituberculosis clinic often saw as many black patients each month as white.[20] Furthermore, community spokesmen favored an expanded role in the future for health units such as the dental facility, which also saw a majority of black clients. The *News* wrote in an editorial that:

> Clinics like these being conducted by the Health Department are eternal reminders in this lopsided social state where armies of dentists and physicians are established to render skilled help to sufferers who are able to pay fees, that some enlightened social state of the future will guarantee to its sons and daughters a normal health condition. This guarantee against preventable disease will be made, not as a charity but in human justice.[21]

In other areas, however, discrepancies in services rendered to Blacks and Whites were substantial; and few voices were raised in the name of human justice to protest the deficiencies. For example, Blacks continued to attend school in inferior facilities, and black public school teachers were paid significantly less than white.[22] The city did not purchase its first municipal park for Blacks until 1941.[23] But no public figure directed his attention to the needs of the black community as had George Ward in the earlier period; the major newspapers were similarly silent. In fact, the black community between 1928 and 1941 had no effective spokesman. A brief article in 1929 announced the formation of the Birmingham Benevolent and Legal Aid Association, established by leading black citizens; but no further reference to this organization was found.[24] Similarly, a Negro Welfare Council was discussed in a single article; its purpose was to publish a bulletin listing agencies that extended welfare services to Blacks. But neither the council nor the publication is mentioned subsequently.[25]

The organization that was most active in behalf of the black community was the Birmingham Branch of the Alabama Inter-racial Commission, an organization led by, and apparently composed exclusively of, Whites. Although brief reference was made to the role of the commission in resolving black complaints of discrimination in employment to the satisfaction of all parties, its main work was in support of improved housing conditions, primarily by means of the New Deal slum clearance and public housing programs.[26] The commission made no complaints against the continuing exclusion of Blacks from political participation or against the increasingly strict policy of racial segregation, illustrated by the 1926 municipal zoning law that established residential zoning as an official means of achieving segregation.[27]

Two incidents from the Depression illustrate the prevailing attitude among public officials toward black citizens. The spring of 1930 witnessed intense discontent among unemployed laborers, including at least one integrated meeting in the main downtown park addressed by black and white speakers and sponsored by local Communists. Speakers advocated a mass meeting of the unemployed and marches upon the city hall and Community Chest for relief; two protested the city laws establishing racial segregation in both public transportation and housing. The city commission promptly enacted an ordinance banning public meetings of anarchists; police then arrested two Whites and three Blacks for "advocating social equality between whites and Negroes" at another park rally.[28]

In January 1939 unemployed workers formed an integrated committee to press for more aggressive local efforts to secure Works Progress Administration projects in the district. When a delegation composed of five Whites and two Blacks called upon the commission president, he shouted, "I don't care to discuss the matter with you. Don't come in here with a mixed committee. Don't bring Negroes in here on a committee."[29]

One reads the local political history of the period and finds a fundamental lack of concern for the black community accompanied by increasing legal segregation. Such protection and assistance as Blacks received came primarily from the professional social work community locally and from New Deal administrators nationally.

Officeholders and Elections

In part the official attitude toward Blacks can be explained by the virulence of the Ku Klux Klan during the 1920s and its impact on local politics. The Klan grew in Jefferson County after 1916, when the Robert E. Lee Klavern Number 1 was established; by 1924 this unit alone had an estimated membership of ten thousand. Klan membership peaked in 1926 with between fifteen and twenty thousand members in the county, including two local judges, the sheriff, most members of the Birmingham police department, and at least twenty other city and county officials.[30] During the decade of the twenties aspiring politicians were virtually compelled to honor, in word if not in deed, the Klan and its program of religious intolerance and racial bigotry. Jimmy Jones, the dominant local politician during the period under review, was no exception to this rule of practical politics. When he first ran for the office of commission president in 1925, he courted the Klan, was endorsed by it, and won an easy victory. Although Jones later proved to be a disappointment to his Klan supporters, as when the commission denied them a parade permit, he was fully aware of the explosiveness of race as an issue in politics and acted accordingly.

Jones served as commission president from 1925 until his death in 1940; his conservative views in matters of both race and welfare mirror well the behavior of city government in these areas during his tenure. Jones also illustrates the type of men who officially ruled Birmingham during the Depression years: unremarkable representatives of the middle class who spent much time either holding local office or trying to. He claimed as his occupation highway construction, though he was also the president of a local trucking company. However, officeholding consumed a greater portion of his time than did private enterprise. Jones was elected city clerk and tax collector in one of the small suburbs that surrounded Birmingham in 1908; two years later, when the Greater Birmingham consolidation act eliminated that post, he became a clerk in the office of the city treasurer. Later he was named city comptroller, a position he held until the 1920 municipal election forced the incumbent commission out of office and led to his replacement as well. Significantly, Jones's political patron throughout his career was N. A. Barrett, the physician who had defeated George Ward in the 1917 commission race with the support of the secret and anti-Catholic True American Society.[31] The intolerance which had first emerged in local politics during that campaign had become full-blown during the twenties and set the tone for the succeeding Depression years.

Jones's two colleagues on the commission in 1928 were also politically active members of the middle class. William E. Dickson had been a public school principal for twenty years, had served as a state legislator, and was finishing his second four-year term as an associate commissioner. The other associate commissioner, John H. Taylor, was also completing his second term; he was the owner of a medium-sized real estate and loan business.[32] The Klan had endorsed all three of the incumbents during the 1925 campaign.

When Jones died, he was succeeded as commission president by W. Cooper Green, who had served one term as a state legislator and seven years as the city's postmaster.[33] Green's public career continued with only brief interruptions until 1974, when he retired from the presidency of the Jefferson County commission.

The other associate commissioners between 1929 and 1941 also reflect the pattern of dominance by middle-class politicians; they include Lewey Robinson, a former newspaper reporter who had served in the state legislature; W. O. Downs, a former sheriff; Jimmy Morgan, the proprietor of a suburban radio company; and Eugene "Bull" Connor, a sportscaster who parlayed his local popularity among radio listeners into a political following and was elected commissioner of public safety in 1937. Connor was to emerge a quarter of a century later as the internationally recognized symbol of the city's racial intransigence.[34]

Defeated challengers came from the same kinds of backgrounds as did elected officials, listing such occupations as druggist, small general store owner, clothing store operator, cafe owner, real estate broker, and lawyer; among them were two former commission candidates and two former commissioners. In the 1929 election, all eight candidates fell into one of these two categories.[35]

It would be an exaggeration to claim that politicians during the 1928–41 period reflected significant differences in background and characteristics from those of the 1900–1917 period, but there were two variations between the periods. First, no figure of the second period had an articulated philosophy of the role of government in society against which to judge the actual performance of local government. George Ward, in annual messages as mayor and as commission president, had advocated a strong municipal government which created a climate favorable to business while supporting an extensive array of services, including educational and cultural services, equitably distributed among citizens. He compared Birmingham's performance against this ideal and found it sadly wanting; he publicly stated his conclusions that the city should increase its revenues, expand its services, and pay greater attention to the needs of Blacks. No public figure in the 1928–41 period spoke of government in anything but managerial terms; discussions of purpose and equity were totally absent.

The second difference between the two periods is that the range of occupations from which politicians emerged was more limited during the latter in terms of traditional rankings of social status. There were no bank presidents, no major local entrepreneurs, and no stock company partners who sought local office—though two lawyers did run unsuccessfully. Men of higher rank had not been driven from public life by any major change in either the regime or the electorate; rather, they seem simply to have retired by personal preference from local politics.

Four general municipal elections were held during the 1928–41 period, with one producing a lively contest, three characterized by an absence of issues, and two by the additional absence of activity.

In 1929 the three incumbents stood for reelection, citing their ability to work together as a team and listing municipal improvements that included the construction of an impressive football stadium, installation of three garbage disposal incinerators, park improvements, an enlarged police force, library additions, street and sewer construction, and a traffic light system.

Opposition to the three commissioners came from two organized sources. First, over one hundred citizens met in the assembly room of the Klan and formed investigating committees to examine the commission's awarding of contracts and to endorse a slate of candidates; though the group denied Klan affiliation, few doubted that the organization was an active force in the election.[36] Credence was lent to this assumption when opponents accused Jones of secretly employing Blacks as special police officers with authority to make arrests. Jones hotly denounced the "ridiculous lies" of the opposition: "They are even saying that we have Negro policemen! No more ridiculous charge could be made against a Southern city, and a man who would tell that when he could tell the truth is beyond contempt."[37] He claimed that the four Blacks whom people accused him of hiring as special officers were in fact janitors at schools helping children cross streets safely.[38]

Other issues raised by the Klan-oriented opposition group included Jones's connection with a trucking firm that held municipal contracts and his assigning two public offices to a single employee. Jones denied that any favoritism had been shown to the transport company and argued that the employee in question was performing both jobs effectively. The entire commission was attacked for refusing to dedicate two hundred acres of outlying city-owned land as a park; the commissioners wished to retain this land as the possible site of a municipal airport.[39]

The second source of organized opposition was the Birmingham Trades Council, an association of thirty-two labor organizations that endorsed four of the challengers. The trades council charged that the commission, especially Jones, had broken promises made to labor during the 1925 campaign by contracting with nonunion firms locally, by unnecessarily using outside companies and workers, by refusing to enforce the eight-hour workday law, and by failing to require more than one operator on each streetcar.[40] Despite this substantial opposition, the incumbents were returned to office without a runoff; each received more than twice the vote of the nearest challenger.[41]

The 1933 election was held after the federal government had developed the Muscle Shoals facility for generating electricity; all eight candidates ran on platforms of decreasing utility rates by means of municipal ownership of the light and power plants.[42] Newspaper accounts of the race indicate an absence of issues until after the primary, when Jones was forced into a runoff for the presidency against North Birmingham businessman C. D. Rogers. That race degenerated into a battle of personal accusations, with Rogers charging Jones with administrative inefficiency and Jones describing his challenger as incompetent in business.[43] Voters returned Jones to office but rejected the other incumbents for reasons that do not emerge from the newspaper reports, selecting instead Lewey Robinson, member of the Alabama legislature and former newspaperman, and W. O. Downs, former sheriff of Jefferson County.[44]

The four-year term of the new team of commissioners was characterized by unprecedented feuding among the three officials; generally the associate commissioners stood in opposition to president Jones. The two newcomers diminished Jones's power by removing various city departments from his supervision and by dismissing employees known to be his supporters; such maneuverings seem to have occupied much of the officials' time, judging by the amount of coverage given them by the press.[45] The peak of hostility was reached in 1934 when a disastrous downtown fire caused $3 million damage to Loveman's, a leading department store. The associate commissioners passed an official commendation for the effective work of the city's fire department and retained an attorney for the duration of an investigation into Jones's charges of inefficiency and drunkenness during the blaze, which he called a "three million dollar monument to cheap politics."[46] While this particular investigation was inconclusive, a second held the following year justified Jones's accusations about cheap politics. The grand jury condemned the two associate commissioners after hearing 110 witnesses in an investigation into charges of

graft in the purchase of fire hoses; it found obvious discrimination against companies employing people known to oppose the two.[47] Although one newspaper began a campaign for the adoption of the city manager plan, the voters
seemed interested in harmony among the commissioners and not a change in
the form of government. The 1937 election saw thirteen candidates enter the
race, but there was virtually no campaigning. No issues emerged, and neither
labor nor any other group made endorsements. One headline summarized the
campaign: "City Commission race apathetic as voting nears."[48] Jones overwhelmed his opposition, polling a majority of more than thirty-eight hundred
over the combined total of the four challengers. Two new associate commissioners, Eugene "Bull" Connor and West End radio dealer Jimmy Morgan,
were chosen, apparently reflecting voter dissatisfaction with the tactics of the
incumbents in disrupting the administration of the city's business.[49]

Tranquility prevailed during the two remaining elections held during the
period. When Jones died in 1940, a special election was held to fill the vacancy,
with the city postmaster, W. Cooper Green, recognized as the leading aspirant
for the office. Seventeen prospective candidates all withdrew from the election;
and the only opposition faced by Green was a token, issueless campaign by a
real estate broker who claimed that he had no intention of running but felt that
the highest municipal office should not be filled by default.[50] The 1941 general
election saw the entire commission returned to office without serious challenge; this time the presidency was retained by default. A *News* editorial said,
"Veteran local politicians declare the city has never seen a campaign as quiet
and uneventful as this one. . . . There is hardly a ripple on the political sea."[51]

During much of the period under review, Birmingham was experiencing
the disastrous effects of the Depression; but electoral politics give not the
slightest hint of this crisis. As will be seen below, New Deal programs did generate controversy locally and did require the attention of local officials; but the
politics of welfare was largely a politics of intergovernmental relations, with
the participants being officials and not the electorate. Welfare was an independent political arena where local issues were manifestations of national policies;
these issues did not lend themselves to local electoral decision and did not
penetrate this arena.

The 1928–41 period resembled the 1900–1917 period in the absence of welfare as an issue in elections but differed in the presence of race as a campaign
topic. The 1929 election culminated a decade of Klan activity, and the charge
that Jones had hired Blacks as policemen reflected its sensitizing the community to race questions. Because no elected officials or challengers made any
efforts to violate the increasingly rigid racial norms of the city, race did not
reemerge as an election issue again before 1941. It did, however, arise as an

issue in the politics of welfare during the Depression and persisted as an important community issue until it erupted as a central electoral issue in the early 1960s.

Routine Operations of Government

The routine operations of Birmingham's city government between 1928 and 1941 can again be conveniently categorized under six headings: (1) establishing the municipal budget, (2) determining the number of offices, (3) selecting the occupants of offices, (4) extending basic services, (5) deciding how to extend these services, and (6) regulating behavior.

Since the turn of the century, Birmingham had been plagued with the problem of an inadequate financial base for the support of essential public services. The already intense budgetary problems, exacerbated by the Depression, forced the city to reduce the total municipal budget from $7,631,840 in 1927–28 to $5,018,244 in 1934–35 before it began a gradual climb upward.[52] The city was compelled to make drastic cuts in personnel, salaries, and services. At least 274 employees were laid off during the crisis, including 50 percent of the officers from a police force that was recognized as inadequate at best. The commission imposed four 10 percent salary reductions and reduced support to facilities such as the public library and the tuberculosis sanatorium. In addition to its previous obligations, the city faced the additional responsibility of providing local funds for direct relief and both financial and in-kind support for work projects; in 1940–41 these expenditures amounted to $110,000 and $42,000, respectively.[53]

Even with stringent economy measures, the commission still needed to generate new revenue for general operations; the most persistent budgetary issue during the period was where to get these funds. Two examples illustrate the dilemma.

In early 1930 the commissioners indicated that they were contemplating levying a temporary one-cent-per-gallon gasoline tax. Immediate opposition came from various "good roads" groups, from automobile dealers, from filling station operators, and from the press—which saw the tax as a violation of the commission's promise not to increase the citizen's tax burden. The commission passed the tax and survived the ensuing fight by the above groups against its imposition.[54]

The commission was not so fortunate when confronted by basically the same problem in 1934. Following the recommendation of a five-member citizens' committee established to advise it on its financial plight, the commission increased taxes on such nonessential items as candy and motion-picture tickets and levied an additional one-cent gasoline tax. Immediately petitions were circulated throughout the city calling for a referendum on the new taxes, with leadership provided by Alabama petroleum industries; over six thousand citizens signed after a brief but intense drive. In the face of this pressure, the commission abandoned its selective taxes, replacing them with a general 1 percent city sales tax. Merchants immediately established an organization that sent twenty-five workers throughout the city full time with recall petitions in a campaign that the newspaper called "unparalleled in the city's political annals"; labor also endorsed the movement.[55] The recall effort was abandoned only when the associate commissioners broke with Jones, repealed all emergency taxes, and delayed the general tax until after the referendum. The tax program was abandoned altogether when voters defeated the proposal by a four-to-one margin.[56]

Examples could be multiplied to illustrate the inability of the city to gain needed revenues through tax increases imposed during a period of economic crisis for businesses and citizens as well as government. It fared better with bond issues for the support of public improvement projects both because of the visibility of such improvements and because of the promise that they could be financed from the sinking fund with no additional taxes. During the 1928–41 period the city commission submitted bond issues to the voters for such projects as a municipal airport, park renovations, and sewer and drainage systems; all were approved by comfortable margins.

Disputes over the number and occupants of offices emerged especially during the 1933–37 term, when associate commissioners Lewey Robinson and W. O. Downs formed a coalition against Jones. Much commission time and newspaper space were devoted to questions such as whether or not the office of chief of police ought to be abolished and replaced by a system of direct supervision of the department by the commissioner of public safety.[57] When this question and others like it but involving lesser offices were answered in favor of maintaining or creating positions, additional time and press coverage were devoted to the subsequent question of who should be appointed to office.

Questions of administrative organization as well as of personnel occupied the attention of the commission, particularly in regard to the fire and police departments. In the face of a crime wave and citizen complaints in 1931, the commission debated the wisdom of establishing an independent detective bureau within the department; the increasing number of automobiles and accidents involving them stimulated discussion about creation of a traffic bureau.[58]

The range of personnel questions coming before the commission was decreased by the passage of a comprehensive civil service law in 1936, which established a unified merit system for Birmingham and Jefferson County. The bill originated among members of the Jefferson County legislative delegation, and the focal point of activity surrounding its passage was the state legislature. Local opposition came from one associate commissioner on the ground that civil service would open the way for the employment of Blacks in city hall; ironically, he was assured that such would not be the case by none other than "Bull" Connor, then a member of the Alabama House of Representatives and an avid supporter of the measure. City and county employees also opposed the civil service bill, while the press encouraged reform-minded legislators to enact the measure.[59]

Birmingham's commissioners regarded the physical improvement of the city and the provision of basic services as the principal functions of city government. Speaking before a civic organization in the spring of 1929, President Jones listed the three major challenges confronting the city as provision of an adequate drainage system, the separation of grade crossings, and the construction of a municipal airport—in that order.[60]

The city began a massive program of storm and sanitary sewer improvement during the 1930s, utilizing federal grants and loans. The system was not completed until the 1980s, and open and overflowing sewers continued to plague both residents and politicians.

A civic problem that had generated continuous controversy for twenty-five years was largely resolved in 1928 when the city and railway companies agreed to a four-million-dollar program of viaduct construction, financed by a bond issue that the companies agreed to pay for in part.[61] Three years later Jones was to say, "I am prouder of getting those grade elimination projects put through than anything else done since I have been in office."[62] And in 1931 Birmingham opened a new municipal airport after a promotional campaign that is reviewed below.

Questions relating to the method of providing services closely resemble those raised during the 1900–1917 period.

Citizen complaints about the quality of service and the rate structure of the street railway company were presented to the commission, as were protests over gas rates. But the most intense efforts were made in behalf of lower rates for electricity in a campaign of major proportions stimulated by the possibility of federally supplied power from the Muscle Shoals plant in the Tennessee Valley. Principal combatants in the controversy were the Birmingham Electric Company, supplier of power to the entire metropolitan area; metropolitan area public officials; civic and labor organizations; and the *Birmingham Post*. Conspicuous by their absence were representatives of the business community. The *Post* reported: "In a session marked by disorder, bitter debate and an attempt to suppress the proceedings from publication, the board of directors of the Junior Chamber of Commerce this afternoon decided to take no stand in the campaign for reduced utility rates."[63]

In an unprecedented example of intergovernmental cooperation, Birmingham and several neighboring municipalities established the Jefferson County League of Municipalities as an instrument to press for lower electric rates before the Alabama Public Service Commission. The league hired rate engineers to prepare its case and established a committee to assess the feasibility of securing a Reconstruction Finance Corporation loan for the purchase or construction of power plants and transmission lines.[64] Birmingham offered the services of its engineering and legal staffs to the league, supplementing them with consulting engineers hired for the case.[65] The *Post* hired rate experts of its own to represent both consumers and municipalities served by the company in an effort to achieve a 50 percent reduction in rates.[66] Various community organizations supported the campaign, using as their vehicle the United Utilities Consumers Association, which included the League of Women Voters, the American Legion, the Birmingham Trades Council, and the Business and Professional Women's Club.[67]

Expert findings that the city could build a new system, reduce rates sharply, and still pay the necessary Reconstruction Finance Corporation loan within twenty years prompted the company to enter into negotiations with city officials for a new ten-year contract at moderately reduced rates that was criticized by the *Post* as offering too little to the consumer.[68]

The result of a complex series of investigations and negotiations was a referendum set for the fall to decide between a new contract or municipal ownership of the electric light plant; included on the same ballot were municipal ownership of the water and streetcar systems.

The Birmingham Trades Council led the campaign for public ownership, sending speakers before every union in the city. All candidates in the concurrent commission race endorsed municipal ownership. The voters, however, rejected all of the proposals for municipal ownership by margins of at least three to two.[69]

Two notable issues stand out in the commission's concern with regulation of behavior. First, it mounted a strict police campaign against vagrants, loiterers, and panhandlers during the Depression years, with a particular concern for keeping the downtown streets clear of drifters who approached shoppers and office workers for money.[70]

Second, the commission failed to mount a strict smoke-abatement campaign in the face of opposition from the larger industries and despite efforts of both the League of Women Voters and the *Post* to secure enforcement of the ten-year-old city ordinance regulating the emission of black smoke.[71] The *Post* described the effects of the frequent smoke episodes, and the *Age-Herald* interpreted their meaning:

> A thick, oily blanket of smoke hung over Birmingham Wednesday—the heaviest by far that the city has experienced in years.
>
> Downtown Birmingham and the north side, particularly, suffered. Up on the top and sides of Red Mountain the sun shone brightly, but was unable to penetrate the smoke in the valley below.
>
> Automobiles and streetcars were using their brightest lights, while pedestrians flitted in and out of the shadows of the smoke blanket like wraiths.
>
> White shirts, donned cleaned and starched early Wednesday morning, took on the appearance of a none-too-clean dust cloth by 9 a.m.[72]
>
> The moral of our black mornings is that a city may become so engrossed in enjoying its prosperity and good fortune that it will permit an ugly and insidious evil to rob it of the fresh, clean and wholesome air, which is the elementary right of every man.[73]

On three occasions the voters were asked to determine what laws would regulate behavior; they voted to allow themselves to drink beer legally and to attend baseball games, but not movies, on Sunday.

The Sunday movie proposal prompted the heaviest vote ever polled in a city election. Ministers were united in their opposition to the measure, and an overwhelming proportion of the vote from outlying boxes supported the clergymen's viewpoint. Voters in the central city narrowly favored Sunday movies.[74]

This vote seemed to illustrate the center-periphery division between a lower-income core and surrounding middle-class neighborhoods that characterized large cities during this period; the periphery was frequently the source of a moral element-suburban coalition that typically produced votes in favor of prohibition and political reform.[75] But on two other issues related to regulation of behavior this coalition failed to support the moralist positions of the community's ministers.

During the summer of 1932 the local topic receiving the greatest newspaper coverage was a proposal to permit Sunday baseball. Again clergymen opposed the measure, but voters by a margin of over two to one favored it.[76] Four years later voters were asked to vote on the twenty-one-year-old ordinance prohibiting the sale and consumption of beer after restaurant owners led a drive to repeal the law, whose enforcement had been a persistent problem for the police. In this case the vote was an overwhelming fifteen to one in favor of repeal. The effectiveness of the defeated prohibition effort can be judged by the newspaper's report that the retail price of beer dropped fifteen cents after the election.[77]

As in the earlier period, those involved in the routine operations and decisions of local government were the public officials with responsibility to act and those private citizens or groups who were immediately affected by their actions. With the possible exception of the electric rate issue, none of the decisions discussed above meet the criteria of a "key" decision; in none of them was the city's economic elite an active participant. The exercise of leadership in public affairs by this elite is encountered only when attention is turned to "important" rather than routine issues.

Important Decisions: Consolidation and the Airport

During the 1928–41 period two issues can be considered "key," using admittedly subjective criteria and viewing local politics from a historical perspective. The first was an unsuccessful attempt to expand the city limits to include adjacent suburbs; this was the Depression-era reflection of a desire held by local leaders throughout the twentieth century. The second was the decision to build a municipal airport, a clear example of "urban imperialism," that is, the warfare waged by cities for regional supremacy, in which transportation facilities were the principal weapons.[78]

At issue in the annexation effort was the consolidation of seven suburbs with Birmingham, which would have expanded the area of the city from fifty-two to one hundred square miles and increased the population from 280,000 to nearly 400,000. The authorizing legislation required that the governing authorities of the affected municipalities present a specific proposal to the voters of each city. In 1928 the Chamber of Commerce of the outlying community of Bessemer took the initiative in establishing the Birmingham District Cooperative Council to promote consolidation. Composed of numerous civic organizations from throughout the metropolitan area, its most prominent members were the Birmingham Chamber of Commerce, the Birmingham Real Estate Board, and their counterparts in the suburbs.[79] The Birmingham Chamber of Commerce established a special annexation committee and secured endorsements from public officials in several of the suburbs; organized citizen opposition appeared simultaneously in the form of civic leagues.[80] The Birmingham newspapers were enthusiastic about expansion, praising "these outlying suburbs that are knocking at our doors," creating the possibility that Birmingham could quickly become "the greatest city in America."[81] Commission president Jones took a diplomatically neutral position; if the suburbs initiated an annexation program, then Birmingham would gladly extend them an invitation to join with the central city.[82] Although the suburbs were promised improved police protection, sanitary sewer service, and public schools, and although the entire district was promised increased industrial growth, opposition mounted among suburban residents. The Chamber of Commerce annexation committee and other supporters of consolidation abandoned their effort to achieve an enlarged Birmingham by referendum before the 1930 census.

The Birmingham Chamber of Commerce board of directors next turned to the possibility of municipal growth through legislative action; but Governor Bibb Graves, after meeting with them, announced his unwillingness to call the special session that would be required to redraw boundaries before the census was taken.[83]

The Chamber of Commerce resumed its leadership role in 1932, meeting with the Birmingham and Jefferson County commissions to explore the possibility of city-county consolidation as a means of reducing the overhead costs of local government. After receiving encouragement from both sets of commissioners and the Jefferson County legislative delegation, the Chamber established a committee of five to review the projected per capita costs of government in eight cities that had city-county merger plans.[84] This fact-finding group concluded that assigning all governmental functions of both the city and county to Birmingham would save local taxpayers almost $1 million each year.[85] Further research into this issue was frustrated by one of the liabilities of depending on newspapers for information about "pet projects" that failed: the press did not detail the apparent opposition to this plan that prevented its enactment. But with decennial predictability the press in 1941 began reporting and endorsing a new drive by Birmingham leaders to attract its suburbs into the city; sources of support and opposition remained the same, as did the outcome of the effort.

Recognition of Birmingham's need for a modern municipal airport marked the impact of technological innovation on local government. As cities in the nineteenth century had fought for choice locations on the nation's emerging rail network, so now they fought with equal determination to be among the cities on the nation's system of airmail routes. The city did have air mail service in 1928 and 1929, but aircraft used a leased private field that lacked adequate lighting and landing facilities. Both the city postmaster and the air mail contractor warned Birmingham that it was in danger of losing this service in the face of a campaign by Montgomery to have the route pass through the capital city.[86]

The Junior Chamber of Commerce was the first public or private group to respond to the warning. Arguing that having no aviation in the future would be like having no railroads in the early 1900s, the Junior Chamber of Commerce conducted a survey that indicated that the city absolutely had to have an improved landing field if it was to remain in competition for air mail service, much less the commercial aviation that was anticipated in the near future.[87] The commission was unwilling to proceed with a bond issue for the facility, however, claiming that the voters did not understand the importance of an airport and would vote the proposal down.[88] Since the supporters of the field were combatting lack of public awareness rather than organized opposition, the *News* made a particularly significant contribution to the campaign by having a reporter fly air mail routes, describe the adequate facilities—especially in rival southern cities, and highlight the deficiencies of the Birmingham airport.[89]

In addition to building support locally, advocates of a municipal airport also had to persuade the United States Postmaster General to reserve a place for Birmingham on the national airmail system. Here the Junior Chamber of Commerce played a crucial role by convening a meeting of postmasters and chamber of commerce representatives from all major cities from Birmingham to Dallas to coordinate their efforts in behalf of a southern transcontinental route. Atlanta, which had fought Birmingham for selection, agreed to join it in opposition to a proposed east-west route that would bypass both cities.[90] At a crucial air mail conference in Washington attended by city officials and representatives of both the Real Estate Board and the Junior Chamber of Commerce, southern cities presented a united front. Birmingham announced its readiness to proceed with development of a new field, which was planned to equal the best in the nation.[91] Based on these promises, national air mail officials developed a New York-Los Angeles air mail route which passed through Birmingham.[92] In early 1930 Birmingham voters approved a $1 million airport bond issue that was presented as both a means of creating jobs and a necessary part of the city's ongoing effort to gain regional supremacy as a transportation center.[93]

In both of the cases presented above, the business community was the focal point of activity in behalf of municipal expansion and development. Because the names of specific leading participants were seldom mentioned in newspaper accounts, it is not possible to determine definitively the presence or absence of a single core group of influential leaders. However, it would seem that different individuals from the same general socioeconomic background were active in the two campaigns, as the consolidation movement was led by area chambers of commerce and real estate boards, while the airport campaign was led almost exclusively by the Junior Chamber of Commerce. In both cases the business community initiated efforts, while local government cautiously awaited adequate support to make the proposals politically "safe." Such support never materialized in the case of consolidation; the movement quietly died without any significant involvement by Birmingham's public officials. The Junior Chamber of Commerce and the press did succeed in stimulating enough public interest in the airport to prompt the commission to pick a site and issue public improvement bonds; amid great ceremony the new municipal field was formally dedicated in the spring of 1931. Appropriately, plans for the three-day celebration were developed by a joint committee of the junior and senior chambers of commerce.[94]

A continuity of patterns that developed early in the century characterized Birmingham's local politics between 1928 and 1941. The middle-class business community, slightly leavened by representatives of the professions, dominated local officeholding. Political candidates did not represent the city's economic elite, but rather its middle ranks; their spheres of influence extended over neighborhoods, or at best the city as a whole. The men whose economic interests extended throughout the region, and in some cases the nation, were not participants in day-to-day local politics but in those few issues that could be classified as "key" or "important." Then they acted not as individuals, but through the private organizations that they dominated, the chambers of commerce.

Politics between 1928 and 1941 was characterized by continuity, but welfare was characterized by change. Part of the change pre-dated the Depression and took the form of a reorganization of private services under the centralized direction of the city's elite. Another part of the change was due to the Depression and took the form of increasing professionalization and public responsibility. The study now turns to this chaotic, but creative, period in the history of welfare in Birmingham.

5

The Depression in Birmingham

O N 27 JUNE 1929 all available Birmingham police officers were dispatched to the downtown City Bank and Trust Company after directors voted to close the bank and to put its affairs into the hands of state officials. That same day three suburban banks also shut their doors.[1] The seriousness of the city's economic condition was now brought home to the public at large for the first time.

Others had seen signs of the Depression at least two years earlier. Roberta Morgan, director of the relief-giving Red Cross Family Service, had detected a significant upturn in applicants for assistance as early as June 1927; the primary problem of most of the new clients was unemployment.[2] The American Federation of Labor issued a report indicating that the Birmingham unemployment rate was 18 percent in February 1928, slightly below the reported average of 21.18 percent for urban areas.[3] Posing as an unemployed worker, a *Birmingham News* reporter was unable to find a job in March 1928.[4] Throughout that year building operations declined slightly over the 1927 level, indicating worsening economic conditions.[5]

Early Public and Private Responses

All of these negative developments were dismissed by optimists as temporary and isolated weaknesses in a basically sound local economy. The city commission anticipated increased revenues for the 1929–30 fiscal year and adopted an operating budget that was $200,000 above the previous year's. The public library and police department enjoyed substantial increases. However, the welfare department, operated by the city in cooperation with the health department and the Community Chest, was abolished; its work was passed over to the police department. As the budget of the welfare department was only $2,500, which paid the salary and transportation of one woman, the saving was modest; but the action indicated the city's belief that the response to the needs of the unemployed should come from another source, namely the Community Chest.[6]

But the budget adopted in October 1929 had to be cut the following month after the stock market collapse had made even optimists realize that the economic weaknesses were neither isolated nor temporary. The commission made the first of a series of retrenchments by dropping twenty employees from the payroll.[7] Over the next five years, municipal budgets declined from $7,764,012 in 1929–30 to the Depression low of $5,018,244 in 1934–35, with corresponding reductions in salaries and the number of public employees.[8] Sixty-two were released by the city in September 1930, including twenty policemen and ten firemen. Seventy-five employees more were cut in February 1931, and all remaining employees were subject to the first of four 10 percent salary reductions.[9] The year 1932 saw another ninety-two employees dismissed, a 50 percent reduction in expenditures for antituberculosis activities, and the closing of all but one of the police department's substations.[10] Meanwhile, building expenditures in Birmingham sank to the lowest level since records were first kept in 1906. From a 1927 figure of $22.8 million, building expenditures had plummeted to $2.3 million in 1931 and to a mere $763,518 in 1932.[11] The program of municipal retrenchments continued through 1934 with another twenty-five employees dismissed, public restrooms closed, and continuing restrictions in all areas of government services.[12] The city's general operating expenses had been cut 37 percent in five years before the commission began gradually restoring personnel, functions, and salaries, starting with a 10 percent pay increase in October 1934.[13]

The formal budgetary actions of the commission were only one reflection of the Depression in Birmingham. Another was the increasing militance of unemployed workers, especially during 1930. The first reported group effort by the unemployed occurred in April 1930, when 100 men formed an organization to assist others in unspecified ways; one tactic that was discussed and publicized but rejected was a mass march on city hall and the county court house demanding $50,000 in temporary relief.[14]

Another meeting the next month was described by the *News* as a "mass protest meeting of the Communist Party, U.S.A., District 17 and Young Communists League, District 17," where an integrated audience of 150 heard black and white speakers advocate racial equality and a march on both city hall and the Community Chest for relief.[15] It was after this meeting that the commission adopted its ordinance forbidding the assembly of anarchists amid reports by the police that Birmingham was the southeastern headquarters of the Communist party, with a local membership of over two thousand, 75 percent of whom were said to be black.[16] The city's response to this type of activity by the unemployed was the disruption of the next rally of 200 in June and the arrest of speakers under the new law.[17] There were further mass meetings of the unemployed in the district in 1932, 1933, 1934, and 1936. The president of the Birmingham Trades Council was later quoted as saying, "Labor demands the right to work" and that action by the public authorities was necessary if the "vast army" of unemployed was to remain good citizens.[18]

Beyond various newspaper and personal accounts of the Depression in Birmingham, it is difficult to determine with accuracy the severity of the crisis. In contrast to the American Federation of Labor's estimate of over 18 percent unemployment in early 1928 is the report of the Census Bureau based upon its April 1930 survey. The bureau's statistics indicated that only 5 percent of the city's once gainfully employed workers were then without work, with another 1 percent laid off without pay; an estimated 5,623 were unemployed and actively looking for a job.[19] These data tend to be confirmed by the records of the Red Cross Family Service, which indicate that an estimated 4,800 individuals were unemployed in Birmingham. According to the Service there was little actual suffering in the area and no evidence of discontent in 1932.[20]

Three other sources disagree dramatically with this rather sanguine assessment of local need in 1932. The city reported that over 12,000 unemployed men had registered for work on municipal improvement projects.[21] The number of people both unemployed and in actual want was also placed much higher than the Red Cross estimate by the head of the League of Women Voters unemployment bureau, who said: "We have 10,900 men and women on our lists, begging for jobs at present. I would also say that from 6,000 to 8,000 persons in this immediate vicinity are suffering from lack of food, fuel, or adequate housing. This number is not exaggerated. I've been in this bureau for two years, and I know what I'm talking about."[22]

The grimmest but perhaps most accurate interpretation of Birmingham's situation in 1932 was made by the district's congressman, George Huddleston, in testimony before a United States Senate relief committee supporting a proposal for one hundred million dollars from the federal government in direct relief to cities. He testified that not more than 8,000 of Birmingham's 108,000 wage earners were receiving their normal incomes, while at least 25,000 had no work at all and the remainder were involuntarily working only part time. The almshouse built for 220 inmates was occupied by 500 indigents. Assessing the local situation and the ability of local agencies to respond to it, he continued:

> There is plenty of political unrest in Birmingham. My people are desperate. They're in an agony of distress and starvation. They are likely to do anything. They have almost lost the power of reasoning. The situation is full of dynamite. There is intense resentment against everybody in public office.

The Roosevelt administration designated Birmingham the "worst hit city in the nation" during the Depression. The district's congressman, George Huddleston, reported to a Senate committee, "My people are desperate. . . . The situation is full of dynamite." (Library of Congress, Farm Security Administration Photographs, Birmingham Public Library)

We are all to blame for the depression and all of us—the whole nation—should and must pay for it. It is unfair to make a local community
like Birmingham, whose industries are largely owned in distant financial
centers, try to take care of its own relief problems. There are, for instance,
hundreds of railroad men out of work, some of them for two years, yet
no railroad company contributed a cent to our local Community Chest.
. . . How are we going to force these people to pay back part of the money
they take from our people, except through Federal taxation?

Hundreds of people are starving, slowly starving, in my district and in
many other parts of the country. The situation is desperate.[23]

In 1932 other politicians from the district were not yet prepared to endorse
Huddleston's proposal for direct federal relief. United States senator Hugo
Black felt that federal funds should be appropriated for relief but that they
should be disbursed through the states and localities: "I want this money administered to the people who need it by their friends and neighbors and not
by a bureau in Washington."[24] Responding to a questionnaire from Senator
Robert L. LaFollette, city commission president Jones took an even more conservative position: "We do not favor a federal appropriation to assist local governments in meeting their emergency relief burdens. We believe that this is a
matter to be handled locally and that the federal government has troubles sufficient of its own to fully engage its attention."[25] Jones initially favored federal
credit relief to cities to assist them in marketing bonds for public works projects; later he advocated a federal bond issue for public improvements administered through local agencies.[26] These proposals reflected Birmingham's inability to market a $.5 million municipal bond issue and the subsequent need for
further budget cuts coupled with a loan from a New York City bank for general
operations.[27]

In fact, the early response to the Depression was much as Jones wanted,
with responsibility placed in the hands of government and private agencies at
the local level. Both were overwhelmed by the task.

By law Jefferson County was the unit of government responsible for care
of the indigent, but its activities were limited to the maintenance of an almshouse that a 1928 grand jury had labeled "a monument to the utter indifference of Jefferson County taxpayers and an indictment of every Board of Revenue that has served in the past twenty-five years." It was "unfit for human
beings."[28]

Various community leaders pointed to the fact that progressive social welfare leaders were advocating old-age pension plans as a more humane alternative to the almshouse; some dozen or more states were closing their residential
facilities and adopting the cash payment plan. Thomas E. Huey, a local busi-

nessman and former member of the Jefferson County board of revenue, even presented a specific pension plan to the board of revenue, but it was rejected as doubling the cost of care per person and leading to graft.[29] County officials instead built an enlarged almshouse, prompting the *News* to write: "Boiled down to the fewest words, the almshouse signifies that our civilized society is not quite stony-hearted enough to execute its aged poor or to let them starve to death, but that it doesn't care to be bothered about them one mite more than it is absolutely necessary."[30]

The county board of revenue seemed reluctant to play any larger role in meeting community needs. When asked to provide funds to the deficit-ridden Red Cross Family Service, they refused, citing legal opinion to the effect that county funds could not be allocated to private organizations.[31] When legislation was introduced in Montgomery at the urging of the Chamber of Commerce and Community Chest permitting appropriations to accredited, nonpolitical, nonsectarian relief agencies, the board of revenue opposed it.[32] Only after enabling legislation was passed in late 1932 did the county agree to provide any funds for relief, and then its monthly allocations became a matter of ongoing controversy—as will be discussed below.[33] At the county level the ideology of local responsibility was accompanied by a paucity of action.

Although city officials seemed more disposed to act in behalf of the needy, their opportunities were severely limited because of the financial crisis. The *Post* captured the mood of city government in the following description:

> The city has no projects underway and none are contemplated. At city hall it is simply a case of holding the fort until the turn of the depression. The street commissioner estimates it will be five years before another street paving venture is undertaken. The weekly city commission meeting long since ceased to be anything but routine affairs. They seldom last more than 10 minutes. There isn't any business to transact.
>
> People continue to come and go, registering complaints about stray dogs, unsprinkled streets and other things, but the city hall isn't what it used to be. The city has no money to spend on expansion and improvement projects. It faces a further cut in its revenues next year.
>
> Not many years ago the big news center of Birmingham, the city hall now runs monotonously along day to day and month to month, attending to routine matters and nothing else.[34]

The earliest responses to human needs caused by the Depression in Birmingham came from a variety of private sources. The first specific project was sponsored in the spring of 1930 by the League of Women Voters, which launched a "clean up, paint up, repair up" campaign to relieve unemployment in the building crafts. Their drive included a telephone solicitation of small jobs and the opening of a free employment bureau for both Whites and Blacks in a downtown office building.[35] Between May 1930 and August 1932 the league claimed to have placed 6,258 with 11,500 additional unemployed workers on its waiting list. As months passed, professional and office workers comprised an increasing proportion of those served.[36] In addition to its employment bureau the league distributed clothes to needy citizens certified by either the Salvation Army or the Red Cross: Whites were served on Wednesday, Friday and Saturday; Blacks on Tuesday and Thursday.[37] The Chamber of Commerce and American Legion also conducted a home-improvement campaign that aided 500 men.[38]

In the suburbs, self-help employment leagues were formed to provide food and clothing to their members.[39] The community pastor in a small mining community began an ambitious self-help program for miners, both black and white, who had marched on the city commission seeking relief. With private funds he began an extensive farming program, opened a saw mill, and offered auto mechanics courses. His efforts received national publicity as a model of voluntary, collective response to the Depression.[40] The large steel companies provided housing, light, water, fuel, groceries, and medical care without charge during the early years of the Depression and allowed their unemployed workers to grow food on company grounds.[41]

The Birmingham Chamber of Commerce undertook a particularly ambitious relief project in December 1930, which included both a food and a work element. The chamber had convened a meeting of two hundred business leaders to discuss the opening of a soup kitchen, a facility bitterly opposed by social workers as providing indiscriminate aid. As an alternative the chamber worked out a plan through which interested citizens purchased meal tickets that could be used at any of the eighteen restaurants that agreed to accept them: fourteen serving Whites only, three Blacks only, and one both races.[42] This project continued throughout the winter months, providing thirty-five thousand meals; then it was discontinued.

The work program was proposed by the president of a large cast-iron pipe company who suggested that wealthy citizens immediately contribute toward a three-hundred-thousand-dollar park improvement project. The city would in turn be asked to submit a bond issue to the voters in early 1931, which, if passed, would permit repayment of the contributions and continuation of the work.[43] Both the city and the business community agreed to this proposition. The businessmen provided forty thousand dollars within three weeks; the city opened a registration bureau in city hall for unemployed black and white men with dependents and set the date for the bond election.[44] The park improvement bond issue was subsequently approved, enabling the city to give part-time employment to about twenty-three hundred men before funds were exhausted eight months later.[45]

For purposes of comparison with relief practices in later years, it is significant to note the procedure followed in assigning workers to the park project. The employment office opened at city hall was under the supervision of the city engineer, who was aided by the personnel director of a utility company on a temporary basis. The social service departments of several churches agreed to investigate applicants to verify need.

> Names of white and colored were cleared through the Social Service Exchange, and if known to the Red Cross accepted without further inquiry. Up to August 1st, 4,455 white and 4,184 colored applied for work and about 4,000 of the former were investigated. The colored were not investigated. The name and occupation of each were filed; the city engineer and park department planned the work; police officers delivered notification of selection.[46]

Thus, white applicants could be hired through either of two processes. If they had previously applied for relief to the Red Cross Family Service and were thereby on record at the Social Service Exchange, Whites were immediately eligible for assignment. If they had not so applied, they were investigated for eligibility by the church workers. Blacks could be certified only if already on record at the exchange. But despite the absence of uniform registration procedures, Blacks did constitute about 35–40 percent of the work force utilized under the project.[47]

The various responses to the Depression discussed above were all planned on short notice and conducted without any effort at coordination with other programs. They were ad hoc activities sponsored by groups or individuals who in most cases had no formal responsibility for meeting local Depression needs. From the earliest days of the crisis until the creation of the department of public welfare in 1933, formal responsibility for relief activities lay with the private agencies of the Community Chest, and most especially with its Red Cross Family Service.

Establishment of the Community Chest

By the time of the Depression, private social welfare work in Birmingham had undergone a drastic reorganization from the arrangement that prevailed at the close of the 1900–1917 period. In 1917 a large number of private agencies functioned independently both in fund-raising and in service delivery. The most ambitious effort at rationalization and improved effectiveness, the Asso-

ciated Charities, had failed; the leading men who had headed the agency requested that the city assume responsibility for all relief. When their request
was met, the Associated Charities turned all of its cases over to what appeared
to be a comprehensive Birmingham department of relief and corrections. But
this 1917 reorganization was only one phase of an ongoing exploration of the
relationship between public authority and private activity in the area of welfare
services. Ten years later these services were totally privatized and supported
by the Community Chest, an organization dominated by the elite that fulfilled
many of the goals of the abortive Associated Charities.

The impetus for creating the Community Chest had come not from the
male civic leaders who were later to direct it, but from the professional social
work community, supported by the League of Women Voters. In 1921 the
league sponsored a survey of social services in Jefferson County that included
all public and private agencies in the county. The survey was undertaken in
cooperation with the Red Cross and the state welfare department and was conducted by professional social workers. This study was initiated specifically because the league felt that the city welfare department was inadequate and
needed to be reevaluated.[48]

The final report of the survey committee was sharply critical of the publicly
administered relief program in Jefferson County. The county board of revenue
lacked legal authority to provide outdoor relief directly or to support it indirectly through appropriations to private agencies. The committee concluded
that the welfare department of the city was inadequately funded and poorly
organized. Its director was a well-intentioned minister who lacked both training in social welfare work and resources adequate to meet local need. Between
1920 and 1923 the city appropriated between $10,000 and $15,000 each year to
the department, a sum supplemented by private donations of between $1,000
and $5,000 each year. Based upon the welfare budgets of other large southern
cities like Louisville, Memphis, and Atlanta, the Birmingham budget should
have been at least $50,000 per year.[49] Lacking funds, the department often sent
applicants to local churches for aid; it also solicited food donations from citizens and peddled rugs door to door.[50] Assessing this haphazard and inadequate relief program, the league survey concluded, "The most glaring social
need for the community is well-organized and managed out-door relief and a
central agency for same."[51] Specifically, the report recommended the creation
of a Community Chest to raise all funds for welfare work, establishment of a
central registration bureau to prevent duplication of services to individuals,
and assignment of relief activities in the county to the Red Cross.[52]

In recommending the creation of a Chest, the survey was reflecting national professional support of community funds and central councils of social agencies, peacetime successors to the war chests that had raised funds and co-ordinated efforts for war relief. Surveying the post-World War I writings of social welfare professionals, Leah Feder observed: "Clearly apparent in the literature of the times is the previously observed reluctance of the private field to regard public departments as having a continuing and developing share in the handling of unemployment relief."[53] By 1920, fifty-two cities had established chests, with only four located in the South.[54] Described by Floyd Hunter as a "rough index of urbanization in the South," the Chest movement spread rapidly through the region in the 1920s.[55]

The survey recommendations were not immediately implemented in Birmingham. The city did promptly reorganize its department and provide it with both increased funds and a professional staff of four, which was expanded to include a black "family visitor" during the winter months.[56] This improved the performance of the public agency but did not meet the recommendation of an overarching privately supported program.

The Community Chest was established in Birmingham in 1923 through the leadership of the Inter-Club Council, a consortium of civic organizations such as the Kiwanis Club, the Business and Professional Women's Club, the Chamber of Commerce, and the Junior Chamber of Commerce.[57] "With grave misgivings" the Chest leaders agreed to allocate $18,000 to the city department for 1924 in addition to $12,000 from Birmingham, thereby providing its first substantial budget; it also authorized the department to hire an additional worker for cases outside the city limits.[58] But Chest leaders stated the position that if the city was unwilling to fund relief adequately, then the private group should assume full responsibility. The city agreed and declared its intent to abandon the relief field, as seen in the following letter to the Community Chest in December 1924 from the city commissioner responsible for overseeing the department:

> The wonderful response of the people to this great opportunity [the Chest] has resulted in a great good to the needy of our city. A duplication of work and authority is a thing to be avoided in all cases and especially in public work and it has been our intention to relinquish welfare work at the city hall to the officers of the Community Chest whenever such action seemed for the interest of charity. I feel that the time has now come. The voluntary contributions have made it unnecessary to burden the taxpayers for the upkeep of an organization which shall be entirely in the hands of the group of officers who are controlling the Community Chest.[59]

In late 1924 the city commission met with the directors and board of the Community Chest to explore the private assumption of the then-public welfare responsibility; they jointly agreed that the commission would abolish the welfare department and that relief activities would be transferred to a newly created Red Cross Family Service. But this arrangement was not at the time regarded as permanent; rather, the private agency was intended to serve as a model of professional case work activity that would be the basis of yet another effort at public welfare, as described by one local historian of social work:

> Mrs. Blynd, then secretary of the local chapter of the American Red Cross, was appointed by the Community Chest to organize a Family Relief Department for the care of the destitute, white and colored, on a county-wide basis. The Red Cross agreed to organize the work and carry it out for a period of five years, at the end of which time the work and the organization, intact with complete records, would be transferred to the city and county as a joint welfare department to be henceforth financed out of tax funds.[60]

The Community Chest through the Red Cross now completely supported all of the relief and rehabilitation work previously conducted by Birmingham and extended it throughout the county. From January 1925 through 1930 the private sector bore complete responsibility for outdoor relief in the district. And when the Jefferson County Department of Public Welfare was created in 1933, it came not as the fulfillment of the 1924 agreement between the city and the Community Chest but rather as the local response to the federal mandate that only public agencies could disburse government funds.[61]

Because the 1925–30 period was so totally an era of private welfare, it is worth examining in detail in order to assess both the strengths and weaknesses of the private sector in this work. The major issues in local social welfare that emerged in the 1960s, such as rational planning and coordination, services for Blacks, and citizen representation on policy-making boards, can all be traced back to this earlier period when the social welfare "establishment" of Birmingham was built. The following analysis of the era of private responsibility deals first with the Community Chest as an organization and then with the Red Cross Family Service—a unique Chest agency that later became the Jefferson County Department of Public Welfare.

Organization and Operations of the Community Chest

The general chairman of the tenth annual Community Chest campaign said much about the organization when he declared, "Birmingham's citizens have always been willing to provide money for the needy as it has been made known to them through the business and social leaders to whom the welfare of our unfortunate neighbors is entrusted."[62] The Chest was from its founding an elite organization. Its leaders were largely responsible for defining the extent of need in the district; in this process, professional welfare workers played a minimal role and the needy no role at all. Its leaders also determined what kind of local response would be made to this perceived need and then raised the funds to finance this response.

The formal governing body of the Birmingham Community Chest was an advisory board whose membership was specified by the articles of incorporation: the president, secretary, and treasurer of fourteen civic clubs; the president, treasurer, and executive director of each agency supported by the Chest; the president of the city commission; the president of the county board of revenue; three judges; the president of the city board of education; the superintendent of schools; and five representatives of the public at large chosen by the city commission. This advisory board was self-perpetuating; its principal function was to elect directors at its annual meeting.[63]

The board of directors consisted of thirty members, ten elected each year for three-year terms. Between 1923 and 1942 116 individuals served on the board, 100 men and 16 women. The women were all prominent by virtue of either their social standing or their previous leadership in social welfare work; they included, for example, the wife of an iron company president and a handful of women who had been active in the Mercy Home or the United Charities. Judges, ministers, and an occasional leading politician also served on the board, but the majority in any given year consisted of a "Who's Who" of the area's business leadership: the heads of both the leading local firms and industries and the huge national corporations. Among the one hundred were the presidents of five banks, two major utility companies, a locally owned steel company, the United States Steel facility in the district, and at least a dozen other prominent manufacturing, retail, banking and real estate interests. Chest membership was regarded as an obligation for the occupants of certain offices; as bank presidents or steel company managers changed, their successors in business also succeeded them on the board. Add to this group the editors of the two leading newspapers, several prominent lawyers, and the first vice-presidents of the largest firms, and one has identified the social, commercial, industrial and professional elite of Birmingham. Three identifiable groups in the community were not represented at all on the board prior to 1942: the medical profession, organized labor, and the black community. Physicians presumably chose not to participate in the Chest. Such was not the case with either labor or Blacks, and how to respond to the wishes of both groups for a larger role in local social welfare was a question unresolved by the board during this period.

The board was characterized by stability of membership from year to year. The articles of incorporation determined that at least twenty members out of thirty during any year would have served the previous year, and limited turnover in each "class" of members increased this number to at least twenty-five. Between the founding of the Chest and the close of the period under review, the advisory board elected ten-member classes eighteen times; at least half of the outgoing group was reelected every year. Chest minutes indicate the following percentage turnovers during this period:

50%—four times
40%—three times
30%—five times
20%—two times
10%—three times
 0%—once

Two factors tended to reduce the impact of even this limited turnover upon the board, its actions, or its thinking. First, new members were deliberately chosen to maintain the fundamental homogeneity of the board; as the campaign chairman had correctly observed, this group was intended to represent the business and social leaders of the community. As will be seen below, lone voices of opposition were raised by members against board policy during discussions of certain important questions, but in general board meetings were characterized by a consensus that would seem virtually inescapable given the recruitment process for members.

Second, there emerged over the years a core leadership group whose members served extensive terms and dominated the most important committees of the Chest. For example, the president of the city's leading bank chaired the Chest budget committee for seven consecutive years. These men so controlled the machinery of the Chest that they could have withstood even a well-organized and serious challenge to their position. But what the Chest minutes reveal is an overwhelming respect for their opinions and a deference to their wishes. Additional insight into the Community Chest can be gained by examining the office of president, the method of raising funds, and the budgeting process.

The presidency of the Community Chest was not an honorific civic position but rather one of considerable influence and power within both the organization and the community. His interpretation of local social welfare needs and programs carried great weight in the deliberations of the board and was extensively reported in the press, particularly during the early days of the Depression. His office gave him the authority to determine who would sit on the major Chest committees, especially the executive, budget, and campaign committees.

As federal programs were developed to meet the Depression crisis, the Chest president was consistently among those who met with local and federal officials to decide what programs would be implemented and at what level. He was, then, able to influence the thinking of the community, the operations of its private welfare system, and the development of publicly aided projects. The men who served as president of the Chest between 1923 and 1942 were men of the highest possible local prestige, including prominent lawyers, bank presidents, industrialists, and commercial leaders. What clearly distinguishes the private welfare sector in this period from the pre–World War I era is the sustained commitment of the city's elite to leadership through the Community Chest.

The Chest was primarily an instrument for the rationalization of fund-raising. This rationalization was intended to serve well both the recipient agencies and the donors. Prior to the creation of the Chest each group had conducted its own fund-raising drive; this method led to situations of overlapping efforts, interagency competition, and multiple visits to the same individuals. Through its annual campaign, the Chest was intended to unify solicitations and broaden the base of giving. Moreover, the Chest was regarded as "substantially a barrier, protecting as it does large contributors against promiscuous appeals which would multiply rapidly under the old plan of financing social work."[64]

The organization largely succeeded in achieving its objectives. Contributors to private agencies had numbered about three thousand before the united drive; this number rose to just over thirty thousand during the first campaign and exceeded seventy thousand by the end of the period.[65] One student of public relief has described the Community Chest as a "voluntary method of self-taxation",[66] a local observer came closer to the mark when she observed that supporting its work was "fairly well recognized as being official duties on the part of citizens."[67] She might have added that supporting it was fairly well recognized as being an official duty of employees, as one part of the Chest's strategy was to recruit major employers as campaign leaders responsible for soliciting in their own firms. Fund-raising was also conducted more efficiently with one well-organized effort. Before the Chest, individual agencies reported spending between 15 and 60 percent of their receipts on administrative costs; the Chest figure was consistently below 5 percent and was consistently among the lowest of major southern cities.[68]

The high point of Chest activity each year was the fall campaign for funds. The chairman of the drive was always a man of social status equal to that of the president, and he selected as assistants high-ranking officials from enterprises representative of the major elements of the local economy. After the board set the campaign goal, the drive would open in the fall amid publicity and often carnival-like hoopla, hopefully to end by Thanksgiving.

The epitome of the successful drive occurred during the fall of 1931, as Chests across the country strained to meet the mounting relief needs of major urban areas. The campaign chairman was a local stockbroker, Mervyn H. Sterne, who was recognized as Birmingham's master fund-raiser; the goal was set at its highest figure ever—nearly $700,000, an increase of 40 percent above the previous year's goal.[69] All of this increase was devoted to relief; the appropriation of every agency but the Red Cross Family Service was reduced 10 percent while the service was allocated $287,000 as opposed to $84,000 the previous year.[70] Spending weeks in careful preparation, Sterne developed a plan by which each member of the executive committee and larger donors agreed in advance to double their last contribution; each potential donor was visited by someone of comparable means who had committed himself to give more than the sum being sought. The result was an oversubscription of nearly $50,000 by the eighth day of the campaign; this still stands as the largest percentage increase in goal and the shortest drive in the history of the Chest.[71]

Not all Community Chest drives were as spirited or as successful as the 1931 campaign. The minutes show that during its first eighteen drives the Chest failed to meet its quotas in 1924, 1925, 1926, 1929, and 1930. Later drives did raise the announced quotas, but it should be noted that the goals were reduced substantially from the pre-Depression level after the beginning of federal relief in 1933. The Chest had first sought more than $.5 million in the fall of 1925, well before relief consumed large amounts of its money; it did not reach the same figure again until the fall of 1941.

Business leaders were not always eager to undertake the task of fund-raising, especially in hard times. One could easily understand the recorded lack of enthusiasm of drive leaders in the fall of 1929, as well as the need for a special committee to solicit from a limited number of large donors "for such amounts as they might be willing to give in the present emergency, but which should not be considered as a basis for renewal in future campaigns."[72] That particular drive missed its goal by nearly $40,000; and the special canvass of prime supporters was judged a failure, as it raised only $2,000.[73] At least two other supplementary solicitations were made during the Depression, neither raising the needed amount.[74] Most campaigns extended well past the target date for conclusion, prompting both Chest leaders and the press to exhort citizens to greater efforts. The purported effectiveness of the Community Chest as a fund-raising instrument is not supported by the organization's record during this period.

Birmingham's goals were not so high that failure to achieve them could be attributed to overzealous board action. For example, Hartford with a population of 172,300 exceeded its 1929 goal of $590,565 by $20,000, while Birmingham with about 250,000 population fell short of its goal of $543,000.[75] Data for six areas for 1935 are as follows:[76]

	Population of Area Served	Goal
Atlanta	371,000	$400,000
Denver	327,000	715,000
Harrisburg	100,000	332,000
Hartford	230,000	787,000
New Orleans	503,000	735,000
Jefferson County	450,000	380,000

Even when the goal was reached in Birmingham, Chest-supported facilities were still unable to function at capacity. The tuberculosis hospital, for example, could use only sixty of its one hundred beds at its 1935 level of support and had a lengthy waiting list; beds also stood vacant at the Children's Hospital.[77]

Goals were recommended to the entire board by the budget committee, which was responsible for detailed reviews of all agency requests. Minutes of the Community Chest indicate how the budgetary process was typically conducted: "The quota was finally set by taking the Red Cross amount plus 50 percent of the requested increases from other agencies, and deducting a collection expectancy of $10,000 from all the years. This gave a sum approaching the amount finally determined of $502,978.47."[78] The budgeting for Chest agencies was incremental rather than rational and reflected the absence of any independent criteria by which the laymen on the committee could evaluate the reasonableness of each agency's request. Unlike many other cities, Birmingham had not coupled voluntary federated fund-raising with a voluntary social welfare planning organization whose roles were to set priorities through research and to evaluate agency budgets. Typically such community welfare councils included representatives of Chest agencies, with public agencies and private non-Chest organizations often represented as well.[79] By contrast, archrival Atlanta had organized such a council in 1923; there as elsewhere it was regarded as a "standard-setting agency for community welfare improvement."[80]

The board did make efforts to engage in planning and evaluation itself through committees that were each responsible for overseeing the work of a group of agencies engaged in common service; agencies were grouped into the following categories: aged, blind, care of children, character building and recreation, prevention of cruelty, relief, and white plague.[81] The committees, first established in 1926, were to meet monthly to examine agency personnel and services and to submit their findings and recommendations to the board.[82] This device, plus the fact that over two-thirds of the board members were also directors of constituent agencies, was viewed as an adequate planning and evaluation procedure.[83] However, the committee system apparently did not work despite efforts at reorganizing it in 1932; there is no record either of written reports or of committee meetings.[84] Without guidance the board, and especially the budget committee, largely determined whether a private agency would survive in the city, for without Chest approval any fund-raising drive was likely to be a failure. Originally the budget committee had approved thirty-two agencies that had submitted for review their previous three years' records as well as lists of contributors. By 1927 the number had grown to forty; new applicants had to meet the criteria of having been in operation one year, not duplicating the work of other agencies, and "being governed by a body of citizens of recognized standing."[85] Periodically the budget committee did require the consolidation of agencies, drop others when public welfare assumed their responsibilities, and deny admission to new applicants.

Professional social welfare workers objected to the procedure of board decision making without professional advice but failed in their effort to establish a planning council. The idea had been mentioned in early 1936, but one year later the Chest director reported that because of a lack of interest by lay leaders in the plan, there had been no subsequent discussion of a permanent council of social agencies.[86] The persistent director next presented information to the board about the work of councils elsewhere, but it showed "no disposition for immediate discussion."[87] The board did ask the president of the Birmingham Social Workers Club to present a statement as to why a social welfare council was needed in Birmingham; this action prompted a request from the professional community for a formal council that would be an integral part of the Chest and its planning, evaluation, and budgeting process.[88] In the face of obvious board hostility to this idea, the club withdrew its proposal in 1938 and instead formed an informal committee—the Jefferson County Coordinating Council of Social Forces.[89] Lacking staff, budget, and formal relationship to the Chest, the council could only recommend changes in programs to the Chest director and agency boards; it was virtually ignored by the board and played no apparent role in its budget process.[90]

The elite leadership of the Community Chest was thus effectively isolated from any challenge to its values or priorities from the professional community. Edward C. Banfield and James Q. Wilson note that in the early twentieth century the old elites in northern cities, driven from politics, dominated instead the new community service organizations, where their political style could still prevail.[91] But this domination in many cities was at least tempered by organized social work groups; in Birmingham the domination was unchallenged, and with significant results. The social work community nationally and locally was generally more interested in meeting determined need than in keeping budgets low and was more inclined to extend additional services to groups like the poor and Blacks. As will be seen below, the effort by professionals to penetrate the lay domination of private agencies continued as an issue within the Community Chest throughout the period under study.

The political style of the lay leaders was clearly seen in the strained relationships that existed between the Chest board and both organized labor and the black community. Only the unique Red Cross Family Service had good working relationships with these two groups; the discussion of the service that follows will indicate that it was a highly professional bureaucracy.

Labor's skepticism of Chest programs first surfaced in the 1927 campaign when the chairman of the railroad employee campaign questioned the support of "character building" agencies, which had largely middle-class clienteles and were not strictly charitable in nature; this same question was reiterated three years later. Although the board promised to respond to labor's question and appointed a committee to draft the reply, no response was ever given.[92]

Then in January 1939 the Birmingham Industrial Union Council and the Birmingham Central Trade Council requested formal representation in the Chest through membership on the advisory board. As this representation would require a constitutional amendment, they were told that the question would be brought up at the January 1940 annual meeting; the record of that meeting indicates no discussion of the request.[93] In August 1940 the Industrial Union Council wrote to the board asking that CIO officials "be given a place in the Chest management equal to those accorded industry, the churches, banking and other groups in our society."[94] The president replied by reviewing the composition of the advisory board, which admittedly included representatives of the Chamber of Commerce but none from labor. He argued, however, that most members were public officials or representatives of service agencies or civic groups. Moreover, he went on, "in raising funds it [the Chest] must discourage the making of pledges by organized groups in substitution for the gifts of individuals."[95] Labor was unimpressed by this line of reasoning; in 1941 the CIO *News Digest* called upon workers not to support the Chest until they were given formal recognition by its leaders.[96] The Chest's attitude toward labor is another issue that persisted into the 1960s.

The speaker's card given to each campaign worker in 1928 proclaimed that "The Chest knows no barriers of creed or color," but the record does not support this statement.[97] The Chest was a modestly redistributive organization, providing services to Blacks that were largely financed by Whites. But these services were found by local evaluators to be inadequate. Moreover, the board only reluctantly allowed Blacks to play even a modest role in Chest management; it refused to support at all the community's only interracial social welfare organization.

The redistributive nature of the Chest is illustrated by data from 1927–28 and 1935–38. In the fall of 1927, 13,172 black donors contributed $21,705 to the Chest, a sum that was 36 percent of what the Chest allocated to agencies serving Blacks. Overall, 42,574 donors contributed a total of $542,180. The Chest budgeted $59,523 to agencies serving Blacks, six of which served Blacks only and five of which served both races (Red Cross Family Service, Salvation Army, Travelers' Aid Society, tuberculosis hospital, and Anti-Tuberculosis Society). Blacks in 1927–28, therefore, constituted 25 percent of the donors, contributed about 4 percent of the total collected, and received nearly 11 percent of the expenditures.[98]

The severe impact of the Depression on the black community is indicated by the sharp decline in quotas for the black division of the campaign, dipping to less than $2,300 in both 1937 and 1938 with black donors representing about 2 percent of all contributors during this period and providing less than .5 percent of all money raised.[99] In 1935 black agencies received slightly less than 7 percent of the Chest budget, with eight agencies allocated $24,981.[100] It should be noted that this reduction does not reflect a decrease in relief funds available to Blacks, as this function by the mid-1930s was performed by the department of public welfare. It does, however, reflect the low priority given by the Chest to serving the black community.

The Chest board was itself aware of the need to extend more services to Blacks and in 1938 encouraged agencies to increase their programs to better meet the "overwhelming needs" among Blacks. At that time the Boy Scouts, for example, had 1,868 boys enrolled in the district, only 184 of whom were Blacks. In response to the board's concern, the Boys Club and YMCA both developed new recreational programs for black youth in separate facilities, and the Children's Aid Society established a "colored advisory board" to work with children reported by the schools to have antisocial behavior.[101]

A 1939 Works Progress Administration (WPA) study of social group work agencies in the Birmingham area indicates that the disparity of opportunities offered to black and white children by the Chest remained great. The study discovered a low participation rate by black children in group work, particularly in areas with the greatest social problems where the fewest programs were operated. Examining the six-to-eighteen-year-old population, the study reported that of 77,252 white youngsters, 12,273 participated in private agency programs; of 60,412 black youngsters, 1,827 participated. Overall in the county, 9.1 percent of the youth were active in organized group work, 13.92 percent of the white population six to eighteen and 2.97 percent of the black. White Chest agencies spent an average of $9.99 per participant; the corresponding figure for black agencies was $5.21. These same white agencies employed thirty-eight leaders while black agencies employed only ten.

The survey examined in detail the twelve largest blighted areas from among the twenty-two such districts identified by the Jefferson County Board of Health, all populated largely by Blacks. It found that white participation was above the 9.1 percent average for the county in these slum neighborhoods, while black participation was strikingly below the already low 2.9 percent figure for black youth in the county.[102] Summarizing its findings about Chest youth programs, the WPA staff wrote: "City-wide agency programs are reaching few Negro boys and girls. . . . The comparatively few white people in blighted areas show unusually high participation. Apparently group work agencies have been successful in their special effort to reach the white population in these areas."[103] In contrast with the Community Chest, United States Steel through its youth programs served 9.2 percent of the potential white clientele and 13.7 percent of the black population. The fact that its seven white and four black paid leaders all had college-level training in group work courses reflects the highly professional nature of the company's social welfare program.[104]

Similar black-white disparities characterize other types of Chest work. A study of private agency leisure-time services by the housing authority showed that 13,592 white families and 1,600 black families participated in these Chest programs; again, services were lowest in areas, largely black, with the highest family problem rate and were highest in areas with the fewest problems.[105] The white Children's Hospital received an average through 1934 of $24,800 per year for its fifty beds; the black Children's Home Hospital received an average of $4,392 per year for its seventeen beds.[106]

Though the board did indicate a desire to provide a broader range of services to Blacks, it was reluctant to allow them to play a significant role in the management of the Chest. In 1939 a former vice-president of the board suggested that a committee of twenty-five Blacks be appointed to work with the campaign organization in securing pledges from Blacks and to advise the board concerning black agencies. This auxiliary group would have only advisory powers; "The suggestions from the Negro Board would be carried to the white Chest Board for final determination on matters of policy."[107] The board accepted the idea of campaign assistance from the black community but rejected even its limited involvement in agency operations.[108] It should be pointed out, however, that individual agencies serving Blacks either had black boards or Blacks advising the white board members; the issue now was participation in the parent Chest organization. The board did create a black advisory committee in the fall of 1939 with responsibility for appointing a campaign chairman and assisting with the drive among Blacks.[109]

The advisory committee immediately tried to strengthen its role in the Chest by requesting that a black staff member be hired to work with it in fund-raising and in a program of education among Blacks about agency activities. This request was denied on the ground that all committee work was voluntary.[110]

The single recorded overruling by the board of a recommendation by the president involved the role of the advisory council. The president had agreed to propose that the council have a separate budget committee to review black agency requests and to submit its recommendations to the Chest budget committee for final joint determination. The board rejected this plan, arguing that white agencies had no such separate budgetary group.[111]

Before questions relating to black involvement in Chest operations arose, the board had already refused to give Chest support to the Birmingham Commission on Interracial Cooperation, the local affiliate of a national commission concerned primarily with improving housing and negotiating charges of racial discrimination. Application for aid was first made in 1928 by two leading white ministers who led the commission.[112] The board listened to the group's presentation but referred the request to the executive committee for further study and a recommendation. The executive committee felt that

> they could not consistently recommend to the Board its inclusion as a Chest supported activity. The conclusion arrived at, it was carefully pointed out, detracted in no way from the excellent work being done locally, and in fact throughout the South. The Board of Directors on receiving the report further discussed the application, and concurred with the Committee that, as Directors of the Chest, they would have to forego the privilege of financing, even in a small way, the work of the Commission. The position of the Directors was in this matter not unlike that toward the support of the Birmingham Safety Council and other groups who have during the past few years applied for financial aid.[113]

By this statement, the board apparently meant that the commission did not qualify for support because its work was not related to health, welfare, or character building. Still, the board's position must have been ambiguous at the time, for the interracial commission applied to the Chest again ten months later. The board stated that it could not give the request serious consideration at the time but would give the commission an opportunity to present the matter again if it so desired.[114]

At the close of the 1928–1941 period the Chest's position concerning black participation in policy-making was firmly established in the negative; so it would remain until the 1960s. But its attitude toward supporting an agency dealing with race relations was ambivalent; in the 1950s the Chest went so far as to lend its aid to a race relations program, which will be discussed later.

During its early years the Chest board also wrestled consciously with the question of what it meant to be a private social welfare organization, particularly in light of the growing governmental role during the Depression era. The severity of the economic crisis forced a substantial change of thinking on this point, a change that was reinforced by new institutional arrangements created by the New Deal.

Public-private distinctions were fuzzy during the first year of Chest operations. The board indicated a willingness to support "any reasonable budget submitted by the Birmingham Sunday School Association for welfare, recreational, and non-sectarian work" but refused to support the city's recreation department because its activities were "not within the scope of the Community Chest."[115] The objection was not to the mixing of public and private funds, nor was it to the private support of a public function. In 1923 the board allocated funds to the city's welfare department, though reluctantly, meanwhile appointing a committee of three "to confer with the city officials to ascertain what would be the relation of the city to the Community Chest and what appropriations the city would make to various charity organizations thru [sic] the Community Chest."[116] The board also contributed money to the state child welfare department and approved in principle supporting a child guidance clinic to be operated in connection with the city schools, though the latter project never was begun.[117]

By 1928 the board was moving toward a definition of which spheres of activity should be privately supported and which publicly; relief was regarded as a private responsibility and health care as a public concern. Thus the campaign chairman that fall would say, "If it is true that there is now somewhat of an industrial depression on, it is our duty more than ever to come to the aid of those who will, as a result of this depression, appeal to us in larger numbers, and everyone of us ought to do more."[118] As the burden of providing relief through the strictly private Red Cross Family Service mounted, the board decided to eliminate its support of the tuberculosis sanatorium, despite the objections of hospital officials that the Chest was willing to give money to people who were well and needed only work while cutting off helpless, bedridden patients.[119] The official statement of the Chest in justifying its action said, "The Chest was not conceived to carry burdens that belong to the body politic."[120] Writing about the crisis that now faced the sanatorium, the *News* endorsed the Chest position:

> the Community Chest was established primarily to relieve just this kind of social malady, poverty that comes when the industrial state is out of joint. The action is unavoidable. . . . It is just as well that responsibility for that establishment [the sanatorium] be placed now exactly where it belongs. Obviously, it is the duty of the county and city to make extraordinary shifts to meet this [health] emergency.[121]

But by January 1931 the Chest had been forced to turn to public funds to supplement private relief appropriations. It received $1,000 monthly from Birmingham and threatened to terminate activities in the county unless the board of revenue accepted "a fair share of responsibility for relief of the unemployed."[122]

Theodore J. Lowi has written that the Depression revealed capitalistic poverty to be systematic in nature, requiring a systematic response.[123] While some in Birmingham may have thought in these terms, the basic insight locally was the pragmatic realization that need was outrunning the ability of the private sector to meet it. The Chest had established an $84,000 relief fund for 1931 but realized by June that this amount would probably meet less than one-quarter of the year's relief load. January through June had seen relief expenditures average $22,000 per month, compared with a comparable monthly figure for 1930 of $9,450. Prepared to support 800 families each month, the Red Cross Family Service was confronted with 5,000 applicants and was carrying a caseload of over 3,900 families—four times the number ever served before. The Chest director said:

> If the crisis is to be averted, and we may as well face the issues quickly, tax funds must be made available through legislation and by other means in such amount as will make possible the adequate care of those rendered jobless and without resources by an economic depression for which they are in nowise responsible, unless extreme suffering and starvation with the attendant physical breakdown result.[124]

However, the local situation only worsened in the short run. The Chest ran a deficit of over $100,000 for 1931; the early months of 1932 saw relief expenditures rise from the $22,000-per-month 1931 level to above $70,000.[125] Relief finally came in the form of Reconstruction Finance Corporation (RFC) loans starting in August 1932, eagerly welcomed by the Chest director:

> In this connection I might point out that but for the foresight of advocates of Federal Aid in the face of exhaustion of local and state resources, this wholesome community of ours would have long since been rendered a highly undesirable place of residence as there would have resulted untold suffering and hardship on many defenseless persons. More than 70,000 persons walking our streets in vain for food is a thing barely averted, the consequences of which make Federal Aid cheap at any cost.[126]

One result of federal aid was an immediate reduction in the 1933 Chest goal by $220,000 to $469,907, the lowest goal since 1923. It was estimated that actual need would be three times the amount sought through private donations, but that any additional funds could be secured from the RFC.[127] When the department of public welfare was established in August 1933, the Chest dropped relief entirely from its budget.[128] Thus the impact of federal assistance was not only to meet local need but also to reduce private efforts in social welfare, leaving relief with no firm private basis of support. The attitude of local leaders in this one deep South city stood in ironical contrast to President Roosevelt's views as stated in October 1934:

> Surely none of you wants to centralize the care of relief either in Washington or your state capitol or in your city hall. The decentralization of relief—the keeping of it in the hands of private organizations as much as we possibly can—means that personal relationships, personal contacts, personal obligations and personal opportunities to do good will be preserved. It is, therefore, without hesitation and with very deep feeling that I ask you to support your local charitable and welfare organization in this 1934 mobilization for human need.[129]

The next problem confronting the Chest in its continuing effort to define public and private areas of responsibility was how to respond to the periodic, apparently arbitrary reductions in federal assistance. When the Federal Emergency Relief Administration withdrew funds in the fall of 1935, leaving thirty-eight hundred employable men who were not on work projects without support, one board member voiced the opinion that the Chest should attempt to increase its quota to absorb part of the burden. "The sentiment of those present seemed to be that it would be impossible to secure enough funds from private sources to take any additional load not already assumed, and that transient relief and resident family relief is a responsibility to be met at present by public funds through state, county and city."[130]

This complete divorce between the public and private sectors continued whenever feasible. When the department of public welfare was about to close its doors because of lack of funds in early 1936 and it was suggested that the Community Chest board help in developing a permanent plan of financing it, no action was taken; the board feared that any involvement might be construed as an indication that the Chest was willing to assume part of the relief load.[131] When the responsibility for transient relief but no funds were transferred to the department, the Chest initially refused to offer any aid, again wanting to keep public authorities "cognizant of their responsibility."[132] Finally, an emergency fund for transients was established by the Chest, but only because these people were literally on the streets without any shelter pleading for aid.[133] The superintendent of schools and PTA were firmly denied Chest funds for free lunches for needy children because this too was a public responsibility. Lest they seem too stony-hearted, though, directors agreed to work with the PTA on this problem on an individual basis; they only wanted to keep the department of public welfare aware that it could not look to the Community Chest as an organization for help.[134]

By the fall of 1938, 92 percent of the nearly $10 million spent that year on social welfare work in Jefferson County came from tax funds; and the Community Chest had developed a different definition of its role from the one given by the campaign chairman a decade earlier when he called for greater private giving to meet greater relief needs. Relief was now seen as a public responsibility because of unemployment compensation, work projects, and the aid available to individuals falling within the Social Security categories of dependent children still in their own homes, the aged outside public institutions, and the mentally and physically handicapped. Chest funds were to be reserved for those cases that existing laws did not allow to be assisted publicly; it supported thirty-five agencies devoted to the care of homeless and sick children and the tubercular and to service and character building.[135]

6

Relief in Birmingham

From the Community Chest
to the Department of Public Welfare

Aʟᴛʜᴏᴜɢʜ ᴀ ᴠᴀʀɪᴇᴛʏ of private agencies like the Chamber of Commerce and
the League of Women Voters sponsored ad hoc programs designed to aid
those who were unemployed because of the Depression, Birmingham turned
to its Community Chest for sustained, organized relief. The responses by the
Chest and several of its agencies were sporadic and partial; as the crisis both
continued and intensified, the Red Cross Family Service emerged as the focal
point of relief activities. Through it, private charity carried the relief burden
unaided until modest local public support was received in January 1931, followed by substantial federal aid in August 1932. Finally, in July 1933, administrative change made official what financing had already made a matter of
fact; the privately governed Family Service was succeeded by the department
of public welfare.

The first Chest agency response to the Depression occurred when the
YWCA opened an employment bureau for women and girls in April 1928; during its initial six months of operation, this bureau placed 193 of its 683 applicants.[1] Worsening business conditions in 1929 led to a sharp increase in the
number of applicants but also to diminishing employment opportunities. Unable to give significant aid, the YWCA abandoned specific efforts to serve Depression victims. This early program was for Whites only; when a black woman
tried to apply, "the director explained, in her quiet and courteous manner, that
the bureau was operated only for white people, but directed Liza to the proper
organization to take care of her difficulties."[2]

Travelers' Aid Society, on the other hand, gave assistance without regard
to race. Offering information about the city to newcomers and helping them
to find jobs, it handled 7,172 cases in 1928, 4,314 white and 2,837 black.[3] Travelers' Aid remained a significant source of relief to nonresidents of both races
until its functions were assumed by the Federal Transient Bureau in 1933.

Whereas Travelers' Aid offered the transient information, the Salvation

Army offered temporary shelter. The Army also served both Blacks and Whites, but none of the available reports about its activities is broken down according to race. It provided emergency housing to transient families and single men upon verification of need through an investigation by the Red Cross Family Service. The Army's mounting caseload is an indication of the growing impact of the Depression on the countryside and small towns, with the resulting migration of the unemployed to big cities in a largely futile search for jobs. In December 1930 it housed 1,457 cases, a 250 percent increase over the previous December. Its annual caseload increased from 7,212 in 1930 to 10,533 in 1931 and then to its peak of 19,384 in 1932.[4]

The counterpart of the Salvation Army for women and children was the residential facility maintained by the Volunteers of America. No reports for this agency could be found; judging from the severe criticism of it by the Chest board and from the fact that it was required to have a new director as a condition of continuing support, its program seems to have been badly mismanaged.[5] In any event, the residential programs of both the Salvation Army and the Volunteers of America were supplanted by the Federal Transient Bureau. The disgruntled Chest board then dropped the Volunteers as a member agency, stating that its work duplicated federal activities, although this harsh fate did not befall the Army, whose work was just as duplicative.[6] Other agency aid was given by the Federation of Jewish Charities, but it played a diminishing role as the Depression wore on. From a 1928 level of $9,000, its Chest budget fell to a minuscule $306 in 1932, reflecting the absorption by the Red Cross Family Service of nearly all relief for residents of the county.[7]

The Community Chest organization itself played a relief role on three separate occasions during the Depression beyond its financing of constituent agencies. When both individuals and families began to flock to the city in the spring of 1928, Birmingham was plagued by the problem of transients soliciting help on the streets; the citizen had no way of determining the true need of these supplicants. Under the headline "War Declared on Charity Frauds," the *News* reported that the Community Chest had developed a plan to protect citizens against impostors. It printed tickets and distributed them to its supporters to be handed to any applicant for aid, referring him to the Community Chest where immediate help would be given if investigation verified real need. The citizen would receive a report on the disposition of the case within twenty-four hours. The Chest director commented: "The Chest, through its forty agencies, stands ready to give immediate relief where there is actual need, and pledges prompt investigation of each case, so that subsequent help may be of lasting benefit. In using these tickets you are not refusing help to needy people; you are making it possible for them to benefit through your contribution to the

Community Chest."[8] This strategy was utilized again in November 1931, accompanied by a police campaign against "panhandlers and undesirables of all kinds" and relief agency assertions that they had resources adequate to meet all real need.[9]

The Chest in February 1932 served as the conduit through which special one-time contributions by businessmen could be channeled to employ "hundreds" of unemployed men on park and recreation projects. These gifts made it possible for the park board to keep open three golf courses, seventeen playgrounds, and eight community centers that would otherwise have been closed.[10]

Supporting all of these other Chest activities and far surpassing their combined efforts in importance was the program of the Red Cross Family Service, a program that received national attention for both administrative excellence and innovative activities.

The Red Cross Family Service

The discussion below of the Red Cross Family Service is set against the following background of statistics: from a pre-Depression monthly caseload level that had not exceeded 680 families, the service served an increasing number of clients until it peaked at 23,208 families in May 1933. Monthly expenditures rose from less than $6,000 per month during 1929 to $180,000 in July 1933. Blacks in 1929 accounted for an average of 24.2 percent of the caseload, up from 10.9 percent in 1925, the agency's first year of operation. In 1932 Blacks constituted 62.8 percent of the caseload.[11]

Prior to 1925 the Birmingham Chapter of the American Red Cross was a distinctly professional agency designed to meet the needs of ex-servicemen and of civilians during times of disaster. Its new secretary, appointed in 1921, reflected the professionalism of the staff; she came to Birmingham after seven years in a social work position at Chicago Commons Settlement House.[12] Red Cross policy that year specified that relief could be given only in cases where there was no other agency able to furnish it; in 1922 the agency did provide free milk, clothes, and money to needy children upon investigation, to enable them to remain in school.[13] But civilian relief proved to be a troublesome diversion from the main activities of the chapter; in May 1923 its board went on record as establishing the policy to withdraw from all such civilian work.[14]

When the Community Chest was established in 1923, Red Cross leaders debated at length the relative merits of joining the new federation of agencies or of continuing their independent and heretofore successful fund drives. When the Chest budget committee allocated the chapter its full request of $12,000 for 1924, the Red Cross board unanimously approved joining.[15] One

year later the Chest executive secretary approached the Red Cross board chairman to ask that the chapter, with its established casework procedures, take
over the work of the city welfare department. The chapter agreed to take over
this activity provided the Red Cross budget was increased by $18,000 for re-
lief payments and suitable additional office space and two automobiles were
made available.[16] Arrangements satisfactory to all parties were made. On 1 January 1925 the Red Cross assumed responsibility through its newly established
Family Service for relief to all who had resided for thirty days or more in Birmingham or Jefferson County under the five-year agreement discussed above;
the Salvation Army and Volunteers of America were assigned the lesser task
of assisting transients.[17] The Chest assumed full responsibility for funding the
relief program operated by these three groups.

The Red Cross Family Service was characterized by a professional, decentralized service delivery system. The director of the agency from mid-1925 on,
Roberta Morgan, had received her training at the Tulane University School of
Social Work and had experience as a social worker with the United States Steel
Corporation, as director of the Red Cross chapter in Montgomery, as a caseworker with the Alabama Child Welfare Department, and as a social worker at
the Walter Reed Army Hospital.[18] She brought to her Birmingham assignment
significant casework and administrative experience and a commitment to establishing and maintaining high professional standards in the family relief program. Her personal philosophy suited her to the task of operating the private
agency as a model for later public administration; she stated that the private
agency's role was to serve as a "pathfinder, turning over the problems they
find to the public."[19] Morgan quickly emerged as a central figure in Birmingham's effort to cope with the Depression, achieving in the process a national
reputation based upon the excellence of the programs she conceived and directed.[20]

Under Morgan's direction the Family Service sponsored a comprehensive
relief program that included clinics, payment for treatment by physicians, public health nurses, prescriptions, legal aid, credit, institutional care, cash relief,
work relief, and commodity distribution.[21] It responded to distress caused by
epidemics, old age, desertion, health problems, and unemployment.

The Red Cross Family Service staff grew to a maximum of over one hundred. Divided about equally between case and clerical workers, this number
included ten full-time black caseworkers who worked exclusively with black
clients and white caseworkers who worked with members of both races. The
Family Service was unique among private agencies in having an integrated
staff.[22]

Few of the staff besides Morgan had formal social work training; lack of proper academic preparation was a deficiency noted in the staff by outside evaluators.[23] However, almost all caseworkers had had some college training, supplemented by in-service instruction in casework. Each worker had a caseload of three to four hundred, well above the accepted maximum of one hundred recommended by the profession; as a result, investigations were less thorough than desirable and follow-up visits less frequent. Still during even the most frenzied periods when new programs were begun on short notice, each case was investigated to verify need and eligibility; home visits were made, previous employers were interviewed, and references were contacted. The investigative process, continued by the successor department of public welfare, clearly kept the number of relief recipients far below what it would have been otherwise; in one typical month only 639 of 1,168 applicants were certified for aid.[24] But a price was paid, not only in terms of staff time but also in terms of personal privacy. When the state relief administration closed, its director commented, "In three years we have tried every test, every system of investigation, every arbitrary ruling that human ingenuity could devise to prove to our own satisfaction that we were aiding the right persons, and the tragedy was that we made them suffer in convincing ourselves."[25]

But no alternative to this careful casework was available in light of the fact that the resources for relief never met local need. In order to overcome client ignorance of and hostility toward the investigations, the agency established case committees in different districts of the city to aid caseworkers; the stated purposes of these citizen groups were to interpret the casework method to the neighborhood, to bring the worker and the community closer together, and to assist the worker in resolving particularly difficult case problems.[26] While there is no indication of how frequently these groups were used in allocating aid and no indication of their abuse, one cannot help speculating about the impact on community life of having one group of citizens in the position of influencing, however slightly, the outcome of relief investigations of applications by other residents. This use of community residents to assist with resource allocation decisions during the Depression resembles to some extent the use of neighborhood advisory councils to assist in staffing local antipoverty centers in the 1960s. It is thus an example of citizen participation in an earlier war against poverty.

Responding to both overcrowded waiting rooms and the hardship experienced by impoverished clients in traveling across town on public transportation, the service opened three offices at least in outlying neighborhoods.[27] Because of the comprehensive range of services that could be provided through the Family Service, these offices can fairly be compared with the neighborhood service centers developed with Office of Economic Opportunity funds in the 1960s.

The administration of the Red Cross Family Service was highly regarded locally and favorably evaluated by outside observers. Perhaps the most prized assessment was that of a staff member of the national Family Welfare Association after a visit to Birmingham in January 1932; she reported that the local program was the most efficient in the South and compared favorably with the best in the nation. She also noted that Birmingham was then unique in the nation in its almost total dependence on private funds for relief purposes.[28]

The Family Service displayed considerable ingenuity and common sense in trying to help the largest number of people. For example, it sponsored a home garden project of twelve thousand plots, utilizing seed packets supplied by the federal government. This project was supplemented by establishing canning centers in some dozen neighborhoods where surplus fruits and vegetables from the gardens were prepared for later distribution to clients during the winter months.[29] This latter program was widely publicized as a local innovation easily replicated elsewhere.[30]

Opposed to giving cash grants in lieu of wages, the service developed a series of public improvement projects that employed up to twenty-six hundred men one to three days a week every other week. Carefully designed not to compete with private enterprise, the work included demolishing abandoned dilapidated houses and saving materials to repair other structures, rebuilding rural schools, draining lowland areas, and repairing discarded toys and shoes for later distribution.[31] Concerned about the psychological hardship for white-collar workers of accepting charity, the service established the Community Placement Bureau for them in December 1931; during its first year the bureau provided employment for 564.[32] Interestingly, these white-collar clients were not subjected to the same detailed investigations as unskilled unemployed workers. Indeed, many were hired by public agencies and paid by their employers without the knowledge that their wages were provided by the Family Service.

The greatest problem faced by the service was inadequate funds. As early as February 1928 the Chest budget committee tried unsuccessfully to persuade the city commission to supplement private contributions in order to meet mounting relief needs.[33] Appeals to both city and county officials were made again during the summers of 1929 and 1930 without avail as Chest deficits mounted. The city finally contributed funds in January 1931, followed by a reluctant county in April 1932. This last public support came at a critical moment, for the $287,000 Chest emergency relief fund was totally spent by April and a $350,000 deficit was projected for the year. The Chest made what appears to have been a completely serious threat: "In light of this interpretation of the Chest's ability to meet the demands, the feeling was that unless additional funds are provided, the Red Cross Family Service has no other course to follow than to close down its relief activities where unemployment is the major problem effective April 1."[34]

With its funds exhausted and $100,000 in unpaid bills on 31 May, the service limped through June and July on emergency local funding and looked forward to the availability of federal Reconstruction Finance Corporation (RFC) money starting 1 August.[35] A formal request was transmitted to the governor by the city, county, and Red Cross asking him to borrow $375,000 for local relief under the RFC provisions of loans for states: no interest with repayment over a five-year period through deductions from federal highway appropriations to the state. Without explanation the governor refused to submit the application, apparently believing that local relief officials were exaggerating local need. He did, however, sign the necessary authorization enabling the city and county to apply for a loan directly, to be paid without time limit at 3 percent interest, Birmingham assuming 60 percent of the obligation and Jefferson County the remainder.[36] The first RFC loan of $75,000 for August was secured after Birmingham social welfare leaders were able to persuade Washington officials that the area was experiencing destitution and suffering and not just unemployment.[37] This money and succeeding federal allocations meant only that relief could be maintained at its current level; there was no provision for improved benefits. And the unsuccessful negotiation with the governor proved to be only the first of a series of troublesome relationships between Birmingham and Montgomery involving relief policy.

Relief payments in Birmingham had consistently been small and below the average for other regional cities. The Russell Sage Foundation compiled comparative data for May 1930 that showed that Birmingham's $9 per family per month was higher than only Fort Worth's $3. Payments for other southern cities were Richmond, $14; Houston, $13; Dallas, $14; Memphis, $12; and Louisville, $21.[38] By August 1932 benefits had worsened; the service allocated no more money for rent and clothing. It provided only food, fuel, and medication; food was rationed at below minimum health standards, and clients were allowed no choice in the items they received.[39] The federal funds allowed at least some relief program to be maintained. By late 1932 the Birmingham Red Cross chapter was managing the largest budget of any chapter in the country during peacetime—nearly $150,000 per month.[40] A dramatic shift had occurred in the sources of funds for this agency that had been totally supported by private funds through 1930; nearly 96 percent of its support was from federal funds.[41]

Because of its experience with relief and its proven ability to administer funds, the Red Cross Family Service was designated the local relief agency by the Alabama Relief Administration, a five-member commission with responsibility for supervising RFC activities in the state. This designation was accompanied by the first of many directives that soon established the framework for local relief: "All aid, whether work relief or direct relief, shall be given on the same basis, the need of the recipient."[42]

To a large extent the Family Service had always awarded relief on the basis of need, although the Community Placement Bureau for unemployed white collar workers had undoubtedly assisted some whose need was relatively less. A dramatic indication of the application of the single criterion of need is the large numbers and high percentage of Blacks served by the Family Service beginning December 1930. The percentage of Blacks among the Service's caseload had increased steadily from its founding in 1925, when the yearly average was 10.9 percent. In 1926 the figure rose to 14.5 percent; figures for 1927, 1928, and 1929 were 15.4 percent, 18.7 percent, and 24.2 percent, respectively. By November 1930 Blacks constituted 32.1 percent of the caseload. In December Blacks constituted over 50 percent of the caseload; they represented 55.5 percent of the 1931 cases, 62.8 percent in 1932, 60.5 percent in 1933, and 63.4 percent in 1934. During the spring and summer of 1931 there was a substantial reduction in the number and percentage of black cases, reflecting an overall removal of childless couples and families with no health problems; this move for some unexplained reason had a disproportionate impact on black clients.[43] The Red Cross minutes contain the following commentary on this action:

> The board held an animated discussion of the reduction of the case load [by the Family Service] and its effect on the community. It was explained that the reduction was mostly in colored families, where no health problems existed and with childless able bodied couples, white and colored. It was also explained that the garden project had made some of its reduction possible. The committee felt that drastic cuts in case loads should not be continued, unless conditions improved. That is, that only those cases should be closed in the future which would be closed in normal times or for good case work reasons. It was decided that the small deficit of something over $1,000 monthly, which would be incurred by continuing approximately to keep the same case load would be worth the forestalling of community criticism.[44]

This situation and the above quotation are of interest because they represent the only recorded instance of the board's urging either higher expenditures or greater attention by professionals to the needs of Blacks; generally the situation was the reverse. This brief period is simply not consistent with the long-term trend of increasing black percentages or the fact that Blacks constituted a majority of cases each year beginning in December 1930. It is also inconsistent with the recollections of both Morgan and a black member of her staff that the agency's relations with the black community were generally excellent throughout the Depression.[45]

A more interesting question is why Blacks waited so long before applying to the Family Service in large numbers and then why they were apparently so readily accepted. No explanation for the delay was found in any of the written material either from or about the Depression era in Birmingham. However, interviews with both Morgan and the director of the Alabama Relief Administration produced the same speculative answer. Both pointed out that large numbers of Blacks had been brought to the area from the countryside by the steel companies as unskilled labor. Through 1929 many of these laborers continued on their jobs, receiving large salaries relative to their previous earnings as farmers. As the Depression intensified, the companies made initial efforts to conduct social welfare programs of their own to keep their labor forces intact. In addition, Blacks brought with them to the city a tradition of dependence on family, friends, and church for aid in times of need. Presumably, the dual resources of company and community, coupled with an unfamiliarity with urban institutions, delayed the influx of black applicants to the Red Cross Family Service until late 1930. The exhaustion of these alternative sources of relief, coupled with an increasing awareness of the relief programs available, is offered as the probable explanation for the increase in black cases from late 1930 onward.[46] If this explanation is correct, the increase in the percentage of Blacks among relief recipients reflects a growing sophistication in the use of city institutions, which can be seen as an indicator of the urbanization of Blacks in the district.

The ready acceptance of black applicants is undoubtedly due to the professionalism of the Red Cross Family Service, especially its director, in applying general rules of eligibility uniformly to members of both races.

In any discussion of agency policy, the personality of Roberta Morgan looms large. Within the limits of available funds and with the exception noted above of board directives concerning caseload reductions, she operated the agency in a highly personal manner.[47] Blacks were first hired as staff members at her initiative, and the friendly atmosphere in agency offices that made them a popular gathering place for unemployed Blacks prevailed because of her directives. The impact of the Depression in Birmingham must necessarily be viewed as the result of institutional forces over which no individual, at least locally, had mastery; but the impact of the relief program can be viewed at least partly in terms of the importance of personal values as a determinant of institutional behavior.

In June 1933 Harry Hopkins, national relief administrator under Roosevelt, informed all state directors, "It is the policy of the Federal Emergency Relief Administrator that whenever federal funds are used in the administration of relief, they must be administered by public officials." This meant that "private organizations [were not permitted to] be designated as administrators of public funds and that applicants for relief [were required to] apply to or be referred to a public official responsible to the State Administration."[48]

Commenting upon this mandate, Hopkins, a former Red Cross executive himself, wrote in _Spending to Save: The Complete Story of Relief_:

> We decided that all sums should be spent only through public agencies. There existed a large army of professional social workers and of public spirited citizens who, as paid or as volunteer workers, had been struggling with this overwhelming burden of dependency before the relief administration opened its doors. We felt that if these persons were to help administer public relief, they should come upon the public payroll and be paid commensurately with other public servants.[49]

To conform with the new federal policy the city and county commissions jointly created the department of public welfare. Following the recommendation of the Chest executive director, they voted that "the organization known as the Red Cross Family Service, stripped of its name, be made the personnel and equipment of the Department."[50] In addition, they appointed a seven-member board of public welfare drawn from the Red Cross and Community Chest boards to oversee the relief program. This creation of the department represented a change of responsibility and bookkeeping but not of program; the same staff continued to operate in the same manner from the same facilities. Though the short-run consequences seemed minimal, the long-run result of this action was of immense importance because it established a permanent agency of local government concerned with welfare activities. It also marked the conclusion of the era of private relief. The Community Chest no longer raised any funds for this purpose, and the Red Cross Chapter restricted itself to its traditional activities.[51] Public authority alone could supply money commensurate with the crisis; from 1933 to 1941 the welfare arena was occupied by public officials engaged in an ongoing struggle over how much funding would be provided by each level of government.

The Department of Public Welfare

The immense changes in philosophy between the Hoover and Roosevelt administrations that would be of central concern in a study of welfare with a national focus had two principal local manifestations. First, federal funding made relief possible on a scale previously unattainable. Thus the Depression maximum of direct relief cases rose to a figure of 33,655 cases in April 1934 at a cost of nearly $250,000 in public funds. With the emphasis later placed on work projects rather than direct relief, monthly public expenditures for work relief rose to about the $.5 million mark during two months in 1935. Basically, however, these increases represented an expansion of the activities carried out in pre-New Deal days. The federal programs specifically designed to deal with unemployment were grander in scale than their predecessors: where before schools had been renovated, hospitals were now built; where before lowlands had been drained, entire drainage systems were now constructed; where before houses had been torn down and others refurbished, entire housing projects were now erected. But the principle remained the same as that which had guided the pre-New Deal Red Cross Family Service: to employ as many unemployed as possible in programs that served the public good without interfering with the private sector.

The second, more significant, change created by the New Deal was the creation of a complex intergovernmental welfare system that removed the power of direction from the hands of local officials and placed it in the hands of federal administrators whose directives, seen from the local level, seemed on occasion to be insensitive if not capricious. Thus, the abrupt beginning and ending of the Civil Works Administration (CWA) caused immense strain on local personnel and resources. With final directives issued on a Saturday in November 1933, welfare officials labored frantically over the weekend to develop public works projects that employed two thousand men the following Monday.[52] The conclusion of the CWA in March 1934 was just as traumatic. The direct relief caseload jumped from 19,554 in March to the record of 33,655 in April; and regulations mandated the reinvestigation of all new cases to verify eligibility. Both in its expanded activities and in its intergovernmental relations, the department of public welfare faced difficulties unknown to its pre-New Deal predecessor.

The department of public welfare experienced criticism on two counts in its administration of New Deal relief programs: it was accused of interfering with private enterprise and was said to favor Blacks in the distribution of aid.

The representatives of private enterprise who felt threatened by welfare programs were members of real estate and grocers' organizations. The Real

Estate Owners Association and the Real Estate Board both argued that the department was encouraging tenants not to pay rents, while bringing pressure on owners to permit welfare recipients to live rent-free. The real estate groups filed complaints with both the city and county commissions but finally withdrew these in favor of a negotiating session with the Alabama Relief Administration, which resulted in a state-wide rent payment policy that was acceptable to all parties.[53]

The wholesale and retail grocers' associations objected to the department's direct operation of seven commissaries, which were said to do business equivalent to that of twenty groceries. Relief officials at both the local and national levels were equally displeased with the commissary system; the food stamp system was developed as a preferable alternative less degrading to the consumer and advantageous to those grocers certified to accept them. Birmingham was one of the first eleven cities in the nation and the first in the South to experiment with the food stamp program, thus satisfying the grocers' organization.[54]

Concerning the impact of New Deal programs on the black community, it is difficult to be precise in determining either the proportion of recipients who were black or the proportion of funds they received. The department of public welfare continued to extend direct relief to a caseload that was over 50 percent Blacks. But with the emphasis on work relief as opposed to direct relief that was reflected in the establishing of the Works Progress Administration (WPA), it becomes impossible to document racial percentages because contemporary reports were not broken down in this manner and because data have been destroyed. Both national and state legislation classified WPA records as "useless papers" to be destroyed upon completion of the program.[55] Interviews indicate, however, that Blacks locally were equitably treated under this program because of both a nondiscriminatory selection process and a uniform wage scale.[56]

Repeatedly, Morgan and her staff faced charges of favoring Blacks, and other New Deal projects encountered criticism on racial grounds. In 1933 the Alabama Division of the Transient Bureau was criticized by the Birmingham Trades Council for permitting a white secretary to take dictation from a black man; the Jefferson County Council of Legion Posts complained that black women and white men were working side by side on CWA projects.[57] The complaint of the Trades Council was upheld; a separate division of the Transient Bureau with a black staff was established to work with Blacks, and Harry Hopkins personally forbade situations of black and white staff members working together. This action illustrates the point that the New Deal in the South extended substantial benefits to Blacks but within the context of the prevailing norms of racial segregation. The accusations of the Council of Legion Posts were voluntarily withdrawn after it investigated both CWA projects and Roberta Morgan, finding the projects run to their satisfaction and Morgan to be "an outstanding social worker of national repute."[58]

Interestingly, the complaints about racial policies were coupled with complaints about the numbers of out-of-state professional staff members imported to fill administrative positions at a time when many local white-collar workers were unemployed. The state relief administrator and Morgan repeatedly pointed to the need for specialized training in casework procedures and to the absence of qualified personnel within the state.[59] The state agency offered special summer training courses for local personnel and leaves of absence with pay for out-of-state study, but it rigidly held to high standards of professionalism even if that meant hiring non-Alabamians and encountering the wrath of local unemployed persons.[60]

Complaints like these against the department were periodic occurrences throughout the New Deal era, but they did not threaten to disrupt the relief program in the area. They involved specific objections from specific groups; in all cases they were either successfully resolved through negotiation or refuted by investigation. A more serious threat to the work of the department came from the politics of welfare as conducted by city, county, and state officials in response to shifting programs and directives from the federal level that necessitated a greater degree of support from within the state.

The heart of the problem was that Alabama's governors were unwilling to commit state funds to the relief program, while Harry Hopkins refused to continue subsidizing Alabama's program fully. The Federal Emergency Relief Administration (FERA) had in fact provided full subsidy from the time of its creation in May 1933 until September 1934. At that time the FERA announced that it would require some relief appropriation from the state, and the political climate in the state in early 1935 seemed favorable to such an allocation.[61] Frank Miller had been succeeded as governor by Bibb Graves, who was expected to recommend a $3 million appropriation made possible by revenues from a 1935 gas tax.[62] The governor in fact refused to release these funds and used them as a bargaining point in a dispute with the Jefferson County legislative delegation concerning his overall budgetary program. The situation reached a crisis when Hopkins could no longer exhort state officials while continuing to give federal assistance. Roosevelt had said in January 1935 that the government "must quit this business of relief."[63] The massive works program began the following March, and all federal direct relief ended in August, thrusting upon the states and localities responsibility for unemployables and employables above the WPA quota.

Birmingham and Jefferson County reluctantly made appropriations for September and October that enabled aid to be given to both unemployables and employables, meanwhile arguing that the state should release funds from the gas tax revenues and carry this burden that federal officials were trying to "unload on city and county governments."[64] In November and December funds were made available for only forty-eight hundred cases that fell within the Social Security categories for unemployables; no funds were allocated to thirty-eight hundred cases classified as employable by the department but in excess of the WPA quota.[65] The new year began with the department's closing two offices, reducing its staff by 25 percent, and announcing that all of its activities would cease 15 January 1936.[66] This was "a time of confusion and near chaos in the history of public relief" in the nation; great human suffering accompanied the new federal program of state and local initiative and responsibility.[67] With a genuine crisis in relief, the city and county held firm, looking to the governor and a possible special legislative session for an increase in the state's meager funding.[68]

By dipping into a mysteriously discovered surplus fund, the department kept a skeleton staff through January. The city and county provided $18,000 of the $55,000 needed for February, the state less than $4,000. For the last half of the month the department sent out $1 relief checks to each case plus grocery orders for surplus commodities.[69] Federal funds were standing idle in Montgomery, but the state had no funds for matching these for the Social Security checks. Funds for welfare previously had been derived from state gas tax collections, but the law authorizing the governor to divert these funds expired 31 January. While relief recipients burned old tires in Birmingham for heat, the governor refused either to initiate new legislation or to borrow.[70]

A $4,000 emergency appropriation by the city and county on 1 March combated documented starvation, while a federal report showed that the state had carried only 1.4 percent of the relief burden as opposed to 92.8 percent federal and 5.8 percent local funding.[71] Alabama was one of only eleven states to receive more than 90 percent of its relief funds from federal sources. The *News* wrote, "Because the people of this state generally emphatically demand economy and no unnecessary and burdensome new taxation does not mean that they can not also consistently demand proper provision for taking care of helpless and afflicted sufferers, old men and women and little children."[72]

The governor announced that he would not act on relief until the legislature approved his revenue program, which would require new general sales taxes; he refused even to appropriate funds from the general fund under an emergency relief measure passed over his opposition. The governor's opponents, headed by the Jefferson County delegation, held out for reduced expenditures through a strict program of economy and no new taxes.[73] The *News* wrote that it was

> as if a great fire were threatening the whole city, and the firemen stood back while those in authority debated the question of how the bills for the water to extinguish the flames would be met. The only difference is that the danger in the relief crisis is less swift than in the case of the fire. . . . It simply takes longer for people to starve to death than it does for people to drown in a flood, or have their homes washed away.

According to the *News* it was simply a case of "playing politics with human misery"; and indeed this seems to have been the case.[74]

The governor finally relented, agreeing to borrow funds if a selective sales tax were passed to support education, which was also in crisis: thirty-eight of sixty-seven counties closed their schools in March for lack of funds. Meanwhile, the county made continuing emergency appropriations of relief; Birmingham made none. Though the tax bill was defeated, the governor finally borrowed $250,000 in April to match idle federal funds. Incredibly, he said that he had not believed reports of actual suffering, considering them to be "grossly exaggerated." Only a visit by an unnamed Birmingham industrialist telling him of actual starvation was said to have changed his mind. Still, the county for April received only $35,000 from all sources for direct relief, while a minimum of $75,000 was needed.[75] Frustrated by the continuing lack of funds, Roberta Morgan resigned.[76] Through the early summer the problem festered. Direct relief recipients in Jefferson County received only $2 per month in July rather than the minimally acceptable $12; the state aided only one-half of the elderly eligible for Social Security and then gave them only one-half of their entitlement. But for present purposes the matter seemed settled locally when the city appropriated $50,000 for the relief program for the fiscal year starting 1 October 1936, to be matched by state and federal funds.[77]

In August 1937 city and county officials proved that the politics of welfare was not confined to intergovernmental disagreements between state and local officials; city and county could spar, and city officials could themselves "play politics with human misery." The controversy erupted when city commission president Jones tried to force the county to accept full responsibility for local relief appropriations, claiming that the county received earmarked taxes from general and liquor sales for this purpose. The county replied that it did not receive enough from these sources to meet local need and added that 85 percent of the recipients from Jefferson County lived in the city and that it was already spending $500,000 on county-wide institutions such as Hillman charity hospital. Jones then secured a ruling from the city attorney that Birmingham lacked legal authority to appropriate funds to a county welfare department; in his view, the state constitution made care of the poor strictly a county responsibility. The other two city commissioners proceeded to make an appropriation for August-October, supported by various attorneys who viewed such aid as perfectly legal. Jones ordered the city comptroller not to disburse the funds until after a state supreme court decision, whereupon the two associate commissioners threatened to suspend the fiscal officer.[78] The governor, meanwhile, refused to release state funds designated for Jefferson County until after the local match was forwarded to Montgomery, commenting on the relief tangle, "That's the city's little red wagon. That's their funeral."[79] A review of local newspapers for this month indicates that welfare had emerged as the central issue of local politics in Birmingham. The *Age-Herald* editorial "Petty politics: Hungry people" seemed to summarize well the local situation.[80] Even the *News*, previously friendly to Jones, noted:

> the citizen unlearned in legal points, however, finds it difficult to believe that a concern over a constitutional right should so belatedly come to some of the city authorities without other influences at work. And here one gets close to political matters that should have no place in welfare appropriations where lives are at stake. . . . When people in need face starvation, it is not a time for quibbling over whose duty it is to carry them food.[81]

The political matters to which the *News* referred were the hostility between the governor and Jefferson County and, more importantly, the personal feud among the three commissioners, which dominated local politics between 1933 and 1937.

While this personal struggle was being resolved, twelve thousand relief cases waited three weeks for their checks, which would be reduced 55 percent without a city appropriation.[82]

For the fiscal year beginning 1 October 1937 the commission appropriated $100,000 for the department of public welfare, a reduction from its previous level of support that caused a 24 percent reduction to clients under the Social Security program.[83] The commission called upon mayors of outlying municipalities to assume their fair shares of the relief burden, but this plea was uniformly rejected. The *News*, which was consistently maintaining the "fundamental principle that relief is a local problem and a local responsibility," was disappointed; if localities were thus negligent, outsiders would be forced to step in and provide aid that was both more costly and less responsive to human needs.[84] "If we are successfully to maintain in this country the strength of local government and avoid the expense and dangers of a centralized bureaucracy, we should begin the fight with the smallest units of government."[85] The issue was now not one of private versus public responsibility but one of which level of government should bear greater responsibility. Philosophies of localism notwithstanding, the county and municipalities were unmoved by newspaper accounts of starvation and overcrowding; those in the Social Security categories received reduced checks, while the able-bodied unemployed received no direct relief at all.[86] The *News* grimly commented, "That human beings can endure so much, that they do endure so much is a tribute to the patience, courage, and loyalty of the American people."[87]

The controversy between the county and the city persisted until the death of commission president Jones brought a resolution to the latest crisis. His successor, W. Cooper Green, Birmingham postmaster since 1933, quickly concluded that relief was the "most acute immediate problem facing the city," and the commission increased its allocation.[88]

Assessment of the New Deal from a Local Perspective

The Depression in Birmingham is almost fondly regarded by those who lived through it as a heroic period in the city's history when people sacrificed for others and suffered immense hardship with quiet dignity. Roberta Morgan, for example, has written:

> The Depression was an interlude, a period of waiting, and a nightmare. For me it was stimulating and all-absorbing. I would not exchange it for any other experience imaginable, but I would not re-live it.
>
> In many ways people were more normal, more humane than in so-called normal times. They rose to the great challenge in a truly remarkable way.[89]

The dramatic Chest drive of 1931 is still cited as an example of what the community can do for itself; stories abound of proud citizens applying for relief for the first time with tears streaming down their faces, desperate for help but ashamed of their plight. An equally imposing number of reports testify to the ingenuity, devotion, and tireless work of many relief workers.

The New Deal did much for Birmingham and its citizens. The first of its relief agencies, the Federal Emergency Relief Administration, clearly saved this and many other communities from literal disaster as private and local public resources for direct relief were exhausted. But Hopkins, particularly, was opposed to direct relief, as was Roosevelt, preferring public works programs. The Civil Works Administration, conceived as a means of tiding the unemployed over the 1933–34 winter, employed fifteen thousand people on projects that left a permanent legacy of storm sewers, parks, and health projects.[90] Additional hundreds found employment on Public Works Administration programs, including a drainage system that employed a maximum of two thousand at one time and an industrial water system that employed five hundred.[91] The Emergency Housing Corporation of the PWA constructed two public housing projects of six hundred units each, one for Blacks and one for Whites, after clearing two of the worst slum neighborhoods. Another three hundred middle-income families were enabled to move to the four homestead projects built outside the city; here industrial workers could supplement their earnings by gardening on the ten acres allotted to each household.[92]

The New Deal also reinforced the preexisting standards of equity and professionalism that had existed under the Red Cross Family Service and extended them significantly. Blacks were apparently treated without any discrimination on both the direct relief and public work programs; only the relatively small efforts of the Community Placement Bureau for white-collar workers and of the homestead program served a predominantly white clientele. The Alabama Relief Administration established high standards of professionalism throughout the state—and then helped workers to meet them. Finally, the New Deal left an institutional structure that implemented the ongoing public commitment to aiding the needy through the Social Security program; most notable are the state welfare department and the network of Alabama State Employment Service offices.

As notable as the New Deal contributions to welfare in the state is one additional fact: the New Deal programs, despite their variety and substantial federal funding, never met local need. Clear examples are offered by the Civil Works Administration and Works Progress Administration programs and by the termination of federal direct relief in 1935.

The Civil Works Administration was a particularly vivid illustration of the hardships worked at the local level by ever-changing federal guidelines because of its hasty beginning, short five-month duration, and then abrupt termination. In addition, it was able to employ only about one-third of the over forty-six thousand eligible registrants certified by the reemployment bureau.[93]

The theory behind the termination of federal direct relief in 1935 was that the able-bodied unemployed would be absorbed into the Works Progress Administration and unemployables would become the responsibility of the localities. But in Jefferson County the unemployables never received even their minimum entitlements, and the WPA quotas left many able-bodied unemployed persons without any source of aid. In August 1935 the number of eligible cases exceeded the quota of 17,000 by 1,100; this figure rose to 3,800 in October. In October 1938 7,500 individuals certified for WPA employment could not work; 3,800 had been waiting at least six months.[94] In June 1941 the quota was reduced by over 1,000 even as 3,100 still awaited the chance to start working.[95] Those most directly involved in the relief effort made no claims of adequacy for their work. Harry Hopkins said of FERA simply, "We have never given adequate relief."[96] The Alabama Relief Administrator wrote as follows in his final report about the varying amounts of relief payments:

> In most cases the fluctuations are largely due to necessary arbitrary action on the part of this office, rather than any marked increase or decrease for the need of relief in Alabama.
> It was recognized that relief was extremely inadequate, and the low averages cannot be fully justified.[97]

Commentaries on the Depression by Lowi and by Piven and Cloward conclude that New Deal relief programs were conceived in fear of civil disorder on the part of the unemployed; it was this emotion rather than humanitarianism that made federal aid both necessary and politically possible.[98] The Birmingham data seem to support this conclusion. Though no violence occurred in Birmingham and the threats of violence were few, judged by available accounts, the threats were heeded by both politicians and welfare workers. Local data also support Piven and Cloward's observation that:

> Once relief-giving had expanded, unrest rapidly subsided, and then aid was cut back—which meant, among other things, that large numbers of people were put off the rolls and thrust into a labor market still glutted with unemployment. But with stability restored, the continued suffering of these millions had little political force.[99]

The political impact of the unemployed locally was negligible as witnessed by the prolonged use of welfare matching payments as a bargaining point in skirmishes between state and local government and between units of local government. Although lack of political influence on the part of the unemployed would be a sufficient explanation for the absence of a fuller welfare program, Piven and Cloward advance a manipulative motive to explain variations in the levels of benefits: once stability had been reestablished, restrictive welfare programs were a means of social control to enforce work norms.[100] They became, in essence, ways of disciplining citizens so that they fulfilled the roles desired of them by the managers of the economy.

There is no indication that this motive in any way guided the actions of those directly involved with the delivery of welfare services in Birmingham; on the contrary, these individuals displayed intense bitterness and frustration at their increasing inability to meet local need. If the politicians and business leaders had such a motive, it was unspoken; one is impressed by their indifference rather than by their cleverness.

Whatever the motives behind public or private actions, the situation in Birmingham did not bode well for the disadvantaged, especially the Blacks among them, in 1941. Their sources of assistance had diminished rather than increased in comparison with the pre-Depression era. There was a permanent public welfare structure, but it served only those in the limited Social Security categories of aged, blind, disabled, or dependent children; furthermore, these programs were not funded adequately for all eligible citizens to be served or for those served to receive full benefits. More importantly, no public aid was extended to the able-bodied unemployed other than WPA, and none at all existed after that program was terminated. The private agencies that had assisted this group before federal programs began had established rigid policies of noninvolvement in the economic problems of clients, justifying their action on the basis of the availability of public aid. Later public programs so discriminated against Blacks that the federal courts intervened in 1976 in the operations of the state welfare department in behalf of black recipients.[101] The only private agency serving Blacks in large numbers, the Red Cross Family Service, returned to its previous traditional activities. Local government abandoned its concern with welfare issues once it was no longer called upon to contribute local funds for this purpose. This retreat by private and public agencies to a pre-Depression level of concern for welfare is illustrated by examining one year midway between the end of the Depression and the beginning of the War on Poverty.

PART THREE

1954

7

The Missed Opportunity
in Race Relations

ALTHOUGH 1954 WAS a momentous year nationally because of the Supreme Court decision in *Brown vs. The Board of Education of Topeka, Kansas*, it was a politically quiet year in Birmingham, producing no issues that occupied unusually extensive space in the newspapers or that divided either the population or its political leaders. A representative example of the major concerns of the city commissioners is an appeal by the city before the Alabama Public Service Commission for an investigation of the three transit companies serving the area, to explore the possibility of consolidating their assets under one company that would then be subject to closer municipal regulation. Another representative example is efforts by the city to attract a new federal office building to Birmingham.[1]

Birmingham did conduct a vote on the question of fluoridating the water supply in 1954, but the referendum produced surprisingly little debate and virtually no newspaper publicity. Predictably, physicians, dentists, public health officials, and the press endorsed fluoridation while a few letters to the editor referred to the ominous possibility of a Communist plot to poison the water supply. Politicians remained silent on the issue, and organized activity was either absent or unreported; the electorate soundly rejected the plan. Even the announcement by the police commissioner that he had discovered widespread corruption in the force failed to generate either political controversy or newspaper concern. The decision by the city commission to repeal the municipal ordinance prohibiting Blacks and Whites from participating in the same sporting event triggered a brief movement of opposition against the commissioners. As the decision affected only professional baseball and made no change in the racial practices of the city otherwise, opposition to it died down quickly.[2]

Indicators of the levels of various services show that Birmingham continued to rank at or near the bottom of listings of cities in its population class. The city continued to maintain a low level of general public services, and even this level caused Birmingham to complete the 1953–54 fiscal year with a deficit of $1.3 million.[3] In large part the fiscal problem was caused by the fact that Birmingham's $10,115,000 total revenue for general services was the lowest in the nation on a per capita basis for cities in the 100,000–300,000 population class; the national average per capita income for the general fund was $55.90, while the corresponding figure for Birmingham was $39.85 in 1953.[4] The city comptroller could rationalize the situation in part by saying, "Of course, it may be and I think quite likely, that through our good administration, we are getting more public service per dollar in Birmingham than most of these places give."[5] Even granting this possibility, the *Post-Herald* wrote of the financial crisis, "It must be met unless we are content to advertise Birmingham to the world as a backward city."[6]

The city commission agreed with this assessment by the newspaper but found its options for generating revenues through new taxes limited. The property tax rate in Jefferson County already stood at the maximum rate of thirty-six mills allowed by the state constitution but produced a small amount for Birmingham relative to other cities. The fact that this rate was among the lowest in the nation was aggravated by the fact that the state received one-quarter of the revenues, a higher percentage than in other states; the city received a correspondingly low 50 percent and the county the remainder. The city commissioners were constrained to recommend either a general sales tax or a tax on salaries and wages as the means for raising the additional $3 million each year needed to balance both the general fund and education budgets. When these alternatives were presented to the voters in a referendum, 75 percent opposed a new tax in either form. Furthermore, the antitax sentiment was general throughout the electorate; the percentage opposed was uniform in all boxes in the city.[7] Once again the voters of Birmingham had affirmed their willingness to accept an inferior level of public services. This affirmation is surely explained in part by the poverty of the community; in family income the Birmingham metropolitan area ranked fifty-first out of fifty-seven areas above 250,000 in population.[8] But poverty alone is not an adequate explanation, since opposition to public spending was as strong in neighborhoods with substantial wealth as it was in neighborhoods characterized by low incomes, and even poverty. One is again driven back to the elusive concept of political culture, with Birmingham's still characterized by that unwillingness to support governmental activities that historian Sam Bass Warner describes as privatism.

Among the most financially starved institutions were the city's public schools. The *Post-Herald* observed that Birmingham was "having to run hard to stay in last place" in school spending.[9] A report issued by the U.S. Department of Health, Education, and Welfare on school spending in thirty-four cities with population above 100,000 showed that Birmingham ranked last in per pupil expenditures during both the 1941–42 and 1951–52 school years. The 1951–52 per pupil figure of $87.74 made the city one of only four to spend less than one hundred dollars per student per year. The system's teachers were among the lowest paid in the nation, and the demands upon the schools were increasing sharply. The 39,073 white and 30,536 black children enrolled during the 1953–54 school term represented increases of 23.8 percent and 27.7 percent, respectively, in four years. The overwhelming defeat of the proposed new tax forced the board of education to consider salary reductions and a shortened school term, but they were spared making this decision when unexpected income was discovered as the result of a bookkeeping error.[10]

Birmingham did not desegregate its schools until the fall of 1963, but in its opposition to the spirit of the Supreme Court's decision the city was in step with much of the rest of the South. Indeed, only two southern states began desegregation in 1954: Texas in one district and Arkansas in two districts.[11] The typical response was enactment of "freedom of choice" plans or adoption of "pupil placement" laws, techniques that appeared to be fair but "proved strongly segregative in practice."[12] Ten years after the *Brown* decision, only 1.17 percent of black school children in the eleven states of the former Confederacy attended school with white classmates.[13]

Little Rock was the exceptional case. There nine black students were able to complete the 1957–58 school year at Central High School only after President Eisenhower had dispatched federal troops to aid in executing a federal district court's desegregation order. The city's entire school system was closed during the 1958–59 school year, reopening in August 1959 after the Supreme Court ruled the closing unconstitutional.[14]

After the 1954 Supreme Court school desegregation decision, Birmingham's public officials were quick to respond to this unwanted federal intrusion into public education policy. State senator Albert Boutwell, later to become the first mayor under the mayor-council form of government adopted in 1962, was quoted as saying, "Our approach is to maintain segregation in the South by legal means . . . [but] since the court has gone outside the law to find a basis for its decision, we can do the same."[15] He then went on, however, to become the state's leading architect of schemes to maintain segregated schools without abandoning the pretense of legality. As chairman of the state interim legislative committee to develop a plan to avoid desegregation, he initially recommended that the legislature vote to abolish the constitutional provision that the state maintain a public school system.[16] When this idea was rejected, he coauthored the "freedom of choice" amendments that permitted parents to request that their children be transferred to schools other than the ones to which they were assigned by the school board.[17] After his initial implication that the law could be ignored, Boutwell steadfastly held to resisting school desegregation and later civil rights demands only by peaceful and lawful means; he emerged in the 1960s as the city's leading racial moderate.

The Birmingham board of education announced that it was exploring ways of obeying the letter but not the spirit of the Supreme Court decision, while Eugene "Bull" Connor, temporarily out of office but soon to return, was widely reported to have boasted, "We're not goin' to have white folks and nigras segregatin' together in this man's town."[18]

However, the most notable local response to the Supreme Court decision was a "wait and see" attitude on the part of all concerned, which resulted in little being said or done during 1954. In a thorough analysis of the response of all of the city's newspapers—daily and weekly, black and white—to the decision, George R. Stewart documents "the silence of Birmingham's two greatest papers in 1954" and observes that "it is inconceivable that so little newspaper comment would have been given."[19] Stewart finds that white educators and white policy-makers were "indecisive" while black Birmingham was characterized by the "staggering" silence of the black community in general and "the silence of the Negro educator" in particular.[20] Only one black weekly, the *Birmingham World*, of all the newspapers attempted to provide leadership to the community in facing the issue of desegregation.[21] As for the rest there was "the silence of a city, of a people, caught in change and truly not knowing what to expect."[22] A lifelong resident of Birmingham, Stewart believes that white Birminghamians found solace in the possibility that the Court order would never filter down to the city.[23]

Two other assaults against racial segregation in Birmingham by means of public policy occurred during 1954, but neither had immediate consequences for the city. Peter Hall, a local black attorney, joined Thurgood Marshall in filing a suit in federal court challenging the racial segregation policies of the Birmingham housing authority. Five prominent black business and professional leaders tried to buy tickets to play on one of the municipal golf courses and were refused; they subsequently filed suit also.[24] Ironically, in a year in which a massive assault against racial segregation in the South was initiated by the Supreme Court, the most significant local activity designed to break down racial barriers occurred in the private sector in a biracial committee that received little publicity and met with no public opposition to its regular meetings. The response to this committee's efforts to provide highly visible public leadership in race relations will be discussed later in this chapter.

Public welfare provided one minor issue in local politics during 1954, and the actions of city officials again reflected their unwillingness to accept this as a legitimate, permanent function of local government.

The welfare-related political issue involved the distribution of surplus food supplied by the federal government to needy families within the city. The Alabama Department of Public Welfare through its county office was responsible for the overall administration of the program, but each municipality was required to certify eligible families within its boundaries and to distribute the commodities. All persons aided under Social Security's categorical assistance programs were automatically eligible, but other applicants had to be screened. In order to process the large volume of cases, the city not only had to assign employees to the project but also had to rely on volunteers; in a time of financial distress the commission expressed understandable displeasure at the estimated ten thousand dollars per month that it spent implementing the plan. Despite the efforts of twenty-five volunteers, lines of eligible recipients stretched four blocks.[25]

The commission was concerned with the costs of the program, but it also felt that at least one-sixth of the thirty-five thousand recipients were "welfare chislers" who would be eliminated by a thorough investigation. Throughout the year the commissioners threatened to terminate the distribution of food altogether unless they received funds from the state; alternatively, they tried unsuccessfully to transfer the program to the county department of public welfare. Still operating the burdensome and expensive system at year's end, the commission terminated its only other welfare activity by eliminating the one-thousand-dollar-per-month allocation to the welfare department for emergency relief.[26]

The health care and welfare programs for the poor in metropolitan Birmingham were both dismally inadequate during the 1950s in comparison with other urban areas, but neither program stimulated concern on the part of public officials. Rather, the private sector took the lead in documenting the extent of need and calling for significant changes in both areas.

In 1958 the Chamber of Commerce appointed a citizens' committee on indigent medical care for Jefferson County in recognition of "more than a decade of inadequate provisions for the care of the indigent sick in an otherwise enlightened community." Extensively documenting "the failure of the community to provide financing and facilities . . . for the sick poor," it released its study with the comment, "It is not an exaggeration to indicate that the results of this study have shocked the membership."[27]

The committee examined in detail the medical programs for indigents in Richmond, Atlanta, Memphis, New Orleans, and Miami, a comparison that reemphasized "the failure of Birmingham and Jefferson County to even remotely approach the health care benefits provided the sick-poor of these latter communities."[28] For example, Jefferson County's population of 630,700 included an estimated 25,000 citizens unable to afford even minimal health care; for these medical indigents a total of 169 beds were made available. By comparison, Memphis, serving a population of 550,000, provided 600 beds; and Atlanta provided 1,000 for 866,200 people. Furthermore, the heavily used emergency room had not been expanded since 1903.[29]

The committee concluded that a minimally acceptable program in Jefferson County would require at least 600 beds and an annual operating budget of over $5,800,000; the total budget for indigent health care at the time was only $1,020,000.[30]

Part of the problem in the area of health care for the poor was the persistent inability of city and county officials to agree on who should accept financial responsibility for operating the hospital, a dispute of fifty years' duration. Commenting that "the indigent patient program has languished for too long in a twilight zone of uncertain responsibility," the committee called for the creation of a Jefferson County medical care commission to plan and administer a program and to own and operate the necessary facilities.[31] The proposed medical commission would be empowered to raise its own revenues by levying a sales tax on public utilities operating in the county.[32] While a new health commission was formed to plan a comprehensive program of medical care for indigents, it lacked the authority to raise revenue. The crisis in medical care for the poor, caused largely by inadequate funds, continued unrelieved into the final decade covered by this study.

The plight of the poor in Birmingham, however, was not limited to health care, as was documented by the Coordinating Council of Social Forces in its survey of health, welfare, and recreation needs and services. The Coordinating Council, which had emerged as a voluntary association of social workers and others interested in social welfare in 1939, was by this time funded by the Community Chest as "the central planning, research, and coordinating social agency of the county."[33] Historically an activist group, the council attracted to its lay board of directors men unique among Chest agencies by virtue of their commitment to developing a rational, comprehensive, and coordinated social welfare program in the county. The initial idea for the survey was put forth by one such board member, Charles F. Zukoski, Jr.; and the study frankly assumed that "no one had a very clear idea of the extent of need, the kinds of needs, the degree to which there was duplication of service, the degree to which some important needs were going unmet."[34] The survey was conducted by a thirty-two-member citizens' committee over a three-year period of time; one Black, A. G. Gaston, was among this group. Aided by fifty consultants, the committee carried out detailed examinations of seventy-one public and private agencies.[35] In its scope, methodology, and conclusions, the survey stands as a unique effort in the history of the community; it was viewed at the time of its release in 1955 as a blueprint for at least the next five years, showing agencies what they must plan to accomplish in order to meet the area's most severe needs. Its prescriptions remain unfulfilled in many cases.

Because of its overriding importance in the field of welfare, the state's program as administered by the Jefferson County Department of Public Welfare received particularly close scrutiny by the citizens' committee. This single agency disbursed over 80 percent of all funds spent for welfare in the county, and its budget was four times the total expenditures by all Community Chest agencies for all purposes.[36]

Payments by the department were confined only to those who fell into one of the four categories of aged, blind, permanently and totally disabled, or dependent children. As payments were determined by the extent to which the state legislature matched federal funds, local communities alone could not influence the levels of categorical aid, which were among the lowest in the nation. Alabama, forty-sixth among the states in per capita income, ranked forty-seventh in average public assistance payments. The average payment in the nation was $53.84 and in the South was $36.69; Alabama paid only $29.88.[37] Payments in each of the categories were determined by the state department on the basis of "budgeted need," a figure that the survey committee found in all cases to be below the amount actually required for subsistence. The state had paid aged recipients at 100 percent of budgeted need for the first time in April 1954; payments to the blind and disabled reached this level the following October.[38] Aid to Dependent Children recipients continued to receive only 50 percent of budgeted need; the Alabama average of $40.17 per case per month was less than one-half the comparable national figure.[39]

The objective poverty of the state, coupled with a generally recognized reluctance on the part of the state legislature to support welfare expenditures, resulted in relatively small state appropriations to the assistance programs. Nationally, federal funds accounted for an average of 50 percent of public assistance payments; in Alabama they constituted 75 percent to 80 percent.[40] In addition, the survey committee noted that "in Alabama available state funds have never been sufficient to obtain federal funds up to the maximum allowable under federal law."[41] The situation was becoming worse rather than better due to recent amendments in the state's welfare legislation. The 1935 act establishing the state department of welfare had required that local funds be used to match state and federal contributions to the categorical aid programs. Amendments to the public welfare law in 1951 had eliminated this requirement for local support, shifting total responsibility for nonfederal funding to the state. State appropriations in each succeeding year had been less than the combined local-state allocations prior to the amendments, thereby reducing the total amount available for welfare purposes in the state. A secondary result of the amendments was a diminished local interest in and control over welfare matters. Prior to the 1951 amendments the citizens' board appointed to supervise the county department of public welfare had met monthly and had involved itself in a broad range of questions related to its operation, including the need for greater local support to increase the level of benefits within the county. After the amendments, which also specified uniform payments throughout the state, the board held perfunctory meetings on a quarterly basis and provided no local leadership in examining local need.[42]

The survey committee found that the greatest need in the area of welfare was for a general assistance program to provide emergency aid to citizens in financial distress who did not fit into any of the four Social Security categories. In the absence of any state funding, the Coordinating Council of Social Forces in 1952 had persuaded the city and county to make appropriations to a twenty-five-thousand-dollar-a-year general assistance fund to be administered by the welfare department. However, Birmingham had eliminated its twelve-thousand-dollar annual appropriation as an economy measure in November 1954; and the committee discovered to its amazement that the department was not spending the remaining amount because both the board and the staff objected to the additional casework required.[43] The committee concluded that the need for a general assistance program was "an urgent one" and noted "the obvious failure of the program [of the department of public welfare] to meet social and economic need."[44]

The survey committee called particular attention to the facts that the black community had the greatest need for services, both public and private, but was receiving a disproportionately small share of these services. With 39.9 percent of its 1950 population of 326,036 black, Birmingham had the largest proportion of minority residents of any large city in the country.[45] The median family income for Blacks in 1949 was one-half the comparable figure for Whites; one-third of the white families in the city earned less than $2,500 per year, while three-quarters of the black families had incomes below this level.[46] Living conditions for Blacks were characterized by poor housing, inadequate recreational facilities, and a high incidence of disease. The maternal mortality rate was 4.7 per 10,000 live births for Whites and 15.5 for Blacks; infant mortality figures were 23.5 per 1,000 live births for Whites and 41.5 for Blacks.[47] The Children's Hospital refused Blacks, and the black Children's Home Hospital was ordered closed by the state health department in 1954 because of unsafe and unsanitary physical conditions. Supported by the Catholic Church, the Holy Family Hospital for Blacks opened that same year. It was the only hospital in the city where black physicians were permitted to treat their patients.[48] Even so, the committee found that "the shortage of beds for Negro children is particularly acute" and recommended the opening of Children's Hospital to Blacks, a step that was taken in 1961.[49] The committee also noted that the community provided no institution for black unwed mothers, though an illegitimacy rate ten to twelve times the white rate pointed to great need. Here, however, the study group recommended creation of a separate institution rather than desegregation of the Salvation Army Home for white girls, a facility supported by the Community Chest.[50]

Data from the recreation and group work areas showed the same type of unmet need in the black community. The city spent less per capita on recreation programs than six other major southern cities and allocated less acreage per person to this purpose.[51] With nearly 40 percent of the population, Blacks had access to only 16 percent of the city's park and recreation space; there was an "especially poignant" dearth of playground facilities for black children.[52] Analysis of facilities for Blacks operated by private agencies revealed a similar lack, while group work programs for youths were found to be most effective in areas with higher levels of income and "social advantages."[53]

In light of later developments during the War on Poverty, the committee's review of the Chest's Children's Aid Society is particularly interesting. It noted with approval that one of the agency's five caseworkers was black, as was one-fifth of its caseload. Furthermore, the society gave limited emergency relief to the families of children whom it was assisting, partially filling the void created by the absence of a general assistance program. Lacking among Chest agencies and particularly needed in the black community was a family counseling agency to identify multiproblem families and coordinate all available public and private services as a demonstration of what could be accomplished through such concerted action.[54] As a result of this recommendation, the Robert R. Meyer Foundation, which funded the original survey, provided a two-year grant to establish the Family Counseling Association, which from the beginning sought to include Blacks, women, and representatives of organized labor on its board and which paid its staff higher salaries than other Chest agencies in order to attract and retain highly qualified professionals.[55] Thus the private sector sought to approach the most severe needs in the community through a highly professional agency that would deliver services directly and also draw upon the array of local public and private agencies to provide a comprehensive, coordinated program.

Begun in 1956, the Family Counseling Association largely failed to achieve its objectives, judging both from its statistical reports and from the subjective evaluations of those who were instrumental in its founding.[56] Its staff of white caseworkers developed a recognized competence as counselors. However, the agency served a largely white middle-class clientele and failed to develop as a focal point for coordinated, comprehensive programs. Originally intended to reach the black community particularly, the agency received an anonymous grant in 1965 to hire a black staff member in order to increase the association's admittedly negligible impact in this very community.[57] The following year the association applied for a grant from the Office of Economic Opportunity to decentralize its services and become one of several Chest agencies that intended to reach clients through neighborhood service centers sponsored by the anti-poverty program.[58] An agency designed to coordinate others sought within a decade to have its own services coordinated by the new community action agency created to fight the local battle of the War on Poverty.

Because of consistent neglect of welfare services by the public sector, the Community Chest faced an unusually large range of needs. Commenting upon the attitude described above as privatism, the committee said, "Due to the failure of public authorities to accept responsibility in appropriate measure for services widely regarded as public responsibilities, the Jefferson County Chest is at present having to spend money for services which long ago have been assumed to be governmental responsibilities in most communities."[59] Specifically, it noted the substantial demands upon the Chest to subsidize indigent hospitalization and emergency relief.

In the face of these exceptional demands, the committee reported that the fund-raising goals set for the Chest were extremely low in relation to both community needs and amounts raised in other southern cities. In 1952, Birmingham had ranked seventh out of nine major southern cities in the per capita amount raised by the Chest; since 1947 the Jefferson County organization had experienced a markedly lower rate of increase in giving than other Chests across the country.[60] Reflecting the concern that goals were set at too easily attainable levels, the committee warned that "a desire for continued achievement of goal should not be permitted to keep campaign goals too low to permit necessary services to be made available."[61]

The survey committee had examined the services of individual Chest agencies and found that they tended not to focus resources in areas of greatest need; it examined the central Community Chest organization and found that it did not even seek to raise resources commensurate with community need. Finally, it examined the board of directors of the Chest and faulted it on grounds of nonrepresentation of significant community interests; here again the study raised a theme that was to be more fully elaborated during the War on Poverty.

The Chest board consistently described itself as a group of leading corporation executives, joined by a lesser number of professional men. It held to its earlier view that the community would respond most generously to need when that need was identified and verified by the leading businessmen in the area.[62] The survey committee confirmed the board's self-description but differed with Chest leaders as to the necessity or desirability of that particular composition. Pointing out that members often served numerous consecutive terms and that the board included no Blacks, one woman, and two county labor officials, the committee observed that "there has been a marked tendency for the Board and the officers to consist of pretty much the same group of people over long periods of time."[63]

Stating that the Chest was community-wide in scope, the committee argued that its board had a responsibility to be "more representative of the overall composition of the population of the county" and to "draw into responsible positions persons from groups with little training in leadership in community affairs."[64] Specifically, it recommended increased representation by local labor unions and, most importantly, representation of black organizations. The committee recognized the problems that would be created for the board if it suddenly included new members unfamiliar with the intricacies of decision making and unaccustomed to dealing with the leading citizens of the community on a person-to-person basis. In words that acquire particular significance in light of later events in Birmingham, the study group said, "However, the committee strongly believes that the future welfare of the Chest, and, indeed, of the entire community depends upon the continued broadening of citizen participation."[65] Responding to the demands of labor and the black community for larger roles in Chest policy-making and management constituted a persistent problem for the Chest board during the decade of the 1950s.

Labor, because of its organized strength at both local and national levels, had already extracted concessions from the board by 1950 and was to gain additional leverage by the end of the decade. James McKee, a student of labor union activity in industrialized communities, observes that organized labor throughout the country sought representation on Chest boards in the 1940s in order to demonstrate their unselfish concern for the community's welfare and thus "to legitimize their very real power in community decision making."[66] According to his analysis, "The primary function of the civic welfare program is not to meet any significant proportion of the community's social needs but to provide a legitimacy for its elite of status and power."[67] Organized labor's drive for representation on Community Chest boards began in 1942 when the national CIO established a separate national fund-raising campaign and urged local affiliates to support it rather than the local Chest.[68] In Birmingham Chest leaders reached a satisfactory arrangement with local labor officials, who did not withdraw their contributions from the drive.[69] The agreement apparently involved the promise of future labor representation on the board, as in 1945 the constitution was amended without discussion to admit to the advisory board representatives of the Jefferson County Trades Council of the AFL, the CIO, and the United Mine Workers of America.[70] The advisory board formally elected the Chest board often from its own membership; and two labor officials were soon so elected.[71]

Labor again asserted pressure for greater visibility in the local Chest in 1951 when the Birmingham Industrial Union Council requested that the Chest employ a full-time CIO labor representative to conduct educational programs and solicitations among unions. The board denied this request and argued that granting it would set the unfortunate precedent of having one staff person specifically representing a single group; both the staff and board, it said, should represent and serve all elements of the community.[72]

Four years later the Union Council renewed its request, pointing out that Birmingham was the only large city in the country without a full-time labor representative on the Chest staff. At this time local labor officials were accompanied by staff members of the national Community Chests and Councils of America, who supported the petition and who, by their presence, underlined the importance of labor's support to the Chest movement. In response to this delegation the board created the position of "staff assistant–labor" and agreed to hire a person nominated by labor.[73] With only two members on the board, organized labor in Birmingham clearly could not influence Chest policy in ways that were unacceptable to the business and professional leaders who dominated the organization. But by having representation on both the board and staff of the Chest, heretofore an agency of the city's elite, labor did gain the kind of recognition of its status and power that McKee indicates it was seeking.

Birmingham's black community also tried to increase its role in Chest operations during this period. Its organizational spokesman in this effort was the Negro Advisory Council of the Chest, a group utilized primarily as a means for increasing contributions from Blacks. Lacking the strength of organized labor at both the local and national levels, Blacks failed to gain the major concessions they sought.

The Negro Advisory Council wrote to the Chest president in 1944 to request membership on the board of directors and to offer various recommendations about the composition of the council and its involvement in Chest operations. In his reply the president pointedly ignored the specific topic of board representation and advised "of the impossibility of carrying out some suggestions which the Negro advisory council had made."[74] The council renewed its efforts in 1946 and requested both board membership and a black staff member. The Chest board denied the staff position, stating that the function of such a person was already being fulfilled by the several Blacks employed by Chest agencies. As for board membership, the council was told that nominations could be made at the next meeting of the Chest's advisory board—a body on which black agencies were represented.[75]

Following this advice, a black agency president in 1947 nominated a respected black dentist from the floor as a substitute for one of the Whites put forward by the nominating committee. The report of the nominating committee had never been challenged in the history of the Chest, and the proposed substitution threw the large public meeting into chaos over which persons in attendance were entitled to vote. The final tally recorded thirty-nine in favor of the committee's slate as presented, with fifteen supporting the black candidate.[76]

In an effort to overcome the resentment of Blacks following this meeting, which had been intensified by critical articles in Birmingham's black weekly newspaper, the Chest president and executive director met with the Negro Advisory Council in recognition of "the seriousness of the problem which faces organizations such as the Chest in its future relationship with Negro citizens."[77]

Future relationships could hardly have been improved by the next official action of the board after this episode. The Chest had been studying the recreational needs of Pratt City, before the 1910 consolidation an independent town, but now merely an identifiable neighborhood of about thirteen thousand people equally divided between the races. The board authorized construction of a community facility adjacent to a school that would be used as a regular school gymnasium with the agreement that it be accessible to the YMCA after school hours. This action, the board concluded, would represent a model for the efficient utilization of space and would meet the recreational needs of the entire white population of Pratt City. The official record shows no concern for the greater recreational needs of the neighborhood's black citizens.[78]

Blacks did not raise the question of board membership again until the 1956 meeting of the Chest's overall advisory board; the Negro Advisory Council itself was quietly disbanded in 1948 because it had been "comparatively inactive" for the past several years.[79] However, the most likely reason for its disbanding is not its inactivity but rather a shift in the focus of black leaders' efforts to influence social welfare and to respond to the particular needs of the black community. Chest minutes record that at the same meeting at which the executive director reported the dissolution of the Negro Advisory Council,

She also told of the planning of some leading Negro citizens and some of the industrialists in the community for some type of Negro organization, possibly the recently organized Urban League, which would have both white and Negro representation and furnish a medium for solving Negro problems. The latter organization would not necessarily have any connection with the Community Chest.[80]

The Effort to Establish an Urban League [81]

For six years the National Urban League had been trying to create a local base of support for a Birmingham affiliate of the organization. As early as 1943, the league's southern field director had corresponded with local leaders, exploring the possibilities of establishing a biracial committee to promote a Birmingham program. Several visits by that staff member failed to generate significant local interest in 1943, and the league abandoned its efforts. Again in both 1945 and 1946 the southern field director met with a select group of black and white citizens, but the local response continued to be negative. The executive director of the Community Chest assured him that funds would not be forthcoming from that source, as the Chest board would disapprove of the league's interracial governing board.[82]

Two Birmingham citizens, however, refused to abandon the effort to establish a local league: Henry M. Edmonds, the retired minister of the prestigious white Independent Presbyterian Church, and Robert Durr, president of the Chest's Negro Advisory Council and editor of the *Birmingham Weekly Review*. Through their efforts, an organizational meeting was held in March 1948 that was attended by twenty-five Blacks and fifteen Whites. The Whites present expressed deep misgivings about aspects of the league's work. In particular, they objected to the practice of hiring local league executive directors from a personnel list provided by the national office and expressed deep concern over the possibility of black and white staff members working together in league offices. To reassure themselves about the kind of support given the league by Whites in other cities, they requested a list of all local board members in the South. But despite these reservations, the Whites present agreed to launch a drive for nine thousand dollars to operate a local Urban League for one year, at the end of which the new agency could apply to the national organization for formal affiliation.[83] At this same meeting twelve white and twelve black citizens were elected to the board of the Birmingham league. The representatives of the elite white leadership, such as would be found on the Chest board, were conspicuously absent from this group; included were four church leaders, four representatives of social welfare agencies, a former school superintendent active in social welfare activities, one lawyer, one physician, and a female employee of a radio station who was active in Democratic Party politics. The black board members included the president of a local college as well as leading businessmen, professionals, and social welfare workers.[84] As there was no Urban League in Alabama, the national office regarded the Birmingham effort as one of its most important activities in the nation.[85] Later the head of the United Mine Workers in the Birmingham district joined the board, signifying the support of organized labor for the program. At no time did any prominent white leader of a major business or industry openly support the organizational effort, though two individuals interviewed indicate that executives of the city's largest bank supported it quietly, as did Mervyn H. Sterne—the stockbroker who had led the dramatically successful drive of the Community Chest in 1931 and who had subsequently emerged as one of the Chest's most influential board members.[86]

A public fund-raising drive was launched in June 1948 under the leadership of Henry M. Edmonds, the white minister, and W. A. Bell, president of black Miles College. A campaign brochure, "Why Birmingham Needs the Urban League Program," stated that the purpose of the organization was "to improve the social and economic condition of Negroes and to prevent misunderstandings arising out of racial conflict." As a means through which to solve community problems, the league would be concerned with employment, health, housing, recreation, juvenile delinquency, family welfare, and race relations generally. The pamphlet pointed out that the national organization was thirty-eight years old, that it included affiliates in fifty-seven cities, and that it was widely credited with relieving community problems and tensions through the educational process of persuasion and the cooperation of members of both races.[87]

The summer of 1948 provided an inhospitable climate for efforts to reduce racial tensions even though events emphasized the intensity of the problem. As lay black leaders of the Girls Service League and the Girl Scouts conducted a mid-June training program at a residential camp on the outskirts of the city, a hundred hooded Klansmen invaded and terrorized the site.[88] This incident was followed by a rash of police shootings in the city that resulted in the deaths of several Blacks. Sixty-six black civic organizations objected in a petition to excessive police actions; Eugene "Bull" Connor, police commissioner and announced gubernatorial candidate for the 1950 election, labeled the petition part of a Communist plot.[89]

In the midst of this heightening racial tension, the Urban League drive faltered for two additional reasons, according to National Urban League staff. First, the leadership of the drive conducted an ineffective canvass characterized by many expenses and few contributions. Second, Robert Durr, the former president of the Chest's Negro Advisory Council, had for some unexplained reason lost the confidence of many in the black community, which now largely withdrew its support for the league. Compounding this problem, Whites were openly promoting Durr as the first executive of the local agency.[90]

The June fund-raising drive proved to be a dismal failure, and the league's southern field director returned to the city to try to salvage the program. There was one sign of new support in the community: the Chest's Coordinating Council of Social Forces had voted to ask the Birmingham Urban League to affiliate with it. Furthermore, the Chest's executive director now expressed approval of the league, after receiving reports from the Chest directors in Atlanta, Louisville, and New Orleans that indicated no negative public reaction to support of the league in those cities.[91]

These advances could not compensate for a widening gulf that separated the black and white supporters of the league. A number of the black board members met separately, apparently to discuss the question of who should direct the league once it was established. Henry Edmonds met separately with a prestigious group of seven white business leaders to explore their willingness to finance the program; among them was Mervyn H. Sterne, the stockbroker mentioned above as a quiet supporter of the league. After this session Edmonds met with the black board members, "reporting that there was a tremendous amount of interest among the white persons in connection with an organization to ease some of the problems of race relations in the community." Edmonds also reported, however, that Sterne had "raised the question about this organization being connected with a national movement and cited his problems in dealing with national organizations. He suggested that it be a local organization, similar to the Urban League, but it should be called something like 'Suburban League.' " According to the field director's report, "It was the unanimous opinion of the Negroes assembled that they wanted no part of a strictly local organization."[92]

Edmonds agreed with his black colleagues as to the desirability of a local affiliate of the national organization. He promised to reconvene the prominent white leaders to secure from them funding for an Urban League and also to solve the national-local organizational issue by 1 January 1949.[93]

During December 1948 Edmonds convened several meetings of the group of seven businessmen previously consulted, now expanded to include the chief executives of four more local companies plus two prominent clubwomen. This elite group pledged nearly one-half of the nine thousand dollars needed to fund a local league for one year; at year's end the prospects of a Birmingham Urban League, guided by a biracial board and supported by leading white business and civic leaders, seemed bright indeed.[94]

Abruptly the course of events changed dramatically during 1949. Precisely what motivated stockbroker Sterne to act as he did cannot be determined, but two persons who knew him and the other white contributors claimed that these donors reacted unfavorably to a story in a national magazine about an Urban League in another city. Included in the article were pictures of Whites and Blacks meeting together socially at a benefit for this other league. Confirming the fears of local white supporters that had already been raised earlier, the article is cited as the immediate cause of the Whites' backing away from the idea of an Urban League.[95]

For whatever reason, Sterne himself now met with the black board members, bypassing Henry Edmonds and apparently acting as the spokesman for the business and civic leaders whose financial support was essential to the league. In his summary of what transpired, the southern field director reports that the stockbroker warned the black board members about membership

> in any subversive organization; such as the NAACP; and in the organization of a League branch that no controversial matters, such as housing, zoning (the Supreme Court declared the Birmingham Ordinance unconstitutional during November [1948]) or any other activities which would disturb the status quo in Birmingham should be part of the program of the Birmingham Urban League. Negro citizens, incensed, indicated that they would have nothing at all to do with any white group with such a point of view. . . .
>
> The attempt by the white group to set up the type of organization which they wanted caused a stalemate.[96]

During the summer of 1949 the executive director of the Chest had worked with the white group to identify a local Black, unidentified in the files, who would be acceptable to both races as the first executive of the Birmingham League. The potential leader's unexpected death in September 1949 merely emphasized the hopelessness of the entire situation to the field director. He now recommended that all activity in the city stop until after the 1950 gubernatorial election had been held. Then he suggested that Birmingham supporters of the league effort should explore a strictly local organization.[97] From 1950 to 1956 the new focal point of local efforts to ameliorate racial tensions was the Community Chest, and most especially its Coordinating Council of Social Forces.

The Interracial Division of the Coordinating Council of Social Forces

The Coordinating Council had been established in 1939 by a group of social welfare workers and civic leaders who were interested in assessing community needs and coordinating the programs of both public and private agencies in response to these needs. Having failed in its initial effort to gain membership in the Community Chest, the council met monthly on an informal basis until the fall of 1947.[98] At that time the University of Alabama agreed to pay one-half of the salary of a director and provide office space for the council if the remaining budget of the organization were paid jointly by the Chest, the Red Cross, the health department, and the department of public welfare. The Chest agreed to appropriate its share of the new agency's budget, regarding the council as a potentially useful planning unit and as a valuable liaison between Chest agencies and the university's proposed new school of social work.[99] After the director had been employed, the president of the council's board was appointed to the Chest board and later to its budget committee in order to link the two groups together at the policy-making level.

The council consisted of over one hundred affiliated agencies including labor, Chest agencies, civic and religious organizations, hospitals, the department of public welfare, the public library, the county board of education, and numerous private citizens. It was described by its president as an "organization of individuals, agencies, and organizations in Jefferson County banded together to inform its members of the social and health needs of the county; to interpret these needs to the community; to provide cooperative planning and promotion of social and health work throughout the county and to promote needed social legislation."[100]

Charles F. Zukoski, Jr., its energetic board president, hoped that the council would become "the great planning medium for the whole community."[101] The three-year community-wide study of health, welfare, and recreation agencies discussed above was regarded as a major step toward the fulfillment of this ambitious objective.

The Coordinating Council conducted its business through a group of lay committees assisted by staff members; its initial standing committees were concerned with health, welfare, recreation, adult education, family and child welfare, housing, and youth guidance. Later an additional committee was established to oversee the operation of the comprehensive survey.[102] The council, upon its funding by the Chest, began to review the operations of Chest agencies and recommended consolidation of services or elimination of entire programs when it found them to be unnecessary from the point of view of rational planning. It also studied all applications for Chest membership and made recommendations about them to the board.[103] The council participated in the budget hearings, though its suggestions for changes were often overridden by lay members who had strong personal attachments to various individual agencies on whose boards they had served.[104]

After the failure of the effort to establish an Urban League, the Chest's executive director and several leading board members felt that the Coordinating Council represented a means by which a strictly local biracial group could be established within the framework of the Community Chest. In August 1950 the entire board approved both additional funds for a full-time director of the council and the creation of an Interracial Division within the council as one of its permanent programs. This new division was recognized as an alternative to the Urban League; the funds that had been raised by the white community for the league were now made available to hire a black staff member to head the Interracial Division.

The board of the Community Chest recognized that it was undertaking a sensitive mission in moving into the area of race relations, and it wanted as director of the parent Coordinating Council a white executive who could communicate effectively with members of both races. Its choice was Roberta Morgan, who as head of the Red Cross Family Service and later the department of public welfare had established a unique record of working effectively with Blacks and Whites both as staff members and as clients.[105] She agreed to return to Birmingham for one year to establish the Interracial Division and remained for a decade.

The members of the Interracial Division were selected with extraordinary care to avoid the kind of bitterness that had surrounded the interracial contacts by members of the Urban League's board. Three prominent black citizens joined an equal number of Whites on the selection committee to choose the division's fifty lay members, also divided equally between the races. No White was appointed unless unanimously approved by the Blacks, and vice versa. Each trio did veto one name put forward by its counterpart. The chairman of the group was Episcopal bishop C. C. J. Carpenter; black attorney Arthur Shores was vice-chairman.[106]

Once the fifty members of the Interracial Division had been appointed, they were assigned to one of the six standing subcommittees established for each of the six principal concerns identified for the group: day care, hospital facilities, housing, police, recreation, and transportation. Additional subjects much discussed by the division were education and welfare, although neither of these had a subgroup established specifically for it.[107] Under Morgan's spirited and sensitive leadership, the division immediately took up two issues of greatest concern to Birmingham's Blacks: the fact that black physicians were not allowed to practice in any hospital except the black one or to belong to the local medical society and the absence of Blacks from the police department.[108]

The full fifty-member group met once a month, with subcommittee meetings similarly scheduled. Many, if not all, of the Interracial Division's sessions were held in the city's leading downtown white Episcopal church, the Church of the Advent, and chaired by Bishop Carpenter. All sessions were open to both the public and the press.[109] It is a measure of the city's racial climate that for several years, at least from 1951 through 1954, these gatherings could be held without overt opposition from any source in the community.

The Interracial Division was productive, and its reports began to have an influence on public officials. For example, it surveyed southern cities to determine how many were employing black policemen; it reported that eighty-two had already integrated their forces and that Birmingham was the only city above fifty thousand to have an all-white department. Atlanta, Memphis, and Nashville had hired black officers in 1948; no city that had desegregated its force had abandoned its plan. The division surveyed leading local citizens and found that virtually all endorsed the hiring of Blacks.[110] The *Birmingham News* lent its support to the campaign, sending a leading reporter to five southern cities to do in-depth studies of law enforcement.[111] The division distributed one thousand copies of its report, which advocated the hiring of black officers in the interest of both better law enforcement and better race relations.[112] The city responded favorably to the report, according to Morgan, by interviewing black candidates for the force; the problem now was that none was willing to be the first to desegregate a department regarded with fear and hostility by the black community.[113]

The major project of the Interracial Division and the primary concern of Morgan as director of the parent Coordinating Council was the holding of an "Educational Institute on Race Relations." Sponsored by the division, the institute was cosponsored by sixteen colleges and universities—public and private, black and white—in the state; an additional fifty-three local organizations listed their support in the official program. Included in this latter category were churches, civic organizations, labor unions, professional and educational associations, and Chest agencies. The institute was held in the spring of 1955 at Birmingham-Southern College and listed eight topics, each of which was addressed by an integrated panel: the role of the church in race relations; progress in Negro health; progress of Negroes in Alabama culture; progress of Negroes in business and industry; Negro police and law observance; Negro housing, public and private; Negroes in the political process; and progress in education and its effect upon race relations.[114]

The institute received favorable publicity in the major newspapers prior to the meeting.[115] Despite the presence of a handful of white pickets who were reportedly out-of-state agitators, the institute was held without incident, attended by a large integrated audience. It was judged by one of its leaders to be "an outstanding success from the point of view of the two races discussing community problems";[116] "for a brief moment, Birmingham achieved some measure of greatness."[117]

From the point of view of future efforts to improve race relations, the institute had unexpected and disastrous consequences. Certain Whites, sensitized by the potential implications for race relations of the 1954 Supreme Court decision, mounted an aggressive campaign against the Interracial Division. An unknown photographer attended one of the group's meetings, photographed Morgan sitting next to a black member, and distributed the photograph in the community amid charges that she was "collaborating with the niggers."[118] The White Citizens' Council and the Ku Klux Klan called upon the Community Chest to drop the Interracial Division or face the consequences of sharply reduced funding.[119] Several major employers predicted that the Council and Klan would be effective in carrying out their threat, as white supremacists were visiting plants in the areas.[120]

Chest minutes report that at the board meeting on 22 March 1956, "the Chair . . . stated that the greater part of the meeting had been reserved for a discussion of the attack made on the Coordinating Council and the Chest by leaders of White Citizens Councils, because of our aid to Negroes, and specifically the support of the Interracial Division of the Council."[121] There followed a lengthy discussion about the possibility of issuing a public statement clarifying the Chest's position on racial integration that would emphasize that "the Interracial Division had always made it clear to our Negro citizens serving on the Council that all work is within the pattern of segregation."[122] The majority of the board opposed such a statement and referred consideration of the future of the Interracial Division to a joint meeting of the executive committees of the Chest and the Red Cross.

The majority of those attending this joint meeting believed that the Interracial Division of the Coordinating Council should be eliminated and its fifty-member committee disbanded in the face of the concerted attack against the Chest by the White Citizens' Council and other white supremacists such as the Klan. At the same time, they were mindful of the disillusionment that such an action would cause in the black community, with an accompanying intensification of interracial tension. All present felt that some other sponsor should be sought for the committee and that it ought not to be eliminated until this alternative sponsor had been identified. Minutes of the meeting state:

At this juncture the president of the Coordinating Council presented an excellent statement proposing a plan for an inter-agency commission on community relations. This plan would include an approach to the city commission to form this inter-agency commission, whose work would be

Negro-white relationships. The commission would in substance replace the present Interracial Committee, but its work would be more narrowly concentrated on the area of concern for health, welfare, and recreation. The primary concern of the commission would be improvements of services and facilities for Negroes, but it would be organized with the clear understanding and agreement that it would not engage, directly or indirectly, in any activity toward desegregation. The commission would be financed by contributions made to it directly by citizens, institutions, corporations and other organizations interested in its work. The Inter-racial Division of the council would not discontinue its existence until the new commission was organized and began to function.[123]

There was a consensus that the interracial committee should be transferred to public auspices "with leading citizens urging the commission's creation." The only objection voiced to the proposal was that "the new commission should not include representatives of the Community Chest, its agencies, or the Red Cross, as that would defeat the present objective of elimination of a campaign hazard."[124]

The motion finally adopted called for the elimination of the Interracial Division with a concurrent effort to persuade the city commission to create a successor to it "representative of all groups in the community."[125] Significantly, the approach to the city was to be a concurrent action; the executive committees were not willing to make dissolution of the division dependent upon a guarantee of continued work in the area of race relations.

The delegation that called upon the city commission to seek its support for a new interracial committee later reported to the Chest board that the mayor would appoint such a group.[126] The Coordinating Council's former president and Morgan both state categorically that the mayor promised to make the appointments.[127] In fact he did not; the interracial committee was disbanded and its black director released. Noting that Atlanta had successfully resisted similar pressure from white supremacists to withdraw Chest support from its Urban League, the former president of the Coordinating Council commented on the tragedy of the city's losing its only interracial forum "when it was most needed" in the days preceding the events of 1963; for him at least, the demise of the Interracial Division was "a very sad day in the life of this community."[128]

Morgan privately wrote of the effect of the division's elimination, coupled with the local reaction to the Supreme Court decision:

we had elicited promises on the part of our public officials that Negro police officers would be engaged in the Birmingham Police Department. Instead there have been evasions, postponements and downright reversal of stated policy and commitments. The committee believes that much progress had earlier been made toward the admission of Negro physicians to the local County Medical Society and to practice in hospitals. In recent months, this progress came to a dead standstill.[129]

It is impossible to state with certainty the extent to which Birmingham's regression in race relations beginning in 1956 was due to the absence of the Chest's interracial program, in light of other nonlocal events that influenced local attitudes toward race questions: for example, the 1955 Supreme Court ruling implementing the 1954 school desegregation decision; the emergence of the civil rights movement in the South; the activities of white supremacist organizations; the increasingly defiant attitude of southern political leaders; and "the pattern of silent assent among those who would be moderate."[130] One thing is certain: Birmingham entered the era of the revolution in race relations lacking channels of communication between Blacks and Whites. On this point, "Some members of the [Interracial] Committee report that probably the greatest achievement of this period has been the improvement of communication within the Committee itself."[131] The city would pay dearly for this lack in the early 1960s, and its significance was quickly grasped by those from outside the South who analyzed Birmingham in 1963 and tried to understand why the events of that summer transpired.[132]

PART FOUR

1962–1975

8

Political and Social Modernization

The striking thing about Birmingham to an outsider is that it seems so advanced industrially and so retarded politically. It has seized the scientific revolution and rejected the social revolution of our time. Accordingly, it is engaged in a remarkable and hazardous experiment: it is trying to back full speed into the future.[1]

T HIS VIEW OF Birmingham, presented to readers of the *New York Times* by James Reston, could be dismissed by angry local leaders on the grounds that he was, after all, an outsider who had spent too little time in the city to assess accurately its true condition. His column and other accounts by the national media concerning the city during the early 1960s have been cited in later years as the source of an inaccurate negative "image" of Birmingham that often has been viewed as the city's greatest liability in its efforts to overcome the reputation gained during the racial demonstrations of 1963. But the generally critical evaluations of Birmingham by national commentators were not the only ones made during these years; a few local spokesmen for change reached basically the same conclusions. One young attorney reviewed the recent history of the city in 1964 and concluded that Birmingham had been a "city whose leadership passionately did not want to lead."[2]

Data from the period support the critics and indicate that Birmingham was maintaining previously established patterns of low revenues, low expenditures, and inadequate services, all earlier identified as indicators of a political culture of privatism. In addition, city officials were resistant to any modification in Birmingham's rigid patterns of racial segregation.

Based on its 1960 figures, the Census Bureau reported that Birmingham's per capita revenue of $64 for general operations was less than one-half the average of all cities in the 300,000–500,000 population class.[3] Of twelve southern cities in this category, Birmingham in both 1962 and 1967 ranked last in property tax receipts, eleventh in total general revenues, and last in general expenditures.[4] A 1963 report by the National Education Association on school systems serving between 50,000 and 100,000 students placed Birmingham thirty-eighth in a list of forty; the city spent $199 per pupil compared with an average for the forty of $348.[5]

As in the earlier time periods, part of Birmingham's poor performance in various areas of fiscal and service activity could be attributed to the relative poverty of the community; in both 1962 and 1967 the area ranked tenth of twelve southern metropolitan areas in its population class in per capita income.[6] The will of the people also was identified by an economist who conducted a fiscal analysis of the county for the decade 1957–1967; he wrote, "A general desire to limit the role of local government in effect also appears to have accounted for low per-capita revenues (and other forms of financial activity) of local government in the county."[7]

Indigent health care continued as a political issue during the early 1960s, with the central actors being the county commission, the city commission, University Hospital, the county's legislative delegation, the medical society, and the health care authority created upon recommendation of the 1954 citizens' survey. Basically, no progress had been made since that report, and the problem had intensified. With a modestly but steadily increasing population, public authorities in 1963 subsidized 107 beds for indigent patients, 7 more than had been provided in 1890. Because of increasing operating losses, University Hospital had actually been forced to convert beds previously allocated to the poor to private use. No local governmental funds were provided for outpatient or emergency services, and the hospital was incurring an annual deficit of $800,000. When the university was forced to charge nearly ten dollars per clinic visit, the hospital's out-patient facilities were effectively closed to the sick poor. Dr. Joseph F. Volker, head of the medical center, noting that the area spent only $2.41 per capita on indigent care compared with at least $3.14 in other southern cities, said, "Birmingham does less than any other city in the nation of comparable size in taking care of its indigent sick"; he called upon the city to accept its moral responsibility and to correct thirty years of neglect. The city commission responded by appropriating $200,000 to emergency-room operations. The president of the county commission called indigent health care "the most serious thing" facing local government; then he and his colleagues reduced the county's 1963–64 appropriation by $120,000.[8]

The health care authority, recognizing the need for a $7 million per year health care system having 450–550 beds instead of a $1 million system with 107 beds, proposed three alternative taxes in 1963 to generate new funding. In the absence of support from either city or county officials, the legislative delegation refused to bring the taxes before the full legislature for a vote in 1963. Disgusted at the lack of concern shown by public officials, the health care authority, which was established to create and administer a comprehensive indigent care program, was dissolved at its own request and its budget directed to the care of the poor. One of its members bitterly observed, "More people will die for lack of medical care, but you don't hear about people who just go off in a corner and quietly die."[9]

The public welfare services available to Birmingham continued to be the categorical assistance programs administered by the state department of public welfare through its Jefferson County office, supplemented by the food stamp program, which was also administered by the state department in conformance with U.S. Department of Agriculture regulations. In the case of the categorical programs, the state continued to provide insufficient funds to match available federal funds; all recipients of benefits were receiving payments below the poverty level throughout the decade.[10] The Aid to Dependent Children (ADC) program, which served over 80 percent black children by 1965, allocated only 35 percent of the minimal survival budget to each family.[11] An additional $12 million in state appropriations would have obtained $53 million in federal funds in 1970, permitting ADC benefits to increase to 100 percent of survival level; but the legislature continued to ignore pleas for greater state support. The state still had no general assistance program; the food stamp program at the end of the decade was reaching only 10 percent of the eligible families in Jefferson County, largely because of a cumbersome application process and the lack of information among potential clients.[12] Between 1957 and 1967 the city actually decreased its total expenditures in the welfare category from $31,000 to $12,000—from .19 percent of the city's general expenses to .04 percent.[13]

In the area of race relations, city officials pursued an uncompromising policy of racial segregation prior to the demonstrations of 1963. The public school system was not yet under court order, and no effort was made to comply with the 1954 decision. Though not required by law, the public library operated a segregated system and would not permit black clients to enter its main downtown facility.[14] When ordered to desegregate its park and recreation programs in 1962, the city chose instead to close its sixty-eight parks, thirty-eight playgrounds, six swimming pools, and four golf courses.[15]

While the first years of the decade witnessed a hardening of racial attitudes by the city commission, they also witnessed the first significant effort at local governmental reform in a half century. This reform movement, led exclusively by white business leaders and professionals, culminated at the same time that civil rights demonstrations, which were led exclusively by Blacks, made the city an international symbol of bigotry and police brutality. These two independent, internally generated movements were shortly reinforced by the externally generated antipoverty and citizen participation programs, which resulted in a combination of pressures for change significantly modifying the city's

long-standing patterns of behavior in politics, social relations, and social welfare services.

Change in the Form of Government, 1962–63

The drive to change the form of Birmingham's city government was initiated by the Birmingham Chamber of Commerce, although the organization's
leadership role was far less public than it had been in important decisions during the 1900–1917 period. In part the Chamber's desire for obscurity was undoubtedly due to the reluctance of its members to become openly embroiled
in an effort that was certain to become intensely controversial. In part it was
due to the fact that Birmingham's business and industrial leaders no longer
lived within the city itself but rather in the affluent suburbs that had developed
in the post-World War I period. Downtown merchants and realtors, in particular, viewed with great concern developments in the city that affected trade and
the value of their investments.

Chamber leaders had three principal objectives that prompted them to
seek significant governmental change. First, they were increasingly dismayed
by the inflammatory and inflexible actions of the commissioners, and especially Eugene "Bull" Connor, in race relations. Particularly offensive to the
business leaders was the Mother's Day 1961 beating of Freedom Riders at the
Trailways Bus Terminal; according to one historian of the period, police were
absent from the site "because of previous arrangements with the Klan, which
were made with the knowledge and approval of 'Bull' Connor himself."[16]
The city's two daily newspapers and the business community had supported
Connor in his successful primary just two weeks before, when he won a land-
slide victory over his three opponents in "the biggest sweep (61%) of his career"; but the attacks on the Freedom Riders so shocked white moderates that
they began to withdraw support from the police commissioner.[17] Most of-
fended of all, and destined to provide leadership to the reform effort, was
Sidney Smyer, president of Birmingham Realty Company, a Dixiecrat in 1948
and a former supporter of the White Citizens' Council, who was the incoming
president of the Chamber of Commerce in 1961. Smyer had been in Tokyo at
the International Rotary Convention when a picture of the beatings appeared
in the Japanese press. "As a result, Smyer found himself the object of cold
stares and perplexed questions from his Japanese hosts and the assembled international businessmen, who had suddenly lost interest in Birmingham's climate for investment."[18] Sidney Smyer became the first economic development
representative of the city to have his efforts thwarted by Birmingham's emerging negative international image. But Smyer had the advantage of being "the

most influential man in Birmingham, influential enough to lead it into a new age."[19] He spearheaded the chamber's effort to reform local government in 1962 and played an additional crucial role during the crisis of 1963. His role in the city's history is pivotal, and his motives were crystal clear. In an interview with Howell Raines, Smyer explained his role: "Well, you might say it was a dollar-and-cents thing. If we're going to have good business in Birmingham, we better change our way of living."[20] Changing the form of government was a convenient way of removing the specific occupants of office prior to the next regularly scheduled general election in 1965.

Second, chamber leaders sought a generally more conciliatory posture by public and private actors alike to the rising demands of black leaders. Third, they wanted to achieve the heretofore elusive goal of merging the suburban communities with the central city; they believed that a new arrangement of public offices was necessary to meet the outlying areas' demands for a more representative form of government.[21] Given the racial climate of the period, the chamber wanted to deemphasize the racial dimensions of its merger effort; but predictably the black-white issue became increasingly central to the movement.

Birmingham had attempted to induce the suburbs to join the city in 1959; this earlier unsuccessful effort justified the contention that the form of government would have to be changed before voluntary consolidation would occur. It also provided a hint as to how race would be injected into the 1962 campaign.

Opponents to the 1959 merger had based their defense of the status quo on the view that the Birmingham city government was "neither adequate nor capable of coping with the affairs of an enlarged metropolis."[22] One leader in a suburb having a mayor-council form of government with representatives elected by districts emphasized the ratios of elected leaders to population; in his community it was 1:1,800; in Birmingham, 1:135,000. Furthermore, he asserted that Birmingham was the only city above 250,000 to have as few as three commissioners; the small number of large cities retaining the commission form all had at least five officers. Consequently, he concluded that Birmingham was incapable of coping with municipal problems and failed to preserve rights of representation and control of affairs at the community level. From the suburbs' point of view, preservation of the benefits of the status quo, which included separate and segregated school systems, warranted a vote against merger.

Advocates of the merger claimed that "the future of Birmingham depends upon the results of this [1959] election and that a failure to annex the two cities involved [Homewood and Mountain Brook] would inevitably result in Birmingham being dominated by a minority group."[23] Both the press and chamber leaders threw their support behind consolidation in 1959, but the proposed reform was soundly defeated by residents of the two outlying communities.

As business leaders living outside the city but having vested interests within it, chamber leaders felt that they could not publicly initiate the effort to change the form of government in the early 1960s. Rather, they thought that the recommendation ought to come from a presumably objective, respected community organization that was not directly connected with the city's business interests. With this in mind, the president of the chamber approached the Birmingham Bar Association in February 1961 with the request that the association appoint a committee to study the present and future governmental needs of a "greater and better Birmingham."[24] At its annual meeting in December 1961, members of the association fought bitterly over whether or not to ask the city to reopen municipal recreational facilities on a desegregated basis in compliance with court orders but voted by a narrow margin to take no position on that issue. At the same meeting they did agree to undertake a study of local government, and the association's president appointed a fifteen-member committee to prepare a report.[25]

The Bar Association committee met biweekly for six months before releasing its recommendation in October 1961 for a strong mayor-council form. Its document carefully avoided any reference to the policies of the commissioners, confining its remarks to what it regarded as defects in the commission form itself. Specifically, it faulted the commission form for failing to provide a single responsible executive in whom could be centralized administrative authority and responsibility. Noting that legislation existed that would enable annexation of neighboring suburbs, the Bar Association recommended amendments that would allow annexed areas to retain initial local jurisdiction over matters pertaining to land use and that would allow municipalities to retain existing independent school systems.[26]

Having secured the desired recommendations for change from a respected professional organization, the chamber was confronted again by the problem that it was not an appropriate group to mount a public campaign to implement the Bar Association's report. At this juncture the Young Men's Business Club adopted the report as a project for its membership, which consisted of young business and professional men committed to staying in Birmingham and changing its politics and racial climate.[27] Two young attorneys assumed major responsibility for promoting the new governmental structure: Erskine Smith, then in his late twenties, and David Vann, who was in his mid-thirties. These two fashioned a reform movement unique in the city's history, and both went on to play significant roles in later reforms discussed below.

The immediate problem facing the Young Men's Business Club was how to secure the seven thousand signatures required on a petition for a referendum, which represented 10 percent of the registered voters in the city. At this point the organization benefited from the success of a previous reform effort. Fourteen members of the club had filed suit in federal court seeking reapportionment of the state legislature for the first time since the adoption of the 1901 constitution; the case had been argued before the United States Supreme Court by David Vann. The court had required the reapportionment of the legislature under a plan that allocated an additional ten positions to Jefferson County; 28 August 1962 was set as the date for the special election to choose candidates for a run-off in November. Shortly before the election, Vann had the idea of putting petitions that called for a referendum on the form of government at booths near polling places within the city on election day. This tactic would guarantee that those signing the petitions were in fact registered voters.[28]

Discussions with Chamber of Commerce officials and others sympathetic with the plan to change the form of government resulted in the decision to establish a blue-ribbon committee of twelve leaders, chosen from a list of twenty-five, to endorse and promote the petition-signing campaign. All twenty-five men on the list, deliberately chosen to represent the area's elite, refused to let their names be used in the campaign. Sidney Smyer, then in his term as president of the Chamber, suggested to Vann that "if we can't get 25 silk-stocking people, let's get 500 anybodies."[29] Accordingly, Vann, Smith, and others began efforts to establish a grass-roots movement supporting the drive. One week before the election, the Young Men's Business Club held a public meeting and successfully sought the names of five hundred people for publication in a newspaper advertisement endorsing the petitions for a referendum in November. At this meeting the supporters of the petition drive adopted the name Birmingham Citizens for Progress; William A. Jenkins, a retired painter from the Birmingham Housing Authority, also a member of the AFL-CIO Committee on Political Education, agreed to chair the citizens' group.[30] On election day, petition booths manned by volunteers from the Citizens for Progress were set up at thirty-five of the city's fifty-two polling places; to avoid later charges by the opposition of a manipulated black vote, no booths were placed at predominately black polls. Supporters of the mayor-council plan were themselves surprised when over eleven thousand registered voters signed petitions. November 6 was set as the date for the referendum.[31]

The prereferendum arguments centered around the questions of effective government and merger; proponents of the mayor-council form called the commission outmoded and saw change as "a vital necessity" in order to establish both executive leadership and a representative legislative branch. Furthermore, they claimed that its adoption "might very well be the change that would induce voluntary merger by adjoining communities. It is certain now that none will voluntarily merge under the present form of government."[32]

The commissioners regarded the drive primarily as a means of bringing racial integration to Birmingham; they claimed to have been invited to closed-door meetings at the Chamber of Commerce where businessmen and the editors of the two daily newspapers tried to persuade them to abandon their resistance to racial accommodation.[33]

Initially denying that segregation was an issue at all in the drive, the Citizens for Progress soon had to argue that, in fact, the mayor-council form had been designed by undoubted segregationists to maintain separation of the races. Reviewing the two enabling statutes under which the referendum would be held, the group argued that

> both of these statutes were carefully drawn by the legislative delegation with the segregation problem sharply in mind. Both were designed by such legislative leaders as Lt. Governor Albert Boutwell . . . to meet the specific problem. Both acts require that candidates for the council must be voted on by all voters in Birmingham—not just the voters in the area where the candidates live.
>   . . . nor is it fair to charge these proven public servants with providing forms of city government for Birmingham designed to elect a Negro to the city council.[34]

Ultimately the issues of race and merger became entangled in a clear demonstration of the way race dominated city politics, forcing racial moderates to engage the segregationists on the latter's own ground. Shortly before the election Vann and Smith both argued that, in fact, merger was a central issue and that only through consolidation could the rising political power of the black community be counteracted in the city. Thus Vann said two weeks before the elections:

> The real question is: do we want this area to become a community of white suburbs, clustered around another city controlled by a Negro block vote?
>   Unless we adopt the mayor-council form of government this is exactly what is going to happen. The white people are moving out, the Negroes are moving in.[35]

When one commissioner charged that as many as five thousand Blacks had signed the petitions, Smith restated the tactic of having no petitions from black neighborhoods and replied that "the only segregation issue in this campaign is to change Birmingham government to an efficient mayor-council form to attract the outlying white communities to join the City of Birmingham and prevent Birmingham from becoming predominantly Negro like Washington, D.C., and other large cities."[36]

Eugene "Bull" Connor, Commissioner of Public Safety, waged an intense but unsuccessful campaign to retain the commission form of government in 1962. Voters rejected Connor in the subsequent mayoral campaign and chose Albert Boutwell to lead the city in 1963. (*Birmingham Post-Herald*, Civil Rights Photographs, Birmingham Public Library)

The commission promised to raise the salaries of public employees 6 percent if retained in office; Connor insinuated that Vann had Communist connections as evidenced by his use of the word *troika* in reference to the commission; and one commissioner under five federal injunctions concerning segregation expressed doubt that any newly elected official would devote such energy to withstanding federal pressure to integrate.[37] At the end of the campaign, Connor played upon the fact that Vann had served as clerk to Supreme Court justice Hugo Black, a Birmingham native: "I came to the conclusion that Bobby Soxer Kennedy sent Freedom Riders to Birmingham and Black sent Vann to Birmingham to brainwash us."[38] Vann cited his family's century-old relationship with the Jefferson County area and reassured voters that "any government elected by the people of this city will reflect their determination to preserve our southern customs and traditions of segregation."[39]

Final election results gave a majority of 777 votes to the mayor-council form; the figures were 18,968 for the mayor-council form, 16,415 for the commission, and 999 for the council-manager form.[40] Analysts have concluded that the margin of victory for change was provided by the black community, which had approximately 12,500 registered voters in 1962.[41] Despite the rhetoric about maintaining segregation, black voters apparently perceived one true motive of the reform effort to be the removal of the commissioners in order to create a governmental climate more conducive to reduced racial tensions and more responsive to the needs and demands of the black community.[42] Furthermore, the reformers, specifically Vann, had established reputations as seekers of change in the community, especially in race relations.

The Young Men's Business Club was regarded as a "maverick" among business organizations because it supported positions that the traditional Chamber of Commerce either opposed or avoided as being too controversial.[43] Vann personally had participated in church-related efforts at reducing racial tensions that had involved him in meetings with Blacks at their churches.[44] Though Vann and Smith made no appeal to Blacks for support, in fact carefully avoided getting their signatures during the petition campaign, and made public statements seemingly supportive of the status quo in race relations, Blacks overwhelmingly supported the change while Whites divided their votes about equally.[45] The significant contributions made by both men in later years to programs that benefited Blacks justified this support.

The commissioners promptly began legal action challenging the validity of the referendum on the grounds that the enabling legislation conflicted with other laws protecting officeholders against removal before their terms of office had expired. The courts held that the referendum was legal, and elections to choose the mayor and council were set for the following March, with the new government to assume office on 15 April 1963. When Commissioner Connor announced that he would run for mayor, it was clear that race would play as central an issue in the upcoming campaign as it had in the one just completed.[46]

In retrospect, it is apparent that the 1962 change in the form of government marked a turning point in the history of Birmingham. For the first time the private concern of the traditional elite over the course of local politics and race relations had been translated into action. The Chamber of Commerce, as it had in previous "key" issues, played a crucial role in suggesting the need for governmental reform and in developing a circumspect strategy for bringing the issue before the community, that is, the use of the Bar Association. But the chamber could not, or would not, provide leadership in the ensuing campaign because most of its members lived outside the city and because many operated businesses that were vulnerable to withdrawal of support by local clients. Consequently, they both needed and used a new political type in local politics: young men, not part of the "establishment" but acceptable to it, who eagerly sought reform, were willing to play highly visible roles in bringing it about, and were able to direct campaigns requiring broad public participation. Organized labor was significantly involved in the reform movement after five years of silence on matters related to moderating race relations in the city.[47] The president of the Birmingham Labor Council was an early supporter of the petition drive, a labor activist served as chairman of the Birmingham Citizens for Progress, and six additional labor leaders were members of the group's steering committee.[48]

Furthermore, the voters of the city demonstrated a willingness to seek moderation in race relations and reject the intransigence of the commission. The petition drive had the characteristics of a citizens' movement with several hundred unnotable citizens joining the new reformers. And at least one-half of the white voters supported significant change. Birmingham in 1962 displayed a new coalition of traditional elite, new reformers, and a significant portion of the electorate.[49]

The Election of 1963

The legislation establishing the mayor-council form of government set a four-year term for the mayor and created a nine-member council elected at large in a nonpartisan election. Four men qualified as candidates for mayor, and seventy-six persons announced for the council. From the outset, greatest interest and press coverage were focused on the campaign for mayor.

The two most prominent candidates were Eugene "Bull" Connor, longtime commissioner and outspoken advocate of segregation by any means, and Albert Boutwell, two-term state senator, lieutenant governor for one term, and coauthor of the "freedom of choice" amendments to the Alabama constitution that were designed to preserve segregated schools without openly defying the 1954 school desegregation decision. Boutwell is described by one historian as "a Birmingham lawyer and [White Citizens'] Council stalwart."[50] Another commissioner, J. T. Waggoner, ran a token campaign based upon the danger of "the black plague" sweeping Birmingham, but his effort was overshadowed by Connor. The fourth candidate, Tom King, a young attorney who had previously run unsuccessfully for the commission as a racial moderate, now adopted a platform similar to Boutwell's in almost every respect. For purposes of this brief analysis of the 1963 election, his activities will not be considered except when they differed notably from the Boutwell position.[51]

Three major issues emerged during the 1963 campaign: the city's response to internal and external demands for desegregation, the condition of the city's economy, and the bad "image" of the city presented in the national media. All four candidates agreed that merger was a necessity for the continued development of the city, and all dealt with this possibility in terms of its implications for the economy of the city. There was no reference in the press to merger as a means of diluting the power of the black community.[52]

All of the candidates for mayor firmly endorsed segregation; the significant difference between Boutwell and Connor was the manner in which each proposed to resist pressures for desegregation. Connor promised a program of open defiance of the law to protect the city's schools from the "Washington blight"; he promised to keep the recreational facilities closed altogether if they could not be open on a legally segregated basis.[53] Boutwell promised resistance but not defiance. He planned to meet desegregation "within the framework of our established traditions and completely within the fabric of the enforcement of law and the maintenance of order. . . . Our resources lie not in disorder but in firm legal resistance."[54] Late in the campaign Boutwell even admitted the possibility that racial barriers ultimately might fall, but he ranked segregation as less important than lawful behavior: "I am determined that we are going to defend, I hope maintain, segregation, but we are not going to be a city of unrestrained and unhampered mockery of the law."[55] Boutwell also favored the partial resumption of the city's recreational program. He would lease or sell the municipal swimming pools to private groups but was willing to reopen golf courses, parks, and playgrounds on a reservation-without-fee basis that would hopefully maintain segregation.[56]

Connor refused to admit that the economy of the city was anything but healthy, and he regarded the low level of public services as a virtue because it enabled Birmingham to have the lowest per capita tax rate of any large city in the country. Boutwell claimed that there had been a 10 percent decline in the city's employment in recent years and that thousands of young people were leaving a city that failed to present them with good job opportunities. He promised to appoint an economic advisory council to promote business and industry within the city and to undertake a program of public improvements including expressways, airport expansion, school modernization, sewer construction, and development of the University of Alabama Medical Center. Once in office, Boutwell promised to invite the mayors of surrounding municipalities to meet with him to discuss merger, another way of strengthening the city's tax base and local economy. Under political leadership in Birmingham that they could trust and respect, he predicted, a voluntary merger with the city would now be a more attractive option for the suburbs.[57]

Boutwell also promised a full-time public relations staff to counteract the negative image acquired by the city under the incumbent commissioners. As though to emphasize the need for such a program, the *Saturday Evening Post* carried a story about Birmingham the week before the election that described it as "the largest city in the United States which adamantly refuses to call its white and Negro citizens together even to try to work out some solution to a problem which the federal government and enlightened public opinion plainly intend to force the city to solve. . . . This makes Birmingham a backward big city by any standards."[58]

In the midst of tornado-like winds and rain, 44,736 voters went to the polls on election day, the largest number ever to participate in a local election. Boutwell led with 39 percent of the votes (17,343), while Connor received 31 percent (13,780); Tom King, the young attorney, received about 26 percent (11,650); and Commissioner J. T. Waggoner, the remaining 4 percent (1,701). Black voters overwhelmingly supported the two reform candidates.[59]

Connor and Boutwell campaigned on the same set of issues in the runoff, but Boutwell received sharply increased support from the leading newspapers and spokesmen for the business community. John Williamson, representative of the Chamber of Commerce, delivered a strong endorsement of Boutwell, saying, "It is brutally clear that we need to do something about Birmingham's image." The only way to change this "false image" was by changing political leadership; the city's dilemma was "rapidly growing worse because some po-litical leaders here have, in effect, volunteered Birmingham for the next big bat-tle ground."[60] The *Post-Herald* was more specific; concerning Connor, it wrote, "Birmingham simply can't afford such leadership at city hall. It has held us back for too long and cost us far too much already . . . to present him to our neighbors and the world at large as Birmingham's first citizen or even as a rep-resentative citizen is unthinkable."[61] Connor replied by attacking the Chamber of Commerce, the newspapers, Communists, and wealthy leaders living in the suburbs who, he felt, were conspiring against him. His supporters circulated cartoons showing Blacks and Whites working side by side in city hall.[62]

The 51,278 ballots cast in the runoff gave Boutwell a victory by the margin of 29,630 to 21,648. As in the referendum, the black vote appeared to be the deciding factor in tipping the election in favor of the reformers. The white vote was about equally divided between the two candidates as illustrated by Connor's home box, where Boutwell led 696–620; Connor led by similar mar-gins in other boxes.[63] Representative black boxes indicated that a large percent-age of the registered black voters cast ballots and that they overwhelmingly supported Boutwell even though he had not overtly sought this support. In one such box with 1,475 registered voters, 1,276 voted for mayor. Boutwell received 1,273 of these votes, Connor only three. At another black box, the vote again was an equally lopsided 1,254–2. Boutwell's margin of victory was prac-tically the same as the total number of votes cast by Blacks.[64]

The city council race is far more difficult to analyze than the mayoral con-test because of the large number of candidates who qualified in the nonparti-san, at-large election. The seventy-six men and women who ran for office in-cluded at least ten attorneys, twenty-eight businessmen, four educators, seven engineers, three public employees, three medical professionals, two laborers, and one labor leader; two of the candidates were black.[65] The newspapers dutifully provided space for each candidate and covered various candidate forums held throughout the city; but the large number of candidates for council, along with the primacy of the mayor's race, resulted in little delineation of substantive issues. Merger, maintaining industrial development, segregated schools, improving medical care for the indigent, and various public works projects were advocated by several; candidates were divided over whether or not to reopen recreational facilities. What was clear from the election results was that voters rejected those candidates who took adamant stands against any accommodation in race relations. Those who advocated keeping recreational facilities closed and closing the schools before integrating them failed to gain sufficient support to enter the runoff. The sixteen Whites who joined the two black candidates in the runoff either avoided race issues altogether or took the comparatively moderate positions of reopening at least some of the recreational facilities and of maintaining school segregation only by lawful means. The two black candidates, Reverend J. L. Ware and attorney W. L. Williams, Jr., supported the hiring of black policemen.[66]

The eighteen candidates in the runoff represented a spread in the initial vote count in the initial election of 20,041 to 7,815; the two black candidates received 8,877 and 8,772 votes.[67] In the runoff the vote spread for the nine winners was 29,691 to 23,100; the two black candidates received 8,829 and 8,698 votes.[68] Thus one can infer that in both elections about 8,600–8,900 black voters went to the polls and that these voters account for Boutwell's margin of 7,982 over Connor. The new city council included two attorneys (Golden and Miglionico), two insurance agents (Drennen and Seibels), an optician (Overton), a retired power company executive (Wiggins), a neighborhood merchant (Woods), a sales representative of a national glass corporation (Hawkins), and the retired superintendent of Jefferson County schools (Bryan).[69]

Runoff candidates with the votes they received in the initial election are listed below. The figures in the right column are the number of votes received in the runoff by the nine winners.

John E. Bryan	20,041	29,691
M. E. Wiggins	19,172	29,164
Nina Miglionico	14,966	23,100
George Seibels, Jr.	14,426	27,400
Alan Drennen	13,168	25,797
John Golden	12,570	23,351
Tom Woods	11,210	24,249

Frank M. James ---------- 11,085
Harwell G. Davis --------- 10,353
Don Watts ------------- 10,261
Don Hawkins ----------- 9,248 ------------ 27,540
Marvin Prude ----------- 9,174
W. L. Williams, Jr. -------- 8,877
Warren Crow ----------- 8,800
J. L. Ware -------------- 8,772
Dan Gaylord ------------ 8,137
Bruce Thrasher ---------- 8,108
E. C. Overton ----------- 7,815 ------------ 23,379

On 2 April 1963 the voters of Birmingham completed a process of internally generated reform by electing to office a mayor and nine city councilors committed to gradual accommodations in race relations, as in recreation, and to resolving the school desegregation issue through the courts while keeping the schools open. The newly elected officials were scheduled to take office the following 15 April. Supporters of the change in the form of government and of the new mayor and councilors looked forward confidently to a new era in local government that would be characterized by moderation on the part of the officials as they tried to maintain segregation and by an ongoing readjustment in the relations between Blacks and Whites. One of the newly elected councilors had cited problems ranging "from closed communication lines to the most negative possible outside image of us."[70] The new officers promised to deal with this range of problems as soon as they had official responsibility.

Two unexpected series of events interfered with the immediate fulfillment of these plans. First, the commissioners refused to leave office, basing their action on an additional legal technicality and maintaining that they had the right to complete their full terms of office. The mayor and council immediately filed suit to clarify the issue, but a final decision was not forthcoming until the Alabama Supreme Court ruled in favor of the new officers on 23 May.[71] The mayor and council were formally inaugurated on the steps of city hall on 15 April; for the next six weeks two bodies, each claiming that it alone had legitimacy, tried to govern Birmingham. Boutwell moved into an empty office adjoining that of the commission president, and both men emphasized the absence of personal animosity. The mayor and council assured citizens that they would take no action that would compel municipal employees or the people to choose between the two governments. The two bodies acted on identical agendas so that no question could arise about the validity of city ordinances or decisions; the commission president and mayor both signed all city checks.[72]

Between 15 April and 24 May Birmingham had too many governors but no recognized government; it was a city government crippled in its ability to act, unable to provide either leadership or a focal point for the resolution of community conflict. At precisely this time, the city faced intense open conflict in its area of greatest sensitivity: race relations.[73]

The Racial Demonstrations of 1963

On 3 April 1963, the day after the runoff election, twenty black men and women changed the nature of race relations in Birmingham by initiating a public demonstration against the strict pattern of segregation that prevailed in both the public and private sectors of the city. They were arrested for trespassing after having ignored warnings by store managers not to seek luncheon service at the counters of five downtown stores. The day after their arrests, all were sentenced in recorder's court to the maximum penalty, 180 days in jail and one-hundred-dollar fines. Even as their cases were being tried, four more Blacks were arrested for sitting in at downtown drug-store lunch counters.[74] Thus, the civil rights movement came to focus on Birmingham, throwing the city into a summer of confusion, violence, bloodshed, negotiation, and change.

In part the Birmingham demonstrations reflected the regional civil rights movement that had begun in Montgomery, Alabama, in December 1955 when Rosa Parks refused to sit in the section of a bus designated for Blacks and was arrested.[75] Her arrest was the direct cause of a massive and successful bus boycott that produced Martin Luther King, Jr., as a significant national civil rights leader and the nonviolent demonstration as an effective strategy by which Blacks could initiate direct action to change historic patterns of segregation. The Montgomery protest also elicited external intervention in an area other than education, because the United States Supreme Court ruled in November 1956 that the segregation of buses was unconstitutional.[76]

Nonviolent direct action was successfully employed by civil rights advocates again when college students sat in at segregated lunch counters in Greensboro, North Carolina, in 1960, and "freedom riders" boarded interstate buses to protest segregation in this form of transportation in 1961. Violence erupted in Alabama in Anniston, Montgomery, and Birmingham during the "freedom rides," resulting in U.S. Attorney General Robert Kennedy's request to the Interstate Commerce Commission that interstate public transportation facilities be desegregated. Recognized as the largest segregated city in the South, Birmingham was a likely candidate for the strategy of peaceful protest against segregation.

Indeed, prior to the 1963 demonstrations, the railroad and bus terminals were the only desegregated facilities in the city. Park and recreation board community centers, closed at the beginning of 1962 in anticipation of a court order to desegregate, were briefly reopened on 1 January 1963 on a reservation basis, only to be reclosed two weeks later. Commissioner Connor was candid about why the doors and windows were again boarded shut: "The colored came and wanted permits and the federal government says you got to give them a permit, too."[77] Aside from areas controlled by public policy, Blacks were excluded from opportunities in the private sector as well; none of the department stores, for example, was willing to hire a Black as a sales clerk or even serve Blacks at lunch counters. And exclusion was accompanied by terrorism; between 1949 and 1960 there had been twenty-two reported bombings of black churches and homes. Though convictions had been obtained in several of these cases, no offender had served a sentence in jail. A black church and three houses had been damaged by dynamite blasts in December 1962; in March 1963 a black home had been wrecked, two people injured, and houses in a two-block area damaged by another blast.[78]

The Birmingham demonstrations were not a spontaneous outburst from the local community; rather, they involved the carefully coordinated efforts of local black leaders, especially Rev. Fred Shuttlesworth, and leaders of the Southern Christian Leadership Conference, headed by Martin Luther King, Jr. King and the other leaders had agreed to delay the demonstrations until after the runoff election in order to avoid influencing the elections but had launched the campaign immediately thereafter, exploiting the period of confusion certain to surround the transition from one regime to another.[79]

Beginning the day after the runoff, the demonstrations proceeded without interruption through the period of Boutwell's inauguration. In addition to the 20 Blacks arrested on 3 April and 4 arrested on 4 April, 10 were arrested on 5 April at drugstore lunch counters and 27 on 8 April after they had tried to march on city hall. The 8 April march climaxed a mass meeting attended by several hundred citizens; the singing, praying marchers were led by A. D. King, brother of Martin Luther King, Jr., down streets lined by hundreds of other Blacks. Twenty-one were arrested on 9 April.[80] On 11 April an injunction was issued by state court judge William A. Jenkins and served at the A. G. Gaston Motel, where Martin Luther King and his colleagues were staying; the order enjoined 8 leaders, the Southern Christian Leadership Conference, the Alabama Christian Movement for Human Rights, and 136 other individuals from picketing in the downtown area. King called the injunction an "unjust, undemocratic and unconstitutional misuse of the legal process"; and 20 were arrested that day for marching in defiance of the court order.[81] King himself was arrested on Good Friday, 12 April, along with more than 50 others, as he tried to lead a march through downtown Birmingham in violation of the injunction.[82] April 14, Easter Sunday, saw Blacks attempt to attend services at five leading white churches; they were admitted at two and turned away at three. That afternoon 30 marchers, led again by King's brother, were arrested as 1,500 watched.[83] Even as Albert Boutwell was delivering his inaugural address on Monday, lines of marchers were again mobilizing for a new demonstration in the downtown area. Before an integrated audience of about 400, including an estimated 100 Blacks, Boutwell pointedly declared that the city government of Birmingham would not submit to intimidation or interference.[84] By this time over 260 Blacks had been arrested during the twelve days of demonstrations; Martin Luther King, Jr., was in jail; and the authority of the new government had been challenged by the commissioners. In the absence of a recognized government with which to negotiate, the black leadership pressed their campaign, hoping to force federal intervention into the local situation.

Controversy will undoubtedly continue for many years, in Birmingham at least, over whether or not the demonstrations of 1963 were a necessary and/or wise strategy on the part of black leaders to achieve their goals of breaking down the barriers of segregation and establishing ongoing communication between leaders of both races. Clearly the communication problem was central to all others; no mechanism for dialogue had been established in the three years since Harrison Salisbury wrote of Birmingham in the *New York Times*: "Every channel of communication, every medium of mutual interest, every reasoned approach, every inch of middle ground has been fragmented, by the emotional dynamite of racism, reinforced by the whip, the razor, the gun, the bomb, the torch, the club, the knife, the mob, the police and many branches of the state's apparatus . . . Birmingham's whites and blacks share a community of fear."[85]

Moderate Whites admitted that the races remained separated but felt that the election of the new officials would lead to efforts at accommodation and negotiation. The Young Men's Business Club issued a plea to local black leaders to use their influence "in a sense of fairness to our newly elected officials" to give the mayor and council the opportunity to solve the race problems of the city. The club's statement argued that

> By voting to change their form of government, the citizens of Birmingham have expressed a new determination to master local problems through the orderly process of law.
>
> Their ability to do so will be hampered if the new government must face harassment from either non-resident Negroes or from non-resident officials.[86]

For the men who had initiated the change in the form of government and who saw the election of Albert Boutwell as the beginning of a new era in Birmingham, the timing of the demonstrations seemed perverse indeed. The white clergy of the city, largely silent until the demonstrations, sharply criticized civil disobedience in an open letter to local black leaders; calling such actions "unwise and untimely," they also called upon the city's Blacks to withdraw support from the demonstrations and "to unite locally in working peacefully for a better Birmingham."[87]

This particular attack by the leading churchmen of the city prompted King's famous "Letter from Birmingham Jail," in which he both argued the moral responsibility of the individual to violate a law perceived to be unjust and stated his rationale for starting the demonstrations the day after the runoff:

> We decided to schedule our direct-action program for the Easter season, realizing that except for Christmas, this is the main shopping period of the year. Knowing that a strong economic-withdrawal program would be the by-product of direct action, we felt that this would be the best time to bring pressure to bear on the merchants for the needed change.
>
> Then it occurred to us that Birmingham's mayoralty election was coming up in March, and we speedily decided to postpone action until after election day . . . so that the demonstrations could not be used to cloud the issues. Like many others, we waited to see Mr. Connor defeated, and to this end we endured postponement after postponement. Having aided in this community need, we felt our direct-action program could be delayed no longer.
>
> You may well ask: "Why direct action? Why sitins, marches and so forth? Isn't negotiation a better path?" *You are quite right in calling for negotiation. Indeed, this is the very purpose of direct action.* Nonviolent direct action seeks to create such a crisis and foster such a tension that a community which has constantly refused to negotiate is forced to confront the issue. It seeks so to dramatize the issue that it can no longer be ignored. . . . I have earnestly opposed violent tension, but there is a type of constructive, nonviolent tension which is necessary for growth. . . . *The purpose of our direct-action program is to create a situation so crisis-packed that it will inevitably open the door to negotiation.*[88] (emphasis mine)

The fundamental problem was that no public or private person or organization emerged with whom King or other black leaders could negotiate. Boutwell, criticizing "irresponsible and unthinking agitators," promised that the new government, when in authority, would give "immediate and determined attention to resolving the differences that face us"; but its authority was not legally established until late May.[89] Meanwhile marches, arrests, convictions, and efforts to worship in white churches continued for the remainder of April; King and ten other leaders were convicted of contempt of court and given maximum sentences of five days in jail and fifty dollar fines.[90]

Ignoring the advice of "nearly every Birmingham leader consulted" not to involve students younger than college age in the demonstrations, King made a strategic decision of fundamental importance. "Having submitted his prestige and his body to jail, and having hurled his innermost passions against the aloof respectability of white American clergymen, all without noticeable effect, King committed his cause to the witness of schoolchildren."[91] Demonstrations intensified in May with six hundred jailed on 2 May during demonstrations near the downtown shopping district. Many of those detained were children absent from school; four hundred youngsters were held in the juvenile court detention home, which had a normal capacity of ninety-six. The marches were carefully directed by black leaders, including King's brother, who led simultaneous rallies in black churches from which orderly groups of demonstrators surged forth. In an article buried in the middle sections of the newspaper, the *Post-Herald* reported: "The demonstrations obviously had been planned down to the finest detail. Not only did pickets move into the downtown area while marches were in progress, but several 'youth leaders' had walkie-talkies that they used to direct their followers."[92]

The following day, King himself addressed a crowd of two thousand, mainly school-age children, at Sixteenth Street Baptist Church, used as a staging ground for the marches. As demonstrators left the church chanting, "We're going to walk, walk, walk. Freedom-freedom-freedom." police dogs and fire hoses were used by authorities for the first time; 220 people were arrested. An Associated Press photograph printed around the world of a police dog burying its teeth in a boy's abdomen was "the sight that came to symbolize Birmingham."[93]

On 4 May 1963 the federal government intervened in the Birmingham situation when Burke Marshall, Attorney General Robert Kennedy's assistant, came to the city to try to play a mediating role. As Harry Holloway observes, King had "succeeded remarkably in nationalizing what began as a local racial conflict."[94] Local events had prompted the attorney general to warn that refusal to grant concessions to Blacks in Birmingham "makes increasing turmoil inevitable." For the record, he emphasized the need for local citizens to assume leadership: "At this moment, primary responsibility for peaceful solutions is with the leaders of business, labor, and the bar, as well as the city officials themselves."[95] In actuality, the diplomacy of Burke Marshall enabled black and white leaders to reach an accommodation at a time when the city appeared to be incapable of resolving the issues involved.

When Marshall arrived, "The first problem that had to be overcome, he found, was the utter lack of communication between the white and negro communities."[96] While massive marches continued, resulting in nearly a thousand new arrests, Marshall met separately with leaders of both sides, trying to clarify the specific demands of the Blacks and to solicit concessions from the Whites. King and his associates listed four demands that would have to be met before they would agree to halt the demonstrations: better employment opportunities for Blacks; desegregation of downtown lunch counters; release of all Blacks jailed as a result of the marches and pickets; and establishment of a biracial committee to plan for the gradual desegregation of the public schools.[97]

Marshall's principal contact in the white community was David Vann, who acted as an intermediary throughout the negotiations between Marshall and white business leaders.[98] The principal white leaders involved at some point in the negotiating process were Roper Dial of Sears and Roebuck; Billy Hamilton, executive secretary to Mayor Albert Boutwell; Edward Norton, chairman of the board of Royal Crown Cola; Sidney Smyer; Erskine Smith, attorney; David Vann; and Burke Marshall, representing the president. Principal black leaders were Arthur Shores, attorney; Ed Gardner, Harold Long, and Fred Shuttlesworth, ministers; A. G. Gaston and John Drew, businessmen; Lucius Pitts, president of Miles College; Andrew Young; and Martin Luther King, Jr. On 7 May Marshall met throughout most of the afternoon with a group of about seventy business and professional leaders, referred to in press reports as a "Senior Citizens Committee," in an effort to gain their support for settlement in the areas of black demands. At the close of this meeting a subcommittee of three local white leaders was designated by the larger group to make contact with "responsible local leaders" to try to develop job opportunities for Blacks and resolve the other demands.[99]

The afternoon of 7 May was crucial, not only because of Marshall's efforts but because events in the streets reflected a rapidly deteriorating situation. Speaking from Montgomery, Governor George Wallace said that he was "tired of lawlessness in Birmingham and whatever it takes will be done to break it up"; he dispatched 575 highway patrolmen to aid local law enforcement officials.[100]

Youthful demonstrators threatened to break the discipline that had characterized the marches theretofore, taunting police to "bring on the dogs. Bring on the water." King's brother used a police megaphone to plead with the crowd to disperse, saying, "You are not helping our cause." Forty were ar-

Martin Luther King, Jr., Fred Shuttlesworth, and Ralph David Abernathy announce the suspension of demonstrations for twenty-four hours on May 8, 1963, in recognition of good faith attempts to resolve Birmingham's racial problems. King and Shuttlesworth announced a formal agreement two days later. (*Birmingham News*, Civil Rights Photographs, Birmingham Public Library)

rested and eight injured before the crowd of about two thousand responded to the warnings of black leaders.[101]

Under Marshall's direction, black and white representatives met together for the first time in the office of Sidney Smyer, the former president of the Chamber of Commerce who had originally suggested the change in the form of government. In a later session that continued until four in the morning, "a blueprint for a settlement" was reached.[102] President Kennedy immediately praised local business leaders for the "substantial steps" that would "begin to meet the needs of the Negro community."[103] Formal announcement of the agreement was made early in the afternoon of 10 May by both King and Shuttlesworth; Smyer issued a statement later the same afternoon acknowledging the settlement.

Scarcely had the tentative settlement been reached before it appeared that it would be negated by new legal actions. Within hours of the agreement, King was convicted and jailed on month-old charges of violating the injunction against marching. His sentencing caused confusion among black leaders, some of whom interpreted the act as an abrogation of the settlement. But the quick release of King on bond resolved this latest obstacle to interracial peace.[104]

The final settlement as reported to the press provided for the desegregation of lunch counters, restrooms, fitting rooms, and drinking fountains at downtown department and variety stores during the next ninety days; upgrading job opportunities for Blacks, including the hiring of at least one sales clerk within sixty days; establishment of communications within the next two weeks between Blacks and the Senior Citizens Committee; and the recommendation that all persons arrested during the disturbances be released either on bond or into their own custodies.[105] Because no public officials were involved in the negotiations, the Whites could only make recommendations to proper authorities concerning jailed demonstrators; but King accepted the recommendation in the belief that "the political power structure always responds to the economic power structure."[106]

Public officials were quick to go on record as having had no involvement in the negotiations and as being bound in no way by the settlement. The commission president and Mayor Boutwell both issued public statements emphasizing their noninvolvement; the commission president labeled the white negotiators "a bunch of quisling, gutless traitors."[107] With the concurrence of Boutwell, the elected-but-not-yet-confirmed city council issued a statement to clarify its position in the proceedings:

> We view with deep concern the implications carried in recent published statements by non-resident agitators concerning civil disorders and demonstrations. The implication that this government has participated in so-called negotiations, or is bound by any action except its own, are [sic] false and untrue.
>
> To make clear, beyond all possible doubt, the council states categorically that at no time did it participate, in any manner, in any of the discussions, conferences or negotiations which reputedly took place between white and colored citizens, nor was it represented at such meetings.
>
> It is therefore plainly impossible to conceive of the council being party to any negotiations or alleged agreements as published by these non-resident agitators . . .
>
> The City Council will maintain segregation to the maximum extent of its powers, and it will insist upon the maintenance of law and order also. . . . There has been no surrender in the past. There will be none in the future.[108]

Sidney Smyer, who remained the spokesman for the white community, confirmed that no public official had been involved in any phase of the settlement. He said that the agreement "was made by private citizens. It involves only private action. It violates no law. It binds no one in the white community except the businesses involved." Furthermore, he reported that the Senior Citizens Committee had not at any time made suggestions to any elected officials, law enforcement agency, school board, or other public body as to how it should carry out its duties.[109] The statements issued after the settlement went to extraordinary lengths to absolve all public officials of playing any role in the resolution of conflict so severe that it not only disrupted the local community but became an international issue as well. Carrying to an extreme a long-standing pattern in the city's politics, public authority positively sought to depend upon private action to resolve what was probably the most critical issue in the history of Birmingham.

Private leaders were nearly as reluctant as public officials to be associated with the settlement. Smyer stated that it would not have been necessary to carry on negotiations by a committee of private citizens had the status of city government been established before the demonstrations:

> We were caught in an emergency and forced to act upon the frightening information from our law enforcement agencies that a situation had been created which could erupt in a holocaust should a spark be struck. What made the problem all the more difficult was the fact that there was no effective governmental agency to deal with the situation.[110]
> The committee was instructed to see what could be done between the private citizens of this community in the absence of any established city government, to re-establish peace in the community and to thus protect the lives which were then in danger.[111]

For nearly one week after the settlement, Smyer was the only White openly identified with the negotiations. When asked why the names of other committee members had not been released, he merely replied, "I would rather not say at this time."[112] He did indicate something of the history and purpose of the Senior Citizens Committee. It was, he said, a group established in August 1962 by the board of directors of the Chamber of Commerce.

After its creation the committee had no further affiliation with the chamber or any other organization. The committee's members included the heads of industries and businesses responsible for 80 percent of the employment in the Birmingham district. The committee was to work on various problems, including highways and expressways, city finance, indigent medical care, and especially school desegregation; but it had been relatively inactive during late 1962 and early 1963. According to Smyer, the whole committee was summoned into emergency session during the demonstrations and voted unanimously to appoint a subcommittee under his chairmanship to try to bring about an end to the demonstrations and to set up a more permanent committee to work with "responsible Negro leadership."[113] He reassured Whites that "the committee which I headed made no agreements inconsistent with plans which already were in the making before these disturbances or contrary to the best interests of the community." It never met with King; it dealt only with Birmingham leaders. Furthermore, the subcommittee that negotiated the settlement fully planned to continue to deal with the issues related to desegregation that had been dramatized during the month of street protests.[114]

Finally, the names of seventy-seven citizens invited to attend meetings of the Senior Citizens Committee were released; there was no indication of who had attended any meetings or of who had played leading roles. The names of the subcommittee on desegregation and of the three negotiators were not made public.[115]

It is apparent that the announced membership list of the committee was a face-saving device by which a large group of prominent Whites, primarily industrialists and professionals, could assume general responsibility for the agreement while obscuring the particular role of any individual other than Sidney Smyer, a large downtown landowner engaged in real estate. Furthermore, none of the downtown merchants whose establishments had been the focal points of the demonstrations was included in the membership; they were thus spared the possible white backlash that might have resulted had they voluntarily planned to desegregate. This omission of merchant representation makes less believable the assertion that the negotiating committee agreed only to actions that were planned to occur in any event; it seems inconceivable that prominent citizens could consider reordering social customs in Birmingham in the absence of those whose establishments would be the location of necessary change. Furthermore, the Senior Citizens Committee did not continue to play the role that it said it would in race relations. After the Alabama Supreme Court confirmed the authority of the mayor and council on 24 May, the city council, after praising the Senior Citizens Committee for its work, approved the formation of a Citizens' Committee on Community Affairs to deal with all issues confronting the city, especially race relations.[116]

Even as the settlement was being explained to the community, new violence erupted in the city; now the location was the black community, and the initiators seem definitely to have been white, though final proof has never been obtained. On the night of Saturday, 12 May, bombs exploded at the black-owned A. G. Gaston Motel, where King had stayed, and at the home of King's brother. Only hours before the blasts, twenty-five hundred Klansmen, many armed, had met around two flaming crosses on the city's outskirts. After the bombings, rioting broke out in a ten-block area of the black community; reporters described hand-to-hand fighting by Blacks and police, with Whites throwing rocks and bricks at Blacks, Blacks stoning firemen as they responded to alarms and breaking windows in dozens of police cruisers, and state troopers using gun butts to beat Blacks, including bystanders. The rioting stopped only after King's assistants and local black leaders appealed to the crowds to disperse; Rev. Ralph David Abernathy urged the classic nonviolent strategy: "We've got to love those who hate us; we cannot stoop as low as they stoop."[117] President Kennedy meanwhile sent federal troops into the state, and Burke Marshall returned in behalf of the attorney general. King also returned and reaffirmed his confidence in the settlement, saying, "I believe the white leaders negotiated in good faith, despite the violence of the bombers."[118] He later toured pool halls in the black community, collecting weapons, and arranged a mass meeting at which sports personalities Jackie Robinson and Floyd Patterson addressed a crowd of two thousand, urging restraint.[119] The rioting stopped, leaving to public officials further analysis of the local situation.

The still-incumbent commission president, Arthur J. Hanes, addressed a crowd of seven hundred, accusing the Kennedys, the Chamber of Commerce, and local newspapers of promoting the change in the form of government, encouraging the demonstrations, and undermining Birmingham by seeking integration; he criticized local law enforcement officials for "backing down" in the face of the crowds.[120]

A local state legislator called for an investigation of the Senior Citizens Committee by the legislative committee already established to investigate racial troubles in Birmingham. The city council unanimously asked President Kennedy to withdraw federal troops, attacking "disorders fomented and organized by nonresident racial agitators and under their malevolent cover colored schools were disrupted, children of all ages were encouraged to disobedience of the law and businesses were intimidated by unlawful acts."[121] Once confirmed in office, Boutwell said that he would refuse to meet with King "or anyone else who shows disrespect for local, state, or federal laws."[122] The United States Civil Rights Commission, meanwhile, opened an investigation into police conduct during the demonstrations and rioting that occurred after the motel bombing.[123]

Violence resumed in Birmingham in late August with the bombing of the home of the city's most notable black attorney, Arthur Shores.[124] This marked the beginning of a new wave of terror, apparently related to the desegregation of the public schools in the face of a federal court order. Boutwell deplored external intervention in local affairs but called for acceptance of the ruling in a lawful and orderly way and for responsible action in "this tragic hour."[125] He also appointed a twenty-three-member citizens committee on public schools, which included three Blacks; this group immediately committed itself to a policy of keeping the schools open and to support of the school board "as they carry out the difficult decisions they have been required to make under court orders."[126] Amid tight security measures, the city prepared to integrate two high schools and one elementary school under the court-approved plan that permitted black parents to apply for the transfer of their children to white schools. The governor ordered highway patrolmen, now renamed state troopers, into the city; included were many who had prevented the opening of Tuskegee High School several days earlier. Two black students registered without incident at Graymont School on the first day of classes, but the apparent success of the school plan was marred by the second bombing of Arthur Shores's home that evening. An ensuing riot left one dead and twenty injured; the board of education closed the three schools involved in the desegregation plan. When the city reopened the schools, state troopers followed desegregation orders of the governor and turned five black students away from all three locations. The school issue was quickly resolved when President Kennedy federalized the Alabama National Guard to ensure both the implementation of the plan and the safety of the five children.[127] Though Whites temporarily boycotted the three newly desegregated schools, the remainder of the school year passed without the extended agony that had characterized Little Rock six years previously.

A brief but more intense agony, however, followed quickly upon the relatively peaceful desegregation of the public schools. The twentieth bombing in eight years killed four black girls as they attended Sunday school at Sixteenth Street Baptist Church, which had served as the headquarters for the demonstrations of the previous spring. This bombing was "the greatest human tragedy that had befallen the movement."[128] Ten days later police investigated two explosions that were apparently part of a plan designed to result in "wholesale slaughter" in a black neighborhood by luring residents from their homes with a decoy bomb and then killing them with a shrapnel bomb.[129] President Kennedy again intervened in the local situation by dispatching two personal representatives to Birmingham on a fact-finding mission: former Army Secretary Kenneth Royall and former West Point football coach Earl "Red" Blaik. He also met at the White House with separate delegations of black and white leaders from the city.[130]

In the face of ongoing tensions and the long series of unsolved bombings, black leaders presented three demands from the White House to white leaders:

a public declaration by the mayor for law and order; establishing a channel of communication between the races; and the hiring of black policemen.[131] The last two points had been objectives of the Interracial Division a decade earlier. The Senior Citizens Committee had promised to continue their discussions with black leaders but had not; the new mayor and council had promised to appoint a committee to deal with race relations but had not done so yet. Issues long avoided came to the fore again in the aftermath of the tragic events of September.

The Young Men's Business Club immediately endorsed the call for black policemen, pointing out that Birmingham remained the only large city in the South with an all white force.[132] More significantly, Martin Luther King, speaking from Richmond, promised new demonstrations in Birmingham unless there was an immediate start of good-faith negotiations between political leaders and black leaders and unless the city hired black policemen. Boutwell refused to comment on King's latest demands, but Councillor Overton reflected the sentiment of that group when he labeled the message "an outrage."[133] Nevertheless, within three days Boutwell announced the appointment of a twenty-five-member Group Relations Committee that included nine Blacks; the bishop of the Episcopal diocese of Alabama, C. C. J. Carpenter, was designated chairman.[134] The appointment of a race relations committee by public authorities occurred over four months after the new administration had promised to create it. At its first meeting in early October, the bishop charged the Group Relations Committee with the "instant goals of improving racial communications and understanding."[135]

Significant support was expressed by the local black community for the demands presented from Richmond by King. The Jefferson County Progressive Democratic Council presented a ten-point program for action to city officials, including the hiring of black policemen, appointment of Blacks to the city's independent boards and agencies, a nondiscriminatory city employment program, the reopening of parks, and removal of segregation signs from municipal buildings.[136] Later 120 black leaders publicly endorsed the leadership of King, counteracting an earlier statement by 2 leaders urging him to stay away from the city. They called for the hiring of black police, saying "the morale of Birmingham's Negro citizens is at least as important as the morale of its police force."[137] Ninety white citizens signed an advertisement calling for black policemen; their petition was endorsed in a second advertisement sponsored by 44 major employers.[138] The Group Relations Committee called upon Boutwell to issue a statement immediately that the city would hire black law officers, while even the council authorized a study by its public safety committee of the possibility of employing Blacks.[139]

The racial tension finally eased in late October, when King abandoned his demand that Blacks be hired on the force within two weeks unless marches were to resume. On the same day that the council flatly rejected this demand, the Reverend Fred Shuttlesworth said that "we must admit that in our zeal to obtain immediate protection for Negroes of our community we have not done the necessary groundwork to bring forward a sufficient number of Negro applicants up to now."[140]

With the lessening of pressure by King, the pace of change in race relations in the public sector slowed. The council committee on public safety did not report on the hiring of black policemen until February 1964, when it presented a favorable review of the experience of over ninety southern cities with desegregated police departments.[141] Another two years were to pass before the first Black became an officer on the force. And not until December 1964 did the council appoint the first Black to an independent board or agency.[142]

In assessing the significance of the demonstrations and other activities in the area of race in Birmingham in 1963, there is no real need to try to explain why Blacks demonstrated or who provided leadership. Unlike the riots later in the decade in northern cities that have stimulated a considerable literature on violence, events in Birmingham are easily explained.

Blacks in Birmingham in 1963 demonstrated for basic civil rights denied them under a repressive political regime and social structure widely recognized as the most segregated in urban America. The local leadership in the 1963 civil rights activities was provided primarily by black ministers. Almost every group of demonstrators arrested for picketing downtown stores included at least one prominent clergyman, and black churches served as the staging ground for the mass demonstrations. The marches and picketings were not only the reflection of long-standing discrimination in Birmingham; they were also part of the regional civil rights movement that had begun in Montgomery eight years previously. Primary leadership in the 1963 activities had come from Martin Luther King, Jr., who drew upon the resources of his Southern Christian Leadership Conference, which included local black ministers in its membership. King's presence in Birmingham was a significant external intervention into the affairs of the city, as were the later mediating efforts of representatives of the Kennedy administration, and especially Burke Marshall; these latter federal interventions at least temporarily ruptured the previously impenetrable barrier to communication between the races.

The greatest immediate impact of the Birmingham events was in Washington, not Birmingham; the local changes resulting from the demonstrations were modest in quantity although of fundamental importance in marking the first modifications in the city's rigid system of segregation. Birmingham is credited, however, with having greatly influenced the thinking and actions of President Kennedy, prompting him to propose the broadest civil rights legislation ever sent to Congress and to identify the presidency more closely than it ever had been before with the objectives of the civil rights movement.[143] Events in Birmingham "initiated a political chain reaction that ultimately produced the Civil Rights Act of 1964."[144]

During the 1960 campaign and the first two years of his administration, Kennedy indicated a preference for executive action rather than civil rights legislation; in June 1963 he proposed legislation encompassing schools, places of public accommodation, and employment. That same month he spoke to the nation: "Are we to say to the world—and much more importantly, to each other—that this is the land of the free, except for the Negroes; that we have no second-class citizens, except Negroes; that we have no class or caste system, no ghettos, no master race, except with respect to Negroes? . . . We face, therefore, a moral crisis as a country and a people."[145]

Blacks in Birmingham gained more from the enforcement of the Civil Rights Act of 1964 than they did as a direct consequence of the demonstrations of 1963, but commentaries on the Kennedy-Johnson years point to these demonstrations, and the white responses to them, as major factors contributing to that legislation. In a way that its traditional leadership never sought, Birmingham profoundly influenced the course of national events, even as its own life was influenced by external factors.

The Return to Normalcy in Politics

With the diminishing of civil rights activities and violence, the political agenda of Birmingham again included the familiar topics of fiscal need, indigent health care, and merger.

Early in 1964 the council approved by a five-to-four vote a 1 percent payroll tax levied on all persons employed within the city, through which they expected to generate $5 million in new funds.[146] A predictably negative response by the business leaders within the city led to the repeal of this tax within one month and the substitution of a one-cent sales tax.[147] By the end of the decade, however, a highly controversial occupational tax was again imposed by a divided council upon recommendation of the mayor, George Seibels, Jr.; furthermore, voters approved a $50 million bond issue in 1967, enabling the largest investment in public improvements in the city's history.[148]

Controversy continued to surround the question of medical care for the indigent and how to finance it. The county commission, objecting to the increasing costs of care provided by University Hospital, finally built Cooper

Green Hospital, a three-hundred-bed charity facility; the commissioners ignored the advice of health professionals that such hospitals were a less effective way of providing care to the poor than supporting a comparable number of beds in general hospitals. The new unit increased the number of beds available to indigents only slightly, due to the reduction of beds in University Hospital; and the area's health care program for the poor remained among the worst in the nation.

A primary argument in behalf of the change in the form of government had been that a new political regime would be an inducement to suburban communities to join the city. The Birmingham Junior Chamber of Commerce secured an adequate number of signatures on merger petitions in six suburbs in May 1964 to have merger elections set for the following August. An additional inducement was offered to the outlying communities when the Birmingham Board of Education agreed to allow all existing school systems to remain if consolidation should occur; the legality of this arrangement was affirmed by the state attorney general in an advisory opinion requested by one of the suburbs.[149]

For each of the suburbs the city developed "contracts" that specified conditions to be met by Birmingham, such as increased services, retention of employees, and noninterference with schools. The press and major civic associations promoted consolidation.[150]

Voters in Fairfield, Midfield, Irondale, and Tarrant City voted against joining Birmingham by decisive three-to-one margins; they rejected consolidation by a 3,177–2,923 vote in the fifth and wealthiest, Mountain Brook. Merger carried by six votes in Homewood (2,423–2,417), but this particular vote was later ruled invalid by the Alabama Supreme Court because of failure to provide adequate legal notice in the press.[151] Merger thereafter emerged as a regular issue in politics, with two particularly intensive campaigns run by the Chamber of Commerce and David Vann in 1970–71. Nevertheless, neither resulted in success for the reformers.

In the area of race relations, the city made no significant progress in its program of fostering communication between the races. When the mayor and council had clear authority for the first time in late May 1963, they promised the immediate appointment of a citizens committee on community affairs that would include a subcommittee on group relations to deal specifically with race issues.

In mid-June the mayor's executive secretary reported that no progress had been made on this subcommittee; in late June the mayor announced that he would soon announce a "completely representative" committee. Finally, in mid-July Boutwell announced a 212-member committee, with subcommittees for economic research and development, finance and revenues, municipal expansion, group relations, public relations, public schools, adult reeducation and job training, public improvements, and youth programs. Of the 212 members, 95 lived outside the city limits; 185 were white and 27 black. The Whites included leaders from industry, commerce, law, education, social welfare, and the clergy. The Blacks included lawyers, ministers, one physician, two dentists, businessmen, public school personnel, and the president of Miles College; at least three of the Blacks had been leaders of the demonstrations. The chairman of the entire committee was the president-elect of the Chamber of Commerce, Frank Newton, a telephone company vice-president. The mayor also appointed a nine-member steering committee, including David Vann, to coordinate the activities of the subcommittees. At his first meeting with the entire committee, Boutwell talked of the problems confronting the city; he said, "The first step in the solution of those problems is to admit they exist, and here among our own people, and with our own talents, seek for their solution."[152]

The Community Affairs Committee appeared to be an ideal instrument created at an opportune time to deal with serious social, economic, and governmental problems facing Birmingham. Its membership included not only the traditional elite of business and the professions but also significant representation from the black community, including several of its most aggressive spokesmen in the area of civil rights. For the first time, public authorities seemed to have endorsed the need for effective biracial communication. New officials at the start of a new administration were in a position to make breaks with past behavior as a way of fulfilling the promises made and implied during the campaign for the change in the form of government. But once again a unique opportunity was allowed to pass without advantage being taken of its possibilities.

As noted above, the Group Relations subcommittee of the larger body was not named by Boutwell until 1 October 1963, at a time when the city was again in the midst of heightened racial tension. The first meeting of the nine-member steering committee with subcommittee chairmen was not held until late November. The mayor himself noted in February 1964 that the committee had not been as active as he had planned, since it had produced only two recommendations for action since being formed: enactment of the sales tax and the hiring of black policemen. When the steering committee recommended that the mayor and council meet with business leaders concerning their hiring and employment practices, Boutwell rejected the suggestion by saying that the authority of the city did not include dealing with private groups that excluded Blacks. Boutwell's narrow definition of what actions public officials might take in race relations prompted Vann to break with Boutwell and charge him with failure even to call most of the subcommittees together.[153]

At the end of April, Boutwell was further criticized by one white member of the Group Relations subcommittee, Rabbi Milton L. Grafman, who observed that the mayor had consistently refused to issue a recommended statement specifically inviting Blacks to apply to the police department. "Every time we have made a report," he said, "we felt like we had our knuckles rapped."[154] Miles College president Lucius H. Pitts grimly commented that further racial demonstrations "are waiting on the outskirts of our town"; apparently he was referring to dissatisfaction among his students, who had been active in the original marches.[155]

Disillusioned by the mayor's inaction, the Group Relations subcommittee asked in vain for a committee of the city council to serve as a liaison between the entire Community Affairs Committee and city government, stating that otherwise the committee was wasting its time.[156]

Reflecting the growing resentment of the black members of the group, one prominent lawyer, Orzell Billingsley, resigned from the subcommittee on adult reeducation, which had not met since being appointed seven months previously. He explained his action: "It seems to be clear and obvious that the Subcommittee on Adult Re-education and Job Training is not going to function, and if it does, then it is likely to try to work within the framework of civic patterns, painful customs, and stagnant ideas which are out of step with the needs or our community and the demands of the new standards of American citizenship."[157]

By the end of 1964 the Community Affairs Committee had passed from the scene as a topic of news and as a potential instrument of change in the several areas in which it had been assigned responsibility. Its chairman had resigned at the end of April in order to take a two-month trip to Europe; eight months later the committee remained leaderless and its subcommittees inactive. Furthermore, Birmingham still had no black policemen and had no plan to hire any.[158] Far from providing active leadership in the resolution of complex issues, Birmingham's city officials adopted anew an attitude of limited government involvement coupled with heavy dependence on the private sector, especially the business community.

Operation New Birmingham

This relationship between public authority and private action was vividly illustrated in April 1969, after twenty-one black leaders sent a telegram to city officials listing areas where they felt the city had to take action to forestall new unrest. The telegram was drafted by the dean of Miles College, Richard Arrington, Jr., who was later to become a two-term city councillor before being elected mayor in 1979.[159] Listed among their concerns were an investigation of police brutality, appointment of black lawyers to city courts and to the city attorney's office, an upgrading of public works and welfare services in black communities, increased employment of Blacks in local jobs, formation of a citizen review board for police affairs, enlargement of the police-community relations division, immediate employment of additional black policemen, racial integration of police and sheriff department squad cars, and human relations training for police and sheriff's department personnel.[160] Unlike the 1963 demands for desegregation in private enterprises, all of the 1969 demands, except increasing job opportunities generally, required public action; the principal concern was clearly in the area of law enforcement.

Though the concerns of the black leaders were directed to city officials, the response to the telegram came from a businessmen's organization, Operation New Birmingham (ONB). The head of this organization, S. Vincent Townsend, invited twenty-seven community leaders to serve on a new community relations committee. Townsend was "officially assistant to the publisher of the *News* but unofficially the most powerful political figure in the city."[161] The committee's membership consisted of nine public officials, both elected and appointed; nine white leaders; and nine black leaders. Appointed as cochairmen were Lucius H. Pitts, president of Miles College, and Cecil Bauer, president of the regional telephone company; included as members were the mayor, the police chief, and two city council members.[162] The major community and governmental issue of the decade had thus been privatized by a businessmen's organization that took the initiative in race relations and invited public officials to join with them in the effort. Playing such a dominant role was not new for Operation New Birmingham. Charles H. Levine observes that "over the decade from 1964 to 1974, there emerged a pattern of ONB influence so pervasive that at times the organization's leadership supplanted the centrality of the mayor and city council in the formulation of public policy and in the selection of appointees to important boards and commissions."[163]

From the beginning, the new Community Affairs Committee (CAC) of Operation New Birmingham insisted that it was, in fact, "a private biracial citizens panel organized to discuss community problems and work to solve them."[164] Its Monday morning breakfast meetings, begun in 1969 and continued without interruption to the present, have consistently been closed to the press on the grounds that it is only a group of concerned citizens gathering to study the problems of the community and to involve the entire citizenry in their resolution. The history and functioning of Operation New Birmingham, however, indicate that it is far more than just another group of concerned private citizens.

Operation New Birmingham is the lineal descendent of the Birmingham Downtown Improvement Association, formed in 1957 from "the dual motive of profit and community pride" by Clarence B. Hanson, Jr., publisher of the *Birmingham News*; Isadore Pizitz and Harold Blach, heads of two major retail stores; and William P. Engel, a realtor specializing in central-business-district property.[165] Its initial membership was confined to those having downtown business interests, men who saw the city's primary need to be the development of a master plan for the renewal of the core city. According to one banker, this business district was experiencing "a private depression," reflected in sharply declining office occupancy rates and declining property values, as retail and service activities decentralized throughout the metropolitan area.[166] The association's first project was to raise $20,000 to retain a consultant to prepare a development plan for the central business district that also included expressways, a new airport, and rapid transit; no consideration was given to either housing or neighborhood revitalization.[167]

Once the master plan was completed in 1961, the Downtown Improvement Association turned to its implementation, persuading sixty architects to donate five thousand hours to redesign the central business district based upon the consultant's report. The association provided the architects with a budget to hire a coordinator and purchase supplies with the understanding that their renderings would be turned over to the property holders involved; the project was christened Operation New Birmingham. Begun in early 1963, the architects' work was completed in mid-1965. Called a "Design for Progress," their plan ambitiously projected $30 million of public expenditures, coupled with $45 million from private sources, to refurbish the city's main thoroughfare and build parking decks, an exhibition hall, a theater, a concert hall, and a trademart.[168]

With the unveiling of the "Design for Progress," ONB entered a new phase in its development. The chairmanship of the organization was now assumed by S. Vincent Townsend, vice president of the *Birmingham News*, a man of immense powers of persuasion who quickly transformed the organization into the instrument of his personal crusade to overcome the "negative image" acquired by the city during the turmoil of 1963. By fall he had established a $160,000 "action fund . . . to ensure brick and mortar improvements to this great city and county"; the city and county governments appropriated $50,000 each to the enterprise, while two hundred private businesses provided the remainder. ONB itself was expanded into a 250-member "brain force and power force" composed of business, labor, government, and black community leadership.[169] To aid the membership, it hired two full-time attorneys to act as liaison between the city, the county, the state legislature, and federal officials relative to the use of federal funds.[170] In 1966 ONB subsumed the parent Birmingham Downtown Improvement Association and broadened its scope to include water, sewer, and road development throughout the county, in addition to its ongoing interest in the central business district.[171] The organization hired a national public relations firm to tell the "Birmingham story" to the nation through "Operation Sell Birmingham." Prizes were awarded to essayists who could tell in less than two hundred words why Birmingham was "A number one-derful" in a campaign "designed to make Birminghamians dwell on the positive attributes of their great city . . . [and] stop comparing itself to other cities."[172] When ONB hired a full-time Washington consultant to serve as the legislative representative of the city and county, its staff seemed equal to the task that its leaders modestly claimed for it: to be "the voice of Birmingham."[173] That voice spoke frequently through the pages of the *Birmingham News*, especially the weekly column of its energetic vice-president.

Prior to the creation of the Community Affairs Committee, ONB had become much more than a private citizens' group. With the bulk of its budget provided by public authorities, it became an extension of local government that performed public relations and intergovernmental relations functions for both city and county. The original focus on downtown redevelopment had given way to an area-wide interest in public works and services, illustrated by its appointment of a committee to examine the consolidation of municipal services in the county. Its offices in Birmingham's city hall were a physical statement of the special relationship that existed between this "private" organization and public authority. This special relationship was emphasized again when a committee of ONB was designated as the official citizen participation advisory committee to Birmingham's Workable Program submitted to the Department of Housing and Urban Development as a condition of receiving further federal funds.[174] When this arrangement was criticized on the ground that most of the committee members lived in the suburbs and were therefore not citizens of the city, ONB redefined its role in the citizen participation area to become the coordinator of various neighborhood-based groups. This change was embodied in ONB's new contract with the city for the 1973 fiscal year; instead of being the citizen participation component itself, ONB was to "advise and assist the Department of Community Development and any other department as necessary relative to citizen participation required in connection with city projects and programs." ONB was to develop and maintain liaison with representative groups, especially poor and minority groups, in all of Birmingham's neighborhoods and to offer technical assistance necessary to give all citizens "a clear and direct access to the decision-making process of the city."[175] To carry out these tasks, ONB hired three full-time field workers supported by a federal grant. The involvement of ONB with neighborhood-based programs became a subject of intense local controversy, as will be seen below in the discussions of the antipoverty and citizen participation programs.

The original twenty-seven members of the Community Affairs Committee were carefully chosen to reflect three major interests in the community: the downtown business community, public officials, and the black community. The public and private white representatives controlled the resources of the community and made decisions as to their allocation, while Blacks were again pressing for their reallocation. The initial agenda for the committee was drawn from the list of concerns identified by the twenty-one black leaders who had sent the telegram to city officials demanding action: police-community relations, problems of poverty, and the hiring of Blacks by city government. Committee members met with neighborhood representatives to discuss matters related to law enforcement, though a broad range of other issues emerged at these sessions, which clearly became a way of communicating citizen demands to public authorities. From this work grew an intensified program of police-community relations, including police athletic teams in low income, primarily black neighborhoods. The committee conducted a special investigation of the local food stamp program in response to complaints about rude treatment of clients, inefficient administration, and inaccessible distribution locations. These efforts resulted in an increased number of distribution centers, supplemented by a mobile van, as well as an improved administration of the county-wide operation.[176] The committee drafted legislation to expand the citizens' governing board of the civil service system to include three black educators and established a special subcommittee that successfully pressed for the appointment of a black lawyer to the municipal court.[177] By the end of 1974 the Community Affairs Committee had been expanded from its original twenty-seven to sixty members, while retaining its tripartite structure. Leadership now rotated among the members with a Black and a White serving as cochairmen for sixty-day terms. The functioning subcommittees reflect the committee's ongoing involvement in a broad range of community issues, dealing with the composition of policy-making boards; hunger, poverty, and welfare; youth services; police athletic teams; law enforcement-community relations; education and training; personnel board; employment; public services; community liaison; and transportation.[178]

The structure and areas of interest of the Community Affairs Committee in 1974 were strikingly similar to those of the predecessor organization of the same name created by Mayor Boutwell a decade earlier; the principal difference between the two groups lay in the public origins of the first and the private creation of the second. For some, the public or private origin of the group was less important than the effectiveness of the effort. The Boutwell committee had largely failed, particularly in the eyes of its black members. The same could not be said for ONB's committee. Lucius H. Pitts, who was cochairman during the early months of the organization, called it "the best committee I have been on in sixteen years"; he said that it had resulted in "real communication between Whites and Blacks."[179] The editor of the *Post-Herald* looked more critically upon the appointment of such an influential community group by a small number of business leaders who reflected the city's traditional elite. Writing of ONB, he asked, "Now that the electorate has been greatly expanded and elections can no longer be manipulated, do the representatives of the old power apparatus tend to surface in consensus committees?"[180]

Birmingham's political system experienced significant reform during 1962–63 through the coincidental initiatives of an increasingly assertive black community, led at critical moments by Martin Luther King, Jr., and an increasingly responsive white business community, hard hit by the boycotts of downtown businesses and the city's increasingly negative international image. Still largely excluded from local electoral politics, black leaders skillfully applied economic pressure in behalf of social and political change. Intermediaries were necessary in a city lacking accepted channels of communication between the races. The intermediary role during this critical period was filled by both local white professionals and representatives of the federal government.

These initiatives were internal in origin, and both related to the racial climate fostered by the city commissioners. Part of the reform effort, the change in the form of government, was permanent; so, too, was the destruction of the city's rigid system of segregation in both public and private affairs. This destruction was aided significantly by two federal interventions: the 1954 Supreme Court school desegregation decision and the Civil Rights Act of 1964. Another product of the reform period, the inclusion of Blacks on public committees established to review significant community problems, was impermanent; within a year the elaborate structure of citizen panels appointed by Boutwell had fallen into complete disuse. When the black leaders again raised major concerns in 1969, it was left to the private sector to respond to these concerns through the creation of a closed committee that regarded itself as a private citizens' group.

But when the Community Affairs Committee was created, it was not the only biracial forum in the Birmingham area. An additional federal intervention, the antipoverty program, established by the Economic Opportunity Act of

1964, had created an interracial organization concerned largely with welfare questions. This program related to two issues of the reform period: black participation in decision making and the quality and quantity of welfare services. Ten years later another federal intervention by the Department of Housing and Urban Development resulted in a citizen participation program developed by the mayor and council that extended the concept of maximum feasible participation to all income groups and expanded the areas of governmental activity to include virtually all functions. These two interventions reinforced the general trend in local politics toward a more open and responsive city government; as a result of the citizen participation program particularly, the power of ONB was sharply eroded. The final chapter deals with the antipoverty and citizen participation programs and with their impact on welfare and politics in Birmingham.

9

The Jefferson County Committee for Economic Opportunity and the Birmingham Citizen Participation Program

WHILE A DETAILED REVIEW of the legislative history of the Economic Opportunity Act of 1964 is not pertinent to this study, two points about its background are relevant to a discussion of its local application.

First, the antipoverty program was in part a response to the civil rights movement and the condition of Blacks in American cities, although the nature of this relationship between race and the War on Poverty is subject to different interpretations. Several observers link the federal initiative against poverty specifically to racial unrest. S. M. Miller and Martin Rein, for example, identify the civil rights demonstrations as the most important political events stimulating a concern for poverty, even though 70 to 80 percent of the poor in the country were white.[1] Those close to the Kennedy administration tend to confirm the central importance of the civil rights movement to the initiation of activities culminating in the act. Sundquist writes of Walter Heller, chairman of the Council of Economic Advisers under Kennedy:

> He believes that an article by Homer Bigart in the *New York Times* describing distress in eastern Kentucky may have triggered the President's decision [to have the War on Poverty be the centerpiece of his 1964 legislative recommendations]. At least the article led Kennedy to initiate a "crash" program to mobilize federal resources to alleviate conditions in that region during the coming winter. Also pressing upon policy makers at all levels, particularly since the Birmingham demonstrations and violence in the spring, had been the demands of the civil rights movement.[2]

This use of legislation with an ostensibly economic focus was consistent with the president's previous efforts at combating racial tension. Recognizing that racial tensions, especially in the North, had their roots in unemployment, Kennedy had proposed expanding the Manpower Development and Training Act to include the "hard-core unemployed" by means of basic skill training and literacy programs; this proposal was made in a message on "Civil Rights and Job Opportunities for Negroes" delivered after a series of White House conferences on racial tension.[3]

Those sympathetic with the Kennedy administration and favorably disposed toward the War on Poverty therefore see in the Economic Opportunity Act the logical extension of legislative efforts to meet the demands of the civil rights movement. Civil rights legislation had dealt with specific behavior that excluded Blacks by virtue of their color; the amendments to the Manpower Act had dealt with the exclusion of Blacks from employment because of inadequate skills. The Economic Opportunity Act is seen as dealing not only with economic disadvantage but also with processes in society that served Blacks poorly, such as the planning and delivery of social services.

Those more critical of the program see it as a means of manipulation, exploitation, social control, and escapism. Francis Fox Piven and Richard A. Cloward tie the antipoverty program not to the idealism of a president or to the demands of Blacks, but rather to a "political imperative": the need of the Democratic administration to gain the allegiance of urban black voters, especially in key industrial states, without alienating white voters.[4] The means of gaining black electoral support was to create a new organization over which Blacks had substantial influence and through which new money could be funneled into the ghettoes of the cities; this strategy would not challenge white control over traditional agencies or reallocate funds from the white to the black community.[5] Piven and Cloward attribute the antipoverty program and other Great Society programs to a "distinctively managerial kind of politics" designed to perpetuate the incumbent administration in office: "In other words, the managerial powers of the presidency were used to forge programs to deal with the political problems of the presidency."[6] In addition to gaining electoral votes, especially in the North, the War on Poverty had the added virtue of defusing protest activity in the South by creating a new arena in which Blacks could expend their energies. "Even more obviously than in the North, Great Society programs in the South channeled protest and turbulence, with the result that much civil rights activity became virtually synonymous with antipoverty activity."[7]

Elinor Graham agrees with Piven and Cloward's analysis of the political needs met by the War on Poverty and adds a psychological dimension to the program: it enabled white Americans to meet the race issue on nonracial grounds. "Emotionally, the nation needed to redefine the racial conflict as a conflict between the 'haves' and 'have-nots.' "[8] She argues that race, like nationalism, is a subject that generates emotional responses and tensions not raised by poverty, a well-understood topic of public concern. "Politically speaking, to *redefine* race and civil rights as a manifestation of conditions of poverty, opens a path for action. . . . White Americans had to raise the poverty issue to relieve the emotional tension and political impasse created by the racial confrontation."[9] These interpreters view the antipoverty program as a means by which Whites could develop and control a political response to the demands of Blacks through opportunity-creating programs well within the traditional scope of American politics that diverted and managed the black-led civil rights movement. Attempting to resolve the conflicting interpretations of the relationship of race to the antipoverty program is not necessary in this study; what is important is to explore this relationship in the context of the Birmingham experience.

The second pertinent consideration about the history of the antipoverty legislation and its early implementation at the national level relates to uncertainty about both its objectives and the means established to attain them. Again, a detailed review of the formulation of the legislation and of ways in which administrators modified legislative intent is not needed; what is important is a recognition of the various standards by which a local antipoverty program could be evaluated.

One recognized objective of the War on Poverty was quite simply to combat economic poverty directly through specific material benefits (money, goods, jobs) or indirectly through services designed to enhance employability (education and training).[10] Related to this objective was the additional one of improving the fragmented service delivery systems in urban areas through the coordination of existing agencies and the rational planning of their programs.[11]

A second objective of the antipoverty program was to combat the poverty of power among the poor by equipping them with the motivation, skills, and forums necessary for them to organize and press their causes.[12] Supporters of this second broad objective recognized that redistributing decision-making power in the community would not directly affect the economic circumstances of the poor; they argued, however, that equipping the poor with power resources would enable them to bring leverage upon the various institutions most relevant to their lives, causing these agencies to be more responsive to the needs of the poor and to increase opportunities for them.[13] Key among these institutions would be the city government itself.

A variety of programs were created by the Economic Opportunity Act to provide benefits and services designed to combat economic poverty and enhance employability; these included youth-oriented projects such as Head Start, the Neighborhood Youth Corps, the Job Corps, and the College Work-Study Program, as well as basic education and small-business assistance programs for adults.[14] The creation of jobs directly by the federal government had been proposed by the Department of Labor but rejected by framers of the act as too costly and inconsistent with President Johnson's program of reducing taxes; the act emphasized children and youth and services to develop their capabilities.[15]

In addition to establishing programs, the act also established a mechanism for local planning, coordination, and service delivery: the Community Action Agency. The nature of this new local entity was left unclear by the legislators, as was the specific content of its program. Sundquist observes, "Rarely has so sweeping a commitment been made to an institution so little tested and so little understood as the Community Action Agency."[16] In general, each community was to establish either a public or private nonprofit umbrella agency to identify the needs of the poor, plan for meeting these needs, and mobilize existing institutions for a concerted attack upon these needs.

The act did state that each community action program would be "developed, conducted, and administered with the maximum feasible participation of the residents of the areas and members of the groups served."[17] This requirement, which provided the foundation for later efforts at the redistribution of political power, was also little understood by Congress. Again Sundquist reports: "One can search the hearings and debates in their entirety and find no reference to the controversial language regarding the participation of the poor in community action programs."[18]

Daniel Patrick Moynihan indicates that the requirement of "maximum feasible participation" was inserted originally into the draft legislation for the purpose of guaranteeing that Blacks in the South would benefit from the local programs; it was not designed to be the basis of redistributing power. "It [the requirement of maximum participation] was intended to do no more than ensure that persons excluded from the political process in the South and elsewhere would nonetheless participate in the *benefits* of the community action programs of the new legislation. It was taken as beneath notice that such programs would be dominated by the local political structure."[19]

This vague requirement was interpreted by those administering the act, especially deputy director Jack Conway, to mandate comprehensive participation in the planning, policy-making, and administration of community action programs. This interpretation led ultimately and logically to local demands that the poor control the programs entirely, demands that triggered much-studied conflicts between the poor, especially Blacks, and existing public and private institutions. The result in each city of this bureaucratic interpretation of legislative intent was a structure "that neither those who drafted it, those who sponsored it, nor those who enacted it ever in any way intended."[20] The success of each local Community Action Agency in achieving maximum feasible participation could be evaluated at several levels, given the comprehensive meaning attached to the phrase; the poor could participate as consumers of antipoverty program benefits, as employees of the program, as advisors in the policy-making process, as policymakers, and as a new political force engaging in social action to achieve institutional change.[21]

The national antipoverty program that enabled the local War on Poverty was thus vague, ambiguous, and even contradictory. It could be analyzed by its academic observers as both a means of social control in behalf of the status quo and as a means of social change in behalf of the poor, particularly Blacks living in the ghettos of large northern cities. The Community Action Agencies were variously expected to cooperate with existing institutions and to confront them; to plan for the delivery of services and to be a service delivery system; to improve the employability of the poor and to employ the poor directly. The antipoverty program has been assessed on the basis of its impact on the local economy and on the basis of its impact on the local polity. Indeed, partly because of the multiplicity of goals that can be attributed to it, the War on Poverty has spawned a large literature evaluating its impact on different cities from the perspectives of economics, political science, and social welfare. Much of the literature by political scientists has focused on northern cities and emphasized the conflict between black leaders, utilizing the program as a power base, and established political and social service structures.[22] The following analysis examines the War on Poverty as it has taken place in Birmingham, permitting a comparison of the experience of this Deep South city with that of the northern cities already documented in several case studies.

The Jefferson County Committee for Economic Opportunity

The initial recorded public reaction in Birmingham to the War on Poverty was largely favorable. The *Post-Herald* editorially endorsed the program in March 1964, five months before the act was signed into law; it described the bill as "well thought out," noting with particular approval the opportunities for communities to design their own action programs: "Local communities should do all possible in this field, reducing the role of the federal government."[23] And immediate interest was expressed in promoting Birmingham's involvement, from three sources.

First, Erskine Smith, the young lawyer who had been a leader of the movement to change the form of government, personally visited Washington several times during the summer of 1964 to gain current information about the program, which he apparently passed on to the mayor and his staff.[24] Smith's personal involvement is particularly interesting because it represents a link between the political reforms of 1962–63 and the antipoverty program.

Second, the Catholic Church in Alabama promoted involvement with national Office of Economic Opportunity (OEO) programs and served as a source of information about them. The archbishop of Mobile-Birmingham established a diocesan antipoverty committee and convened a conference of clergymen, social welfare leaders, educators, and public officials in Montgomery in October 1964 to initiate activity in the state.[25] This session was followed by a community meeting held in Birmingham in January 1965 for the same purpose.[26]

Third, the city of Birmingham officially expressed interest in the program in the fall of 1964; as the city's plans were developed, the local Catholic antipoverty group, established as a result of the local meeting, deferred to local public officials. The antipoverty organization in the Birmingham area was established as a result of actions taken by the mayor with concurrence by the city council.

Mayor Boutwell himself conferred with federal officials in September 1964 about the antipoverty program, exploring particularly its possibilities as a stimulus for the local economy. The city had previously received several million dollars under the Accelerated Public Works Program but because of a declining unemployment rate would be ineligible for further such aid. The antipoverty program was viewed as an alternative source of federal aid. Boutwell stated that the most serious problems confronting Birmingham were economic; he saw as the most important aspect of the new legislation the upgrading of education and job skills of the entire area through training "so that with a pool of available skilled and educated workers we can attract permanent jobs which private enterprise is anxious to create in an area where skilled workers and raw materials are available."[27] Birmingham's ineligibility for Accelerated Public Works funds was deceptive, he thought, because there were still pockets of poverty in the city, and unemployed miners were entering the area from surrounding counties. Furthermore, much of the steel manufactured in the district was being shipped to other parts of the country for finishing by skilled workers. In addition to holding the promise of addressing these economic deficiencies, the antipoverty program was attractive to the mayor because "projects under the act are locally initiated and controlled."[28] He enthusiastically projected plans for improving a local park with federal funds intended to create new jobs for young workers sixteen to twenty-two years old, who would be given skill training on the job. Boutwell talked with federal officials about Birmingham becoming "a command headquarters" for the War on Poverty in Alabama and expressed interest in hosting one of the urban Job Corps centers.[29]

In mid-December 1964 Boutwell formally asked the council for authority to apply for a project development grant under the Economic Opportunity Act. Funds would be used to establish a staff in city hall consisting of a director, researchers, field workers, and secretaries, whose chief function would be to assist local agencies, both public and private, which dealt with the problems of poverty and of unskilled workers. The staff would help these agencies apply for funds to train workers from low income families in the metropolitan area. The objective was clearly economic advancement for the region through the cooperative efforts of existing agencies under the leadership of city hall.[30]

The council promptly authorized the mayor to submit the application. Boutwell indicated that he would appoint a two-hundred-member Birmingham Area Committee for the Development of Economic Opportunity; this group would form a nonprofit corporation to make the initial application for funds and to sponsor projects under the Economic Opportunity Act. While Boutwell still maintained that the overriding objective of the effort was to upgrade business and industrial opportunity, he expanded the range of concerns that the committee might have. In addition to "the development of skills which are basic to modern industry," the new group was to seek "the eradication of those conditions of poverty—poverty of education, poverty of physical fitness and general health, and all the other conditions which chain men and women to a bare existence in a land of vast wealth and hope . . . and which chain this great city and its people to an economy based largely on heavy and common labor."[31]

In January 1965 Boutwell did create a twenty-member Birmingham Area Committee for the Development of Economic Opportunity and reaffirmed that the city would not administer the program directly but rather would designate a nonprofit corporation. The mayor appointed Erskine Smith, a leader of the political reform movement and an early advocate of the War on Poverty, as chairman of the new group.[32]

The mayor's initial decision to create a new private nonprofit agency was consistent with the long-term tendency of Birmingham's public officials to avoid public responsibility for programs wherever possible and to rely instead on private sector organizations. There was no identifiable demand from any sector of the community that he select this option. Because the local and national antipoverty programs were not yet embroiled in controversy, there is no reason to believe that the city sought to avoid direct association with a politically sensitive program. Indeed, the new corporation was to be housed in city hall.

Erskine Smith was faithful to Boutwell's conception of the antipoverty program, stating that it would coordinate the work of other agencies that would develop projects and present them to the committee for consideration; a specific example was a proposal from the University of Alabama medical center to train medical technicians. He also recognized the requirement of maximum feasible participation, stating that members would be added to the committee to represent the "entire community"; he proposed a special subcommittee on "grass roots involvement" that would identify neighborhood leaders and work through them to reach the people and to involve them in projects.[33]

One week after the creation of the committee, the city council approved its charter, which authorized the organization to participate in more than forty programs mentioned in the Economic Opportunity Act. The board of directors would have from twenty to forty-one members, all appointed by the mayor for staggered three-year terms. The only objection to the charter was voiced by George Seibels, Jr., the councillor who was to succeed Albert Boutwell as mayor; he argued that the corporation "could be used rather dangerously" by future city administrations and that it could not be controlled by the council once established as an independent entity.[34] The mayor's assistant and the city attorney countered that the council could abolish the committee at will by dismissing the directors and refusing to appoint successors; they said that the charter was broad because the law was broad and that "the charter is designed to follow the law."[35]

Created in January 1965, the Committee for the Development of Economic Opportunity had become the object of intense controversy by late February because of its sponsorship of a state-wide informational conference on the Economic Opportunity Act. Without consulting either the mayor or his own board, Erskine Smith agreed to have the Urban League serve as cosponsor of the event. Still without an affiliate in the state, the league looked upon the conference as a way of reestablishing a foothold in the Birmingham area; Smith, wishing to support the league's efforts, agreed to the arrangement with what his successor as chairman feels was "an apparent disregard" of its consequences for the local program.[36]

Upon learning of the Urban League's cosponsorship, Governor Wallace's appointed coordinator of antipoverty programs in Alabama refused to give official recognition to the meeting and refused to attend. After the session had been held in a Birmingham hotel, strong criticism was expressed to the mayor from Montgomery, including the recommendation that Smith be discharged as chairman. Boutwell asked Smith to resign, charging failure to communicate with the appointing authorities about the conference; Smith complied, but the committee itself refused to accept his resignation.[37] Thus the question of committee leadership was unclear in April 1965, with conflict created by an activity that was distinctly peripheral to the actual program of the local committee; at the same time, Washington approved the committee's application for a project development grant to establish a small central staff in city hall and forwarded it to the governor for his review.[38] Significantly, federal officials attached a special condition to the grant that stipulated that no change could be made in the board members.[39] Clearly Washington was throwing its influence behind Erskine Smith.

Governor Wallace promptly vetoed the Birmingham grant in the first exercise of this prerogative, which was written into the Economic Opportunity Act. A principal reason for the veto was surely Smith's local leadership, as he was not only regarded as dangerously liberal by Wallace but also had openly opposed the governor in his campaign for office.[40] For the record, Wallace based his veto on the grounds that the antipoverty program was intended to serve entire areas, while the Birmingham proposal was limited to the city only. He promised to approve programs representative of the entire community if asked to do so by the various local governing bodies. His office then did, in fact, extend immediate recognition to a competing antipoverty agency formed by the mayors of other municipalities in the county and chaired by a mayor long recognized as a loyal Wallace lieutenant, Jess Lanier of Bessemer.[41]

The result of this obvious impasse was an agreement negotiated by Boutwell and the county commission to establish a single, expanded countywide Community Action Agency; the mayors who had created the competing county agency accepted this plan on condition that Smith not serve as chairman.[42] The articles of incorporation were amended and approved by both the county commission and city council in June 1965; a new Jefferson County Committee for Economic Opportunity (JCCEO) was created with a board of forty-one members, twenty-one appointed by the city and twenty by the county.[43] Seven of the county's appointees were black, as were eleven of those designated by the city.[44] The new president, Sheldon Schaffer, was an economist employed by Southern Research Institute, a local private research corporation. With Erskine Smith's knowledge and support, Schaffer had met with both the mayor and the president of the county commission asking for the presidency and promising to communicate fully with both officials.[45] The new committee's first action was to resubmit the previously vetoed proposal requesting project development funds; presumably this proposal would be quickly reapproved by Washington and cleared by the governor. At the 27 August board meeting, the chairman reported that the Birmingham application had been cleared by the Atlanta regional office "with flying colors. Some discussion has arisen about the board membership but I have been assured that our proposal is progressing satisfactorily."[46]

Washington, however, delayed approval of the proposal until late fall on the ground that it failed to meet the requirement of "maximum feasible participation" of the poor and their representatives. JCCEO projected three specific ways of meeting the participation requirement. First, there would be "representation on the governing board of the Applicant Corporation by persons whose employment, civic activities, normal personal contacts, residence, or income make them personally knowledgeable about the problems of disadvantaged groups." Second, there would be

> participation by residents of disadvantaged areas or members of disadvantaged groups in the direction of the program and in the formation of program policy. This will be assured primarily by the formation of grassroots or neighborhood committees composed of disadvantaged persons and local persons familiar with the problems of disadvantaged persons. These local committees will normally work with the Jefferson County Committee for Economic Opportunity in an advisory capacity and in some instances as possible subcommittees.

The third method of participation would be "employment of disadvantaged persons as employees of the Jefferson County Committee for Economic Opportunity or its subcontractors."[47]

Although JCCEO promised this apparently substantial role for representatives of the poor, it failed to satisfy the national office, which finally notified the group by telephone after a two-month delay that target area representatives had to be included on the board; this requirement was reiterated by the deputy associate director of the Office of Economic Opportunity during a visit to Birmingham in late September.[48] What seemed inconsistent to local leaders was the fact that just twelve days before his deputy's visit to Birmingham, OEO director Sargent Shriver had announced a $6 million grant to Atlanta, pronouncing that city's effort "a shining example" even though no poor were on the board. Shriver defended this absence of poor by saying that their involvement in policy making would be an evolutionary process and noting that the law did not require that board members themselves be low income persons.[49]

It would seem, however, that the real problem with Birmingham's application centered around the Erskine Smith episode and the Wallace veto rather than around the issue of representation of the poor. In October, Shriver asked Smith and Orzell Billingsley, a black lawyer, to come to Washington to advise him on the application.[50] Specifically, he sought assurances from these two men on three points: that JCCEO was not dominated by forces representing Governor Wallace; that the two endorsed the proposed director and associate director of the agency; and that the mayor and county commission would be willing to appoint two representatives of poverty areas to the board in the future.[51]

Shriver was apparently satisfied by Smith and Billingsley, as OEO approved the Birmingham application contingent upon amendment of the articles of incorporation to provide for representation of target areas on the board. Specifically, JCCEO was to establish a network of neighborhood advisory councils in the county; the charter amendment specified that

> to fill vacancies created by the expiration of the terms of office of the thirteen members of the Board of Directors of the Jefferson County Committee for Economic Opportunity whose terms expire January 1, 1966, no less than twelve names of residents of target areas to be served by the Office of Economic Opportunity grant shall be submitted by such Neighborhood Advisory Councils to the appropriate appointing authorities as candidates for membership on the Board of Directors of the Jefferson County Committee for Economic Opportunity. In designating the names of these target area candidates, the Neighborhood Advisory Councils will utilize traditional democratic approaches and techniques.[52]

From the names submitted by the advisory councils, the city was to appoint at least three and the county at least three to the board. Thus, at least six of the forty-one board members would be target area representatives by 1 January 1966. The same process was to be used in succeeding years, which would have resulted in at least eighteen target area representatives by the start of 1968. The board of directors approved the stipulated amendments at its November meeting; funds were received for the Community Action Agency staff a full ten months after the first request had been submitted by the predecessor of JCCEO.[53]

Launching the War on Poverty in Birmingham was clearly a highly political process, but the politics were not related to competing interests within the city itself so much as they were to conflict between Birmingham and Montgomery, centered around the personality of Erskine Smith and the involvement of the Urban League in the February workshop. This conflict was enlarged to include the national OEO office, which continued to support Smith and apparently delayed funding Birmingham until after OEO director Shriver was persuaded that Wallace did not control the local program. The substantive changes required by OEO reflected no local discontent with the role of the poor in the program; they were demands of the national staff that seemed arbitrary in light of the funding of the Atlanta program. Though the issue of representation of the poor did arise, the question of control did not. The poor would constitute only a small proportion of the board, at least during the first year; the mayor and county commission retained the power of appointment over all positions.

In January 1966, one year after Boutwell had established the initial Community Action Agency, JCCEO president Schaffer reviewed the events and accomplishments of the first year of the War on Poverty in Birmingham. Accomplishments were limited because of the delay in funding the community action program; only the Head Start program for preschool children and the Neighborhood Youth Corps programs for teenagers were operational.[54] However, Schaffer could report that the foundation for a broadly expanded program had been established. During December 1965 the staff had created fifteen neighborhood advisory councils; 60 percent of their members were low income residents, while 25 percent were white. In the future, the councils would be selected by democratic elections and special efforts would be made to increase the proportion of low income persons and Whites. Already six individuals recommended by the councils had been appointed board members by the mayor and the county commission. The staff hired under the project development grant was designing a decentralized neighborhood service center program wherever possible; the provision of specific services was to be subcontracted to "already existing, experienced, and competent local agencies."[55] In addition, a county-wide child development committee composed of target area parents, professionals, and members of the board had been appointed to supervise the various preschool projects.

Finally, the president noted that "the committee can claim the distinction of being one of the first, if not the first, effective quasi-public interracial group in the community, a feat of no small consequence."[56] Unmentioned throughout all of the discussions and controversy surrounding the local antipoverty program was the fact that from the beginning its board had included Blacks. In light of the repeated failures of both private and public officials to establish an ongoing interracial organization and in light of the continuing racial tensions in the city, the uninterrupted existence of the local Community Action Agency as a forum for black-white communication should be recognized. Indeed, the capacity of the board to function effectively during the early years of the program is regarded by three early board presidents as perhaps the principal accomplishment of the agency. Speaking of the board, one said, "This was the real black-white forum in the community."[57] Another stated, "Trying to build up a little black-white faith was the damn thing we needed."[58] More elegantly, a third viewed the board as "an outstanding example of how in this period of adjustment to the new place of the black people the two races can work together."[59] Significantly, Erskine Smith's companion on his trip to Washington in behalf of the JCCEO application was the same black attorney, Orzell Billingsley, who had bitterly condemned Boutwell's 1963 Community Affairs Committee upon submitting his resignation from it; he was an active JCCEO board member for a full three-year term.[60]

Between 1965 and 1975 the programs sponsored by JCCEO expanded dramatically. The agency operated or cosponsored twenty-four different service programs and managed a budget that exceeded $5 million every year after 1967. Annual reports list more than fifty thousand beneficiaries served in typical years. The paid staff ranged from 450 to 550 each year, with most of them being inexperienced subprofessionals. During its first decade of existence JCCEO became a major source of employment in the human services area, had measurable impact on the local economy through its expenditures and job training programs, and emerged as a significant social welfare agency. No comprehensive evaluation of JCCEO or its programs will be undertaken in this study; rather, general observations will be made in areas relevant either to previous material on Birmingham or to assessments of other local community action agencies.

The Board of Directors and the Role of the Poor

The original Birmingham Area Committee for the Development of Economic Opportunity was governed by a twenty-one member board, all of whose members were appointed by the mayor; no specific provisions were made for including representatives of the target area population. After the Wallace veto, the organization was restructured to include the county, with the county commission appointing twenty members of a forty-one person board; again, no mechanism assured representation of the poor. At this point, the national OEO stipulated the creation of neighborhood advisory councils composed of target area representatives and the appointment to the board in January 1966 of at least six nominees presented to public officials by these councils; a total of eighteen were to be appointed by January 1968. The power of appointment still rested fully with the mayor and council.

The 1966 amendments to the Economic Opportunity Act modified this administrative requirement, advancing the date by which the full complement of representatives of the poor must be appointed but lowering their proportion on the board. In these amendments Congress required that at least one-third of the board members be democratically elected representatives of the poor by 1 March 1967; a maximum of one-third of the board could be public officials or their representatives, and the remaining one-third would represent other major community interests.[61] In a further exercise of administrative rule-making, the Atlanta regional office of OEO set more precise requirements for the composition of the JCCEO board: sixteen board members would be public officials or representatives of public agencies; sixteen would be representatives of other community groups; and sixteen should be representatives of the poor. The

JCCEO board of directors itself was given responsibility for designating the six-teen public and sixteen private agencies, each of which would select one rep-resentative. One representative of the poor was to be elected by each of the sixteen neighborhood councils; members of these councils, in turn, were to be chosen in general elections. For purposes of these elections, the entire county was divided into districts; candidates had to live in the area in which they ran.[62] One month after the OEO requirements had been received locally, the newly constituted board met in the presence of a national OEO representative.[63]

The OEO regional office interpreting the 1966 amendments accomplished by letter a major reorganization of the Birmingham agency, including a dra-matic redistribution in power over it. Whereas the mayor and county commis-sion had appointing power prior to February 1967, this power was suddenly decentralized to forty-eight separate units. Furthermore, the JCCEO board it-self selected two-thirds of the agencies to be represented; the mayor and com-mission now were designated by the board as two of the sixteen public orga-nizations entitled to one representative each, where before they had designated board members. The poor were to elect their sixteen representatives directly, rather than recommending them to other appointing authorities. Most striking is the fact that this reorganization, which exceeded the requirements of the law, took place without recorded protest by the public officials whose formal au-thority was drastically diminished and without any recorded demand for it by the poor. This board structure prevailed in Birmingham until 1972, when new amendments restored some of the power of the mayor and commission. Whereas the JCCEO board had designated various public bodies like the uni-versity, housing authority, and the health department for board representa-tion, Congress in 1972 mandated that all public representatives be elected pub-lic officials or individuals designated by them and not by independent public entities.[64]

JCCEO was governed by basically the same kind of tripartite board from 1967 to 1975, advised by sixteen neighborhood advisory councils democrati-cally elected in biennial balloting; an additional requirement by the regional office resulted in the subdivision of councils into "area blocks."[65] Furthermore, the sixteen heads of the neighborhood advisory councils formed yet another advisory group, the Neighborhood Advisory Council Committee.

Aside from electing representatives to the board, the neighborhood advi-sory councils, ranging in size from ten to twenty-five members, functioned "to provide the vehicle for representatives of the poor to participate in planning, conducting, and evaluating anti-poverty programs and services required in their neighborhoods."[66] These councils were the starting point in the agency's long-range planning process, identifying neighborhood problems that they recommended to the board as areas for agency action in the coming one to five years. This function of the poor, however, appears relatively insignificant to actual agency operations for two reasons. First, the final priorities for each program year tended to represent a compendium of often vaguely worded objectives with no indication of how they were to be achieved. Thus, one such priority was "to develop and implement programs of housing for the poor"; additional priorities dealt with education, health care, and other services where real change would require not only massive infusions of money, but also significant changes by autonomous bureaucracies.[67] More important as a factor in reducing the power of the poor in planning was the long-term trend toward reduced "versatile" funds available to local communities to allocate and a corresponding increase in "national emphasis" programs initiated and directed from national or regional offices.[68]

More meaningful roles were played by the neighborhood advisory councils within the context of programs already funded. Although project directors were selected by the board, permanent subprofessional staff members were hired upon recommendation of the council in whose geographic area they would be working.[69] The councils thereby achieved significant power over one area of immense concern to the poor: the employment of target area residents in JCCEO programs. An Emergency Assistance Program allocated $1,000 to each council for distribution to residents eligible for but not yet receiving food stamps or in need of immediate medical care; again the councils had power over specific tangible benefits.[70] The Head Start program adopted as policy the recommendations of the neighborhood advisory council committee as to the location of centers in the county, and neighborhood committees largely determined the locations of service centers within their boundaries.[71]

One specific unfulfilled request of the neighborhood advisory council representatives dealt with gaining greater control over local programs and their material benefits; the representatives wanted one neighborhood advisory council to be incorporated as an independent delegate agency administering OEO funded projects.[72] In general, throughout the history of JCCEO the neighborhood advisors representing the target area residents consistently sought a larger role in program development and a greater voice in the selection of employees at both the professional and subprofessional levels.

In assessing the functioning of representatives of the poor on the board of directors itself, one is hindered by the fact that the minutes of the meetings fail to indicate the alignment of members on controversial issues. However, by supplementing the minutes with interviews, the strong impression emerges that the target area representatives formed a cohesive bloc on two specific questions relating to material benefits: selection of personnel and setting wage and salary levels. In the area of personnel, the poor were typically opposed by a coalition of professionals from social welfare agencies and public representatives; at stake were questions of both professionalism and race.

A major early crisis in the agency's history occurred in the summer of 1967 when the first executive director, John H. Carr, a white social worker previously employed by a Community Chest agency, resigned. Amyle F. Boykin, the black female associate director, was a serious contender for the vacant position; she was opposed by various white board members on the grounds of inadequate qualifications and an uncooperative attitude. Target area representatives, a large majority of whom were black, endorsed her appointment; a black civic leader said, "If the white community finds a way to disqualify her, the Negro community will take it as a racial issue."[73] Ultimately, the white board president, acutely aware of the racial implications of the question, persuaded enough public and private agency representatives to support Boykin to gain a majority vote. Other appointments at the project director level stimulated similar board divisions at infrequent intervals; typically, the decisions favored the preferences of target area representatives.[74]

The target area representatives were less successful in the area of salaries and wages than they were with staff appointments. Here they sought to have JCCEO employees paid the maximum allowable amount, rather than permitting the executive to follow a flexible schedule. The board in this case upheld the discretionary authority of the director.[75]

Although a detailed analysis of board functioning has not been attempted in this study, the minutes and interviews indicate that the representatives of the poor participated effectively in both board and committee meetings, emerging as a unified bloc only on the personnel and wage questions discussed above, where they pressed for more material benefits for their constituencies. Neither the advisory council nor board members in any way disrupted either the policy-making process or the operations of the agency. Such disruption did occur, but the initiators were clients within the program; some of their strongest opposition came from black board members who were otherwise advocates of the target area residents.

Two major protests were launched by the poor involved in JCCEO programs, but in both cases their demands related to the quality of services received rather than to the distribution of decision-making power. The first was begun by the Poor Peoples Action Committee, described by one of its leaders as "a relatively small number of very brave black women."[76] Their grievances were directed toward the Concentrated Employment Program, which was designed to coordinate the services of several public and private agencies into a comprehensive training project for unskilled and poorly educated low income residents. The women charged that they had been promised employment in human relations occupations but instead were placed in a chicken-packing plant; in addition, they claimed that they had been intimidated by two staff members and threatened with termination if they followed through with their protest. One of the staff members was the white project director; the other, a black assistant director. Affidavits documented their charges of inadequate training, unsuccessful placements, and staff abuse; the OEO-funded Legal Services Program represented the women before a joint committee of the JCCEO executive committee and the Concentrated Employment Program governing board.[77] The frequently noted fact that the federal government, in funding community action agencies, often supported protests by the poor against agencies of local government had a unique dimension in Birmingham; OEO here supported a protest against one element of the War on Poverty itself. This semijudicial procedure, which involved both sides being represented by attorneys before the JCCEO executive committee, had three immediate consequences. A special investigating committee confirmed the deficiencies in the Concentrated Employment Program that were alleged by the clients; the black assistant director was formally disciplined by the JCCEO board; and the white director resigned, although he subsequently received the full support of the clients who had attacked him.[78] The clients later filed a federal court suit against JCCEO, the state employment service, and the state department of education. Represented by the OEO-funded attorneys, they pressed their charges of deficiencies in training and placement. This case was finally dismissed by the courts.[79]

The second client protest was brought by the United Neighborhood Improvement Association, which picketed the JCCEO headquarters in the spring of 1971 in behalf of two dismissed black employees and demanded the firing of the white executive director and two black project directors. Later the association sent a telegram to the executive committee demanding a meeting with it to present its charges of discriminatory employment practices, which it refused to document, saying that this was the responsibility of the executive committee.[80] The executive committee, committed to a policy of accessibility, agreed to the meeting. The only objection to the session was voiced by a black board member, newspaper editor Emory Jackson, regarded as a champion of the poor, who refused to attend it and wrote to the president: "Let me make it as clear as words can convey that no group or any individual, black or white, poor or powerful, learned or unlearned, is going to intimidate me."[81] An ad hoc committee of the board developed a comprehensive statement of existing personnel policy as a reply to the United Neighborhood Improvement Association; in its report the board committee pointed out that meeting the demand for equal numbers of black and white neighborhood service center directors would in fact reduce the number of Blacks in senior positions.[82] In the face of this response the protestors shifted the grounds of their grievances, filing a new formal complaint that said, "We as a people know and will prove in any federal court of law that these hard-core people are not being reached wherever the fault lies the courts will have to decide [*sic*]."[83] After another special board committee met with the disgruntled clients, the episode concluded with no court cases actually filed.

The poor and their representatives in the JCCEO program were not quiescent; they had both demands and objections that they voiced politely in board meetings and forcefully through picket lines. What distinguishes the activity of the poor is its narrow focus upon issues of employment and the quality of services rendered; there were no generalized demands relating either to the policy-making process of JCCEO or to the distribution of decision-making power elsewhere in the community. This focus can perhaps be explained as the understandable consequence of two facts. First, the poverty of the clients was extreme; as with immigrants served by the political machine in previous generations, the clients had such pressing material needs that concern for a paying job far outweighed considerations about power and participation in decision-making. Second, the black community in Birmingham was just gaining a foothold in community affairs in the mid-1960s. The willingness of the white community to sustain any significant interracial organization was still in doubt, and Blacks had gained basic rights of citizenship only within the past five years as a result of the Voting Rights Act of 1965. The political development of Birmingham's black community thus lagged behind that of the black communities in northern and many other major southern cities.[84] The local antipoverty program did produce significant demands for the redistribution of decision-making power in the social welfare arena; these demands, however, came not from the poor but rather from the regional and national offices of OEO.

The Role of the Regional and National Offices

John Wofford has noted that OEO wanted to give a major role in shaping programs to the local community without detailed federal specifications, but that the very absence of these specifications made the federal representatives of the War on Poverty significant figures on the local political stage.[85] The previous discussion of intervention from Washington and Atlanta concerning the composition of the first JCCEO board reviewed only the first of several such actions aimed at restructuring the decision-making processes within OEO-related activities. The instrument used to achieve the desired restructurings was the list of special conditions attached to specific grants; failure to comply with these stipulations would result in no funds for the project under review.

In November 1966 the regional office approved a grant for support of the central staff but required amendments to the articles of incorporation relating to the executive committee and the standing committees of the board; the net effect of these amendments was to increase the role of target area and black representatives. The executive committee was to be expanded and to have the same tripartite composition as the entire board, including adequate minority representatives; to meet this requirement three target area representatives were appointed. Previously, the board president had had power to appoint standing committees; the amendments specified nomination by the enlarged executive committee and confirmation by the board.[86] In later grant awards the regional office mandated a youth policy-making group for recreation programs and a Head Start policy advisory committee with significant functions in program management, at least 50 percent of whose members were to be parent representatives.[87] The most interesting and aggressive efforts by OEO administrators to modify decision-making structures involved the controversial Legal Services Program. The applicant for funds in this project was the Birmingham Legal Aid Society, whose membership was the same as the Birmingham Bar Association. Disagreement over the precise composition of the board for the Legal Services Program resulted in prolonged and complex negotiations among the JCCEO board, the Legal Aid Society board, and the OEO regional office.[88] In June 1973 OEO announced that local bar associations were to appoint 75 percent of the board members and that in the future the Birmingham Legal Services Program would be funded directly from Washington to the Legal Aid Society, bypassing the Community Action Agency entirely.[89]

A final example of intervention by the regional office into the operations of the local antipoverty program deals with the racial composition of its client group. Ironically, in light of Moynihan's account of the origin of the "maximum feasible participation" requirement, OEO officials constantly pressed for greater white involvement. It is understandable, given the rigidly segregated nature of Birmingham's society until the eve of the War on Poverty, that Whites would be reluctant to participate in a program that guaranteed interracial contact at least and perhaps interracial group activities; probably most offensive to potential white clients was the possibility of being served by black staff members. In typical years Whites constituted only 3 to 5 percent of the participants in antipoverty projects; the figure rose to 10 to 30 percent in the Neighborhood Youth Corps, Legal Services, Emergency Food and Medical, and Parent-Child Development Center programs.[90] The latter project involved a limited number of infants and their mothers in an intensive enrichment and training program;

the racial composition of the project was maintained at fixed proportions through the selection process.

From an early date the agency itself attempted to increase the rate of white participation, recognizing that about half of the county's forty-one thousand low income families were white. A senior-level white staff member was assigned in June 1966 to meet with white neighborhood leaders who had contact with low income Whites and white ministers whose churches might be rented for use by JCCEO.[91] The refusal of the latter, coupled with the refusal of the Birmingham Board of Education to make school space available, resulted in an initial Head Start program based in black churches and the white Unitarian church. Consequently, 95 percent of the youngsters in the much-publicized Head Start program were black, making future efforts at racial balance in this and other OEO programs all the more difficult.[92]

In light of the dominance of black clients, the regional office in 1969 began stipulating greater efforts by the agency to recruit Whites. With yearly regularity this condition was attached to program grants; with equal regularity the agency attempted to devise new ways to increase the proportion of white clients but failed to meet its objectives.[93] A decade after its founding, JCCEO continued to be an agency whose program beneficiaries were overwhelmingly black.

JCCEO was thus perceived from its beginning primarily as a service delivery system serving low income Blacks, though governed by a stable biracial board and operated by an integrated staff. The program did generate public demands for change on the part of the poor and their representatives, but these demands were confined to the operations of the agency itself, to the quantity and quality of benefits received by the poor. Demands for changes in the policy-making structures of the agency itself and others funded through it were made, but by regional and national administrators at their own initiative and not in response to local sentiment seeking these modifications. JCCEO did not emerge as a threat to local power-holders in either the social welfare or the larger political arenas. As will be seen below, the lack of impact by the antipoverty program on Birmingham's politics was matched by a similar lack of concern by the city's politicians to establish control over the Community Action Agency.

Relations with Local Public Officials

The War on Poverty began in Birmingham officially because of the initiatives of Mayor Boutwell, who viewed the program largely as a stimulus to the local economy directly through employment and indirectly through skill-training programs that would create a labor force attractive to employers. However, after the controversy surrounding Erskine Smith as board chairman, the mayor did not maintain an active involvement in the development of the Community Action Agency. Sheldon Schaffer, Smith's successor as chairman, reported in an interview that by mid-1965 Boutwell regarded the antipoverty program as a "thorn in the side" and sought to dissociate himself from it; he did not, however, attempt to thwart its further progress. The new chairman had promised to keep the mayor fully informed about the activities of JCCEO; receiving this information and designating one member of the board constituted Boutwell's only further involvement with the program.[94]

The 1967 Green Amendment to the Economic Opportunity Act, which created the opportunity for local governments to assume control of Community Action Agencies, raised anew the question of the relationship between JCCEO and the city. Boutwell's successor, George Seibels, Jr., turned to Thad Holt, his representative on the JCCEO board, for advice about whether to maintain the agency as an independent corporation or to bring it directly under the city's supervision. As the former director of New Deal relief programs in the state, Holt had a predisposition to favor public responsibility for operating the program; he urged this position upon the mayor.[95] The agency was opposed to this recommendation, as were the two major newspapers. The *News* wrote: "We agree that the War on Poverty needs some overhauling. But we have our doubts that city hall is the place to get it done."[96] Public control, it later editorialized, would in fact be detrimental, as the board was now functioning effectively and had gained valuable experience, while the agency as a whole "has gained increased acceptance as currently run."[97]

In May 1968 the city and the county designated JCCEO as the local Community Action Agency, stipulating two major changes in the constitution and by-laws: the executive committee was enlarged to include the mayor and the president of the county commission or their representatives; and the agency's purchasing and financial operations were to be supervised by the city's purchasing department and finance director. In addition the city requested that the neighborhood advisory councils be given greater responsibility in planning and administering programs in their respective target areas. Despite strenuous objections from the staff, the board concurred with the specified amendments, with the understanding that it retained sole authority over the selection of programs to fund, agencies to sponsor them, staff members, and overall budgeting.[98]

The request for greater power for the neighborhood advisory councils, which would have weakened the ability of board, staff, and local government alike to manage antipoverty programs, was never met. The representatives of the mayor and the president of the county commission on the executive committee did influence the agency's future operations as will be discussed below. The city never utilized the control of purchasing or the supervision of JCCEO's overall fiscal operations as a means of regulating the agency; the agency continued to manage its own affairs without any interference, although it did submit reports regularly to city and county officials for their review, including minutes of board and executive committee meetings. This failure by the city to assert its prerogatives occurred despite repeated comments by the mayor that the city was going to assume fiscal control of JCCEO "and straighten things out."[99]

Two incidents reflect the seeming indifference of both city and county to the activities of the antipoverty agency and their lack of information about it despite its submission of reports and minutes. In December 1970 the county commission reduced its annual appropriation to JCCEO from the usual $5,000 to $2,500, citing increasing costs in other areas "of greater importance on a county-wide standpoint."[100] The city maintained its $25,000 appropriation but refused to increase it as requested. In order to increase the financial support from these governments, meetings were held with officials of both. JCCEO minutes report:

> The city and county officials stated that they were personally unaware of what is going on in JCCEO. Mr. Singleton (executive director) stated that minutes of the Executive Committee and Board of Directors meetings are mailed to the mayor and county commission each month. Mr. Cooper (board member) further suggested that a one-page summary could be sent each month to these governmental officials and that personal conferences be held with these people.[101]

The impression that JCCEO confronted the apathy of public officials rather than their hostility is confirmed by both interviews and a management study of the agency submitted in June 1974 by a nationally recognized consultant. The report noted that the city and county as "parent bodies" had "legal powers" over the purchasing and fiscal operations of the organization. Yet, the consultants "noted no formal definition by the parent bodies of JCCEO's responsibilities with respect to these legal powers" and no formal or informal acknowledgement by them of receipt of the regularly submitted reports and minutes. The report urged JCCEO to take the initiative in fostering greater responsiveness by public officials by requesting either a written acceptance of these documents or a statement of their deficiencies.[102]

Though the agency was free of intrusions from city hall and the county courthouse, it received ongoing criticism from the representatives of the mayor and commission president. However, it seems certain that these two men were not implementing directives from their appointers. Rather, they imported into their JCCEO work the same criteria of efficiency, economy, and fiscal account-ability that characterized their business careers; in the case of Thad Holt, the mayor's representative, these criteria had been the hallmarks of his tenure as state relief administrator during the New Deal. By these criteria, the agency proved to be vulnerable, not because its administrators were dishonest, but because they valued different objectives more highly and had too few re-sources to manage carefully what became an intricate social service system. On these grounds the agency was repeatedly attacked by both business-oriented board members and detractors in the community; JCCEO was troubled more by the audit than by opposing political power.

Much of the legitimate criticism of JCCEO's administration seems due to the fact that it was an exceedingly complex organization with a small and largely inexperienced central staff more interested in program operation than in careful accounting. Part of its complexity was the result of the extensive net-work of relationships that it had established with both private and public agen-cies in the metropolitan area, relationships necessary to fulfill its dual role of coordinator of services and stimulator of change in other institutions.

Relations with Other Agencies

JCCEO's maze of relationships with other local agencies can fruitfully be examined in terms of four different functions: modifying the services of other agencies in behalf of greater benefits for low income citizens; promoting more rational planning for the delivery of services; serving as coordinator of related services provided by discrete agencies; and serving as the source of advocates for the poor.

The executive director of JCCEO summarized the organization's attitude to other groups when he stated in his 1970 annual report, "There is emphasis on close cooperation with other helping agencies in making the most effec-tive impact on the problems associated with poverty in Jefferson County."[103] JCCEO did not openly confront existing agencies in an effort to change their behavior; rather, it offered financial incentives to those that were willing to deliver services on the terms set by either the local board or the OEO admin-istration.

The initiative to apply for funds generally came from agencies themselves and reflected a desire to extend their traditional services to a new clientele by locating staff members in the decentralized system of neighborhood service centers operated by JCCEO. In the first program year, the board reviewed and approved unsolicited proposals from the county health department to conduct preventive health programs in the centers, from the Visiting Nurses Association for a home health aid program, from Planned Parenthood for a mobile unit to serve the centers, from the Family Counseling Association for additional staff members to be housed in the centers, from the Tuberculosis Association for testing children in the target areas, and from University Hospital to offer medical services to persons certified by the center directors.[104] Yet none of these projects was funded, not because of failure to comply with JCCEO's requirements but because funds were frozen, compelling the board to select only two from among the proposals submitted to it. The two projects funded were a day-care center operated by St. Vincent's Hospital and an adult education program operated by Miles College.[105] In the case of Birmingham, at least, there was consistently a greater willingness by agencies to undertake new programs than there were funds to support these activities. Even so, JCCEO did stimulate the development of a decentralized service delivery system in low income neighborhoods that brought together in differing combinations such diverse activities as Head Start, legal services, community-based casework by both the juvenile court and Bureau of Pardons and Parole, housing counseling, emergency food and medical services, job placement through the state employment service, Planned Parenthood, and alcoholism counseling. For agencies whose leadership voluntarily sought to change their traditional methods of operation, JCCEO played a facilitating role.

In the case of national emphasis programs such as Head Start, Neighborhood Youth Corps, and the Concentrated Employment Program, JCCEO was required to cooperate with established public bureaucracies; here it encountered resistance that it lacked the resources to overcome fully. The agency could not criticize too harshly those agencies whose cooperation was needed, and it lacked any sanction to change behavior other than delaying or withholding grants. Thus the boards of education involved with Head Start and Neighborhood Youth Corps resisted hiring nonprofessionals, integrating classrooms, and working with agency staff in program development, leading the JCCEO board on several occasions to examine alternative means of providing the needed instruction.[106] In each case, however, the school systems made sufficient changes to warrant their continued participation, as in the case of the Fairfield school superintendent who agreed to integrate Head Start classrooms rather than have funds allocated to community churches, though angrily commenting, "It is becoming increasingly clear that the Office of Economic Opportunity is more concerned with the integration of students and faculty than with alleviating pockets of poverty."[107] Though relations were always strained between JCCEO and such bureaucracies, the agency did extract precedent-setting modifications in their standard operating procedures; in the words of one former president, JCCEO was "an icebreaker in some respects for the community."[108]

JCCEO did not establish itself as the focal point for program planning, although it played a direct role in stimulating the formation of planning bodies in the areas of health and manpower. In the area of health, the agency contracted with the Community Chest's Community Service Council to develop a comprehensive plan of services for the poor. The council had already become involved in other phases of health planning and had previously cooperated extensively with JCCEO in identifying neighborhoods of greatest need for the neighborhood service centers program. Furthermore, John Carr, the first JCCEO executive director, had been recruited from the staff of the Community Service Council.[109] JCCEO's willingness to aid in establishing the council as the recognized planning unit in the health area reflected the positive relationships that had historically existed between the two bodies.

In the area of manpower, a competitive organization successfully wrested primacy from JCCEO. Capitalizing on the deficiencies in the manpower programs, the business community, through the Chamber of Commerce and National Alliance of Businessmen, proposed that an alternative body be designated by the mayor and council to develop and monitor a master plan for the metropolitan area as required in the 1968 Vocational Education Act.[110] Though JCCEO wanted this designation, it could not mobilize the necessary support in the business community and city hall. Ultimately, the agency agreed to have four representatives on the new thirty-six-member organization and to retain responsibility for the operation of several programs.[111] By 1970 it was clear that comprehensive planning would be required by law in several functional areas and that Birmingham would establish autonomous planning bodies for each area; neither JCCEO or any other public or private agency emerged as the coordinator of these planners.

In fact, JCCEO failed most dismally in its attempts to coordinate other agencies, although in this failure it reflected the experience of community action agencies across the country.[112] The most dramatic effort at coordination occurred in the Concentrated Employment Program; here clients were recruited through the neighborhood service centers, oriented to "the world of work" by the Opportunities Industrialization Center, provided basic education by the board of education, given on-the-job training by the recently organized Birmingham Urban League, and placed in jobs by the state employment service.[113] Lacking both the staff and authority to compel cooperating agencies to develop quality programs or to coordinate their activities, JCCEO was coordinator in name only. Furthermore, it was dependent on local employers to hire program graduates; the employers refused to employ many, claiming that they were not motivated, not dependable, and not trained adequately.[114] The staff countered with charges that employers refused to make any concessions in unreasonably stringent employment standards and refused to be nondiscriminatory in hiring.[115] As mentioned above, investigation by a committee of JCCEO board members determined that deficiencies did exist throughout the program. And while staff and program changes were made by participating agencies, JCCEO continued to be plagued by the weaknesses of a complex project over which it lacked clear management authority.

JCCEO did succeed notably in producing advocates for the poor and in establishing a constituency in the community for programs serving low income residents. When food stamp recipients claimed inadequate service, the board appointed an ad hoc committee that pressed for reform and gained significant publicity for the situation.[116] To call attention to the plight of low income residents who lacked water, both black and white, the agency conducted a comprehensive survey through its neighborhood service centers for the waterworks board and then publicized its results.[117] Acting as the "voice of the poor," the agency intervened in a dispute between the county commission and the university, which had delayed the opening of the new charity hospital.[118] While one cannot assess the influence of these actions in bringing about subsequent changes in each of the areas mentioned, it is apparent that JCCEO had emerged as the institutional spokesman for the poor in the community.

The most striking example of JCCEO's creating a constituency for the poor occurred in the summer of 1973, when it appeared that the Nixon administration's hostility to the War on Poverty would result in the termination of all federal funds to community action agencies. Upon request of the board, the mayor and county commission jointly appointed a fifteen-member citizens' task force to evaluate JCCEO's program and to recommend whether or not local government should maintain the organization. Headed by a businessman and comprised of recognized civic leaders, the task force met eight times; visited programs; and held meetings with staff, clients, and representatives of other social welfare agencies.[119] In its final report it noted program weaknesses, which it felt reflected less on the quality of the staff than on the fact that the agency "simultaneously pursues goals which are often in conflict with one another." Concerning possible duplication of services offered by other agencies, it concluded, after meeting with their representatives, that there was "no competition for clients between JCCEO and other agencies. In fact, it is very often the case that JCCEO provides a liaison between clients and established service agencies." While recognizing that it could not evaluate the quality of JCCEO's services, the task force nonetheless reported that "the partnership of advisory council members and Neighborhood Service Center staff has implemented an impressive variety of services on behalf of poor residents throughout the county." Based upon its research and the testimony of both agency representatives and clients, the task force called for the continuation of JCCEO as an independent agency "organized substantially as it is at present" as "a delivery system with a central control and policy making capability and decentralized service delivery capability"; it also recommended maintenance of the governing board as then structured.[120]

Three different ad hoc groups endorsed the task force report and called upon local government to guarantee the survival of the threatened agency. First, the past presidents of JCCEO informally organized and presented arguments for continuation to both the task force and public officials.[121] Second, a black minister formed the JCCEO Supporters Club, which held public meetings in the black community and also made a presentation to the task force.[122]

Finally, a "Future of JCCEO Committee," composed of several influential board members, made overtures to local authorities for continued support from General Revenue Sharing funds.[123] The result of the task force report and the activities of JCCEO advocates was an immediate increase in the city's support from $25,000 to $65,000, coupled with a pledge by the city council to provide $405,000 from the Revenue Sharing funds in the event other federal funds were terminated.[124] What had been clearly demonstrated during this process of evaluation were the facts that JCCEO had created a base of support for itself among those who had been involved with its programs and that the agency's program could favorably impress an ad hoc group, most of whose members were largely unfamiliar with its work prior to their appointment to the task force. The pledge of financial support by city government reflected public officials' acceptance of the agency as a useful addition to the already existing public and private institutions in the community.

An assessment of Birmingham's experience with the War on Poverty in relation to that of other, particularly northern, cities supports two generalizations about its impact on local politics and welfare. First, after it was finally established, the antipoverty program in the Birmingham area was conducted largely within the social welfare arena and did not erupt as an issue in local politics as it did in many other cities. Second, while the War on Poverty in Birmingham had special implications for the black community, its influence on black-white relations was of a different kind from that most frequently found in northern cities.

As a reform movement in social welfare, the War on Poverty differed drastically from its predecessor reform effort, the New Deal, in three notable respects. First, the New Deal had emphasized change in the public sector and had required that all of its funds be spent by public authorities. During the

Great Society "traditional notions of the lines that divided public and private institutions seemed outmoded."[125] Critics of the War on Poverty have lamented the demise of this distinction and pointed to potentially deleterious consequences.[126] Others more sympathetic to the antipoverty program have been impressed with its impact upon both public and private agencies, sensitizing them to the needs of low income residents and introducing participatory practices into their own administrative structures.[127]

Second, the New Deal emphasized centralization of program administration at the state level and of rule-making at the national level. New Deal relief programs operated by the county welfare departments were tightly controlled by the state relief administrator who was, in turn, guided by specific guidelines developed in Washington. OEO programs, on the other hand, emphasized decentralization of program administration even within metropolitan areas, while much rule-making was carried out at the regional as well as national level.

Third, the New Deal in Alabama contributed to the professionalization of social welfare as trained social welfare administrators filled senior positions at the county level or above. The War on Poverty deliberately "deprofessionalized" its programs through its emphasis on hiring indigenous personnel from the neighborhoods and others presumably sensitive to the needs of the poor through prior experience rather than professional training.

Yet the New Deal and the War on Poverty had one similar result in Birmingham: both offered Blacks sharply increased opportunities to share in the benefits of their programs. The antipoverty program went beyond the New Deal in that it additionally afforded Blacks the opportunity to participate with Whites in the development of social welfare policy. It did not, however, have significant immediate impact upon the participation of Blacks in city politics.

In Birmingham, the antipoverty program followed immediately after a significant political reform that had challenged the traditional political culture of the community. The change in the form of government had been sought in part for the purpose of gaining greater responsiveness by local government to the aspirations and needs of the black community. The War on Poverty, with a similar objective, coincided with and reinforced a major break with the historic political patterns of the community; it reinforced reform initiated by local Whites prior to the massive demonstrations of the summer of 1963. In one way, the account of JCCEO presented above does conform to the traditional pattern of local politics in Birmingham: the role of public authorities in this, as in many other issues discussed earlier in the study, was extremely limited; one again gets the impression that local officials sought to play as minor a role as possible in influencing the outcome of an important community issue. But the break with the historic pattern of local politics accomplished by creating and sustain-

ing a biracial policy-making board is of far greater consequence than this simi-
larity. It was the forces of reform and not defenders of the status quo who benefited most from the War on Poverty in Birmingham; the personal involvement
of Erskine Smith and Orzell Billingsley testifies to the shared outlooks of those
who supported political change and those who supported JCCEO.

In the northern setting, the principal actors in the decision-making process
concerning Community Action Agencies were big-city mayors, aggressive
black leaders, and reform-oriented Whites; the relationship between local public officials and supporters of a participatory antipoverty program was typically
one of conflict. The characteristic "life cycle" of a Community Action Agency
involved creation of a local organization by the mayor, followed by a challenge
to that organization by militant black spokesmen seeking to utilize the War on
Poverty as a means of establishing a local base of political power; finally, a
compromise was struck, reflecting the relative strength of the contestants.[128]

In the northern experience, the question of representation of the poor on
the Community Action Agency board was a significant public policy question
engaging the attention of both local politicians and major politically active interest groups. The issue was resolved within the context of the local polity,
reflecting the historic political culture and the current relative strengths of competing groups. The key figure was the mayor, whose "ideology and preferences set the agenda for discussion and policy formation" in the antipoverty
program.[129]

The Birmingham case was substantially different from that outlined above,
particularly in regard to the salience of the issue of black/poor representation
and the manner in which it was resolved. First, neither the War on Poverty in
general nor the question of representation in particular was a major issue in
local politics during the time when this question was being resolved. Mayor
Boutwell had been instrumental in establishing the first Community Action
Agency; but after the gubernatorial veto, he did not appear to play an active
role or to have much interest in the program. His successor, George Seibels,
Jr., took much the same position with regard to JCCEO. Newspaper articles
and agency records alike seldom mention the mayor, and where he is mentioned it is never in the context of attempting to gain control over the policy-
making process of the organization.

One could argue that it was politically in the interest of Birmingham's
mayor to assume this stance toward the antipoverty program, given both the
traditional political culture of the city, especially as it related to Blacks, and the
events of 1962–63 concerning political reform and civil rights activities. For it
was apparent that the War on Poverty nationally, regionally, and locally was
intimately related to questions of race; the episode in February 1964 concerning

a workshop cosponsored by the Community Action Agency and the Urban League had underscored that connection. Indications that the mayor actively supported or even wanted to control a program so clearly associated with the needs of the black community could have been a serious political liability in the white community. On the other hand, mayoral opposition would have been inconsistent with the new government's desires to be more responsive to the black community and might have posed electoral liabilities in a city whose black population constituted 40 to 50 percent of the population. Thus, allowing the antipoverty program to function in an autonomous arena largely unfettered by city hall could be viewed as the course of political wisdom.

Interviews with past agency presidents, the mayor's representative on the board, and a former senior staff member of JCCEO tend toward a somewhat different conclusion, but one not necessarily in conflict with the above speculation based on mayoral interest; they suggest that Birmingham's mayors were not particularly interested in the War on Poverty, though they were generally sympathetic to improving social services. They were simply content to leave it alone so long as it did not become a disruptive force in local politics. Boutwell and Seibels, particularly the latter, reportedly had little information about the programs of JCCEO and little interest in becoming involved with its administration; the city's failure to exercise fiscal control over the agency after the Green amendment supports this impression. As one past president put it, the mayor's position was "just keep us informed and pull no surprises."[130]

While the mayor played a lesser role in Birmingham than in northern cities, businessmen played a larger role, particularly the two who served on the board as representatives of the mayor and the president of the county commission. That politicians should turn to businessmen was consistent with the dependence public officials had historically had on the judgment of the business community; the frequent attacks by the business representatives on the management capabilities of the agency and its staff seem to have reflected their personal values only and not those of the appointing authorities.

In Birmingham, the agenda for decision making in the antipoverty program was largely set by OEO bureaucrats at the regional and national levels. It was they who mandated the composition of the board in 1965 requiring one-third representation of the target area population; and it was they who confronted the Legal Aid Society with demands to reform its governing board. Instead of emerging as a significant issue to be resolved through local political processes, the antipoverty program constituted an avenue for ongoing intervention by external forces, intervention that supported the continued opening of new opportunities to the black community.

The antipoverty program also represented the culmination of a progression begun during the New Deal, when Blacks were treated equitably for the first time as clients receiving benefits through relief programs. They played no role in policy-making and clearly subordinate roles as staff members in New Deal programs. The Voting Rights Act of 1957 and later related acts enabled Blacks to have a greater voice in the selection of policymakers, an enlarged power that was a crucial element in the vote to adopt the new form of government and in the subsequent election of Boutwell over Connor. Still, as the reformers themselves made clear, Birmingham's political regime had been carefully constructed to exclude Blacks as policymakers. In the private sector, social welfare policy-making also excluded Blacks until early 1967, when the Community Chest elected its first two black board members, leaving only Jackson, Mississippi, with a segregated board.[131]

With the advent of JCCEO, Blacks participated as board members in policy formation. The appointment of a black executive director in August 1967 created the first situation in either the public sector or the private social welfare field in which a Black headed an integrated staff. When this director resigned her position to return to graduate school, the *News* recognized the significance of her tenure and of the antipoverty program for race relations in the city; it editorialized that JCCEO

> has been living, breathing proof that effective biracial cooperation can be a reality in Birmingham.
>
> Mrs. Boykin's service as JCCEO director proves that a Negro can be appointed to a high, responsible executive position and receive the support and cooperation of the whole community.
>
> Indeed, the entire anti-poverty program in Jefferson County has been a demonstration first of the willingness of the community to give Negroes an important—even dominant—voice in decision-making and, second, of the ability of Negro citizens of the county to produce the kind of leadership such a challenge demands.[132]

JCCEO had a significant impact upon the social welfare services in metropolitan Birmingham, but its greatest local significance lies in its dual impact on race relations. First, it created in the JCCEO board of directors the only stable forum in the area for communication between the races. The creation of this forum followed the failures of the Urban League effort, the Interracial Division of the Coordinating Council of Social Forces, and the elaborate Community Affairs Committee of Albert Boutwell; it preceded by four years the biracial committee of Operation New Birmingham. Thus, JCCEO filled a vacuum in the community.

The second primary contribution of the antipoverty program to race relations was its function as a training ground for the development of black leadership that emerged from the agency and moved into other major community institutions. Former JCCEO employees later held senior positions in the business community, the local comprehensive health planning commission, the University of Alabama at Birmingham, and local offices of the Departments of Defense and Housing and Urban Development.[133] Notable is the absence of former antipoverty program workers from local elected or appointed office, an absence that underscores the separation in Birmingham between city politics and the War on Poverty. Only one person with JCCEO connections, a senior black administrator, sought elective office after having established a base of community support through the agency; he was defeated in his bid for a city council seat.[134] On the other hand, none of the three Blacks sitting on the Birmingham City Council in 1976 had significant involvement with the War on Poverty prior to election to public office, nor did any black candidates in later years. The increased involvement of the community, especially the black community, in local politics was encouraged not through the War on Poverty, but through an independent external intervention that resulted in the city's elaborate citizen participation program.

The Birmingham Citizen Participation Program

The Birmingham Citizen Participation Program merits brief review for four reasons. First, it stands as another example of significant change at the local level stimulated by federal intervention. Second, the program extends into local politics the participatory principles underlying the War on Poverty; it fuses citizen participation and city politics in a way that JCCEO never did. Third, the program represents a decisive rejection by citizens of leadership by the local business community; it signals a shift of responsibility from private organizations to public authority. Finally, the program illustrates the potential for effective biracial coalitions.

As mentioned above in the discussion of Operation New Birmingham, that organization had been designated by the city as the official citizen participation structure for programs funded by the Department of Housing and Urban Development. In late 1972 a newly formed organization composed of city residents objected to this designation on the grounds that most members of ONB lived in the suburbs and that ONB had not actively participated in the development of the required workable program and comprehensive land use plan.[135] Aware of the mounting discontent with ONB's role in the programs of the department, the Birmingham area office of the Department of Housing and Urban Development (HUD) reviewed the city's application for recertification of its workable program in early 1973. The result of this evaluation was a letter from the HUD area director to the mayor stipulating changes in the workable program, including its citizen involvement component. Specifically, the area director said:

> No later than January 1, 1974, the city will have developed, *under direct city control*, the functional capacity to involve its citizens directly in the community development process. Such involvement must be continuous, and should emphasize involvement of the poor, minorities, and those most likely to be affected by community development activities. The mechanism chosen to develop this functional capacity should, at a minimum:
>
> 1. Provide direct access of citizen representatives to the office of the mayor;
> 2. Represent the ethnic, age, economic and business characteristics of the community at large;
> 3. Be integrally involved, on a continuous basis, in all phases of the community development process (planning, implementation and execution);
> 4. Be provided up-to-date and timely information on all events of importance to citizens;
> 5. Be provided a defined set of roles and responsibilities for local government officials and citizens that will maximize opportunities for complementary relationships to exist; and
> 6. Provide mechanisms to assure accountability of citizen representatives to their constituencies.
>
> The accomplishment of these performance criteria will necessitate at a minimum modification of the city's present contract [with ONB] for citizen participation.[136] (emphasis mine)

This letter initiated a policy-making process within the executive branch, especially the Community Development Department, to produce a satisfactory plan by the required date. According to one of the two officials within the department principally responsible for fashioning the city's response, the mayor was for the most part represented by the director of the Community Development Department and its staff in subsequent activities related to the Citizen Participation Program.[137] The mayor, as he did with the JCCEO, lacked detailed information and did not intervene in the development of the citizen participation plan, even though this program, unlike JCCEO, was clearly a responsibility of his office.

The staff of the Community Development Department produced a document by the 1 January 1974 deadline that proposed a complex, three-level citizen participation structure.[138] The first level would be ninety neighborhood citizen committees, with membership open to all residents sixteen years of age and above. The boundaries of the neighborhoods were to be those established by the Birmingham Planning Department for its land use, transportation, and public improvement planning activities. The second level was to be a smaller number of community citizen committees. Each community would be composed of several neighborhoods; each neighborhood would be represented at the community level by three democratically elected officers. Finally, the elected presidents of the community-level committees, as well as eight representatives appointed directly by the mayor, would constitute the Birmingham Citizens Advisory Board, which would meet regularly with the mayor and the city council.

The proposal listed ten functional areas of local government activity in which the structure would be active: education; housing; health services; economic development; public safety and consumer protection; transportation, communication, and utilities; recreation and culture; natural resources; social services; and general municipal government.[139] It specified methods of communication between city officials and the citizen participation structure and within that structure. The proposal also included a major role for ONB, although its drafters anticipated opposition from citizen groups to this involvement and recognized that they were "playing an appeasement game with ONB."[140] Specifically, the proposal stated that ONB would "have primary field responsibility for developing, organizing, and maintaining viable citizen participation groups in the neighborhoods and communities throughout Birmingham."[141] In short, the organization objected to by both the Department of Housing and Urban Development and vocal citizens was to receive a contract to represent city government in the neighborhoods and to help fashion an operational citizen participation structure. The proposal recognized the importance of ONB's role, noting that "a great deal of responsibility for the success of the proposed program rests with Operation New Birmingham. . . . The city is relying heavily on ONB and is confident that it can fulfill its key role in helping achieve a successful Citizen Participation Program."[142]

After the mayor had released this plan and it had been presented to various audiences, the city council scheduled a public hearing, as requested by citizens, on 1 April 1974 to consider the document. An estimated crowd of over five hundred braved torrential rain to attend the session, which had to be moved from the council chambers to the municipal auditorium. Thirty individuals addressed the council, not one of whom endorsed the plan as presented. While several substantive points in the proposal were touched upon in the comments and strong objections were raised to having the mayor appoint representatives directly to the Citizens Advisory Board, universal criticism was directed by the speakers to the role of ONB.[143] This meeting reflected not only careful preparation for the meeting by already existing civic groups, mainly black, but also the degree of hostility to ONB on the grounds that it represented only the interests of the white business establishment and that several of its officials reportedly had played leading roles in a "get out the white vote" campaign in the 1973 city elections.[144]

After analyzing the statements of citizens delivered on 1 April, the staff of the Community Development Department recommended that the mayor invite all of the critics of the proposal to a workshop in city hall.[145] Later that month nearly one hundred citizens met to recommend modifications in the plan. One of the most significant changes discussed was the elimination of ONB from the citizen participation program. The staff incorporated most of the citizens' recommendations into a revised proposal that omitted ONB completely. When aired at a second public hearing on 1 October, the revised plan was praised by all who commented upon it, including several of its severest critics at the earlier meeting. The leaders of ONB made no public objection to their elimination from the plan, apparently recognizing the degree of antagonism toward the organization—especially in the black community.

In mid-November 1974, nearly eighty-five hundred residents voted in their neighborhoods to elect officers for their citizen participation committees, about one-third the number who voted in the most recent city council election.[146]

At the end of the study period, the Birmingham Citizen Participation Program was based upon a foundation of eighty-four neighborhoods grouped into nineteen communities. The neighborhood and community boundaries and names were not those adopted by other city departments but rather those identified by residents after hundreds of hours of interviewing by field workers employed directly by the Community Development Department. Each neighborhood decided how it would spend an allotment of federal Community Development Block Grant funds provided to it through the city under the Housing and Community Development Act of 1974. Ranging from about one thousand to over ten thousand residents in size, each neighborhood received between fifteen and seventy-five thousand dollars based upon a formula related to both population and need. Most expenditures were upon improvements in streets, lighting, and recreation, reflecting the city's historic pattern of underexpenditure in these areas relative to other cities. Regular meetings were also held on the community and city-wide levels; the first city-wide committee, chaired by a black minister and composed of eleven Blacks and eight

Whites but no representatives appointed by the mayor, held bimonthly sessions with the mayor and the city council.[147]

Four observations can be made about the city's early experience with its Citizen Participation Program. First, citizen interest increased during the first year as judged by participation in neighborhood elections, and this interest appeared to be shared by Blacks and Whites of all income levels. Over twelve thousand residents cast ballots in the second year's election, an increase of nearly 50 percent over the previous election. The vote had been heaviest in 1974 in black neighborhoods where candidates faced strong opposition; in 1975, the vote was more evenly distributed over all the neighborhoods, and white participation increased substantially. Unlike JCCEO, the program had avoided identification with either the black or the white community alone and retained a distinctly biracial constituency, a fact undoubtedly due in part to the strategy of allocating funds to all neighborhoods. No organization or group of organizations loomed as an especially strong supporter of the program; active participants emerged from neighborhood organizations, churches, parent-teacher associations, and the War on Poverty. The latter did not play a conspicuous role in the program, reflecting the continuing separation of the antipoverty program and city politics.[148]

Second, the Citizen Participation Program ranged far beyond the expenditure of Community Development Block Grant funds to consider a broad spectrum of topics that included the zoning of individual parcels of land and the persistent issue of creating a citizens review board to study charges of police brutality. City officials promised to involve the citizen participation structure in an increasingly varied set of decision-making processes, including development of the city's housing program and capital and operating budgets.[149] In short, it appeared that many of the city's policy-making and administrative activities would be subject to the scrutiny of the citizen participation apparatus, giving access to officials to every geographic area in the city and to interest groups, like the handicapped, that had never before played active roles in local politics.

Third, the Citizen Participation Program served as a training ground for political candidates, exceeding in one year the cumulative record of the antipoverty program. Five of twenty-four candidates running for city council in the fall of 1975 emerged from the program, including the president of the city-wide committee; none of these five had had previous political experience. While only the city-wide committee president reached the runoff, where he was defeated, the program demonstrated its potential role as a recruitment channel for political leadership in future years.[150]

Finally, the city-wide committee particularly functioned as a biracial group without open divisions along racial lines; in this it resembled the JCCEO board, only with a much more extensive range of topics coming before it. Thus, the program raised the possibility that biracial politics might be possible in Birmingham.

The simultaneous functioning of JCCEO and the Citizen Participation Program indicates that biracial organizations and political activity had emerged as real possibilities in Birmingham in 1975; the continued functioning of ONB's Community Affairs Committee also supported this conclusion. Furthermore, the 1975 city council and mayoral elections indicated the potential for biracial coalitions in electoral politics. Richard Arrington, Jr., the incumbent black city councilman who was outspoken in his criticism of the police department and in his concern for the interests of the black community, was easily reelected to a second term, finishing second in a field of twenty-four candidates and gaining substantial support in upper-middle-class white neighborhoods on the city's southside.[151] Already regarded by many as a potential candidate for mayor, Arrington chose instead to campaign actively in behalf of a white fellow councilman who succeeded in winning the mayorship, gaining the support of the overwhelming majority of black voters and a significant proportion of the southside white vote.[152] Birmingham's new mayor, inaugurated twelve and one-half years after Albert Boutwell initiated the mayor-council form of government, was David Vann.

As the above three chapters indicate, politics and welfare in Birmingham were dramatically transformed after 1962; although the political and social welfare arenas were largely separated from one another, changes in both brought to the city a new pluralism resting on the principles of greater citizen participation and greater responsiveness to the needs of constituencies previously neglected or unrecognized. This transformation in local affairs rested upon four key issues.

The first two issues, the change in the form of government and the resolution of the racial crisis of 1963, were intertwined and reflected both the emergence of Blacks as significant local political actors and the significance of race relations to the stability of the local polity. While the change in the form of government can be viewed as a locally generated reform, the demands of Blacks, which influenced this reform, received external support from the civil rights movement, specifically from the activities of Martin Luther King, Jr. His involvement elevated local events to international significance and stimulated direct federal intervention. The third issue, the War on Poverty, not only added new resources to the community but also created the institutional means to allocate them. The result was the creation of a stable, biracial, tripartite policy-making group; a major social service delivery system; and a constituency for the needs of low income residents of the community, especially low income Blacks.

The fourth issue, the Citizen Participation Program, reflected additional concern by the federal government specifically for the poor and minorities and their participation in the political decision-making process related to the expenditure of federal funds provided by the Department of Housing and Urban Development. The local mechanism created in response to this latest federal intervention reinstated neighborhoods as entities of political significance and formally established new constituencies; they and their elected representatives became involved in political matters extending beyond the allocation of federal funds into virtually all areas of local government.[153] The program can, therefore, be viewed as an additional basic change in local political structures. While the Community Affairs Committee of ONB continued as a strong force in the community, concerned with many of the same subjects discussed by Citizen Participation Program participants, its parent organization suffered a significant defeat, based largely upon widespread discontent with it in low income and black neighborhoods, when ONB was eliminated from the Citizen Participation Program. The managed pluralism of the Community Affairs Committee was supplemented by the unmanaged, and sometimes unmanageable, pluralism of the Citizen Participation Program; the closed meetings of a purportedly private organization reflecting particularly the interests of the business community were supplemented by the numerous open meetings at all three levels of the Citizen Participation Program, a clearly public institution. A city characterized prior to 1962 by a relatively inactive local government and a heavy dependence on private leadership and organizations in 1975 had a twice-reformed local government whose new responsibilities were assumed partly at the expense of influential private actors. While it would be premature to pronounce the city's traditional culture of privatism dead, it would be fair to state that privatism was being so seriously confronted by public, biracial, participatory bodies that Birmingham was in transition to a new era of politics characterized by both increased pluralism and increased public responsibility.

Epilogue

ANY ATTEMPT TO continue the story of Birmingham's development since 1975 would require a separate, complex, and lengthy volume.[1] I would, however, offer some concluding observations about this distinctive community based not upon traditional scholarship but rather upon close observation of the community since 1975, coupled with the unique opportunity which I had to serve as a senior staff member for Mayor Richard Arrington, Jr., from 1979 to 1987. I would suggest that two of the major concluding themes of this study have been carried forward from 1975 to the present: increasing the responsibility of local government and making it more inclusive in its personnel and policies. The potential for biracial cooperation remains strong but still often unfulfilled.

Two men have occupied the mayor's office since 1975: David Vann (1975–1979), lawyer, political reformer, and city councillor from 1971 to 1975, and Richard Arrington, Jr. (1979–), biologist, educator, and city councillor from 1971 to 1979.

During the Vann-Arrington era, Birmingham has ceased to stand out as a unique large city stubbornly resisting relentless pressures of social, economic, and political change. Instead, Birmingham has become a reflection of urban America more generally, coping with civic issues related to diversity of the population and economic change. The two men have shared a political philosophy and a public policy program that have carried forward two main themes from the earlier period: promoting a more responsible, active city government and increasing opportunities for participation by Blacks in both the political and economic arenas. These twin policy objectives have led to a city government that has become increasingly intertwined with the private sector in economic development activities, while putting pressure on that same private sector to provide more opportunities for black citizens. Thus, David Vann entered into a partnership with the downtown business community to undertake a master plan for downtown revitalization that hinged upon an activist city government using its planning authority and public improvements program to undergird private-sector development within the downtown area. Similarly, his administration initiated a program of using federal funds made available through the Urban Development Action Grant Program to stimulate home-building and home renovation by private-sector owners. At the same time, Vann pressed forcefully for the greater inclusion of minority businesses in the economic life of the community and minority employees in the operations of the city government. He initiated a 10 percent minority participation require- ment in city contracts, a policy that resulted in a legal conflict between the city and the Associated General Contractors of America that was not resolved until 1989. Vann's appointment of James Baker, a prominent black attorney, to the post of city attorney illustrated his commitment to the inclusion of minorities in public-sector positions from which they had previously been excluded. In these efforts to grapple with economic change and promote minority partici- pation, Vann was joined by his friend and political ally on the city council, Richard Arrington, Jr. Both men also shared a commitment to the revitalization of the neighborhoods of the city and to a significant and expanding role for the Citizen Participation Program.

Richard Arrington challenged David Vann in the 1979 municipal election even though the two men shared both a close personal relationship and a simi- lar public policy agenda. The reason for this unexpected challenge called forth images from the city's troubled past. A white police officer shot and killed a black woman at the scene of a robbery. An outraged black community de- manded that Mayor Vann dismiss or at least severely discipline the white of- ficer involved. Vann, however, concluded that the officer had fired his weapon "within policy" and therefore should not be the subject of any sanctions. In a true draft, Arrington was approached by a group of black ministers who pre- vailed upon him to enter the upcoming mayoral contest. Arrington did enter the race and won in the runoff, capturing the vote of the strongly united black community and approximately 10 percent of the white vote—primarily from the city's south side. While the media now turned to Birmingham with re- newed interest, hailing the election of a black mayor in the city once recognized as the international symbol of racial intransigence, careful analysis of the local situation points to a somewhat harsher conclusion. Richard Arrington's elec- tion did not, in my view, represent the culmination of an ongoing process of progressive change within the Birmingham community. Rather, his election represented the resurgence of a difficult issue from the city's past, police bru- tality, coupled with the new demographic reality of a city approaching a ma- jority black population and electorate—a black population that had acquired dramatic new political power after the Voting Rights Act of 1965.

Richard Arrington as mayor carried forward the philosophy that local gov- ernment should be an effective participant in key economic development activities in Birmingham. A major commitment of his first term was implemen- tation of the downtown revitalization plan initiated by David Vann; this downtown renewal was contingent upon a combination of public and private investment. Though implementation of the master plan for downtown revitalization did not achieve all of its desired goals, the mayor nonetheless clearly established city government as a principal actor in local economic development. This policy was emphasized by significant revitalization of neighborhood commercial districts; acquisition, development, and sale of industrial park properties; and perhaps the most aggressive municipal program of assistance to single-family home owners in the nation.

Arrington also carried forward the Vann commitment to expanding opportunities for minorities in both private and public sectors. Throughout his years in office his policy program has included increasingly sophisticated forms of financial assistance to disadvantaged entrepreneurs, with particular emphasis on Blacks and women. The program of assistance to "disadvantaged business enterprises" has moved from an entirely publicly funded loan program to one in which the city and local financial institutions cooperate. Indeed, Arrington has emphasized the notion of public-private partnerships in many areas of community life, ranging from the construction of major physical facilities like the Museum of Art, the Birmingham Civil Rights Institute, and the Race Course to developing neighborhood-based programs to expand opportunities for low income youth. Arrington has also made a significant commitment to opening new opportunities for Blacks in the public sector. Under the terms of a consent decree approved by the federal district court, the city's workforce—most notably the fire and police departments—has been integrated in terms of both race and gender. The electoral process has reinforced these changes in personnel policy; six of nine city councillors are now black and three are women.

The Birmingham Citizen Participation program remains a model in the nation and a training ground for aspiring local politicians. Ninety-nine neighborhood associations are regular participants in matters related to municipal budgeting, zoning, and land-use planning; some have created sophisticated community development corporations undertaking housing revitalization and other improvements within their boundaries.

Birmingham city government since 1975 has increasingly become a partner with the private sector in a significant erosion of privatism as the community's dominant political ideology and the extension of public authority and responsibility. Part of this fundamental change is due, undoubtedly, to the fact that throughout most of this period federal programs of assistance to cities have been progressively diminished; cities have increasingly been called upon to undertake locally initiated efforts. But the erosion of privatism and the expansion of public responsibility began before this growing federal indifference to cities, and they exist independent of it. There is now a view in the community—widely shared by corporate leaders, public officials, and citizens—that local government can and should become an active participant in an increasingly wide range of community endeavors.

The city's experience with biracialism since 1975 has been alternately promising and problematic. A widely shared perception at the time of Arrington's election was that Birmingham had achieved a new level of biracial cooperation. Though his election had grown out of an interracial police incident and had polarized the community to a significant extent, his administration began amid extensive favorable publicity and very high hopes. The newly inaugurated mayor signaled his intentions to the community by appointing a staff which was 50 percent black and 50 percent white and included women for the first time in important policy-making positions. He likewise made overtures to the overwhelmingly white business community, which gradually became more accepting of his administration and of the expanded role in economic development that now characterizes city government in Birmingham. This "era of good feelings" suffered a significant jolt when the Jefferson County Citizens Coalition, a predominately black political organization founded by Arrington, endorsed an all-black slate in the 1981 city council elections.

In time the mayor both acknowledged the problems created by this slate and worked hard to overcome its negative impact, particularly among white business leaders. Though he campaigned hard in predominately white neighborhoods in his 1983 reelection bid, his percentage of the white vote hovered at approximately 12 percent, only 2 percent greater than during the 1979 campaign for mayor; there was only a slight increase in support from the white community even though the city had objectively carried out more public improvement programs in predominately white neighborhoods than during any previous administration. The reelection campaigns of 1987 and 1991 followed basically the same voting pattern.

The Arrington years have been characterized by continuity in public policy, with continuing emphasis upon the main themes outlined above. Three significant developments point to both the advances that have been made and the obstacles to progress that have arisen during recent years.

First, in 1989 Arrington and business leaders fashioned a voluntary response to the ongoing litigation between the city of Birmingham and Associated General Contractors over the issue of minority participation in construction. After U.S. Supreme Court rulings that made mandatory municipal programs extremely difficult to maintain, a significant public-private partnership labeled "The Birmingham Plan" resulted in major contractors agreeing to set minority participation goals on an annual basis for both public and private

The Birmingham Civil Rights Institute, dedicated November 15, 1992, is located in Birmingham's Civil Rights District across the street from both Sixteenth Street Baptist Church and Kelly Ingram Park. The park, site of demonstrations in 1963, is now designated "A Place of Revolution and Reconciliation." (Photograph courtesy of W. E. Ricker)

construction in a multicounty area. The Birmingham Plan stands as a nationally significant effort to expand economic opportunities for Blacks and women, carrying forward the themes of city government as a partner in economic development and greater inclusion of minorities in economic activities.

The unifying tendencies of the Birmingham Plan were more than offset by the divisive effects of a series of investigations by federal agencies into alleged corruption in the Arrington administration that extended over approximately an eight-year period of time beginning in 1984. Ultimately the integrity of the mayor was called into question amid allegations that he had accepted a bribe. Arrington and his supporters charged that the investigations were without foundation and represented systematic harassment of the mayor and his administration by a hostile federal district attorney; administration critics anticipated vindication of their charges that public funds had been mismanaged and the public trust abused. Division over this matter in the community largely followed racial lines; the negative impact upon the city's economic development efforts was incalculable as many potential partners shied away from business relations with an administration under investigation.

The end of 1992 suggested that Birmingham might be again embarked upon a path characterized by greater harmony within the community, especially across racial lines. The first major development in this direction was the conclusion of the federal investigation into the Arrington administration, which cleared Arrington of any wrongdoing, thereby creating a more favorable environment for private sector involvement with the city in economic development efforts. Second, the new Birmingham Civil Rights Institute was dedicated on 15 November 1992 as a memorial to the civil rights movement in the South and especially in Birmingham, and as an active center of research and education dealing with national and international questions of human rights and justice. The enthusiastic response to opening week activities and the institute suggested that the Birmingham Civil Rights Institute might indeed fulfill the dreams of its supporters by serving as a place of both learning and healing. The city basked in favorable national publicity reporting the events of the opening, describing the program of the institute, and suggesting for the first time since Arrington's election in 1979 that Birmingham is a city that has reached a milestone in race relations. Unlike the 1979 election, however, the opening of the Civil Rights Institute reflected a significant degree of cooperation within the community, knitting together diverse groups such as the veterans of the civil rights period and the mainstays of the corporate community in promoting a common effort. Though skeptics remain to be convinced, optimists hope that the institute represents a partial fulfillment of the perpetual promise which *Harper's Magazine* writer George R. Leighton had noted fifty-five years before.

Notes

Preface

1. U.S. Department of Commerce, Bureau of the Census, *Fifteenth Census of the United States, 1930: Population*, 1:18.
2. George R. Leighton, "Birmingham, Alabama: The City of Perpetual Promise," *Harper's*, August 1937, pp. 225–42.
3. Ibid., p. 227.
4. Ibid., p. 239.
5. Ibid., p. 225.
6. Ibid., p. 230.
7. Sam Bass Warner, Jr., *The Private City: Philadelphia in Three Periods of Its Growth* (Philadelphia: University of Pennsylvania Press, 1968), pp. 176, 208.
8. Wilson discusses professionalization and bureaucratization in his essay "The Police and the Delinquent in Two Cities" in *City Politics and Public Policy*, ed. James Q. Wilson (New York: Wiley, 1968), pp. 173–95 and especially pp. 175–76.

1. Birmingham, Alabama

1. John R. Hornady, *The Book of Birmingham* (New York: Dodd, Mead, 1921), p. 169.
2. Martha Carolyn Mitchell Bigelow, "Birmingham: Biography of a City of the New South" (Ph.D. dissertation, University of Chicago, 1946), p. 13.
3. Ibid., p. 15.
4. Hornady, *Book of Birmingham*, p. 20.
5. Ibid., p. 20; Bigelow, "Birmingham," p. 21.
6. Bigelow, "Birmingham," pp. 21–22.
7. Ibid., pp. 24–25.
8. Ibid., pp. 28, 35.
9. Ibid., pp. 30–31.
10. Ibid., pp. 37, 40.
11. Ibid., p. 45.
12. Joseph M. Farley, "The Greater Birmingham Struggle of 1907–1910" (Birmingham, n.d., typewritten), p. 2.
13. Bigelow, "Birmingham," p. 279.
14. Ibid., p. 50.
15. *Birmingham News*, 30 November 1914, 21 February 1915.
16. Ibid., 30 April 1915.
17. Ibid., 7 May 1907, 7 January 1908.
18. Bigelow, "Birmingham," p. 76.
19. *Birmingham News*, 9 December 1914.

20. Ibid., 24 May 1907.

21. Ibid., 1 May 1907.

22. Ibid.

23. Hornady, *Book of Birmingham*, p. 105.

24. Edward S. LaMonte, *George B. Ward: Birmingham's Urban Statesman* (Birmingham: Birmingham Public Library, 1974), p. 31.

25. *Birmingham News*, 24 April, 24 May, 3 October 1911.

26. Ibid., 19 October 1913.

27. Ibid., 16 November, 13 December 1913.

28. Ibid., 2 June 1914.

29. Ibid., 25 February, 12 July 1915.

30. Ibid., 8 August 1915.

31. Ibid., 19 November 1916.

32. Ibid., 17 July 1917.

33. Ibid., 29 November 1914.

34. Ibid., 18 December 1914.

35. Ibid., 19 January 1915.

36. Ibid., 10 January 1916.

37. Ibid., 28 December 1915.

38. Ibid., 28 March 1903.

39. Ibid., 19 October 1913.

40. Ibid., 12 July 1907; 13 April 1913.

41. Ibid., 15 January 1902.

42. Ibid., 28 February 1903.

43. Ibid.

44. Ibid., 26 March 1916.

45. Ibid., 12 February 1916.

46. Ibid., 11 October 1902.

47. Ibid., 24 January, 8, 12 February 1906.

48. Ibid., 3 April 1907.

49. Ibid., 27 September 1916.

50. Ibid., 3, 6 December 1916.

51. Ibid., 30, 31 January 1917; also Citizens Committee on Indigent Medical Care for Jefferson County, Alabama, "Draft of Final Report" (Birmingham, 22 September 1958), p. 4.

52. *Birmingham News*, 4 November 1917.

53. Sara Griffith, "Birmingham: The Magic City" (B. S. project, Northwestern University, 1938), p. 3; Don H. Doyle, *New Men, New Cities, New South: Atlanta, Nashville, Charleston, Mobile, 1860–1910* (Chapel Hill: University of North Carolina Press, 1990), p. 13.

54. Bigelow, "Birmingham," p. 220.

55. Ibid., p. 223.

56. Ibid., p. 229.

57. Ibid., p. 236.

58. *Birmingham News*, 1 May 1907.

59. Ibid., 4 September 1901.

60. Ibid., 5 November 1903.

61. Ibid., 22 November 1905.

62. Ibid., 5 November 1903.

63. Ibid., 6 November 1905. Similar data from Nashville and Atlanta are found in Doyle, *New Men, New Cities, New South*, pp. 276–78.

64. *Birmingham News*, 10 February 1908.

65. Ibid., 3 August 1908.

66. Ibid., 7 March 1905.

67. Ibid., 1 May 1907.

68. Ibid., 1 May 1909.

69. Bigelow, "Birmingham," pp. 236, 240.

70. *Birmingham News*, 21 March 1912.

71. Ibid., 17 April 1913.

72. Ibid., 5 August 1917.

73. Bigelow, "Birmingham," p. 271.

74. *Birmingham News*, 23 July 1901.

75. Ibid., 3 September 1903.

76. Bigelow, "Birmingham," p. 271.

77. *Birmingham News*, 24 June 1914.

78. Ibid., 22 September 1914.

79. Ibid., 21 April 1910.

80. Ibid., 13 August 1913.

81. Ibid., 4 February 1916; Robert Gaines Corley, "The Quest for Racial Harmony: Race Relations in Birmingham, Alabama, 1947–1963 (Ph.D. dissertation, University of Virginia, 1979), p. 24.

82. *Birmingham News*, 25 September 1911.

83. Ibid., 22 August 1912.

84. Ibid., 27 June, 12 July 1913.

85. Ibid., 18 October 1916.

86. Ibid., 18 September 1916.

87. Ibid., 3 December 1914.

88. Ibid., 16 November 1913, sec. A, p. 6.

89. Bigelow, "Birmingham," p. 79.

90. Malcolm Cook McMillan, *Constitutional Development in Alabama, 1798–1901: A Study in Politics, the Negro, and Sectionalism* (Chapel Hill: University of North Carolina Press, 1955 [vol. 37 of James Sprunt Studies in History and Political Science]; Spartanburg, S. C.: Reprint Company, 1978), pp. v, 370.

91. *Birmingham News*, 19 February 1902.

2. Politics and Decision Making

1. *Birmingham News*, 28 February 1903; Martha Carolyn Mitchell Bigelow, "Birmingham: Biography of a City of the New South" (Ph.D. dissertation, University of Chicago, 1946), pp. 80–88; Carl Vernon Harris, *Political Power in Birmingham, 1871–1921* (Knoxville: University of Tennessee Press, 1977), p. 60.

2. John R. Hornady, *The Book of Birmingham* (New York: Dodd, Mead, 1921), p. 321.

3. Bigelow, "Birmingham," p. 55.

4. *Birmingham News*, 23 April 1900, 22 October 1904, 21 January 1907, 17 January 1908; also Harris, *Political Power in Birmingham, 1871–1921*, p. 60.

5. *Birmingham News*, 28 February 1903.

6. Ibid., 26 June 1908, 13 September 1914, 15 October 1915.

7. Ibid., 13 July 1913.

8. Charles N. Glaab and A. Theodore Brown, *A History of Urban America* (New York: Macmillan, 1967), pp. 212–15.

9. *Birmingham News*, 27 May, 9 June 1910.

10. LaMonte, *George Ward*, pp. 24–27.

11. *Birmingham News*, 2 February 1907.

12. LaMonte, *George Ward*, pp. 24–27.

13. *Birmingham News*, 21 August 1917.

14. Ibid., 19 September 1917.

15. Ibid., 6 October 1917.

16. Ibid., 9 October 1917.

17. LaMonte, *George Ward*, p. 40.

18. Virginia Van der Veer Hamilton, *Hugo Black: The Alabama Years* (Baton Rouge: Louisiana State University Press, 1972), pp. 278–79. Wayne Flynt states that more than one-half of Birmingham's ministers belonged to the Klan in the 1920s. (Flynt, *Mine, Mill & Microchip: A Chronicle of Alabama Enterprise* [Northridge, Calif.: Windsor Publications, 1987], p. 134). An overview of the Klan in Birmingham is William R. Snell, "Masked Men in the Magic City: Activities of the Revised Klan in Birmingham, 1916–1940," *Alabama Historical Quarterly* 34, no. 3–4 (Fall and Winter 1972): 206–27. A general overview of the Klan during this period is Kenneth T. Jackson, *The Ku Klux Klan in the City, 1915–1930* (Chicago: Ivan R. Dee, 1992).

19. Glaab and Brown, *History of Urban America*, pp. 217–20; Edward C. Banfield and James Q. Wilson, *City Politics* (New York: Vintage Books, 1963), p. 139. A similar conflict between the center city and suburban fringe during a temperance crusade is documented in Don H. Doyle, *Nashville in the New South 1880–1930* (Knoxville: University of Tennessee Press, 1985), p. 162.

20. *Birmingham News*, 1 May 1909.

21. Ibid., 13 July 1913.

22. Ibid., 24 August 1913, sec. C, p. 16.

23. Ibid., 5 December 1904, 29 November 1910, 13, 15 March 1934.

24. Harris, *Political Power in Birmingham, 1871–1921*, p. 120.

25. A similar pattern is noted in Sam Bass Warner, Jr., *Streetcar Suburbs: The Process of Growth in Boston, 1870–1900* (New York: Atheneum, 1974), pp. 2–3.

26. *Birmingham News*, 15 September 1905.

27. Graham T. Allison, *Essence of Decision: Explaining the Cuban Missile Crisis* (Boston: Little, Brown, 1971), p. vi.

28. Blaine Allison Brownell, *The Urban Ethos in the South, 1920–1930* (Baton Rouge: Louisiana State University Press, 1975); Harris, *Political Power in Birmingham, 1871–1921*; and Bigelow, "Birmingham."

29. *Birmingham News*, 20 March 1902.

30. Ibid., 16 September 1914.

31. Ibid., 8 February 1900.

32. Ibid., 8 February 1900, 3 January 1903.

33. Ibid., 6 August 1903.

34. Ibid., 15, 19 August 1903.

35. Ibid., 20 September 1906.

36. Ibid., 23, 29 January 1907.

37. Ibid., 23 January, 26 September 1907.

38. Ibid., 30 January, 4, 20 February 1908.

39. Ibid., 28 April 1909.

40. Ibid., 2 March, 5 October 1910; 8 February 1911.

41. Ibid., 31 May 1911, 10 February 1912.

42. Ibid., 25 September 1911. The Birmingham Trades Council represented white workers. The council had delegates from black locals and was integrated until 1903, when the Colored Central Labor Council was formed with twenty affiliated unions. An alliance between the two councils prevented the use of members of either organization as strikebreakers. Most workers during this period were in segregated locals, though some United Mine Workers locals were integrated (Philip S. Foner, *Organized Labor and the Black Worker, 1619–1973* [New York: Praeger, 1974], p. 87).

For a discussion of integrated United Mine Workers of America locals in the Birmingham district during the 1908 strike, see Ronald L. Lewis, *Black Coal Miners in America: Race, Class, and Community Conflict, 1780–1980* (Lexington: University Press of Kentucky, 1987), pp. 51–55. Also of interest is part 2 of Lewis's book, which deals with convict leasing and focuses on Alabama.

43. *Birmingham News*, 29 September, 6, 28, 29, 31 October, 9, 12 November 1912, 13 January, 30 March 1913, 23 October, 5, 6, 17, 21 November 1914, 16 January, 20, 21, 23 February, 8 June 1915.

44. Ibid., 12 June, 14 December 1900.

45. Ibid., 4, 22, 29, 30 January, 15 February 1902.

46. Ibid., 18 February 1902.

47. Ibid., 7 April 1903.

48. Ibid., 8 January, 18 April 1903.

49. Ibid., 26 September, 1 October 1903.

50. Ibid., 1, 2, 8, 19, 20 September 1905.

51. Ibid., 29 July 1907.

52. Ibid., 5 August 1907.

53. Ibid., 9 August 1907.

54. Ibid., 3, 4, 7 January 1908.

55. Ibid., 13, 23 January, 17 June, 5, 6, 18, 19 August, 16 December 1909.

56. Jere King, "Formation of Greater Birmingham" (Birmingham, n.d., typewritten), p. 1.

57. *Birmingham News*, 26 July 1906.

58. Ibid., 24 October 1907.

59. Ibid., 17, 19, 21 November 1908.

60. Ibid., 4 December 1908.

61. Ibid., 7 December 1908.

62. Ibid., 10 December 1908.

63. Ibid., 3 April 1909.

64. Ibid., 10, 12 August 1909.

65. Ibid., 13 August 1909.
66. Ibid., 13 May 1910.
67. Ibid., 6 May 1910. This municipal league was a new organization, distinct from the Birmingham Municipal Ownership League, established in 1907, that was discussed earlier in this chapter.
68. Ibid., 21 June 1910.
69. Ibid., 10 December 1910.
70. Ibid., 28 February 1911.
71. Ibid., 27 February 1911.
72. Analyses were made but not included in the study for the following issues: installation of an area-wide sewer system (1900), police administration (1907–08), smoke control (1905–13), prohibition (1906–11), and civil service legislation (1910–12).
73. *Birmingham News*, 18 February 1902; see *Birmingham Post-Herald*, 9 May 1975, for a more recent and similar U.S. Steel case.
74. Harris, *Political Power in Birmingham, 1871–1921*, p. 281.
75. *Birmingham News*, 30 April 1934.
76. Wilson, *City Politics*, p. 12.
77. Sam Bass Warner, Jr., *The Private City: Philadelphia in Three Periods of Its Growth* (Philadelphia: University of Pennsylvania Press, 1968), p. 4.
78. Ibid., p. 208.
79. Ibid., p. 3.
80. Ibid., pp. 109, 176.
81. Warner, *Streetcar Suburbs*, p. 33.
82. *Birmingham News*, 20 June 1915.
83. Ibid., 23 January 1917.
84. Ibid., 11 August 1917.
85. Ibid., 1 March 1916.
86. Ibid., 2 August 1914.
87. Ibid., 18, 23 December 1914.
88. Ibid., 10 January 1916; 21 June 1910.
89. In his study of Atlanta, Nashville, Charleston, and Mobile, Doyle describes differing attitudes held by the dominant "urban business class." For example, Charleston is characterized by a "torpid spirit of enterprise" and "a view of life that accepted leisure and sociability to be as important as the art of making money was in Atlanta" (Doyle, *New Men, New Cities, New South*, pp. xiii, 118–19).
90. Political scientists find the concept of "privatism" helpful in discussions of urban government generally. The authors of one text cite Warner in their review of "sociocultural forces that make Americans somewhat indifferent to the problems of cities" when they refer to "an ethos of privatism—whereby decisions in the private sector are presumed to be superior to and immune from government actions" (Clarence N. Stone, Robert K. Whelan, and William J. Murin, *Urban Policy and Politics in a Bureaucratic Age* [Englewood Cliffs, N.J.: Prentice Hall, 1986], pp. 13, 15).
91. Goldfield concludes that in southern cities generally, "government provision for social services was deemed unnecessary" (David R. Goldfield, *Cotton Fields and Skyscrapers: Southern City and Region, 1607–1980* [Baton Rouge: Louisiana State University Press, 1982], p. 5).

3. Welfare Services

1. Leah Hannah Feder, *Unemployment Relief in Periods of Depression: A Study of Measures Adopted in Certain American Cities, 1857 through 1922* (New York: Russell Sage, 1936), pp. 37–70 passim; Elizabeth Wisner, *Social Welfare in the South from Colonial Times to World War I* (Baton Rouge: Louisiana State University Press, 1970), pp. 93, 115.

2. Feder, *Unemployment Relief*, p. 26.

3. Josephine Chapin Brown, *Public Relief 1929–1939* (New York: Henry Holt, 1940), p. 1.

4. The term *outdoor relief* refers to aid provided outside the institutional setting of a "poorhouse" or almshouse.

5. Brown, *Public Relief 1929–1939*, p. 8.

6. Nathan Irvin Huggins, *Protestants against Poverty: Boston's Charities, 1870–1900* (Westport, Conn.: Greenwood, 1971), p. 9.

7. Ibid., p. 157.

8. Brown, *Public Relief 1929–1939*, p. 50.

9. Feder, *Unemployment Relief*, p. 223.

10. Anita Van de Voort, "Public Welfare Administration in Jefferson County, Alabama" (M.A. thesis, Tulane University, 1933), p. 7.

11. Ibid., p. 8.

12. Ibid., p. 19.

13. Ibid., p. 22.

14. Martha Carolyn Mitchell Bigelow, "Birmingham: Biography of a City of the New South" (Ph.D. dissertation, University of Chicago, 1946), p. 143.

15. Feder, *Unemployment Relief*, p. 136.

16. Charles Allen Brown, *The Origin and Development of Secondary Education for Negroes in the Metropolitan Area of Birmingham, Alabama* (Birmingham: Commercial Printing, 1959), p. 13; *Birmingham News*, 16 January 1900.

17. *Birmingham News*, 6 May 1901, 9 January, 13 February 1916.

18. Ibid., 24 March 1900, 16 February 1903, 24 January 1906, 20 February 1907, 14 December 1910, 24 November 1912, 16 March 1913.

19. Ibid., 28 August 1901, 10 September 1906.

20. Ibid., 30 August 1906.

21. A. G. Gaston, *Green Power* (Birmingham: Birmingham Publishing, 1968), p. 22.

22. *Birmingham News*, 14 November 1915; Brown, *Secondary Education for Negroes*, pp. 15, 17; Gaston, *Green Power*, p. 1.

23. Mark H. Elovitz, *A Century of Jewish Life in Dixie: The Birmingham Experience* (University: University of Alabama Press, 1974), pp. 45, 58, 85, 104, 111, 112; *Birmingham News*, 21 October 1905.

24. *Birmingham News*, 23 April 1900, p. 55, 8 April 1901, p. 25, 24 November 1902, 21 June 1905, 25 May 1908, 6 January, 13 December 1910, 16 January 1911, 24 November 1912.

25. Ibid., 23 April, 8 June, 1, 9 August, 18 October 1900, 2 January 1906, 5 October 1907.

26. Ibid., 28 November 1903.

27. Ibid., 23 April, 22 May 1900, 29 May 1901, 18 February 1911, 26 January 1913.

28. Ibid., 17 May 1914, sec. C, p. 9, 15 November 1914, 6 June 1917.

29. Ibid., 25 February 1917.

30. Ibid., 7 December 1913, sec. E, p. 5, 22 March 1917, sec. C, p. 11, 6 June 1917.

31. Ibid., 7 December 1913, sec. E, p. 5.

32. Ibid., 26 May 1902, p. 79, 28 September, 28 November 1904, 28 January 1905, 12 April 1907, 23 May 1912, 6 June 1917.

33. Ibid., 3 May, 12 October 1905, 17 August 1907, 25 March 1909, 12 January, 24 April 1911, 20 September 1912, 4 May, 29 June, 10 August 1913.

34. Ibid., 7 November 1908, 13 January 1912, 29 April, 6 October 1917.

35. Ibid., 18 September 1911, 20 March 1912, 27 June 1914, 11 October 1917; and E. M. Henderson, Sr., "Relief in Jefferson County: A Brief Survey" (Birmingham: 1934, typewritten), p. 76.

36. *Birmingham News*, 9 February 1911, 15 December 1912, 6 June 1917.

37. Ibid., 3 February 1912.

38. Ibid., 19 November 1915.

39. Ibid., 29 March, 4 November, 19 December 1911; 19 June, 20 October 1912, 8 March 1913, 27 June 1916.

40. Ibid., 26 May 1902, p. 69, 4 May 1903, 5, 15, 18, 22 February 1904; Bigelow, "Birmingham," pp. 145–48.

41. *Birmingham News*, 27 September, 24 November 1900, 8 November 1902, 25 November 1905, 23 July 1907, 20 February 1908, 9 December 1910.

42. Ibid., 10 September, 1904, 22 December 1912.

43. Ibid., 16 June 1910, 7 April 1911, 4 July, 6 October 1912, 5 April 1914, sec. D, p. 5, 4 June 1916.

44. Ibid., 23 June 1916.

45. Harris, *Political Power in Birmingham, 1871–1921*, p. 160.

46. Mollie Beck Jenkins, "The Social Work of the Tennessee Coal Iron and Railroad Company" (M.A. thesis, University of Alabama, 1929), p. 27. A comprehensive review of the company's health care program is Marlene Hunt Rikard's "An Experiment in Welfare Capitalism: The Health Care Services of the Tennessee Coal, Iron and Railroad Company" (Ph.D. dissertation, University of Alabama, 1983).

47. Roberta Morgan is the most notable example of a prominent social worker who began her career with the company. Her later work is discussed in subsequent chapters.

48. Bigelow, "Birmingham," p. 145.

49. *Birmingham News*, 10 November 1906.

50. Ibid., 20 March 1909. Activist women established a United Charities in Nashville in 1901 (Doyle, *Nashville in the New South, 1880–1930*, p. 129).

51. *Birmingham News*, 28 April 1909.

52. Ibid., 21 October 1909.

53. Ibid., 28 April 1909.

54. Ibid., 15 March 1914.

55. Ibid., 17 November 1912.

56. Ibid., 21 October 1909.

57. Ibid., 3 December 1913.

58. Ibid., 14 May 1916.

59. Ibid., 17 January 1915.

60. Ibid., 30 July 1916.

61. Ibid., 3 May 1905.

62. Ibid., 31 January 1907.

63. Ibid., 17 March 1914.

64. Ibid., 1 April 1914.

65. Ibid., 29 May 1901.

66. Ibid., 31 January 1907.

67. Ibid., 5 October 1914.

68. Ibid., 4 March 1912.

69. *Birmingham Age-Herald*, 4 July 1907.

70. *Birmingham News*, 6 February 1913, 29 November 1914, 11 July 1915, 24 December 1916.

71. Ibid., 27 June 1913; Van de Voort, "Public Welfare Administration," p. 41.

72. *Birmingham News*, 6 February 1913.

73. Ibid.

74. Ibid., 25 August 1914.

75. Ibid., 17 January 1915.

76. Ibid., 13 June 1915.

77. Ibid., 18 August 1916.

78. *Birmingham Age-Herald*, 11 March 1917.

79. *Birmingham News*, 14 October 1917.

80. Van de Voort, "Public Welfare Administration," pp. 56, 59.

4. Politics and Government in Birmingham

1. Blaine Allison Brownell, "Birmingham, Alabama: New South City in the 1920's," *Journal of Southern History* 38 (February 1972): 24.

2. Blaine Allison Brownell, "The Corporate-Expansive City: Concepts of Growth and Community in Southern Cities in the 1920s," paper presented at the Institute of Southern History Seminar, Johns Hopkins University, 14 April 1972, p. 50.

3. Brownell, *Urban Ethos*, p. 59.

4. Ibid., p. xix.

5. Brownell, "Birmingham, Alabama," p. 45.

6. Brownell, *Urban Ethos*, p. 161–62.

7. *Birmingham Post*, 20 January 1928.

8. Ibid., 25 December 1931.

9. *Birmingham News*, 24 October 1937, 30 March 1941.

10. Ibid., 18 May 1936.

11. *Birmingham Post*, 16 May 1935.

12. *Birmingham News*, 20 May 1931, 18 June 1934.

13. Ibid., 2 March 1934, 20 November 1940.

14. Ibid., 24 June 1928.

15. Griffith, "Birmingham."

16. *Birmingham News*, 8 September 1929, 30 March 1941; *Birmingham Post*, 15 September 1936.

17. *Birmingham Post*, 19 May 1938.

18. Ibid., 23 December 1941; *Birmingham Age-Herald*, 6 August 1932.

19. Griffith, "Birmingham."

20. *Birmingham News*, 24 June 1928, 10 January 1930, 23 January 1931.

21. Ibid., 10 January 1929.

22. Ibid., 20 June 1938, p. 69.

23. Ibid., 13 November 1941.

24. Ibid., 23 June 1929.

25. Ibid., 15 January 1928.

26. *Birmingham Post*, 1 December 1933.

27. Ibid., 17 February 1931.

28. *Birmingham News*, 23 May, 17 June 1930. Nell Irvin Painter offers remarkable insights into the activities of the Communist party and the life of working-class Blacks in Birmingham generally in *The Narrative of Hosea Hudson: His Life as a Negro Communist in the South* (Cambridge: Harvard University Press, 1979). A more comprehensive history of the Communist party in Alabama is Robin D. G. Kelley, *Hammer and Hoe: Alabama Communists during the Great Depression* (Chapel Hill: University of North Carolina Press, 1990). See pp. 15, 31–33, and 71–73 for reviews of demonstrations in Birmingham in 1930, 1932, 1933, and 1934.

Angelo Herndon, who moved to Birmingham as a child of thirteen, became a black Communist activist after he attended his first party meeting in 1930. Recognized by Birmingham police as a leading Communist, Herndon was arrested periodically and finally moved to Georgia in late 1931 or early 1932 to carry on his party work. Herndon's arrest in Atlanta on 11 July 1932 ultimately led to a landmark 1937 Supreme Court decision declaring the Georgia "insurrection" statute unconstitutional (Charles H. Martin, *The Angelo Herndon Case and Southern Justice* [Baton Rouge: Louisiana State University Press, 1976], pp. 9–10).

29. Ibid., 30 January 1939. At the first convention of the Southern Conference for Human Welfare, held in Birmingham in November 1938, black and white delegates sat together during the first day's sessions. Acting on orders from commissioner of public safety Eugene "Bull" Connor, Birmingham police required strict observance of the city's segregation ordinances on subsequent days (Thomas A. Krueger, *And Promises to Keep: The Southern Conference for Human Welfare, 1938–1948* [Nashville: Vanderbilt University Press, 1967], p. 26; Linda Reed, *Simple Decency & Common Sense: The Southern Conference Movement, 1938–1963* [Bloomington: Indiana University Press, 1991], pp. 15–19).

30. Brownell, "Birmingham, Alabama," p. 3; interview with Mervyn H. Sterne of Sterne, Agee, and Leach Stockbrokers, 8 March 1973; and William R. Snell, "Masked Men in the Magic City: Activities of the Revised Klan in Birmingham, 1916–1940," *Alabama Historical Quarterly* 34, no. 3–4 (Fall and Winter, 1972): 206–27.

31. *Birmingham Post*, 19, 20 May 1931.

32. *Birmingham Age-Herald*, 20 May 1928.

33. *Birmingham Post*, 10 February 1940.

34. *Birmingham Age-Herald*, 5 May 1937. Connor's career is fully reviewed in William A. Nunnelley, *Bull Connor* (Tuscaloosa: University of Alabama Press, 1991).

35. *Birmingham News*, 25 August 1929.

36. Ibid., 28 May 1929.

37. Ibid., 4 September 1929.

38. Ibid., 9 October 1929.

39. *Birmingham Post*, 5 June, September 1929; *Birmingham Age-Herald*, 8 June 1929; *Birmingham News*, 6 June 1929.

40. *Birmingham Post*, 12 September 1929; *Birmingham News*, 26 September 1929.

41. *Birmingham News*, 15 October 1929.

42. *Birmingham Age-Herald*, 25 April 1933; *Birmingham Post*, 1 August 1933.

43. *Birmingham Post*, 17 August 1933.

44. Ibid., 30 May, 24 July 1933; *Birmingham Age-Herald*, 30 August, 13 September 1933.

45. *Birmingham Post*, 28 November 1933, 26 February 1935; *Birmingham Age-Herald*, 12 December 1933.

46. *Birmingham News*, 13 February 1934; *Birmingham Post*, 17 March 1934.

47. *Birmingham News*, 4, 25 September 1935.

48. Ibid., 19 April 1937.

49. Ibid., 19 May 1937.

50. Ibid., 15 February 1940.

51. Ibid., 11 April 1941.

52. Ibid., 21 October 1928, 18 December 1935.

53. *Birmingham Post*, 23 December 1941.

54. *Birmingham News*, 23 February 1930; *Birmingham Age-Herald*, 26 February 1930; *Birmingham Post*, 25, 26 February 1930.

55. *Birmingham Post*, 23 February 1934.

56. Ibid., 27 February 1934; *Birmingham Age-Herald*, 21 March 1934.

57. *Birmingham News*, 9 January 1934.

58. *Birmingham Post*, 18 August, 19 September 1931.

59. *Birmingham News*, 3 April 1935; *Birmingham Post*, 27 July 1935; *Birmingham News*, 25 August 1935.

60. *Birmingham News*, 1 March 1929.

61. *Birmingham Age-Herald*, 21 February 1928.

62. *Birmingham Post*, 20 May 1931.

63. Ibid., 16 May 1933.

64. Ibid., 16 March, 9 May 1933.

65. Ibid., 13 June 1933.

66. Ibid., 12 May 1933.

67. *Birmingham Age-Herald*, 20 May 1933.

68. *Birmingham Post*, 14 July 1933.

69. *Birmingham Age-Herald*, 10 October 1933.

70. *Birmingham Post*, 18 August 1931.

71. Ibid., 16 November 1928.

72. Ibid., 19 December 1928.

73. *Birmingham Age-Herald*, 22 December 1928.

74. Ibid., 25 April 1928.

75. Harris, *Political Power in Birmingham, 1871–1921*, pp. 84–89.

76. *Birmingham Post*, 13 July 1932.

77. *Birmingham News*, 19 August 1936.

78. The concept of "urban imperialism" is developed in Richard C. Wade, *The Urban Frontier: Pioneer Life in Early Pittsburgh, Cincinnati, Lexington, Louisville, and St. Louis* (Chicago: University of Chicago Press, 1959), pp. 322–36.

79. *Birmingham News*, 19 August 1928.

80. Ibid., 18 September 1928.

81. Ibid., 19 September 1928.

82. Ibid., 18 September 1928.

83. *Birmingham Post*, 15 May 1930.

84. *Birmingham News*, 17 February 1932.

85. Ibid., 14 August 1932.

86. *Birmingham Post*, 9 February 1929.

87. Ibid., 15 February 1929.

88. *Birmingham News*, 22 February 1929.

89. Ibid., 21 May 1929.

90. *Birmingham Post*, 4 June 1929.

91. Ibid., 10 June 1929.

92. *Birmingham News*, 25 September 1929.

93. *Birmingham Age-Herald*, 12 February 1930.

94. *Birmingham News*, 27 April 1931.

5. The Depression in Birmingham

1. *Birmingham News*, 27 June 1929.

2. Jefferson County (Alabama) Community Chest, Inc., Minutes and Other Documents, 1923–1973, 14 vols. (typewritten), Advisory Board meeting of 9 June 1927.

3. *Birmingham News*, 27 March 1928.

4. Ibid., 25 March 1928.

5. Ibid., 2 July 1928.

6. *Birmingham Post*, 30 October 1929.

7. *Birmingham News*, 5 November 1929.

8. *Birmingham Post*, 2 November 1929; *Birmingham News*, 18 December 1935.

9. *Birmingham News*, 9 February 1931.

10. *Birmingham Post*, 5 August, 1932; *Birmingham News*, 19 February 1932.

11. *Birmingham Post*, 31 December 1932.

12. Ibid., 12 January 1934.

13. Ibid., 9 October 1934.

14. *Birmingham News*, 5 April 1930.

15. Ibid., 23 May 1930.

16. Ibid., 17 June, 14 November 1930. Hosea Hudson estimates that in 1933–35 there were 600–700 members of the Communist party in the Birmingham area, mainly Blacks. By the late 1930s membership stood at approximately 250. (Painter, *The Narrative of Hosea Hudson*, pp. 17, 114).

17. *Birmingham News*, 29 June 1930.

18. Ibid., 27 July 1931.

19. Ibid., 12, 13 February 1931.

20. *Birmingham Post*, 6 January 1932.

21. Ibid.

22. Ibid.

23. *Birmingham Age-Herald*, 6 January 1932.

24. *Birmingham News*, 9 May 1932.

25. Ibid., 2 February 1932.

26. *Birmingham Post*, 27 May 1932.

27. Ibid., 22 June 1932; *Birmingham News*, 7 July 1932.

28. *Birmingham Post*, 14 June 1928.

29. *Birmingham News*, 4 August 1930.

30. Ibid., 9 November 1930.

31. Ibid., 3 May 1931.

32. Ibid., 21, 28 June 1931.

33. Community Chest, Minutes, 2:151.

34. *Birmingham Post*, 7 May 1932.

35. Ibid., 25 April 1930.

36. *Birmingham News*, 17 August 1932.

37. Ibid., 16 December 1930.

38. *Birmingham Age-Herald*, 17 March 1932.

39. *Birmingham News*, 28 February 1933.

40. Ibid., 9 May 1931.

41. Ibid., 20 December 1931; 21 January 1932.

42. Ibid., 11 December 1930.

43. Ibid., 14 December 1930.

44. Ibid., 28, 30 December 1930.

45. Ibid., 16 August 1931.

46. Bessie A. Brooks, *A Half Century of Progress in Family Welfare Work in Jefferson County* (Birmingham: Roberts, 1936), p. 33; Anita Van de Voort, "Public Welfare Administration in Jefferson County, Alabama" (M.A. thesis, Tulane University, 1933), p. 67.

47. *Birmingham News*, 25 June 1931.

48. Van de Voort, "Public Welfare Administration", p. 42.

49. Ibid., p. 46; Brooks, *Progress in Family Welfare Work*, p. 22.

50. E. M. Henderson, Sr., "Relief in Jefferson County: A Brief Survey" (Birmingham, 1934, typewritten) p. 49.

51. Ibid., p. 50.

52. Ibid., p. 55.

53. Feder, *Unemployment Relief*, p. 300.

54. Floyd Hunter, "Community Organization: Lever for Institutional Change?" in *The Urban South*, ed. Rupert B. Vance and Nicholas J. Demerath (Chapel Hill: University of North Carolina Press, 1954; Freeport, N.Y.: Books for Libraries, 1971), p. 254.

55. Ibid., p. 255.

56. Van de Voort, "Public Welfare Administration," p. 54.

57. *Birmingham News*, 7 November 1933.

58. Brooks, *Progress in Family Welfare Work*, pp. 23–24.

59. Ibid., pp. 2–3.

60. Van de Voort, "Public Welfare Administration," p. 60.

61. Ibid.

62. *Birmingham News*, 17 October 1932.

63. Ibid., 8 January 1928.

64. Community Chest, Minutes, Board of Directors meeting of 18 September 1929.

65. Lucile Higgins, "A History of Charity in Birmingham" (B.A. thesis, Howard College, 1928), p. 83; and Community Chest, Minutes, Advisory Board meeting of 19 January 1938.

66. Brown, *Public Relief 1929–1939*, p. 78.

67. Higgins, "A History of Charity in Birmingham," p. 3.

68. Community Chest, Minutes, Board of Directors meeting of 20 October 1926.

69. *Birmingham News*, 2 September 1931.

70. Community Chest, Minutes, Advisory Board meeting of 15 September 1931.

71. Interview with Mervyn H. Sterne, Sterne, Agee, and Leach Stockbrokers, Birmingham, Ala., 13 March 1973; Community Chest, Minutes, Advisory Board meeting of 14 January 1932.

72. Community Chest, Minutes, Board of Directors meeting of 3 December 1929.

73. Ibid., Advisory Board meeting of 14 January 1930.

74. Ibid., Board of Directors meeting of 31 May 1932.

75. *Birmingham News*, 30 November 1929.

76. Ibid., 29 October 1935.

77. Ibid., 31 October 1935.

78. Community Chest, Minutes, 4:135.

79. Sanford Kravitz, "The Community Action Program—Past, Present, and Its Future?" in *On Fighting Poverty: Perspectives from Experience*, ed. James L. Sundquist (New York: Basic Books, 1969), p. 53; and Sanford Kravitz and Ferne K. Kolodner, "Community Action: Where Has It Been? Where Will It Go?" in *Annals of the American Academy of Political and Social Science* 385 (September 1969): 31.

80. Hunter, "Community Organization," p. 257.

81. Community Chest, Minutes, 1:195.

82. Community Chest, Minutes, Board of Directors meeting of 19 May 1926.

83. Ibid., Advisory Board meeting of 14 January 1930.

84. Ibid., Board of Directors meeting of 17 February 1932.

85. Higgins, "A History of Charity in Birmingham," p. 7.

86. Community Chest, Minutes, Advisory Board meeting of 25 January 1937.

87. Ibid., Board of Directors meeting of December 1937.

88. Ibid., 3:193, 212.

89. Ibid., Advisory Board meeting of 18 January 1939; Beatrice Weaver, "Community Welfare Councils in Nine Cities: A Comparative Study for Application in Birmingham, Alabama" (M.A. thesis, University of Alabama, 1948), p. 6.

90. Weaver, "Community Welfare Councils," p. 66.

91. Banfield and Wilson, *City Politics*, p. 39.

92. Community Chest, Minutes, Board of Directors meeting of 21 December 1927; Advisory Board meeting of 14 January 1930.

93. Ibid., Advisory Board meetings of 18 January 1939 and 16 January 1940.

94. Ibid., Executive Committee meeting of 14 August 1940.

95. Ibid.

96. Ibid., 4:111.

97. Higgins, "A History of Charity in Birmingham," appendix B.

98. *Birmingham News*, 7 October 1928.

99. Ibid., 1 October 1937, 22 October 1938; Community Chest, Minutes, Advisory Board meeting of 12 January 1934.

100. *Birmingham News*, 3 September 1935.

101. Community Chest, Minutes, Advisory Board meeting of 19 January 1938.

102. Jefferson County Commission, *Social Group Work Agencies in Birmingham and Jefferson County—1939* (a report prepared with the assistance of the Works Progress Administration), pp. 6, 29, 55, 57, 66.

103. Ibid., p. 62.

104. Ibid., pp. 76, 78.

105. Duncan Nolan, *Social and Economic Survey of the Birmingham District* (Birmingham: Housing Authority of the Birmingham District, 1943), pp. 15, 18.

106. Henderson, "Relief in Jefferson County," pp. 85–86.

107. Community Chest, Minutes, Executive Committee meeting of 26 May 1939.

108. Ibid., Executive Committee meeting of 6 June 1939.

109. Ibid., Advisory Board meeting of 16 January 1940.

110. Ibid., Executive Committee meeting of 18 January 1940.

111. Ibid., 4:121.

112. Ibid., Board of Directors meeting of 20 December 1928.

113. Ibid., Board of Directors meeting of 20 February 1929.

114. Ibid., Board of Directors meeting of 18 September 1929.

115. Ibid., Board of Directors meetings of 7 November and 9 November 1923.

116. Ibid., Board of Directors meeting of 19 November 1923.

117. Ibid., 1:14, 17.

118. *Birmingham News*, 12 August 1928.

119. Ibid., 6 May 1930.

120. Ibid., 12 May 1930.

121. Ibid., 7 May 1930.

122. Ibid., 28 June 1931.

123. Theodore J. Lowi, *The End of Liberalism: Ideology, Policy, and the Crisis of Public Authority* (New York: W. W. Norton, 1969), p. 216.

124. *Birmingham News*, 28 June 1931.

125. Ibid., 14 January, 31 March, 1 May 1932.

126. Community Chest, Minutes, Advisory Board meeting of 12 January 1933.

127. *Birmingham News*, 11 October 1932.

128. Community Chest, Minutes, 2:193.

129. *Birmingham News*, 23 October 1934.

130. Community Chest, Minutes, Board of Directors meeting of 27 September 1935.

131. Ibid., Board of Directors meeting of January 1936.

132. Ibid., Executive Committee meeting of September 1936.

133. Ibid.

134. Ibid., Executive Committee meeting of September 1937; Board of Directors meeting of September 1938.

135. *Birmingham News*, 2 December 1937.

6. Relief in Birmingham

1. *Birmingham News*, 30 September 1928.
2. Ibid., 19 April 1928.
3. Ibid., 16 January 1929.
4. Ibid., 14 January 1931, 25 February 1933.
5. Jefferson County (Alabama) Community Chest, Inc., Minutes and Other Documents, 1923–1973, 14 vols. (typewritten), 1:126.
6. *Birmingham News*, 16 January 1935.
7. Ibid., 22 January 1928, 31 March 1932.
8. Ibid., 8 April 1928.
9. *Birmingham Age-Herald*, 19 November 1931.
10. *Birmingham News*, 14 February 1932.
11. Brooks, *Progress in Family Welfare Work*, pp. 42–45, 66–68.
12. Jefferson County (Alabama) Chapter, American Red Cross, Minutes and Other Documents, 1921–1942 (typewritten), Executive Committee meeting of 16 August 1921.
13. Ibid., Board of Directors meeting of 19 December 1922.
14. Ibid., Board of Directors meeting of 15 May 1923.
15. Ibid., Board of Directors meeting of 18 September 1923.
16. Ibid., Board of Directors meetings of 21 October, 15, 23 December 1924.
17. Ibid., Board of Directors meeting of 20 January 1925.
18. Interview with Roberta Morgan, former director of the Red Cross Family Service and later of the Jefferson County Department of Public Welfare, Heflin, Ala., 8 March 1974; *Birmingham News*, 20 April 1936.
19. *Birmingham News*, 6 August 1930.
20. Ibid., 11 November 1932.
21. Ibid., 29 January 1928.
22. Interview with Roberta Morgan, 8 March 1974; *Birmingham News*, 11 April 1932.
23. Interview with Roberta Morgan, 8 March 1974.
24. Community Chest, Minutes, Advisory Board meeting of 7 January 1931.
25. *Birmingham News*, 10 January 1936.
26. Red Cross, Minutes, Board of Directors meeting of 13 November 1929.
27. Ibid., Board of Directors meeting of 15 December 1931.
28. Ibid., Board of Directors meeting of 13 January 1932.
29. *Birmingham News*, 3 August 1931.
30. Ibid., 11 November 1932.
31. Ibid., 11 April, 11 November 1932.
32. Brooks, *Progress in Family Welfare Work*, p. 36.
33. Red Cross, Minutes, Board of Directors meeting of 21 February 1928.
34. Community Chest, Minutes, Executive Committee meeting of 9 March 1932.
35. *Birmingham News*, 7 June 1932.

36. *Birmingham Post*, 3 August 1932.

37. *Birmingham Age-Herald*, 18 August 1932.

38. Community Chest, Minutes, 1:207.

39. *Birmingham News*, 19 August 1932.

40. Ibid., 11 November 1932.

41. Van de Voort, "Public Welfare Administration," p. 70.

42. *Birmingham News*, 12 January 1933.

43. Brooks, *Progress in Family Welfare Work*, pp. 42–45, 66–68.

44. Red Cross, Minutes, Board of Directors meeting of 16 June 1931.

45. Roberta Morgan, "Social Implications and the Human Side," *Journal of the Birmingham Historical Society* 1 (January 1960): 15; interview with Roberta Morgan, 8 March 1974; interview with Clara Moses Barton, former caseworker for the Jefferson County Department of Public Welfare, Birmingham, Ala., 15 February 1975.

46. Interview with Roberta Morgan, 8 March 1974; and interview with Thad Holt, former Alabama Relief Administrator, Birmingham, Ala., 28 March 1974.

47. Interview with Roberta Morgan, 8 March 1974.

48. Henderson, "Relief in Jefferson County," p. 29.

49. Harry L. Hopkins, *Spending to Save: The Complete Story of Relief* (New York: W. W. Norton, 1936), p. 100.

50. Henderson, "Relief in Jefferson County," p. 31.

51. *Birmingham News*, 18 July 1933; Community Chest, Minutes, 2: 193.

52. Interview with Roberta Morgan, 8 March 1974; and interview with Mervyn Sterne, Sterne, Agee, and Leach Stockbrokers, Birmingham, Ala., 13 March 1973.

53. *Birmingham News*, 10, 15 June 1934.

54. Ibid., 12 September 1934, 20 November 1939.

55. Interview with Thad Holt, 28 March 1974.

56. This tentative conclusion for Birmingham contradicts Goldfield's conclusions that Whites in southern cities received preference for both employment and relief during the Depression and that Blacks did not receive an equitable share of welfare funds through federal relief (Goldfield, *Cotton Fields and Skyscrapers*, p. 165).

57. *Birmingham News*, 22 December 1933, 6 January 1934, 28 December 1933.

58. Ibid., 19 January 1934.

59. Ibid., 26 December 1933.

60. Alabama Relief Administration, *Two Years of Federal Relief in Alabama* (Wetumpka, Ala.: Wetumpka Printing, 1935), p. 82.

61. *Birmingham News*, 28 September 1934.

62. Ibid., 14 January 1935.

63. Brown, *Public Relief 1929–1939*, p. 312.

64. *Birmingham News*, 31 August, 11 September 1935.

65. Ibid., 26 September 1935.

66. Ibid., 3 January 1936.

67. Brown, *Public Relief 1929–1939*, p. 325.

68. *Birmingham News*, 26 September 1935.

69. Ibid., 14 February 1936.

70. Ibid., 26 February 1936.

71. Ibid., 4 March 1936.

72. Ibid., 1 March 1936.

73. Ibid., 12, 13 March 1936.

74. Ibid., 13 March 1936.

75. Ibid., 22, 17 March, 9 April 1936.

76. Ibid., 20 April 1936; interview with Roberta Morgan, 8 March 1974.

77. *Birmingham News*, 30 June, 10 November, 12 October 1936.

78. Ibid., 9 June, 5 August 1937.

79. *Birmingham Post*, 29 July 1937.

80. *Birmingham Age-Herald*, 2 September 1937.

81. *Birmingham News*, 19 August 1937.

82. Ibid., 22 August 1937.

83. Ibid., 3 November 1937.

84. Ibid., 28 August 1937.

85. Ibid., 9 November 1937.

86. Ibid., 5 December 1937.

87. Ibid., 1 December 1937.

88. *Birmingham Post*, 28 February 1940.

89. Morgan, "Social Implications and the Human Side," p. 17.

90. *Birmingham News*, 20 February 1934.

91. *Birmingham Post*, 1 December 1933; *Birmingham News*, 6 January 1936.

92. *Birmingham News*, 15 August 1934, 25 October 1933.

93. Ibid., 11 January 1934. For a general history of the Civil Works Administration, see Bonnie F. Schwartz, *The Civil Works Administration, 1933–34: The Business of Emergency Employment in the New Deal* (Princeton: Princeton University Press, 1984).

94. *Birmingham News*, 29 August, 30 October 1935, 26 September 1939.

95. *Birmingham Post*, 28 June 1941.

96. Hopkins, *Spending to Save*, p. 99.

97. Alabama Relief Administration, *Federal Relief in Alabama*, pp. 2, 29.

98. Lowi, *The End of Liberalism*, p. 217; Frances Fox Piven and Richard A. Cloward, *Regulating the Poor: The Functions of Public Welfare* (New York: Pantheon, 1971), pp. xiii, 45.

99. Piven and Cloward, *Regulating the Poor*, p. 45.

100. Ibid., p. viii.

101. *Birmingham Post-Herald*, 5 August 1976.

7. The Missed Opportunity in Race Relations

1. *Birmingham Post-Herald*, 22, 17 July 1954.

2. Ibid., 9 September, 3 November, 28 January 1954.

3. Ibid., 14 September 1954.

4. Ibid., 8 October 1954.

5. Ibid., 23 September 1954.

6. Ibid., 3 November 1954.

7. Ibid., 25 August, 3 November 1954.

8. Jefferson County Coordinating Council of Social Forces, *The Jefferson County Survey of Health, Welfare, and Recreation Needs and Services* (University, Ala.: University of Alabama Press, 1955), p. 1.

9. *Birmingham Post-Herald*, 17 February 1954.

10. Ibid., 17 February, 14 August, 4 December 1954.

11. Juan Williams, *Eyes on the Prize: America's Civil Rights Years, 1954–1965* (New York: Penguin, 1988), p. 92.

12. Richard Kluger, *Simple Justice: The History of Brown v. Board of Education and Black America's Struggle for Equality* (New York: Vintage Books, 1977), p. 752.

13. Ibid., p. 758.

14. Williams, *Eyes on the Prize*, p. 118.

15. George R. Stewart, "Birmingham's Reaction to the 1954 Desegregation Decision" (M.A. thesis, Samford University, 1967), p. 19.

16. *Birmingham Post-Herald*, 9 September 1954.

17. Ibid., 26 March 1963.

18. Charles Morgan, Jr., *A Time to Speak* (New York: Harper and Row, 1964), p. 49; *Birmingham Post-Herald*, 25 March 1954.

19. Stewart, "Birmingham's Reaction to the 1954 Desegregation Decision," p. 34.

20. Ibid., pp. 60, 70.

21. Ibid., p. 67.

22. Ibid., p. 36.

23. Ibid., p. 71.

24. *Birmingham Post-Herald*, 8 June, 20 August 1954.

25. Ibid., 10 June, 3, 11, 14 September, 9 November 1954.

26. Ibid., 9 November 1954.

27. Citizens Committee on Indigent Medical Care for Jefferson County, Alabama, "Draft of Final Report" (Birmingham, 22 September 1958, typewritten), p. 2.

28. Ibid., p. 3.

29. Ibid., pp. 7, 17, 21.

30. Ibid., pp. 19, 24.

31. Ibid., pp. 9, 58.

32. Ibid., p. 87.

33. Coordinating Council, *Survey of Needs and Services*, v.

34. Ibid., v.

35. Ibid., v–vii.

36. Ibid., p. 172.

37. Ibid., pp. 177–78.

38. *Birmingham Post-Herald*, 24 November 1954.

39. Coordinating Council, Survey of Needs and Services, p. 178.

40. Ibid., p. 179.

41. Ibid., p. 177.

42. Ibid., pp. 174–80.

43. Ibid., pp. 183, 191.

44. Ibid., p. 183.

45. Ibid., p. 1.

46. Ibid., p. 3.

47. Ibid., p. 17.

48. Ibid., p. 17; *Birmingham Post-Herald*, 1 April 1954.

49. Coordinating Council, *Survey of Needs and Services*, pp. 19, 101; Jefferson County (Alabama) Community Chest, Inc., Minutes and Other Documents, 14 vols. (typewritten), 1923–1973, 9:135.

50. Coordinating Council, *Survey of Needs and Services*, p. 19.

51. Ibid., p. 226.

52. Ibid., pp. 223, 235.

53. Ibid., pp. 258–65.

54. Ibid., p. 130; Annie Laurie Fulcher, *The History, Structure, and Program of the Family Counseling Association of Jefferson County, Alabama* (Birmingham: Jefferson County Coordinating Council of Social Forces, 1967), p. 21.

55. Fulcher, *Family Counseling Association*, pp. 14, 16, 22.

56. Interview with Charles F. Zukoski, Jr., former president of the Coordinating Council of Social Forces, retired bank official and attorney, Birmingham, Ala., 2 October 1975; data in the personal files of the author, accumulated during his term as a member of the board of directors of the Family Counseling Association.

57. Community Chest, Minutes, Executive Committee meeting of 6 August 1965.

58. Ibid., Executive Committee meeting of 15 February 1966.

59. Coordinating Council, *Survey of Needs and Services*, p. 39.

60. Ibid., pp. 322, 325.

61. Ibid., p. 322.

62. Community Chest, Minutes, 5:107.

63. Coordinating Council, *Survey of Needs and Services*, p. 319.

64. Ibid.

65. Ibid.

66. James B. McKee, "Status and Power in the Industrial Community: A Comment on Drucker's Thesis," *American Journal of Sociology* 58 (January 1953): 364–70.

67. Ibid., p. 369.

68. Community Chest, Minutes, 4:188.

69. Ibid., 4:190.

70. Ibid., 5:141.

71. Coordinating Council, *Survey of Needs and Services*, p. 314.

72. Community Chest, Minutes, Executive Committee meeting of 18 September 1951.

73. Ibid., Executive Committee meeting of 12 January 1955, 7:142.

74. Ibid., Executive Committee meeting of 21 July 1944.

75. Ibid., Executive Committee meeting of March 1946.

76. Ibid., Advisory Board meeting of January 1947.

77. Ibid., Board of Directors meeting of 26 February 1947.

78. Ibid., 5:207.

79. Ibid., Board of Directors meeting of 16 December 1948.

80. Ibid.

81. The following case history has been reconstructed by drawing primarily upon staff reports in the National Urban League papers deposited in the Library of Congress. While the possibility of bias in these reports cannot be overlooked, their independent confirmation in interviews with Roberta Morgan and Charles Zukoski, Jr., two knowledgeable sources long active in efforts to improve Birmingham's race relations, suggests that the account is accurate.

82. National Urban League Papers (Washington, D.C.: Library of Congress), selected letters dealing with Birmingham, 28 February 1950.

83. Ibid.

84. Ibid., 16 March 1948.

85. Ibid., 28 February 1950.

86. Interview with Charles F. Zukoski, Jr.; interviews with Roberta Morgan, Heflin, Ala., 8 March 1974 and 6 August 1974.

87. Urban League Papers, campaign pamphlet, "Why Birmingham Needs the Urban League Program."

88. Ibid., selected letters, 28 June 1948; Community Chest, Minutes, Executive Committee meeting of 16 June 1948.

89. Urban League Papers, selected letters, 28 February 1950.

90. Ibid. Robin D. G. Kelley indicates that Robert Durr moved to Birmingham in 1931 and engaged in "radical" activities until about 1934, when the Tennessee Coal, Iron and Railroad Company (TCI) offered him money to begin an antiunion black newspaper, the *Weekly Review*. His reputation as a conservative editor may have attracted him to the Whites while alienating many Blacks (Kelley, *Hammer and Hoe*, p. 110).

91. Urban League Papers, selected letters, 10 December 1948.

92. Ibid.

93. Ibid.

94. Ibid., 28 February 1950.

95. Interview with Charles F. Zukoski, Jr.; interviews with Roberta Morgan.

96. Urban League Papers, 28 February 1950.

97. Ibid.

98. Interviews with Roberta Morgan.

99. Community Chest, Minutes, Executive Committee meeting of 3 September 1947.

100. *Birmingham Post-Herald*, 12 May 1954.

101. Ibid.

102. Ibid.

103. Community Chest, Minutes, 7:6, 47.

104. Interviews with Roberta Morgan.

105. Ibid.; Community Chest, Minutes, Board of Directors meeting, August 1950.

106. Interviews with Roberta Morgan. S. Jonathan Bass, "Bishop C. C. J. Carpenter: From Segregation to Integration," *Alabama Review* 45, no. 3 (July 1992): 191.

107. Coordinating Council, *Survey of Needs and Services*, p. 303.

108. Interviews with Roberta Morgan.

109. Ibid.

110. "Report on a Study of Negro Police Made by the Jefferson County Coordinating Council of Social Forces," September 1953, Roberta Morgan Papers, Birmingham Public Library, Birmingham, Alabama. At least in Atlanta, black police officers did not have the authority to arrest Whites until 1962 (Pat Watters and Reese Cleghorn, *Climbing Jacob's Ladder: The Arrival of Negroes in Southern Politics* [New York: Harcourt, Brace, and World, 1967], p. 85).

111. Interviews with Roberta Morgan.

112. Summary of activities of the Coordinating Council, 1952–53, Roberta Morgan papers.

113. Interviews with Roberta Morgan.

114. Program of the Educational Institute on Race Relations, Roberta Morgan Papers.

115. *Birmingham Post-Herald*, 30 September 1954.

116. Interview with Charles F. Zukoski, Jr.

117. Transcript of ceremony honoring Roberta Morgan upon her retirement, December 1960, Roberta Morgan Papers.

118. Interviews with Roberta Morgan.

119. Ibid.; interview with Charles F. Zukoski, Jr. The White Citizens' Council emerged in 1954 as "eminently respectable" opponents of school desegregation and other advances for Blacks, boasting "prestigious membership rosters" that included public officials and civic and business leaders. One historian of this movement concludes "that what the Klan sought to achieve through violent mob action, the more cautious Councils sought to achieve through appeals to states' rights, southern regionalism, and obstructive legislative tactics" (Francis M. Wilhoit, *The Politics of Massive Resistance* [New York: George Braziller, 1973], pp. 111, 113–14).

In Birmingham, the North Alabama Citizens' Council attracted many laborers, often union members, primarily from the industrial suburbs (Neil R. McMillen, *The Citizens' Council: Organized Resistance to the Second Reconstruction, 1954–64* [Urbana: University of Illinois Press, 1971], p. 47).

The Councils peaked in membership in 1957 and then declined steadily in membership and influence through the rest of the decade.

120. Interviews with Roberta Morgan.

121. Community Chest, Minutes, Board of Directors meeting of 22 March 1956.

122. Ibid.

123. Ibid., Executive Committee meeting of 6 April 1956.

124. Ibid.

125. Ibid.

126. Ibid., Board of Directors meeting of April 1956.

127. Interviews with Roberta Morgan; interview with Charles F. Zukoski, Jr.

128. Interview with Charles F. Zukoski, Jr.

129. Letter from Roberta Morgan to Merrill F. Krughoff, 2 March 1956, Roberta Morgan Papers.

130. Anthony Lewis and the *New York Times, Portrait of a Decade: The Second American Revolution* (New York: Random House, 1964), p. 58.

131. Coordinating Council, *Survey of Needs and Services*, p. 303.

132. Birminghamians themselves compared their city with Atlanta frequently, self-consciously, and most often unfavorably. Three works document the dramatic differences that did in fact exist between the two cities: Doyle, *New Men, New Cities, New South*; Bradley R. Rice, "If Dixie Were Atlanta," in *Sunbelt Cities: Politics and Growth since World War II*, ed. Richard M. Bernard and Bradley R. Rice (Austin: University of Texas Press, 1983); and Clarence N. Stone, *Regime Politics: Governing Atlanta, 1946–1988* (Lawrence: University Press of Kansas, 1989).

Atlanta, emerging from defeat and devastation during the Civil War, had by 1910 become "the quintessential symbol of the New South," with a broad, diversified manufacturing and commercial base; its status as the "financial metropolis of the Southeast" was affirmed when the city was chosen as the site of the regional

Federal Reserve bank in 1914 (Doyle, pp. 46, 50). With its strong local economy and collection of black institutions of higher education, Atlanta early had a prosperous black middle class.

Blacks became politically potent during the 1940s, when a sophisticated voter registration drive in 1945 increased the number of black voters from 3,000 to 21,000 the following year, from 4% of the registered voters in the city to 27.2%. Thereafter the voting rate among Blacks consistently exceeded that of Whites; aligned with middle and upper class Whites, the black electorate emerged as an effective force in behalf of racial moderation. Of Mayor William B. Hartsfield, one commentator wrote, "He was just as liberal as necessary to get the black vote" (Rice, p. 47). His election in 1949 was "a victory made possible only by the huge majorities he received in black precincts" (Stone, p. 30).

Stone describes governance by "civic cooperation" in Atlanta, an "informal partnership between city hall and the downtown business elite." He notes that "one of the remarkable features of Atlanta's urban regime is its biracial character" (Stone, pp. 3, 5, 11).

A bloody race riot in 1906 led to efforts to promote biracial understanding, culminating in 1919 when white ministers and a local banker formed the Commission on Interracial Cooperation, "providing a means whereby communication and negotiation could be conducted across racial lines in Atlanta" (Stone, p. 18). An Urban League chapter was organized in 1919, funded in part by the Community Chest; the Urban League thereafter "was a central connector in the city's governing coalition" (Stone, pp. 33–34). The league, along with the local chapter of the NAACP and several professors at Atlanta University, was instrumental in conducting the effective 1945 voter registration drive.

Stone concludes that a series of biracial agreements emerged in the mid-1940s that lasted until the student-led protests of the 1960s; these agreements represented "a form of group reciprocity in which the mayor and white business executives promoted racially responsible behavior by whites, in exchange for which black leaders acquiesced in a policy of massively reordering land use in central Atlanta" and in other policies favored by those promoting the city's economic growth (Stone, pp. 26, 162).

8. Political and Social Modernization

1. Lewis, *Portrait of a Decade*, p. 198.

2. Morgan, *A Time to Speak*, p. 154.

3. *Birmingham Post-Herald*, 5 September 1962.

4. Southern Research Institute, *Evaluation of the Alternatives for Achieving Improved Local Government: A Preliminary Statistical Analysis of Local Government Activity in Jefferson County Compared to Other Areas in Alabama and the United States, 1957–1967* (Birmingham: Southern Research Institute, 1970), p. 65, table 12.

5. *Birmingham Post-Herald*, 2 September 1963.

6. Southern Research Institute, *A Preliminary Statistical Analysis*, p. 61.

7. Ibid., p. 7.

8. *Birmingham Post-Herald*, 18, 10 November 1963, 17 April 1964, 29 August 1963, 21 July 1964, 29 August, 2 October 1963.

9. Ibid., 10 November 1963, 3 November 1964, 24 September, 12 November 1963.

10. Community Service Council, *Family and Children Study of Jefferson County: Priorities and Recommendations* (Birmingham: Community Service Council, 1970), p. 19.

11. *Birmingham Post-Herald*, 17 October 1963.

12. Community Service Council, *Family and Children Study*, p. 11.

13. Southern Research Institute, *A Preliminary Statistical Analysis*, p. A 25.

14. *Birmingham Post-Herald*, 4 December 1963. Buses were legally desegregated: Under the leadership of the Reverend Fred L. Shuttlesworth, the Alabama Christian Movement for Human Rights had carried out a one-day boycott of the city's segregated buses by hundreds of black riders in December 1956. Rev. Shuttlesworth's January 1957 federal court suit challenging the legality of the city's segregation ordinance was dismissed in October 1958 after the city commission repealed the law and passed a new ordinance authorizing the company to set its own rules. The company's Jim Crow regulations led to a new federal suit; Judge H. Hobart Grooms upheld the company's segregation policies. The fifth circuit court voided the city's ordinance in July 1960 and thereby the company's policies. After city police continued to enforce segregated seating, the federal court issued an injunction in June 1962 barring police from enforcing Jim Crow policies on city buses (Catharine A. Barnes, *Journey from Jim Crow: The Desegregation of Southern Transit* [New York: Columbia University Press, 1983], pp. 126–27, 189).

15. Morgan, *A Time to Speak*, p. 107.

16. Robert Gaines Corley, "The Quest for Racial Harmony: Race Relations in Birmingham, Alabama, 1947–1963" (Ph.D. dissertation, University of Virginia, 1979), p. 217.

17. William A. Nunnelley, *Bull Connor* (Tuscaloosa: University of Alabama Press, 1991), pp. 92, 109.

18. Taylor Branch, *Parting the Waters: America in the King Years 1954–1963* (New York: Simon and Schuster, 1988), p. 426.

19. Howell Raines, *My Soul Is Rested: The Story of the Civil Rights Movement in the Deep South* (New York: Penguin, 1983), p. 162. Birmingham is one of fourteen case studies of the role of businessmen in meeting the challenges of the civil rights movement in Elizabeth Jacoway and David R. Colburn, eds., *Southern Businessmen and Desegregation* (Baton Rouge: Louisiana State University Press, 1982). Other cities studied are Little Rock; Greensboro, N.C.; Columbia, S.C.; New Orleans; Norfolk; Atlanta; Dallas; Augusta, Ga.; Louisville; St. Augustine; Jackson, Miss.; Tampa; and Memphis.

20. Ibid., p. 165.

21. *Birmingham Post-Herald*, 9 October 1962.

22. Irvine Porter, "Statement Opposing Annexation of Homewood to Birmingham," speech delivered at a meeting of the directors of the Birmingham Area Chamber of Commerce, Birmingham, Alabama, 23 April 1959, p. 6.

23. Ibid.

24. *Birmingham Post-Herald*, 3 April 1963.

25. David Vann, "The Change from Commission to Mayor-Council Government and the Racial Desegregation Agreements in Birmingham, Alabama 1961–

1963" (Birmingham: Center for Urban Affairs, University of Alabama at Birmingham, 1988), p. 13.

26. *Birmingham Post-Herald*, 26 October 1962.

27. Morgan, *A Time to Speak*, p. 9.

28. Vann, "The Change from Commission to Mayor-Council Government," pp. 15–16.

29. Ibid., p. 18.

30. Ibid., p. 20.

31. *Birmingham Post-Herald*, 30 August 1962.

32. Ibid., 16 August 1962.

33. Ibid., 19 October 1962.

34. Ibid., 5, 29 September 1962.

35. Ibid., 24 October 1962.

36. Ibid., 27 October 1962.

37. Ibid., 19, 31 October, 2 November 1962.

38. Ibid., 31 October 1962.

39. Ibid., 3 November 1962.

40. Ibid., 7 November 1962.

41. Harry Holloway, *The Politics of the Southern Negro: From Exclusion to Big City Organization* (New York: Random House, 1969), p. 159; and Donald S. Strong, "Alabama: Transition and Alienation," in *The Changing Politics of the South*, ed. William C. Havard (Baton Rouge: Louisiana State University Press, 1972), p. 445.

42. Strong, "Alabama: Transition and Alienation," p. 445.

43. Morgan, *A Time to Speak*, p. 9.

44. Interview with David Vann, Mayor, City of Birmingham, Birmingham, Ala., 7 November 1975.

45. Holloway, *Politics of the Southern Negro*, p. 59.

46. *Birmingham Post-Herald*, 5 January 1963.

47. Corley, "The Quest for Racial Harmony," p. 175.

48. Vann, "The Change from Commission to Mayor-Council Government," pp. 16, 20, 21.

49. Analysis of voting data prior to 1962 suggests that the Birmingham electorate was divided into three identifiable clusters: blue collar, typically more segregationist Whites living in the working class precincts of Ensley, West End, Central Park, and East Lake; an approximately equal number of racially moderate Whites living in the more affluent neighborhoods of Forest Park, Roebuck, Crestwood, and Southside; and a relatively small number of Blacks. Affluent Whites had already moved in large numbers to the city's burgeoning suburbs. In the early 1960s approximately 10% of voting-age Blacks were registered, "the lowest level of any major city in the South" (Neal R. Peirce, *The Deep South States of America: People, Politics, and Power in the Seven Deep South States* [New York: W. W. Norton, 1974], p. 296). The division in the white community was clearly seen in the June 1957 runoff election between "Bull" Connor and moderate Robert Lindbergh, when the candidates received 15,891 and 15,788 votes respectively (Corley, "The Quest for Racial Harmony," p. 162). The same division was seen again in the 1962 referendum on adopting the mayor-council form of government; the commission form received support from precincts where Connor had done well in the past.

In January 1966 the U.S. Department of Justice sent federal examiners into Jefferson County, where Birmingham is located, under the provisions of the 1965 Voting Rights Act. Fourteen thousand Blacks registered in less than four weeks; the increase in black voters led to "changes in the climate of Alabama politics unlike any seen before" (David J. Garrow, *Protest at Selma: Martin Luther King, Jr., and the Voting Rights Act of 1965* [New Haven: Yale University Press, 1978], pp. 185, 187).

After 1965 Birmingham had three voting blocs of approximately equal size: working-class white conservatives, middle-class white moderates, and Blacks. Local elections frequently saw two-bloc coalitions with moderate white and black voters aligned, as they had been in the referendum to change the form of government and would be in the 1963 election (Charles H. Levine, *Racial Conflict and the American Mayor: Power, Polarization and Performance* [Lexington, Mass.: Heath, 1974], p. 90).

The late emergence of a large black electorate stands in sharp contrast to Atlanta, where Blacks became politically potent during the 1940s and became effective partners in that city's biracial governing coalition, which also included city hall and the downtown business elite (cf. chapter 7, note 132).

The Birmingham experience prompts Harold W. Stanley's conclusion that moderate leadership emerged in Birmingham prior to the presence of a large black vote, in contrast to the view of Watters and Cleghorn that moderate white leadership emerged simultaneously with the first sizable black electorate. Moderates had already changed the form of government and would support moderate Albert Boutwell over "Bull" Connor in the upcoming 1963 mayoral race in the absence of a large black vote but in the face of economic pressures created by unfavorable media coverage and increasingly effective boycotts by local black activists (Stanley, *Voter Mobilization and the Politics of Race: The South and Universal Suffrage, 1952–1984* [New York: Praeger, 1987], pp. 135 and 147 [n. 6]); Pat Watters and Reese Cleghorn, *Climbing Jacob's Ladder: The Arrival of Negroes in Southern Politics* (New York: Harcourt, Brace, and World, 1967), p. 86.

50. McMillen, *The Citizens' Council*, p. 314.
51. *Birmingham Post-Herald*, 21, 18, 11 January 1963.
52. Ibid., 25 February 1963.
53. Ibid., 23 January 1963.
54. Ibid., 22 January 1963.
55. Ibid., 27 February 1963.
56. Ibid.
57. Ibid., 23 January, 14 March, 21 February 1963.
58. Ibid., 25 February 1963.
59. Ibid., 6 March 1963.
60. Ibid., 5 March 1963.
61. Ibid., 25 March 1963.
62. Ibid., 26 March 1963.
63. Ibid., 3 April 1963.
64. Morgan, *A Time to Speak*, p. 99.
65. Biographical data gathered from newspaper articles published throughout the campaign.
66. *Birmingham Post-Herald*, 2, 9 February 1963.
67. Ibid., 7 March 1963.

68. Ibid., 3 April 1963.

69. Ibid.

70. Ibid., 28 March 1963.

71. Ibid., 4 April 1963.

72. Ibid., 17, 15, 29 April 1963.

73. Atlanta offers an interesting and instructive contrast to Birmingham in its response to the rising demands for desegregation. Atlanta Chamber of Commerce president Ivan Allen, Jr., included in his six-point program in 1960 keeping the public schools open in the face of integration. When ten black students entered Atlanta's high schools in September 1961, Mayor William Berry Hartsfield held a racially mixed cocktail party for 200 visiting reporters at the Biltmore Hotel; the Chamber of Commerce purchased a full-page advertisement urging calm. "The result was peaceful, if token, integration for blacks and a giant public relations coup for Atlanta" (Bradley R. Rice, "If Dixie Were Atlanta," in *Sunbelt Cities: Politics and Growth since World War II*, ed. Richard M. Bernard and Bradley R. Rice [Austin: University of Texas Press, 1983], pp. 44, 47). Hartsfield's career is reviewed in Harold H. Martin, *William Berry Hartsfield: Mayor of Atlanta* (Athens: University of Georgia Press, 1978).

On his first day in office in 1962, new Atlanta mayor Ivan Allen, Jr., removed the "colored" and "white" signs from city hall drinking fountains. Later he threw out the first ball at the city's first integrated professional baseball game. In Birmingham, meanwhile, the signs remained up, the parks remained closed, and the Birmingham Barons baseball team disbanded instead of complying with integration in the Southern Association (Branch, *Parting the Waters*, p. 592).

74. *Birmingham Post-Herald*, 4, 6 April 1963.

75. The most detailed recounting of the civil rights movement is in Branch, *Parting the Waters*. The following account draws heavily on this work, supplemented by Anthony Lewis' earlier *Portrait of a Decade*.

76. Martin Luther King, Jr., *Stride toward Freedom: The Montgomery Story* (San Francisco: Harper and Row, 1958). For a review of the Women's Political Caucus, a driving force behind the Montgomery bus boycott, see Jo Ann Gibson Robinson, *The Montgomery Bus Boycott and the Women Who Started It: The Memoir of Jo Ann Gibson Robinson*, ed., with a foreword, by David J. Garrow (Knoxville: University of Tennessee Press, 1987).

77. *Birmingham Post-Herald*, 12 March 1963.

78. *Birmingham Post-Herald*, 28, 25 March 1963.

79. Martin Luther King, Jr., *Why We Can't Wait* (New York: New American Library, 1964), p. 79.

80. *Birmingham Post-Herald*, 6, 8, April 1963.

81. Ibid., 12 April 1963.

82. Ibid., 13 April 1963. The decision to violate the state court injunction had been an excruciatingly difficult one for King to make. Andrew Young later said: "Not knowing how it was going to work out, he walked out of the room and went down to the church and led a demonstration and went to jail. That was, I think, the beginning of his true leadership" (Williams, *Eyes on the Prize*, p. 186).

83. *Birmingham Post-Herald*, 15 April 1963.

84. Lewis, *Portrait of a Decade*, p. 179.

85. Ibid., p. 175.

86. *Birmingham Post-Herald,* 9 April 1963.

87. Ibid., 13 April 1963. This letter is typically viewed as a direct criticism by the white ministers of King's decision to march in violation of the court injunction. S. Jonathan Bass argues that the white ministers have been misunderstood. Bass writes that on the day of King's arrest, the eight ministers issued a statement against civil disobedience addressed not to King but specifically to local black leaders. An aide smuggled a newspaper carrying the text of the letter to King in jail; King interpreted it as "a personal attack on his work" and wrote the "Letter from Birmingham Jail" in response. The eight signers of the statement were Bishop C. C. J. Carpenter (Episcopalian); Bishop George Murray (Episcopalian); Rabbi Milton L. Grafman; Bishop Joseph A. Durick (Roman Catholic); Bishop Paul Hardin (Methodist); Bishop Nolan B. Harmon (Methodist); Presbyterian moderator Edward V. Ramage; and Earl Stallings, pastor of First Baptist Church of Birmingham (Bass, "Bishop C. C. J. Carpenter," pp. 184–215).

88. King, "Letter from Birmingham Jail," in *Why We Can't Wait,* pp. 79–80.

89. *Birmingham Post-Herald,* 4 May 1963.

90. Ibid., 27 April 1963.

91. Branch, *Parting the Waters,* pp. 752, 755.

92. *Birmingham Post-Herald,* 3 May 1963. The newspaper was correct in its observation about careful planning, a hallmark of the work in Birmingham by King's assistant Wyatt Tee Walker (Williams, *Eyes on the Prize,* p. 182; Branch, *Parting the Waters,* p. 756).

93. *Birmingham Post-Herald,* 4 May 1963; Branch, *Parting the Waters,* p. 760.

94. Holloway, *Politics of the Southern Negro,* p. 167. Cotman analyzes federal civil rights legislation in terms of Thomas R. Dye's elite model of politics. The core of Cotman's work is tape recordings from the Kennedy Library of discussions among the president, attorney general, Burke Marshall, and other federal officials that include the crisis in Birmingham (John Walton Cotman, *Birmingham, JFK, and the Civil Rights Act of 1963: Implications for Elite Theory* [New York: P. Lang, 1989]).

95. *Birmingham Post-Herald,* 4 May 1963.

96. Lewis, *Portrait of a Decade,* p. 182.

97. *Birmingham Post-Herald,* 7 May 1963.

98. Interview with David Vann, 7 November 1975; Vann, "The Change from Commission to Mayor-Council Government," p. 31; Branch, *Parting the Waters,* pp. 779–80; David J. Garrow, *Bearing the Cross: Martin Luther King, Jr., and the Southern Christian Leadership Conference* (New York: Random House, 1988), pp. 253, 255.

99. *Birmingham Post-Herald,* 8 May 1963.

100. Ibid.

101. Ibid.

102. Ibid.; interview with David Vann, 7 November 1975; Branch, *Parting the Waters,* p. 781; Garrow, *Bearing the Cross,* p. 255.

103. *Birmingham Post-Herald,* 9 May 1963.

104. Ibid.

105. Ibid., 10, 11 May 1963; slightly different terms of agreement are presented in Garrow, *Bearing the Cross,* p. 259, and Branch, *Parting the Waters,* p. 791.

106. *Birmingham Post-Herald,* 11 May 1963.

107. Ibid., 10 May 1963; Lewis, *Portrait of a Decade*, p. 183.

108. *Birmingham Post-Herald*, 13 May 1963.

109. Ibid., 16 May 1963.

110. Ibid., 11 May 1963.

111. Ibid., 16 May 1963.

112. Ibid., 14 May 1963.

113. Ibid., 10 May 1963.

114. Ibid., 11, 14, 10 May 1963.

115. Ibid., 16 May 1963. To this day the Chamber of Commerce has retained the closed records of the Senior Citizens Committee.

116. Ibid., 29 May 1963.

117. Ibid., 13 May 1963.

118. Ibid.

119. Ibid., 14 May 1963.

120. Ibid., 14, 16 May 1963.

121. Ibid., 15 May 1963.

122. Ibid., 24 May 1963.

123. Ibid., 16 May 1963.

124. Ibid., 21 August 1963.

125. Ibid., 13 July, 20 August 1963.

126. Ibid., 28 August 1963.

127. Ibid., 30 August, 4, 5, 10, 11 September 1963.

128. Ibid., 16 September 1963; Garrow, *Bearing the Cross*, p. 291.

129. *Birmingham Post-Herald*, 26 September 1963.

130. Garrow, *Bearing the Cross*, p. 295.

131. *Birmingham Post-Herald*, 20 September 1963.

132. Ibid., 27 September 1963.

133. Ibid., 28 September 1963.

134. Ibid., 1 October 1963.

135. Ibid., 5 October 1963.

136. Ibid., 2 October 1963.

137. Ibid., 18 October 1963.

138. Ibid., 7 October 1963.

139. Ibid., 12 October 1963.

140. Ibid., 23 October 1963.

141. Ibid., 14 February 1964.

142. Ibid., 30 December 1964.

143. Lewis, *Portrait of a Decade*, p. 5.

144. Earl Black and Merle Black, *Politics and Society in the South* (Cambridge: Harvard University Press, 1987), p. 108. Other authors linking the demonstrations in Birmingham with the 1964 Civil Rights Act include Watters and Cleghorn, *Climbing Jacob's Ladder*, p. 239; Hugh Davis Graham, *The Civil Rights Era: Origins and Development of National Policy 1960–1972* (New York: Oxford University Press, 1990), p. 4; Ralph David Abernathy, *And the Walls Came Tumbling Down* (New York: Harper and Row, 1989), p. 229; E. Culpepper Clark, *The Schoolhouse Door: Segregation's Last Stand at the University of Alabama* (New York: Oxford University Press, 1993), p. xi; and Adam Fairclough, *To Redeem the Soul of America: The Southern Chris-

tian Leadership Conference and Martin Luther King, Jr. (Athens: University of Georgia Press, 1987), pp. 133–35.

145. Lewis, *Portrait of a Decade*, p. 121.

146. *Birmingham Post-Herald*, 22 January 1964.

147. Ibid., 26 February 1964.

148. Ibid., 31 December 1967. The 1967 bond issue provided funds for the Birmingham Green beautification program on Twentieth Street in downtown; the Birmingham-Jefferson County civic center complex; restoration of Morris Avenue; Red Mountain (now Elton B. Stephens) expressway; expansion of the municipal airport; and expansion of Legion Field, the city's football stadium (Flynt, *Mine, Mill & Microchip*, p. 196).

149. *Birmingham Post-Herald*, 19 June 1964.

150. Ibid., 16 July 1964.

151. Ibid., 12 August 1964.

152. Ibid., 12 June, 17 July, 6 August, 25 July 1963.

153. Ibid., 26 November 1963, 21 February, 1, 16 April 1964.

154. Ibid., 30 April 1964.

155. Ibid.

156. Ibid., 9 May 1964.

157. Ibid., 27 June 1964.

158. Ibid., 21 December 1964.

159. Jimmie Lewis Franklin, *Back to Birmingham: Richard Arrington, Jr., and His Times* (Tuscaloosa: University of Alabama Press, 1989), p. 61.

160. *Birmingham News*, 12 May 1969. The first black police officers had been hired in 1966.

161. Levine, *Racial Conflict and the American Mayor*, p. 90.

162. *Birmingham News*, 20 April 1969.

163. Levine, *Racial Conflict and the American Mayor*, p. 94.

164. *Birmingham News*, 17 September 1973.

165. Ibid., 19 December 1971.

166. *Birmingham Post-Herald*, 4 December 1963.

167. *Birmingham News*, 20 August 1961.

168. Ibid., 9 February 1963; *Birmingham Post-Herald*, 9 June 1965.

169. *Birmingham News*, 12 October 1965.

170. *Birmingham Post-Herald*, 21 September 1965; *Birmingham News*, 19 October 1965.

171. *Birmingham News*, 3 November 1966.

172. *Birmingham Post-Herald*, 3 May 1967.

173. *Birmingham News*, 19 January 1968; *Birmingham Post-Herald*, 14 August 1968.

174. *Birmingham News*, 1 May 1972.

175. Ibid., 8 November 1972.

176. Ibid., 28 June 1971, 17 July 1972, 12 May 1969, 12 May 1971.

177. *Birmingham Post-Herald*, 19 August 1969; *Birmingham News*, 31 October 1971.

178. *Birmingham News*, 11 August 1974.

179. *Birmingham Post-Herald*, 17 August 1969.

180. Ibid., 11 May 1974. Neal R. Peirce shared the enthusiasm of Pitts for the Community Affairs Committee. "Notorious old Birmingham," he wrote, "has begun to form a solution that could also be a model for other Southern states and the rest of the nation" (Peirce, *The Deep South States of America*, p. 241). Birmingham's gradually improving race relations prompted *Look* magazine and the National Municipal League to name Birmingham an "All American City" in 1971 (Levine, *Racial Conflict and the American Mayor*, p. 100; Raines, *My Soul Is Rested*, p. 185).

A less sanguine view of the role of ONB and the committee is offered by Charles Morgan, Jr.: "Birmingham changed because the law changed and the people had to obey. That was more basic than Operation New Birmingham and all the rest" (Peirce, *The Deep South States of America*, p. 290).

9. The Jefferson County Committee for Economic Opportunity and the Birmingham Citizen Participation Program

1. S. M. Miller and Martin Rein, "The War on Poverty: Perspectives and Prospects," in *Poverty as a Public Issue*, ed. Ben B. Seligman (New York: Free Press, 1965), p. 276. Patterson, however, believes that the Kennedy administration was primarily concerned with problems in Appalachia and wanted to focus on white poor as a disadvantaged group to complement civil rights activities in behalf of Blacks (James T. Patterson, *America's Struggle against Poverty 1900–1980* [Cambridge: Harvard University Press, 1981], p. 134).

2. James L. Sundquist, *Politics and Policy: The Eisenhower, Kennedy and Johnson Years* (Washington, D.C.: Brookings, 1968), p. 136.

3. Ibid., p. 131.

4. Piven and Cloward, *Regulating the Poor*, p. 254.

5. Ibid., pp. 272, 276.

6. Ibid., pp. 249 (n. 1), 257.

7. Ibid., p. 381.

8. Elinor Graham, "The Politics of Poverty," in *Poverty as a Public Issue*, ed. Seligman, p. 244.

9. Ibid., p. 245.

10. Miller and Rein, "War on Poverty," p. 307.

11. James L. Sundquist, "Origins of the War on Poverty," in *On Fighting Poverty: Perspectives from Experience*, ed. James L. Sundquist (New York: Basic Books, 1969), p. 23.

12. Ibid.

13. Mario Fantini, Marilyn Gittell, and Richard Magat, *Community Control and the Urban School* (New York: Praeger, 1971), p. 11.

14. Sar A. Levitan, *The Great Society's Poor Law: A New Approach to Poverty* (Baltimore: Johns Hopkins University Press, 1969), p. 50.

15. Sundquist, "Origins of the War on Poverty," p. 26.

16. Ibid., p. 29.

17. Daniel Patrick Moynihan, *Maximum Feasible Misunderstanding: Community Action in the War on Poverty* (New York: Free Press, 1969), p. 89.

18. Sundquist, "Origins of the War on Poverty", p. 29.

19. Moynihan, *Maximum Feasible Misunderstanding*, p. 87. Jeffrey M. Berry et

al. disagree with Moynihan's assertions and argue that legislators wanted "meaningful and recurrent participation of the poor" that went far beyond simply participating in benefits of the program (Jeffrey M. Berry, Kent E. Portney, and Ken Thomson, *The Rebirth of Urban Democracy* [Washington, D.C.: Brookings, 1993], pp. 25–29).

20. Moynihan, *Maximum Feasible Misunderstandings*, p. 98.

21. Ralph M. Kramer, *Participation of the Poor: Comparative Community Case Studies in the War on Poverty* (Englewood Cliffs, N.J.: Prentice Hall, 1969), p. 4.

22. See J. David Greenstone and Paul E. Peterson, *Race and Authority in Urban Politics: Community Participation and the War on Poverty* (New York: Russell Sage, 1973); Peter Bachrach and Morton S. Baratz, *Power and Poverty: Theory and Practice* (New York: Oxford University Press, 1970); Dale Rogers Marshall, *The Politics of Participation in Poverty: A Case Study of the Board of the Economic and Youth Opportunities Agency of Greater Los Angeles* (Berkeley: University of California Press, 1971).

Zarefsky evaluates the War on Poverty in terms of the language in which its programs were presented, especially by President Johnson. He concludes that the language created a symbolic world in which the programs would be judged failures because they did not perform at the levels promised by the rhetoric. However, the War on Poverty did legitimize several new ideas: "Citizen participation, for example, emerged as a key idea in the process of social change" (David Zarefsky, *President Johnson's War on Poverty: Rhetoric and History* [University: University of Alabama Press, 1986], pp. 192, 207).

23. *Birmingham Post-Herald*, 17 March 1964.

24. Jefferson County (Alabama) Committee for Economic Opportunity (JCCEO), Minutes and Other Documents, 1965–1975 (typewritten), Board of Directors meeting of 4 January 1966.

25. Birmingham Area Committee for the Development of Economic Opportunity (BACDEO), Minutes of Meetings of the Board of Directors, 1965 (typewritten), letter of 27 October 1964 from the Most Reverend T. J. Toolen, archbishop of Mobile-Birmingham.

26. Ibid., letter of 30 December 1964 from Rev. Edward L. Foster.

27. *Birmingham Post-Herald*, 19 September 1964.

28. Ibid.

29. Ibid.

30. Ibid., 19 December 1964.

31. Ibid., 23 December 1964.

32. Ibid., 5 January 1965.

33. Ibid., 9 January 1965.

34. Ibid., 13 January 1965.

35. Ibid.

36. Interview with Sheldon Schaffer, Southern Research Institute, former president of the Jefferson County Committee for Economic Opportunity, Birmingham, Ala., 12 November 1975.

37. BACDEO, Minutes, meetings of 12 March and 18 May 1965.

38. Ibid., meeting of 23 April 1965.

39. *Birmingham News*, 12 May 1965.

40. *Birmingham Post-Herald*, 21 October 1965.

41. *Birmingham News*, 12 May 1965.

42. *Birmingham Post-Herald*, 15 May 1965.

43. BACDEO, Minutes, meeting of 18 May 1965.

44. Interview with Sheldon Schaffer; interview with Odessa Woolfolk, University of Alabama at Birmingham, Birmingham, Ala., 31 October 1975.

45. Interview with Sheldon Schaffer.

46. JCCEO, Minutes, Board of Directors meeting of 27 August 1965.

47. Ibid., 1965 application for a Community Action Program.

48. *Birmingham News*, 26 September 1965.

49. *New York Times*, 14 September 1965.

50. *Birmingham News*, 18 October 1965.

51. *Birmingham Post-Herald*, 19 October 1965.

52. JCCEO, Minutes, amended Articles of Incorporation.

53. Ibid., Board of Directors meeting of November 1965.

54. Ibid., Board of Directors meeting of 27 August 1965.

55. Ibid., Board of Directors meeting of 4 January 1966.

56. Ibid.

57. Interview with Sheldon Schaffer.

58. Interview with John Dunbar, University of Alabama at Birmingham, former president of JCCEO, Birmingham, Ala., 22 July 1975.

59. Interview with Charles F. Zukoski, Jr., retired bank official and attorney, Birmingham, Ala., former president of JCCEO, Birmingham, Ala., 2 October 1975.

60. *Birmingham News*, 18 October 1965.

61. John G. Wofford, "The Politics of Local Responsibility: Administration of the Community Action Program, 1964–1966," in *On Fighting Poverty*, ed. Sundquist, p. 82; *Annals of the American Academy of Political and Social Science* 385 (September 1969): 8.

62. JCCEO, Minutes, Board of Directors meeting of 3 January 1967.

63. Ibid., Board of Directors meeting of 13 December 1966.

64. Ibid., Board of Directors meeting of 31 July 1973.

65. Ibid., Board of Directors meeting of 25 March 1969.

66. Ibid., 1969 statement on the functions of neighborhood advisory councils.

67. Ibid., Board of Directors meeting of 30 July 1971.

68. Lillian B. Rubin, "Maximum Feasible Participation: The Origins, Implications and Present Status," *Annals* 385 (September 1969): 26.

69. JCCEO, Minutes, 1969 statement on the functions of neighborhood advisory councils.

70. Ibid., Board of Directors meeting of 9 September 1968.

71. Ibid., Board of Directors meeting of 29 July 1969.

72. Ibid., Board of Directors meeting of 30 July 1971.

73. Interview with John Dunbar.

74. JCCEO, Minutes, Board of Directors meetings of July 1967 and October 1967.

75. Ibid., Board of Directors meeting of 22 April 1966.

76. Ibid., Executive Committee meeting of August 1969.

77. Ibid.

78. Ibid., Executive Committee Meeting of 2 September 1969; *Birmingham News*, 29 July 1969.

79. JCCEO, Minutes, Executive Committee meetings of 1 December and 17 June 1970.

80. Ibid., Executive Committee meeting of 27 July 1971.

81. Ibid., Board of Directors meeting of 17 August 1971.

82. Ibid.

83. Ibid., Ad Hoc Committee meeting of 20 September 1971.

84. See Holloway, *Politics of the Southern Negro*.

85. Wofford, "Politics of Local Responsibility," in *On Fighting Poverty*, ed. Sundquist, p. 91.

86. JCCEO, Minutes, Board of Directors meeting of 29 November 1966.

87. Ibid., Executive Committee meeting of 18 November 1969; Board of Directors meeting of 27 October 1970.

88. Ibid., Board of Directors meetings of 24 September 1968, 21 October 1971, 28 March, 25 July, 29 August, 28 November 1972; Executive Committee Meetings of 15 February, 20 August, 3 October 1972.

89. Ibid., Board of Directors meeting of 26 June 1973.

90. Ibid., Executive Committee meeting of 19 August 1969.

91. *Birmingham Post-Herald*, 30 June 1966.

92. JCCEO, Minutes, Executive Committee meeting of 14 July 1966.

93. Ibid., Executive Committee meeting of 21 April 1970; Board of Directors meeting of 27 October 1970.

94. Interview with Sheldon Schaffer.

95. *Birmingham News*, 11 January 1968.

96. Ibid.

97. Ibid., 12 May 1968.

98. JCCEO, Minutes, Executive Committee meeting of 28 May 1968.

99. Ibid., Executive Committee meeting of 4 November 1968.

100. Ibid., letter from the president of the Jefferson County Commission to the executive director of JCCEO, 19 October 1970.

101. Ibid., Executive Committee meeting of 1 December 1970.

102. Ibid., Management Study, June, 1974, pp. 5, 6.

103. Ibid., Board of Directors meeting of 25 May 1971.

104. JCCEO, Minutes, Board of Directors meeting of 22 April 1966.

105. Ibid., Board of Directors meeting of 25 October 1966.

106. *Birmingham News*, 21 March 1968; and JCCEO, Minutes, Executive Committee meeting of 6 May 1969.

107. *Birmingham News*, 21 March 1968.

108. Interview with Sheldon Schaffer.

109. JCCEO, Minutes, Board of Directors meeting of 18 June 1965.

110. *Birmingham News*, 25 March 1969.

111. *Birmingham Post-Herald*, 23 April 1969.

112. Kramer, *Participation of the Poor*, p. 32.

113. JCCEO, Minutes, 1967 Annual Report.

114. *Birmingham News*, 18 March 1969.

115. Ibid., 23 February 1969.

116. JCCEO, Minutes, Executive Committee meeting of 5 January 1971.

117. Ibid., Board of Directors meeting of 30 March 1971.

118. Ibid., Executive Committee meeting of 15 February 1972.

119. Citizens Task Force on the Jefferson County Committee for Economic Opportunity, *Report to the Mayor and County Commission* (Birmingham, 1973), p. 1.

120. Ibid., pp. 5, 9, 10, 21.

121. Ibid., statement of past presidents, n.p.

122. Ibid., statement of Supporters Clubs, n.p.

123. JCCEO, Minutes, Board of Directors meeting of 26 February 1974. Federal General Revenue Sharing funds were made available to units of local government as entitlements that could be spent on virtually any governmental activity.

124. Ibid., Board of Directors meetings of 27 March and 25 June 1974.

125. Levitan, *Great Society's Poor Law*, p. 49.

126. Lowi, *The End of Liberalism*, pp. 233–36.

127. Levitan, *Great Society's Poor Law*, p. 49; Sundquist, "Origins of the War on Poverty," in *On Fighting Poverty*, ed. Sundquist, p. 31.

128. Wofford, "Politics of Local Responsibility," in *On Fighting Poverty*, ed. Sundquist, p. 80; Kenneth Clark and Jeanette Hopkins, *A Relevant War against Poverty: A Study of Community Action Programs and Observable Social Change* (New York: Harper and Row, 1969), p. 212.

129. Greenstone and Peterson, *Race and Authority*, p. 269.

130. Interview with John Dunbar.

131. Community Chest, Minutes, Board of Directors meeting of 16 December 1965; interview with David Orrell, executive director, United Way of Jefferson-Shelby-Walker Counties (Alabama), Birmingham, Ala., 15 August 1974.

132. *Birmingham News*, 17 April 1968.

133. Interview with W. C. Patton, National Association for the Advancement of Colored People, former President of JCCEO, Birmingham, Ala., 12 November 1975.

134. Interview with John Dunbar.

135. *Birmingham News*, 8 November 1972. The term "workable program" refers to the locally developed plan for the use of federal funds submitted by the city to the Department of Housing and Urban Development.

136. Jon Will Pitts, Birmingham area director, Department of Housing and Urban Development, letter to Birmingham mayor George Seibels, Jr., 6 July 1973, in Community Development Department, Citizen Participation Folder, City of Birmingham, Birmingham, Alabama.

137. Interview with Charles Lewis, principal human resource officer, Birmingham Community Development Department, Birmingham, Ala., 5 December 1975.

138. Ibid.; second draft of "Proposed Citizen Participation Plan" in Citizen Participation Folder, n.d.

139. Second draft of "Proposed Citizen Participation Plan", p. 3.

140. Interview with Charles Lewis.

141. Second draft of "Proposed Citizen Participation Plan", p. 4.

142. Ibid., p. 18.

143. *Birmingham News*, 2 April 1974.

144. The Birmingham Action Group was the vehicle established for mobilizing mainly white voters in the 1973 elections. With one exception, its officers were also officers of Operation New Birmingham; ONB was reportedly billed for expenses of the Birmingham Action Group (*Birmingham Post-Herald*, 26, 27 October, 27, 28, 29 November 1973).

145. Interview with Charles Lewis, 17 July 1993. Lewis, whose thoughtful and energetic staff leadership of the Citizen Participation Program during its formation has left an indelible mark on it, assembled other staff members after the 1 April meeting to review systematically the tape-recorded remarks of each speaker. Each staff member wrote what he or she heard each speaker say, and the group did not move on until they had reached consensus as to the specific concerns of each speaker. The goal of this meeting was to enumerate the speakers' concerns and group them into problem areas, which finally numbered six.

Next the staff convened a workshop to which all speakers at the 1 April meeting were invited. Each attendee was randomly assigned to one of six groups, each of which dealt primarily but not exclusively with one of the six problem areas. Each group later offered "citizen generated recommendations" to the problems.

This highly participatory method of responding to citizens' concerns became a hallmark of the Birmingham program.

146. Interview with Charles Lewis, 5 December 1975.

147. Ibid. The Birmingham Citizen Participation Program is one of five exemplary programs analyzed by Berry et al. in *The Rebirth of Urban Democracy*; the other cities included are Dayton; Portland, Oregon; St. Paul; and San Antonio.

148. Interview with Charles Lewis, 5 December 1975.

149. *Birmingham Post-Herald*, 16 September 1975.

150. *Birmingham News*, 5 October 1975. The effectiveness of this channel of recruitment is indicated by the fact that four of the nine city councillors serving in 1994 had Citizen Participation Program experience. Roosevelt Bell, Linda Coleman, Aldrich Gunn, and Antris Hinton had all been neighborhood presidents.

151. Franklin, *Back to Birmingham*, p. 84. Arrington had first been elected to the city council in 1971.

152. Interview with Carol Nunnelley, political reporter, *Birmingham News*, Birmingham, Ala., 15 January 1976; Franklin, *Back to Birmingham*, p. 90.

153. Most publicly funded welfare activities were not directly affected by these local changes because the state and counties, rather than municipalities, have primary responsibility for welfare activities in Alabama.

Epilogue

1. Three useful accounts of this period are "Birmingham: The Mayor" in Margaret Edds, *Free at Last: What Really Happened When Civil Rights Came to Southern Politics* (Bethesda, Md.: Adler and Adler, 1987), pp. 99–123; "Birmingham: A Magic City" by Ernest Porterfield in *In Search of the New South: The Black Urban Experience in the 1970s and 1980s*, ed. Robert D. Bullard (Tuscaloosa: University of Alabama Press, 1989), pp. 121–41; and Franklin, *Back to Birmingham*.

Bibliography

Abbott, Carl. *The New Urban America: Growth and Politics in Sunbelt Cities.* Chapel Hill: University of North Carolina Press, 1987.

Abernathy, Ralph David. *And the Walls Came Tumbling Down.* New York: Harper and Row, 1989.

Alabama Relief Administration. *Two Years of Federal Relief in Alabama.* Wetumpka, Ala.: Wetumpka Printing, 1935.

Allen, Robert S., ed. *Our Fair City.* New York: Vanguard, 1947.

Allison, Graham T. *Essence of Decision: Explaining the Cuban Missile Crisis.* Boston: Little, Brown, 1971.

American Academy of Political and Social Science. *Evaluating the War on Poverty. Annals of the American Academy of Political and Social Science* 385 (September 1969).

Armes, Ethel. "The Spirit of the Founders." *The Survey: A Journal of Constructive Philanthropy* 27, no. 1 (January 1912): 453–63.

Atkins, Leah Rawls. "Senator James A. Simpson and Birmingham Politics of the 1930s: His Fight against the Spoilsmen and the Pie-men." *Alabama Review* 41, no. 1 (January 1988): 3–29.

———. *The Valley and the Hills: An Illustrated History of Birmingham and Jefferson County.* Woodland Hills, Calif.: Windsor Publications, 1981.

Autrey, Dorothy. "The National Association for the Advancement of Colored People in Alabama, 1913–1952." Ph.D. dissertation, University of Notre Dame, 1985.

Bachrach, Peter, and Morton S. Baratz. *Power and Poverty: Theory and Practice.* New York: Oxford University Press, 1970.

Banfield, Edward C., and James Q. Wilson. *City Politics.* New York: Knopf, 1963; Vintage Books, 1963.

Barnes, Catharine A. *Journey from Jim Crow: The Desegregation of Southern Transit.* New York: Columbia University Press, 1983.

Bass, Jack, and Walter DeVries. *The Transformation of Southern Politics: Social Change and Political Consequence since 1945.* New York: Times Mirror, 1977.

Bass, S. Jonathan. "Bishop C. C. J. Carpenter: From Segregation to Integration." *Alabama Review* 45, no. 3 (July 1992): 184–215.

Bernard, Richard M., and Bradley R. Rice, eds. *Sunbelt Cities: Politics and Growth since World War II.* Austin: University of Texas Press, 1983.

Berry, Jeffrey M., Kent E. Portney, and Ken Thomson. *The Rebirth of Urban Democracy.* Washington, D.C.: Brookings, 1993.

Bigelow, Martha Carolyn Mitchell. "Birmingham: Biography of a City of the New South." Ph.D. dissertation, University of Chicago, 1946.

Biles, Roger. *Memphis in the Great Depression*. Knoxville: University of Tennessee Press, 1986.

Black, Earl, and Merle Black. *Politics and Society in the South*. Cambridge: Harvard University Press, 1987.

Branch, Taylor. *Parting the Waters: America in the King Years 1954–1963*. New York: Simon and Schuster, 1988.

Brooks, Bessie A. *A Half Century of Progress in Family Welfare Work in Jefferson County*. Birmingham: Roberts, 1936.

Brown, Charles Allen. *The Origin and Development of Secondary Education for Negroes in the Metropolitan Area of Birmingham, Alabama*. Birmingham: Commercial Printing, 1959.

Brown, Josephine Chapin. *Public Relief 1929–1939*. New York: Henry Holt, 1940.

Brownell, Blaine Allison. "Birmingham, Alabama: New South City in the 1920's." *Journal of Southern History* 38 (February 1972): 21–48.

———. "The Corporate-Expansive City: Concepts of Growth and Community in Southern Cities in the 1920's." Paper presented at the Institute of Southern History Seminar, Johns Hopkins University, 14 April 1972, p. 50.

———. *The Urban Ethos in the South, 1920–1930*. Baton Rouge: Louisiana State University Press, 1975.

———. "The Urban Mind in the South: The Growth of Urban Consciousness in Southern Cities, 1920–1927." Ph.D. dissertation, University of North Carolina at Chapel Hill, 1969.

———, and David R. Goldfield, eds. *The City in Southern History: The Growth of Urban Civilization in the South*. Port Washington, N.Y.: Kennikat, 1977.

Browning, Rufus P., Dale Rogers Marshall, and David H. Tabb. *Racial Politics in American Cities*. New York: Longman, 1990.

Bullard, Robert D., ed. *In Search of the New South: The Black Urban Experience in the 1970s and 1980s*. Tuscaloosa: University of Alabama Press, 1989.

Button, James W. *Blacks and Social Change: Impact of the Civil Rights Movement in Southern Communities*. Princeton: Princeton University Press, 1989.

CBS Reports. "Who Speaks for Birmingham?" Typed manuscript as broadcast over the CBS Television Network, Thursday, 18 May 1961.

Center for Urban Studies, University of Alabama at Birmingham. *An Evaluation of the Community Health Planning Commission 1969–1972*.

Citizens Committee on Indigent Medical Care for Jefferson County, Alabama. "Draft of Final Report." Birmingham, 22 September 1958. Typewritten.

Citizens' Task Force on the Jefferson County Committee for Economic Opportunity. *Report to the Mayor and County Commission*. Birmingham, 1973.

Clark, E. Culpepper. *The Schoolhouse Door: Segregation's Last Stand at the University of Alabama*. New York: Oxford University Press, 1993.

Clark, Kenneth, and Jeanette Hopkins. *A Relevant War against Poverty: A Study of Community Action Programs and Observable Social Change*. New York: Harper and Row, 1969.

Colburn, David R. *Racial Change and Community Crisis: St. Augustine, Florida, 1877–1980*. New York: Columbia University Press, 1985.

Community Service Council. *Family and Children Study of Jefferson County: Priorities and Recommendations*. Birmingham: Community Service Council, 1970.

Corley, Robert Gaines. "The Quest for Racial Harmony: Race Relations in Birmingham, Alabama, 1947–1963." Ph.D. dissertation, University of Virginia, 1979.

Cotman, John Walton. *Birmingham, JFK, and the Civil Rights Act of 1963: Implications for Elite Theory*. New York: P. Lang, 1989.

Dahl, Robert A. *Who Governs? Democracy and Power in an American City*. New Haven: Yale University Press, 1961.

Davidson, Chandler. *Biracial Politics: Conflict and Coalition in the Metropolitan South*. Baton Rouge: Louisiana State University Press, 1972.

Davidson, Roger H. "The War on Poverty: An Experiment in Federalism." *Annals of the American Academy of Political and Social Science* 385 (September 1969): 8.

Davis, Feather Ann. "Welfare Effort in the United States, 1950: An Analysis of Interstate Variation." M.A. thesis, Vanderbilt University, 1967.

DeSario, Jack, and Stuart Langton, eds. *Citizen Participation in Public Decision Making*. Westport, Conn.: Greenwood, 1987.

Doyle, Don H. *Nashville in the New South 1880–1930*. Knoxville: University of Tennessee Press, 1985.

———. *Nashville since the 1920's*. Knoxville: University of Tennessee Press, 1985.

———. *New Men, New Cities, New South: Atlanta, Nashville, Charleston, Mobile, 1860–1910*. Chapel Hill: University of North Carolina Press, 1990.

Edds, Margaret. *Free at Last: What Really Happened When Civil Rights Came to Southern Politics*. Bethesda, Md.: Adler and Adler, 1987.

Elovitz, Mark H. *A Century of Jewish Life in Dixie: The Birmingham Experience*. University: University of Alabama Press, 1974.

Fairclough, Adam. *To Redeem the Soul of America: The Southern Christian Leadership Conference and Martin Luther King, Jr*. Athens: University of Georgia Press, 1987.

Farley, Joseph M. "The Greater Birmingham Struggle of 1907–1910." Birmingham, n.d. Typewritten.

Feder, Leah Hannah. *Unemployment Relief in Periods of Depression: A Study of Measures Adopted in Certain American Cities, 1857 through 1922*. New York: Russell Sage, 1936.

Flynt, Wayne. "Dissent in Zion: Alabama Baptists and Social Issues, 1900–14." *Journal of Southern History* 35 (November 1969): 523–42.

———. *Mine, Mill & Microchip. A Chronicle of Alabama Enterprise*. Produced in cooperation with the Business Council of Alabama. Northridge, Calif.: Windsor Publications, 1987.

———. *Poor but Proud: Alabama's Poor Whites*. Tuscaloosa: University of Alabama Press, 1989.

———. "Religion in the Urban South: The Divided Religious Mind of Birmingham, 1900–1930." *Alabama Review* 30, no. 2 (April 1977): 108–34.

Foner, Philip S. *American Socialism and Black Americans: From the Age of Jackson to World War II*. Westport, Conn.: Greenwood, 1977.

———. *Organized Labor and the Black Worker, 1619–1973*. New York: Praeger, 1974.

Franklin, Jimmie Lewis. *Back to Birmingham: Richard Arrington, Jr., and His Times*. Tuscaloosa: University of Alabama Press, 1989.

Fulcher, Annie Laurie. *The History, Structure, and Program of the Family Counseling Association of Jefferson County, Alabama*. Birmingham: Jefferson County Coordinating Council of Social Forces, 1967.

Funigiello, Philip J. *The Challenge to Urban Liberalism: Federal-City Relations during World War II.* Knoxville: University of Tennessee Press, 1978.

Garrow, David J. *Bearing the Cross: Martin Luther King, Jr., and the Southern Christian Leadership Conference.* New York: Random House, 1988.

———. *Protest at Selma: Martin Luther King, Jr., and the Voting Rights Act of 1965.* New Haven: Yale University Press, 1978.

———, ed. *Birmingham, Alabama, 1956–1963. The Black Struggle for Civil Rights.* Brooklyn, N.Y.: Carlson Publishing, 1989.

Gaston, A. G. *Green Power.* Birmingham: Birmingham Publishing, 1968.

Gelfand, Mark I. *A Nation of Cities: The Federal Government and Urban America, 1933–1965.* New York: Oxford University Press, 1975.

Glaab, Charles N., and Theodore A. Brown. *A History of Urban America.* New York: Macmillan, 1967.

Goldfield, David R. *Black, White, and Southern: Race Relations and Southern Culture, 1940 to Present.* Baton Rouge: Louisiana State University Press, 1990.

———. *Cotton Fields and Skyscrapers: Southern City and Region, 1607–1980.* Baton Rouge: Louisiana State University Press, 1982.

———. *Promised Land: The South since 1945.* Arlington Heights, Ill.: H. Davidson, 1987.

Grace, D. B. "Official Life of George B. Ward." Birmingham, n.d. Typewritten.

Graham, Hugh Davis. *The Civil Rights Era: Origins and Development of National Policy 1960–1972.* New York: Oxford University Press, 1990.

Greenberg, Stanley B. *Race and State in Capitalist Development: Comparative Perspectives.* New Haven: Yale University Press, 1980.

Greenstone, J. David, and Paul E. Peterson. *Race and Authority in Urban Politics: Community Participation and the War on Poverty.* New York: Russell Sage, 1973.

Griffith, Sara. "Birmingham: The Magic City." B.S. project, Northwestern University, 1938.

Haeberle, Steven H. *Planting the Grassroots: Structuring Citizen Participation.* Westport, Conn.: Praeger, 1989.

Hamilton, Virginia Van der Veer. *Hugo Black: The Alabama Years.* Baton Rouge: Louisiana State University Press, 1972.

Harris, Carl Vernon. "Economic Power and Politics: A Study of Birmingham, Alabama, 1890–1920." Ph.D. dissertation, University of Wisconsin, 1970.

———. *Political Power in Birmingham, 1871–1921.* Knoxville: University of Tennessee Press, 1977.

Havard, William C., ed. *The Changing Politics of the South.* Baton Rouge: Louisiana State University Press, 1972.

Haveman, Robert H., ed. *A Decade of Federal Antipoverty Programs: Achievements, Failures, and Lessons.* San Diego: Academic Press, 1977.

Henderson, E. M., Sr. "Relief in Jefferson County: A Brief Survey." Birmingham, 1934. Typewritten.

Henley, John C., Jr. *This Is Birmingham: The Story of the Founding and Growth of an American City.* Birmingham: Birmingham Publishing, 1960.

Higgins, Lucile. "A History of Charity in Birmingham." B.A. thesis, Howard College, 1928.

Holloway, Harry. *The Politics of the Southern Negro: From Exclusion to Big City Organization.* New York: Random House, 1969.

Hopkins, Harry L. *Spending to Save: The Complete Story of Relief.* New York: Norton, 1936.

Hornady, John R. *The Book of Birmingham.* New York: Dodd, Mead, 1921.

Huggins, Nathan Irvin. *Protestants against Poverty: Boston's Charities, 1870–1900.* Westport, Conn.: Greenwood, 1971.

Hunter, Floyd. *Community Power Structure: A Study of Decision Makers.* Chapel Hill: University of North Carolina Press, 1953.

Jackson, Kenneth T. *The Ku Klux Klan in the City, 1915–1930.* Chicago: Ivan R. Dee, 1992.

Jacoway, Elizabeth, and David R. Colburn, eds. *Southern Businessmen and Desegregation.* Baton Rouge: Louisiana State University Press, 1982.

Jefferson County Commission. *Social Group Work Agencies in Birmingham and Jefferson County—1939.* A report prepared with the assistance of the Works Progress Administration.

Jefferson County Coordinating Council of Social Forces. *The Jefferson County Survey of Health, Welfare, and Recreation Needs and Services.* University: University of Alabama Press, 1955.

Jenkins, Mollie Beck. "The Social Work of the Tennessee Coal Iron and Railroad Company." M.A. thesis, University of Alabama, 1929.

Katz, Michael B. *In the Shadow of the Poorhouse: A Social History of Welfare in America.* New York: Basic Books, 1986.

Kelley, Robin D. G. *Hammer and Hoe: Alabama Communists during the Great Depression.* Chapel Hill: University of North Carolina Press, 1990.

Key, V. O., Jr., with the assistance of Alexander Heard. *Southern Politics in State and Nation.* New York: Knopf, 1950.

King, Jere. "Formation of Greater Birmingham." Birmingham, n.d. Typewritten.

King, Martin Luther, Jr. *Stride toward Freedom: The Montgomery Story.* San Francisco: Harper and Row, 1958.

———. *Where Do We Go from Here: Chaos or Community?* New York, Bantam, 1968.

———. *Why We Can't Wait.* New York: New American Library, 1964.

Kluger, Richard. *Simple Justice: The History of Brown v. Board of Education and Black America's Struggle for Equality.* New York: Vintage Books, 1977.

Kousser, J. Morgan. *The Shaping of Southern Politics: Suffrage Restriction and the Establishment of the One-Party South, 1880–1910.* New Haven: Yale University Press, 1974.

Kramer, Ralph M. *Participation of the Poor: Comparative Community Case Studies in the War on Poverty.* Englewood Cliffs, N.J.: Prentice Hall, 1969.

Krueger, Thomas A. *And Promises to Keep: The Southern Conference for Human Welfare, 1938–1948.* Nashville: Vanderbilt University Press, 1967.

LaMonte, Edward S. *George B. Ward: Birmingham's Urban Statesman.* Birmingham: Birmingham Public Library, 1974.

Larsen, Lawrence H. *The Rise of the Urban South.* Lexington: University Press of Kentucky, 1985.

———. *The Urban South: A History.* Lexington: University Press of Kentucky, 1990.

Lawson, Steven F. "Freedom Then, Freedom Now: The Historiography of the Civil Rights Movement." *American Historical Review* 96, no. 2 (April 1991): 456–71.

Leighton, George R. "Birmingham, Alabama: The City of Perpetual Promise." *Harper's,* August 1937, pp. 225–42.

————. *Five Cities: The Story of Their Youth and Old Age.* New York: Harper and Bros., 1939.

Lesy, Michael. *Real Life: Louisville in the Twenties.* New York: Pantheon, 1976.

Levine, Charles H. *Racial Conflict and the American Mayor: Power, Polarization and Performance.* Lexington, Mass.: Heath, 1974.

Levine, Robert A. *The Poor Ye Need Not Have with You: Lessons from the War on Poverty.* Cambridge: M.I.T. Press, 1970.

Levitan, Sar A. *The Great Society's Poor Law: A New Approach to Poverty.* Baltimore: Johns Hopkins University Press, 1969.

Lewis, Anthony, and the *New York Times. Portrait of a Decade: The Second American Revolution.* New York: Random House, 1964.

Lewis, Ronald L. *Black Coal Miners in America: Race, Class, and Community Conflict, 1780–1980.* Lexington: University Press of Kentucky, 1987.

Lowi, Theodore J. *The End of Liberalism: Ideology, Policy, and the Crisis of Public Authority.* New York: Norton, 1969.

McKee, James B. "Status and Power in the Industrial Community: A Comment on Drucker's Thesis." *American Journal of Sociology* 58 (January 1953): 364–70.

McMillan, Malcolm Cook. *Constitutional Development in Alabama, 1798–1901: A Study in Politics, the Negro, and Sectionalism.* Chapel Hill: University of North Carolina Press, 1955 (vol. 37 of James Sprunt Studies in History and Political Science); Spartanburg, S.C.: Reprint Company, 1978.

McMillen, Neil R. *The Citizens' Council: Organized Resistance to the Second Reconstruction, 1954–64.* Urbana: University of Illinois Press, 1971.

Marris, Peter, and Martin Rein. *Dilemmas of Social Reform: Poverty and Community Action in the United States.* 2d ed. Chicago: Aldine, 1973.

Marshall, Dale Rogers. *The Politics of Participation in Poverty: A Case Study of the Board of the Economic and Youth Opportunities Agency of Greater Los Angeles.* Berkeley: University of California Press, 1971.

Martin, Charles H. *The Angelo Herndon Case and Southern Justice.* Baton Rouge: Louisiana State University Press, 1976.

Martin, Harold H. *William Berry Hartsfield: Mayor of Atlanta.* Athens: University of Georgia Press, 1978.

Metcalf, George R. *From Little Rock to Boston: The History of School Desegregation.* Westport, Conn.: Greenwood, 1983.

Mohl, Raymond A., ed. *Searching for the Sunbelt: Historical Perspectives on a Region.* Knoxville: University of Tennessee Press, 1990.

Morgan, Charles, Jr. *A Time to Speak.* New York: Harper and Row, 1964.

Morgan, Roberta. "Social Implications and the Human Side." *Journal of the Birmingham Historical Society* 1 (January 1960): 11–17.

Moynihan, Daniel Patrick. *Maximum Feasible Misunderstanding: Community Action in the War on Poverty.* New York: Free Press, 1969.

————, ed., with the assistance of Corinne Saposs Schelling. *On Understanding Poverty: Perspectives from the Social Sciences.* New York: Basic Books, 1969.

Nolan, Duncan. *Social and Economic Survey of the Birmingham District.* Birmingham: Housing Authority of the Birmingham District, 1943.

Norrell, Robert J. *James Bowron: The Autobiography of a New South Industrialist.* Chapel Hill: University of North Carolina Press, 1991.

Nunnelley, William A. *Bull Connor*. Tuscaloosa: University of Alabama Press, 1991.

Painter, Nell Irvin. *The Narrative of Hosea Hudson: His Life as a Negro Communist in the South*. Cambridge: Harvard University Press, 1979.

Patterson, James T. *America's Struggle against Poverty 1900–1980*. Cambridge: Harvard University Press, 1981.

Peirce, Neal R. *The Deep South States of America: People, Politics, and Power in the Seven Deep South States*. New York: Norton, 1974.

Perry, David C., and Alfred J. Watkins, eds. *The Rise of the Sunbelt Cities*. Beverly Hills: Sage, 1977.

Pioneers Club. *Early Days in Birmingham*. Birmingham: Birmingham Publishing, 1968.

Piven, Frances Fox and Richard A. Cloward. *Poor People's Movements: Why They Succeed, How They Fail*. New York: Pantheon, 1977.

———. *Regulating the Poor: The Functions of Public Welfare*. New York: Pantheon, 1971.

Porter, Irvine. "Statement Opposing Annexation of Homewood to Birmingham." Speech delivered at a meeting of the directors of the Birmingham Chamber of Commerce, Birmingham, Alabama, 23 April 1959.

Preston, Howard L. *Automobile Age Atlanta: The Making of a Southern Metropolis, 1900–1935*. Athens: University of Georgia Press, 1979.

Rabinowitz, Howard N. *Race Relations in the Urban South, 1865–1890*. New York: Oxford University Press, 1978.

Raines, Howell. *My Soul Is Rested: The Story of the Civil Rights Movement in the Deep South*. New York: Penguin, 1983.

Reed, Linda. *Simple Decency & Common Sense: The Southern Conference Movement, 1938–1963*. Bloomington: Indiana University Press, 1991.

Rikard, Marlene Hunt. "An Experiment in Welfare Capitalism: The Health Care Services of the Tennessee Coal, Iron and Railroad Company." Ph.D. dissertation, University of Alabama, 1983.

Robinson, Jo Ann Gibson. *The Montgomery Bus Boycott and the Women Who Started It: The Memoir of Jo Ann Gibson Robinson*, edited, with a foreword, by David J. Garrow. Knoxville: University of Tennessee Press, 1987.

Rubin, Lillian B. "Maximum Feasible Participation: The Origins, Implications and Present Status." *Annals of the American Academy of Political and Social Science* 385 (September 1969): 26.

Sautter, Udo. *Three Cheers for the Unemployed: Government and Unemployment before the New Deal*. New York: Cambridge University Press, 1991.

Schnore, Leo F., ed. *The New Urban History: Quantitative Explorations by American Historians*. Princeton: Princeton University Press, 1975.

Schwartz, Bonnie F. *The Civil Works Administration, 1933–34: The Business of Emergency Employment in the New Deal*. Princeton: Princeton University Press, 1984.

Seigel, Harriet. "Public Assistance Programs in the Southeast, 1936–40." M.A. thesis, University of Alabama, 1941.

Seligman, Ben B., ed. *Poverty as a Public Issue*. New York: Free Press, 1965.

Sikora, Frank. *Until Justice Rolls Down: The Birmingham Church Bombing Case*. Tuscaloosa: University of Alabama Press, 1991.

Silver, Christopher. *Twentieth-Century Richmond: Planning, Politics, and Race*. Knoxville: University of Tennessee Press, 1984.

Sitkoff, Harvard. *The Struggle for Black Equality, 1954–1992.* New York: Hill and Wang, 1993.

Smith, Douglas L. *The New Deal in the Urban South.* Baton Rouge: Louisiana State University Press, 1988.

Snell, William R. "Masked Men in the Magic City: Activities of the Revised Klan in Birmingham, 1916–1940." *Alabama Historical Quarterly* 34, no. 3–4 (Fall and Winter 1972): 206–27.

Southern Research Institute. *Evaluation of the Alternatives for Achieving Improved Local Government: A Preliminary Statistical Analysis of Local Government Activity in Jefferson County Compared to Other Areas in Alabama and the United States, 1957–1967.* Birmingham: Southern Research Institute, 1970.

———. *Evaluation of the Alternatives for Achieving Improved Local Government in Jefferson County, Alabama.* Birmingham: Southern Research Institute, 1971.

Stanley, Harold W. *Voter Mobilization and the Politics of Race: The South and Universal Suffrage, 1952–1984.* New York: Praeger, 1987.

Stewart, George R. "Birmingham's Reaction to the 1954 Desegregation Decision." M.A. thesis, Samford University, 1967.

Stone, Clarence N. *Regime Politics: Governing Atlanta, 1946–1988.* Lawrence: University Press of Kansas, 1989.

Stone, Clarence N., Robert K. Whelan, and William J. Murin. *Urban Policy and Politics in a Bureaucratic Age.* 2d ed. Englewood Cliffs, N.J.: Prentice Hall, 1986.

Sundquist, James L. *Politics and Policy: The Eisenhower, Kennedy and Johnson Years.* Washington, D.C.: Brookings, 1968.

———, ed., with the assistance of Corrine Saposs Schelling. *On Fighting Poverty: Perspectives from Experience.* New York: Basic Books, 1969.

Trexler, Harrison A. "Birmingham's Struggle with Commission Government." *National Municipal Review* 14 (November 1925): 662–63.

U.S. Department of Commerce. Bureau of the Census. *Fifteenth Census of the United States: 1930 Population.* Vol. 1. Washington, D.C.: Government Printing Office, 1931.

U.S. Department of Commerce. Bureau of the Census. *Relief Expenditures by Governmental and Private Organizations, 1929 and 1931.* Washington, D.C.: Government Printing Office, 1932.

U.S. Department of Health, Education, and Welfare. Social and Rehabilitation Service. Office of Research, Demonstrations, and Training. *Perspectives in Public Welfare: A History,* by Blanche D. Coll. Washington, D.C.: Government Printing Office, 1969.

U.S. Department of Labor. Children's Bureau. *Trends in Different Types of Public and Private Relief in Urban Areas, 1929–35,* by Emma A. Winslow. Children's Bureau Pubn. no. 237. Washington, D.C.: Government Printing Office, 1937.

Van de Voort, Anita. "Public Welfare Administration in Jefferson County, Alabama." M.A. thesis, Tulane University, 1933.

Vann, David. "The Change from Commission to Mayor-Council Government and the Racial Desegregation Agreements in Birmingham, Alabama 1961–1963." Birmingham: Center for Urban Affairs, University of Alabama at Birmingham, 1988.

Wade, Richard C. *The Urban Frontier: Pioneer Life in Early Pittsburgh, Cincinnati, Lexington, Louisville, and St. Louis.* Chicago: University of Chicago Press, 1959.

Warner, Sam Bass, Jr. *The Private City: Philadelphia in Three Periods of Its Growth.* Philadelphia: University of Pennsylvania Press, 1968.

———. *Streetcar Suburbs: The Process of Growth in Boston, 1870–1900.* New York: Atheneum, 1974.

Watters, Pat, and Reese Cleghorn. *Climbing Jacob's Ladder: The Arrival of Negroes in Southern Politics.* New York: Harcourt, Brace, and World, 1967.

Weaver, Beatrice. "Community Welfare Councils in Nine Cities: A Comparative Study for Application in Birmingham, Alabama." M.A. thesis, University of Alabama, 1948.

Wedell, Marsha. *Elite Women and the Reform Impulse in Memphis, 1875–1915.* Knoxville: University of Tennessee Press, 1991.

Wilhoit, Francis M. *The Politics of Massive Resistance.* New York: George Braziller, 1973.

Williams, Juan. *Eyes on the Prize: America's Civil Rights Years, 1954–1965.* New York: Penguin, 1988.

Wilson, James Q., ed. *City Politics and Public Policy.* New York: Wiley, 1968.

Wisner, Elizabeth. *Social Welfare in the South from Colonial Times to World War I.* Baton Rouge: Louisiana State University Press, 1970.

Wolters, Raymond. *The Burden of Brown: Thirty Years of School Desegregation.* Knoxville: University of Tennessee Press, 1984.

Worthman, Paul. "Black Workers and Labor Unions in Birmingham, Alabama, 1897–1904." In *Black Labor in America*, ed. Milton Cantor. Westport, Conn.: Greenwood, 1969.

———. "Working Class Mobility in Birmingham, Alabama, 1880–1914. In *Anonymous Americans: Explorations in Nineteenth-Century Social History*, ed. Tamara K. Hareven. Englewood Cliffs, N.J.: Prentice Hall, 1971.

Zarefsky, David. *President Johnson's War on Poverty: Rhetoric and History.* University: University of Alabama Press, 1986.

Scrapbooks, Collected Papers, and Minutes

Birmingham (Alabama) Public Library. The Administration of Cooper Green, President of the Birmingham City Commission, February 29, 1940–April 14, 1953. Scrapbooks of newspaper clippings and other materials. Compiled in the office of the President of the Commission. Vols. 1 and 2.

———. The Administration of J. M. Jones, Jr., President of the Birmingham City Commission, November 2, 1925–February 7, 1940. Scrapbooks of newspaper and other clippings. Compiled in the office of the Commission. Vols. 2–14.

———. George Ward Collection of Scrapbooks Relating to the History and Government of Birmingham, June 1, 1899–December 23, 1923, and January 1, 1930–April 24, 1939.

———. Roberta Morgan Papers.

Birmingham Area Committee for the Development of Economic Opportunity. Minutes of Meetings of the Board of Directors, 1965. Typewritten.

———. City of Birmingham (Alabama). Community Development Department. Citizen Participation Folder.

Jefferson County (Alabama) Chapter, American Red Cross. Minutes and Other Documents, 1921–1942. Typewritten.

Jefferson County (Alabama) Committee for Economic Opportunity. Minutes and Other Documents, 1965–1975. Typewritten.

Jefferson County (Alabama) Community Chest, Inc. Minutes and Other Documents, 1923–1973. 14 vols. Typewritten.

National Urban League Papers; selected letters dealing with Birmingham, microfilmed by the Library of Congress Photoduplication Service. Collection is in Manuscript Division, Library of Congress.

Interviews

Barton, Clara Moses. Former caseworker, Jefferson County Department of Public Welfare. Interview by author. Birmingham, Ala., 15 February 1975.

Dunbar, John. University of Alabama at Birmingham. Interview by author. Birmingham, Ala., 22 July 1975.

Holt, Thad. Operation New Birmingham. Interviews by author. Birmingham, Ala., 28 March, 28 June 1974.

Lewis, Charles. Principal human resource officer, Birmingham Community Development Department. Interviews by author. Birmingham, Ala., 5 December 1975, 17 July 1993.

Morgan, Roberta. Heflin, Alabama. Interviews by author. Birmingham, Ala., 8 March, 6 August 1974.

Nunnelley, Carol. Political reporter, *Birmingham News*. Interview by author. Birmingham, Ala., 15 January 1976.

Orrell, David. Executive director, United Way of Jefferson-Shelby-Walker Counties (Alabama). Interview by author. Birmingham, Ala., 15 August 1974.

Patton, W. C. National Association for the Advancement of Colored People, Birmingham, Ala. Interview by author. Birmingham, Ala., 12 November 1975.

Schaffer, Sheldon. Southern Research Institute, Birmingham, Ala. Interview by author. Birmingham, Ala., 12 November 1975.

Sterne, Mervyn H. Sterne, Agee, and Leach Stockbrokers, Birmingham, Ala. Interviews by author. Birmingham, Ala., 1 March, 8 March, 13 March, 29 March, 3 April 1973.

Vann, David. Mayor, City of Birmingham. Interview by author. Birmingham, Ala., 7 November 1975.

Woolfolk, Odessa. University of Alabama at Birmingham, Birmingham, Ala. Interview by author. Birmingham, Ala., 31 October 1975.

Zukoski, Charles F., Jr. Retired bank official and attorney, Birmingham, Ala. Interview by author. Birmingham, Ala., 2 October 1975.

Newspapers

Birmingham News. 1 January 1900–31 December 1917; 1 January 1928–31 December 1941; and miscellaneous later dates.

Birmingham Post-Herald. 1 January 1954–31 December 1954; 1 August 1962–31 January 1965; and miscellaneous later dates.

Index

ABOUT THE AUTHOR

EDWARD SHANNON LAMONTE is Howell Heflin Professor of Political Science at Birmingham-Southern College. He received his bachelor's degree from Harvard and his master's and his doctorate degrees from the University of Chicago. Besides working in a number of administrative and teaching positions, LaMonte served as Executive Secretary to Birmingham's Mayor Richard Arrington, Jr.